D0411591

WHEN REPORTERS CROSS THE LINE

WHEN REPORTERS CROSS THE LINE

THE HEROES, THE VILLAINS, THE HACKERS AND THE SPIES

STEWART PURVIS and **JEFF HULBERT**

Biteback Publishing

LIS - LIBRARY

Date	Fund
2.10.2013	t-War

Order No.

02445384

University of Chester
36135265

First published in Great Britain in 2013 by
Biteback Publishing Ltd
Westminster Tower
3 Albert Embankment
London SE1 7SP
Copyright © Stewart Purvis and Jeff Hulbert 2013

Stewart Purvis and Jeff Hulbert have asserted their rights under the Copyright, Designs and Patents Act 1988 to be identified as the authors of this work.

All rights reserved. No part of this publication may be reproduced, stored in a retrieval system or transmitted, in any form or by any means, without the publisher's prior permission in writing.

This book is sold subject to the condition that it shall not, by way of trade or otherwise, be lent, resold, hired out or otherwise circulated without the publisher's prior consent in any form of binding or cover other than that in which it is published and without a similar condition, including this condition, being imposed on the subsequent purchaser.

Every reasonable effort has been made to trace copyright holders of material reproduced in this book, but if any have been inadvertently overlooked the publishers would be glad to hear from them.

Quotation from the unpublished diaries of Harold Nicolson by kind permission of Juliet Nicolson.

ISBN 978-1-84954-583-9

10 9 8 7 6 5 4 3 2 1

A CIP catalogue record for this book is available from the British Library.

Set in Sabon and Heroic

Printed and bound in Great Britain by
CPI Group (UK) Ltd, Croydon CR0 4YY

MIX
Paper from
responsible sources
FSC
www.fsc.org   FSC® C020471

CONTENTS

Introduction   vii

1. John Simpson   1
2. W. N. Ewer   41
3. Walter Duranty   59
4. Guy Burgess   89
5. John Peet   123
6. Reg Foster and Brendan Mulholland   147
7. Charles Wheeler   177
8. Frederick Forsyth   191
9. Martin Bell   213
10. Sidney Bernstein   229
11. Sandy Gall   247
12. Lindsey Hilsum   263
13. Andrew Gilligan   287
14. The Hackers   325
15. The Morals of the Stories   339

Appendix   347
Endnotes   349
Index   377

INTRODUCTION

British journalists are not very interested in reading rules that someone has written for them. One of the country's most respected correspondents, the late Charles Wheeler, once admitted he'd never seen and never read a copy of the BBC's editorial guidelines. His own guideline was 'push it as far as you can but make sure you get it right'.

Rather than quoting guidelines, regulatory codes or media laws, reporters and editors prefer to talk about 'crossing a line'. But in the fiercely competitive world of daily print and broadcast journalism there has rarely been the time or the inclination to agree where this 'line' is. No one even seems to have tried to define it.

So our title *When Reporters Cross the Line* is, in part, a rhetorical device. If no one agrees where the line is how can anybody decide whether it has been crossed or not?

We have found media men and women who have accidentally or deliberately strayed across loosely defined ethical lines but also those who proudly and defiantly marched across conventions believing their cause was justified.

This investigation is therefore part celebration of British print and broadcast journalism and part exposure. The case studies do not claim to be representative of journalism or journalists; instead they help us, in our concluding chapter, to point towards where exactly such a line should be.

Most of the chapters are the story of an individual reporter who made a decision which created controversy. We set out to find more about these people than was previously available. The more we researched the more we discovered that some of those regarded as heroes by journalists had less than heroic moments. And others thought to be villains may have had a case for their defence. Often the people we researched turned out to be caught up in moments when the worlds of media, propaganda, politics, espionage and crime collided or overlapped. In one case a reporter was at various times, and sometimes simultaneously, a distinguished newspaper correspondent, a Russian spy and a secret British propagandist.

Some of these case studies may appear to be issues from an analogue past but they still have implications in this digital world where audiences – readers, viewers and listeners – increasingly have to make their own judgements about the credibility of the media they consume. This is a long view of journalism that looks back to try to help us look forward.

Jeff Hulbert and I have combined archive research with new interviews which we have conducted with those involved in episodes over the past eighty years. We have also added my own experiences in the news business over the second half of that period. When I offer those personal thoughts I write in the first person and am happy to accept any credit or blame for them.

It is ten years since Paddy Coulter, then at the Reuters Institute at the University of Oxford, nursed me through my four Visiting Professor lectures on 'Crossing the Line: borderline judgements in broadcast news'. I am grateful to him and to Simon Albury, then chief executive of the Royal Television Society, who encouraged me to believe that the Oxford lectures had an after-life, initially as a one-off lecture at the RTS in London.

My thanks to Martin Rosenbaum and Helen Grady at BBC Radio, who converted my pitch for a series of 'Crossing the Line' programmes into a single well-received programme. And to the unnamed BBC scheduler who thought *When Reporters Cross the Line* was a better title.

Our editor at Biteback, Sam Carter, gave us the invaluable advice 'write the book you want to write', which is what we've done.

Most of all my thanks to Jeff Hulbert, who has been my partner in this project from the first night at Oxford when he manned the video projector through the countless days he spent researching in British archives to the hours we have spent together writing and subbing this book. I know he would also want me to thank his partner, Lesley Newman, for being so understanding and supportive. Jeff and I are very grateful to Angela Frier, who read the manuscript and made many helpful suggestions. We are also grateful to the many archivists at the National Archives and the BBC Written Archives Centre, Caversham and to Anna Sander at Balliol College, Oxford for their help. And I'm deeply grateful for the support of my wife Jacqui Marson, whose own book *The Curse of Lovely* was also published this year and will undoubtedly outsell this volume.

Stewart Purvis
City University London
2013

JOHN SIMPSON

In October 2012 the BBC was facing 'its worst crisis in fifty years'. The judgement came from a BBC reporter whose reputation and status were so high that he could make that kind of bold statement about his own employers without worrying about the impact on his career prospects.

The crisis was the BBC's handling of the allegations that the late Jimmy Savile, a TV and radio star made by the BBC, had sexually molested children on its premises for many years.

The pundit was John Simpson, the world affairs editor of the BBC, now a stocky, white-haired man, wearing a sad, even downcast, expression, talking to a BBC programme investigating the BBC. Variously billed as a 'veteran foreign correspondent' (*The Times*) and a 'respected BBC correspondent' (*The Sun*), what he said on the *Panorama* programme was picked up by all the major newspapers and broadcast news bulletins.

For that brief moment, rather than reporting the news, John Simpson was the news. As someone who had absolutely no involvement whatsoever in the scandal, he was the respectable unofficial, but decently authoritative, voice of the BBC; a voice of calm reason, of reassurance. In short, a person that one could still trust to uphold the BBC's standards in time of crisis.

Yet six months before, as if to prove that none of us in journalism is perfect, John Simpson had decided after many years to say 'sorry' for something he had done. He had accused rivals of 'profoundly misleading' reporting giving rise to 'a false impression about one of the major events of the decade'. And he had been proved wrong.

The decade in question was the 1990s and the event was the battle for Bosnia. The country, if at the time it could be called that, was in the grip of a bloody and horrific civil war; and much of it was being played out nightly on the world's television screens.

At the start of the decade the former Yugoslavia was crumbling into chaos and civil war. A decade before, and after delivering four decades of strong leadership, Josip Broz, known as Tito, had died. During his battles with the Nazis the partisan leader had delivered his orders in his native Croat: 'Ti to, ti to', which translates as 'you will do this, you will do that'. His staff heard it so many times that it became a natural nickname for him.[1] His subsequent autocratic presidential style meant that there were no natural successors waiting in the wings to take over; in the resulting power vacuum that followed his death in 1986 there was little prospect of keeping the state together. The tensions between the very diverse ethnic and cultural populations soon saw separatist processes spiralling out of control; and eventually they became unstoppable. Very swiftly the parts of the Yugoslav federation that were rather more ethnically and culturally homogenous, Slovenia and Croatia, seceded although even then it was not without a bloody fight with the Yugoslav National Army (JNA), which was Serb dominated.

Then in 1992 Bosnia and Herzegovina broke away. But, unlike Slovenia and Croatia, it was highly diverse ethnically and culturally; and a long, bloody and brutal civil war ensued in which Muslim Bosniaks were pitched against Bosnian Serbs, who were Eastern Orthodox Christians. To this was added the complication posed by a sizeable Bosnian Croat minority, which was predominantly Roman Catholic and populated western and southern parts of the state. Everywhere there were close-knit ethnic communities, 'enclaves', which were dotted around larger swathes of land that were predominantly populated by people from the opposing ethnic community. It was as if the pattern on a pedigree Dalmatian's coat had been transformed into geographical reality.

But there was a further complication: Bosnian Serbs declared themselves separate from the rest of Bosnia and formed a state within a state that was to become known as Republika Srpska. It was a part of a plan that had been mooted several years earlier to create a greater Serbia, to unite Serb-speaking peoples who had been deliberately divided by the Yugoslavian Communist regime.[2] It was led by a former psychiatrist, Radovan Karadžić; he and his military chief, a former Yugoslav army general, Ratko Mladić, were unofficially aided and abetted in their political and military activities by the rump of the former Yugoslavia, which was then led by the Serbian nationalist politician and supporter of a Greater Serbia, Slobodan Milošević. To achieve ethnically homogenous statehood would mean encouraging people from other ethnic groups to move to other parts of the country so that they could live among their own ethnic group, but it would not be easy. Such a simple if questionable concept very quickly came to be translated into a brutal reality. The world's media picked up the plans and with it the description 'ethnic cleansing'. The term was a hygienic way of describing a reality that was far removed from that: a reality where force, intimidation and murder became widespread and ethnic tensions, rivalries and hatred boiled over, quid pro quo.

The Bosniak Muslim side, which was led by Alija Izetbegović, sought to defend itself and to hold on to territory it feared would be lost, thus threatening its very viability. Izetbegović's administration also received help and support from outside, from countries including Iran, Pakistan, Saudi Arabia and Turkey; and sometimes various Western powers also lent a hand, but less overtly.[3]

There were times when the fight became an uneasy alliance between Bosniak Muslim and Bosnian Croat against Bosnian Serb, and other occasions where it was a three-cornered fight. The terrain was harsh and difficult to take: a fact already acknowledged by the Roman Emperor Trajan's legions in the first century AD and by Hitler's armies over 1,800 years later. There were massacres, war crimes and devastations. No side was entirely blameless, although some were seen as being less blameworthy than others.

Sarajevo, the Bosnian capital, which still showed some of its former Austro-Hungarian provincial heritage, was overlooked by hills which, when the city was put under siege by the Bosnian Serbs, formed vantage points for many snipers and artillery emplacements. The world watched as pictures, sanitised to spare television audiences the brutal reality of war, illustrated stories about snipers, the mortaring of market places and the devastations to which the city's population were subjected.[4] The pathos of stories about people killed as they dashed to fill up water bottles or shopped for food put many of the world's politicians under pressure about why they appeared not to be doing anything to stop the slaughter. Stories about other places in Bosnia were less widespread because there was the considerable and recurring problem confronting journalists when reporting from the world's danger zones: access.

Access was a real problem: not only getting access, but when there being able to gather evidence and eyewitness testimonies to support the stories and keep safe; then there was the problem of getting the stories out and into the public domain. Without access the stories that circulated could be, and often were, taken only as rumour or exaggeration. This suited many – including politicians who wished to remain incurious, for whatever 'higher' policy reasons – since they could be dismissed and the lack of evidence cited precisely as the reason for not taking action at all, while others were posturing and looking for political advantage.[5] To this was added the fact that many journalists were not entirely trusted by the combatants precisely because they did not take sides, and so were considered potentially hostile to individual causes.

As the civil war developed stories of dark deeds and dreadful conditions were emerging, but for many of them it was impossible to check the details. And as is so often the case with conflicts details were frequently denied, obfuscated, invented or exaggerated by combatants, their opponents and their supporters; and the problem was compounded by others who had interests in muddying the waters and keeping what they or others were doing hidden from view. This created a problem of perception and understanding, according to Oxford academic John Burns. He wrote that among the news media 'few would admit to deliberate bias and yet the Yugoslav civil wars ... demonstrate the clearest examples of one-sided reporting from a pack psychology among journalists'.[6] His assertion was supported by John Simpson, who wrote that it was 'certainly true that there was a powerful pro-Muslim lobby among the British and American journalists in Bosnia' and they were fiercely competitive when it came to uncovering 'wrongdoing on the part of the Serbs, which was very considerable, and not all the facts were checked too carefully'.[7]

Camps

Shortly after the civil war began rumours were circulating about populations being forcibly uprooted from their homes and moved to other parts of the country: ethnic cleansing – then still a new term – in action. In July 1992, two journalists, Roy Gutman of New York *Newsday* and Maggie O'Kane of *The Guardian*, revealed to the world the existence of Bosnian Serb-controlled camps. Gutman wrote about a camp at Manjača, which he said was called by Republika Srpska's army a prisoner-of-war camp, but he also attributed to an unnamed US embassy official in Belgrade the description of the Bosnian camps as concentration camps.[8] Two days later, on 21 July, he wrote about the cleansing of Banja Luka, where Muslims were moved out of the city 'in sealed freight trains'.[9]

Maggie O'Kane, in her report which was published in *The Guardian* on 29 July, used the term 'concentration camp' to describe a camp at Trnopolje. In total she used the term four times.[10] On 2 August 1992 Roy Gutman wrote an article headlined 'Death Camps'. It began, 'The Serb conquerors of northern

Bosnia have established two concentration camps in which more than a thousand civilians have been executed or starved and thousands more are being held until they die...'[11]

'Concentration camps', that chilling expression from those reports, would inevitably have conjured up in many people's minds a direct association with the camps operated by the Nazis before and during the Second World War. The mental pictures produced by those two words would have been the iconic images that circulated widely after the war depicting hollow-eyed skeletal inmates dressed in broad-striped camp garb. But historically that was not what other concentration camps had been. The Nazi model had been a distortion, a gross perversion.

Concentration camps had been developed decades before the Second World War, as a policy response to handling large numbers of civilians caught up in zones of conflict.[12] They had been used by the Spanish when suppressing a revolt in Cuba at the end of the nineteenth century and a couple of years later the idea was taken forward by the British in the Boer War. The British had originally intended them to provide shelter and sustenance for a refugee population that had fled, or been forcibly removed by General Kitchener's forces, who were conducting scorched earth warfare against Boer guerrilla forces. They had been 'rough and ready' constructions situated along railway lines to aid removal of inmates away from the war zone. There had been separate camps for black and white. However, a mix of harsh regimes, management incompetence, food shortages and overcrowding led to insanitary conditions, disease and death. There was also the point that the camps – undoubtedly for some of the inmates – applied pressure and sought to break the Boer spirit, the will to resist. What had started out as a relatively humanitarian policy became a disaster, in real terms, but in London, the imperial capital, they were a disaster in political and propaganda terms too.[13]

A couple of decades later the Nazi experience was an altogether different and much darker story. Concentration camps had been established soon after Adolf Hitler took office as Germany's

Chancellor in January 1933. Initially, they were designed to hold political opponents, but as time moved on their role quickly changed and they became the places where all of Nazi society's 'undesirables' were sent, usually for some form of harsh treatment and punishment. By the war's end – just twelve years after Hitler's rise to power – it is known that there had been hundreds of concentration camps, and many of their names became synonymous with true hell on earth. In that relatively short time, and as peace changed into war, the numbers of inmates, executions and deaths increased massively, aided by uncompromisingly criminal and brutal camp regimes. The numbers dying from hunger, disease, overcrowding, neglect and overwork rocketed. But maybe surprisingly these were not death camps, in the sense of being centres where mass murder was practised as a deliberate policy. Many were labour camps and detention centres where inmates were expected to work on industrial production lines. The distinction between death camps and labour camps may have been relatively fine, however, when it came to death, as labour camp inmates faced only overwork, undernourishment and, usually, a slower death from malnutrition and disease.[14]

Extermination camps were distinct from concentration camps. They were industrial killing facilities and were few in number; they drove forward the Nazis' 'final solution' plans. Three operated under what became known as Operation Reinhard. They were purpose-built extermination centres – Belzec, Sobibor and Treblinka. Each was operational for two years or less but in that time they were responsible for the deaths of millions. A powerful and uncompromising description of what happened in them is provided by Gitta Sereny's book about Franz Stangl, the commandant of Treblinka.[15] When those camps' work was deemed complete they were bulldozed and hidden from view: farmsteads were built and settled, trees and flowers were planted to cover their traces.[16] Three other industrial killing centres, Auschwitz-Birkenau, Majdanek and Chełmno, also operated, but they were a part of the wider concentration camp system.[17]

For years after the Second World War many hoped that the words concentration camp had been consigned to history, although variants – looking to their original purpose: centres for concentrating civilians forcibly moved or fleeing from zones of unrest – did emerge, for instance, during the Malayan emergency as British forces battling with Communist insurgents moved domestic populations into camps.

But when the existence of camps emerged during the Bosnian civil war a collective chill passed down people's spines. O'Kane's report described the northern Bosnian city of Banja Luka, which was one of the principal cities of Republika Srpska but whose population was partly Bosniak Muslim, as a 'a city waiting to be cleansed'. The despatch also mentioned camps at Omarska – to which the International Committee of the Red Cross (ICRC) had been trying to get access, but without success – and Bratunac. She wrote that one camp, Trnopolje, was 'the best one to be sent to' because food was provided and villagers could take in supplies. But her report quoted an eyewitness account of trains plying between Trnopolje and elsewhere, comprising largely cattle trucks, but whose cargo was very much human. The eyewitness had spoken of seeing women and children being taken away from the camp in those trains. And in a direct parallel with witness testimonies from the Second World War about concentration camp transport trains, her report described fully laden trucks that were left in blazing sunshine for a whole day while the people locked inside called for water that was not forthcoming. That was just the sort of casually inhuman thing that the Nazis had perpetrated decades before, without giving their human cargo's needs a second thought. Gutman, interviewed on the US National Public Radio two weeks after his first report was published, spoke about Omarska and another camp at Brčko. He spoke about a former Omarska inmate, an escapee, who had told him that in the camp 'they would execute people in groups of ten or fifteen. They would shoot them. They would slit their throats...' With stories like these filtering out the world's politicians and news consumers alike became greatly concerned to find out more, to have the details checked, to discover whether there could possibly be other camps too, and to see whether anything needed to or could be done about them.

'I invite foreign journalists to visit...'

As Maggie O'Kane's story about concentration camps broke Radovan Karadžić happened to be in London to discuss a European Union-sponsored peace plan: one of many that failed to get anywhere. While Karadžić was making preparations for a press conference that he would be holding later in the day, senior editorial staff at Independent Television News (ITN) seized on the report and began discussing what might be done. The company supplied the news programmes for Independent Television (ITV) and Channel 4, doing so by means of completely separate and discrete editorial and news-gathering operations.

In the *Channel 4 News* morning editorial meeting, foreign editor Sue Inglish raised Maggie O'Kane's story and it was decided that diplomatic editor Nik Gowing should go to Karadžić's press conference in London and ask him about the camps.[18]

Gowing recorded an interview with Karadžić, who had been handed a copy of that morning's *Guardian*. Gowing challenged him about the camps. Karadžić replied, 'There is no ethnic cleansing going on in Bosnia ... there is no evidence that people are being forced to leave ... civilians get full rights under Geneva Convention.'[19] But he then went on, 'I invite foreign journalists to visit and look for concentration camps.'[20] Was that a touch of bravado? Was it calling Gowing's bluff – a 'put up or shut up' sort of reaction? Or was it an ill-thought-out knee-jerk reaction? Events would soon provide an answer.

As soon as the interview was over Gowing quickly called Sue Inglish and told her that Karadžić had just issued an invitation to foreign journalists to go and see for themselves.[21] Immediately after she had spoken to him she called Karadžić's London press representative, John Kennedy, and told him that Karadžić had issued an invitation, that she was accepting and had a team ready to go. She then absorbed herself with making the arrangements, including briefing the Moscow correspondent, Ian Williams, to ready himself for the journey to Belgrade.[22]

The Guardian also busied itself, although later in the day. Ed Vulliamy tells that after seeing Karadžić's challenge on *Channel 4 News* that evening the newspaper's foreign editor, Paul Webster, called Karadžić straight away, reaching him on his car phone as he travelled to Heathrow, and told him that he would be sending Vulliamy to check out the story. Just afterwards Vulliamy was briefed by Webster and O'Kane, whom he was already scheduled to replace on rotation, while they shared a drink in a pub near *The Guardian*'s offices.

So over the next days, preparations were made for the departure of two ITN teams, which would be led by very experienced reporters, Penny Marshall (for ITN's news service to ITV) and Ian Williams (*Channel 4 News*).They would travel to Bosnia via Belgrade and ultimately Ed Vulliamy would accompany them. When there they hoped to be taken to Omarska and Trnopolje and to be able to see the camps for themselves, to see what conditions were like and how the camps functioned. Failing that they hoped to be able to provide more eyewitness accounts like O'Kane's and Gutman's. Shortly after they arrived Roy Gutman's 'death camps' article about Omarska was published.

After spending some frustrating time in Belgrade while officials hastily made arrangements and delivered endless briefings the ITN teams and Vulliamy were flown to Pale in Republika Srpska on 3 August 1992 and from there driven to Banja Luka. At Banja Luka the journalists faced further delays as yet more officials and, this time, military commanders pondered what to do with them.[23] It appeared to the reporters to be a delaying tactic, the result of Karadžić's knee-jerk reaction. Having issued the invitation, which only ITN and *The Guardian* had taken up, Karadžić's colleagues then faced up to the task of preparing the camps and their inmates so that they could be shown in a good light. Eventually it was agreed that the journalists would be taken to see some camps, but it was proposed that instead they should see a camp at Manjača, which had already received an ICRC inspection, instead of Omarska. Manjača was known to be 'a ghastly place', but they declined the invitation because from what they had already heard Omarska remained 'a terrible mystery' and everyone wanted to check it out.[24] Ian Williams takes up the story:

> We made it very clear that the reason we were there was to visit these camps. We reminded them of the promise that had been made to us by Karadžić. We reminded them of the importance of verifying what sort of camps these were and we told them that. Although it was dangerous we were prepared to take that risk.

Asked about the reaction with which these points were greeted, Williams said,

> A number of phone calls was [sic] made. There was much shuffling of feet and eventually, once again, we were loaded back into the green army bus, although I think by then Channel Three [ITN on ITV] had a VW van which they had arranged to have bought in from Belgrade so were travelling separately from us.[25]

Finally they set out on their journey on 5 August. But on the way they experienced what appeared to be a gun battle by a small bridge. Williams and Vulliamy both speculated later that it may have been faked: an attempt to persuade faint-hearted journalists to ask to turn back without seeing the camps. It just happened there were no faint-hearted journalists in the party.[26] It is also possible that it could have been used to create a context in which the journalists might have been injured or even killed, all of which could then have been attributed to hostile forces.[27] This was a dirty war, after all.

What they may not have realised because communications

from the war zone were difficult was that the day before their trip *The Guardian* had published another story about the camps. In Geneva on 3 August the International Committee of the Red Cross (ICRC) had said publicly that 'all sides in the Yugoslav conflict were violating human rights conventions in their treatment of civilians from other ethnic groups'. Relief organisations were quoted as saying that the 'Croat–Muslim alliance as well as the Serbs had set up what were in effect concentration camps'.[28] In response, a US State Department spokesman, Richard Boucher, was quoted saying that the US government, while 'deeply concerned' about the camps, was not going to make detentions 'a special issue'. Likewise, a UN spokesman had said that people

> think it is just the Serbs but that is not the case. Serb civilians who have fled, or been forced to flee, Croat and Muslim-held areas also give convincing accounts of mistreatment. The fact that the Serbs are better-armed and hold much more territory certainly makes the size of the problem greater where they are in control. The Serb militias are certainly ferocious, but the Croat militias are no angels either.[29]

What would the journalists discover when they got to see the camps?

Eventually, the party was taken to see Omarska and Trnopolje. At each location the journalists were allowed to spend an hour moving about the camps, filming and talking to camp inmates; while they did so they were in turn filmed by Republika Srpska military cameramen. What the reporters brought out with them would cause a stir. While at Trnopolje Penny Marshall had been handed a roll of film by Dr Idriz Merdžanić, a Muslim inmate, who was acting as a camp doctor. The film, when developed, would show the marks left on several prisoners by beatings.

Of the camp at Omarska, Ian Williams said,

> What confronted us was, frankly, an appalling scene. The silence perhaps spoke volumes. No one spoke, terrified sunken eyes,

dishevelled filthy prisoners, eating like famished dogs while over them stood well-fed fat Serbian guards with their guns cocked. It was an appalling vision of inhumanity. These people had been starved. They were in a disgraceful state.[30]

Ed Vulliamy found inmates, or internees, who were 'horribly thin, raw-boned; some are almost cadaverous, with skin like parchment folded around their arms; their faces are lantern-jawed, and their eyes are haunted by the empty stare of the prisoner who does not know what will happen to him next'.[31]

When later the party was moved onto Trnopolje, a journey that took them around half an hour, the party found what was described as a civilian-controlled transit camp. The ITN team, driving in their VW minivan, arrived first. Vulliamy wrote that there was

> complete confusion – political and physical. The camp is a ramshackle fenced-in compound around a former school. The men stand stripped to the waist, in their thousands, against the wire in the relentless afternoon heat; the women and children seek shade upstairs in the crowded, smelly building. They wait, stare at nothing, sweat – and wonder what will happen next.[32]

Williams said of that camp, 'The physical condition of the men penned in was very bad. Many had been brought from another camp that day. Some had come from Omarska, some had come from a camp called Kheratam [sic].[33] They were in a very bad physical condition, emaciated, dirty and clearly very, very frightened.' [34]

As the visits ended the journalists faced a long journey back to Belgrade. They knew that what they had seen was important and they also knew that they were potentially in danger for that very reason. Their particular concern was simple – get the tapes out of the country. They decided to travel first to Belgrade and piled into the ITV News VW minivan: the four-strong *Channel 4*

News team, the three-strong ITV News team, plus Ed Vulliamy, two fixer/interpreters and the driver, Misha.

Penny Marshall highlighted the problem:

> I was very keen to get out of Bosnia safely with all our tapes, because you are often stopped in these circumstances at road blocks and very often they'll confiscate all your tapes from you, sometimes even take your equipment, which happened to me on a subsequent trip about two weeks later. So we were actually extremely anxious and there's nobody to my knowledge who had made that journey across that particular area before safely. We were just very anxious to do it.[35]

Ed Vulliamy shared the concern, remembering that they all tried to occupy themselves with the distraction of remembering how much of the Beatles' *Sgt Pepper* album they could each remember.[36]

Ian Williams remembered:

> I think everybody was pretty stunned. We had seen some pretty harrowing images. We had seen some pretty clear evidence of inhumanity. We were stunned and there was also a sense of 'Are they going to let us get out of here with these tapes?' because we knew the material we had was powerful. We knew the material we had was the first evidence, the first-hand evidence of inhumanity in this part of Northern Bosnia and, frankly, at one point, we wondered if we would actually get out of Bosnia with those tapes.[37]

They reached Belgrade at around midnight – after some hairy moments along the way, including passing between two battle fronts. Shortly after they arrived they were asked to meet Liberal Democrat leader Paddy Ashdown in the Belgrade Hyatt hotel. Ashdown had just arrived in Belgrade on a fact-finding visit with his party's foreign affairs spokesman, Sir Russell Johnston, and wanted to know what they had found out.[38] After the meeting they parted company: Vulliamy would be staying in Belgrade to write his report, and the ITN and Channel 4 teams would have some food and snatch a couple of hours of much-needed rest before travelling separately to the Hungarian capital, Budapest, where they were scheduled to edit their stories and send them on to London via satellite link. But before they sorted themselves out Penny Marshall and Ian Williams telephoned their respective editors in London to tell them what they had seen and filmed. Penny Marshall said, 'We knew we had established something extraordinary was taking place that needed to be reported on, as clear from the rushes [uncut video material], and on the basis of that I rang London and they sent out a team.'[39] After making the call she was intent on getting a good night's sleep 'to make sure ... I had a whole day to do an edit'.[40] Ian Williams called Sue Inglish: 'I told her that we had very powerful pictures, that we had a very strong story which went some way to confirm the rumours, the allegations that had existed about what was happening in North-East Bosnia.'[41] The next morning, at the crack of dawn, each team set off for Budapest.

When they reached their destination they met Bill Frost, a video editor who had flown out from London especially to assist Marshall's team with their story. The *Channel 4 News* footage would be edited by James Nicholas, who had shot it. Their bosses in London had also organised separate local professional production facilities for them to use, so that they could work with maximum speed and the minimum of disruption. Over the course of the next few hours each worked intensively and independently of the other, shaping their stories and pictures to show what they had found. They did not discuss their stories, share 'angles' or details.[42] Among other things, there just wasn't the time for them to discuss their approaches.

Xylophone ribs

London was keen for the reporters to tell their strong stories. Penny Marshall's first filmed story was scheduled for ITV's *News at 5.45* and she was also to do a live two-way interview about what she had seen. Ian Williams's report was scheduled to be broadcast around seventy-five minutes later, during the early part of *Channel 4 News*, and he too would be interviewed live on air; later Penny Marshall's main report would be broadcast on *News at Ten*.

Ian Williams takes up the story: 'We had strong images and in a sense there was a desire to hear less of me and to be able to just allow people to see the visual evidence of what we had found in Omarska and Trnopolje.'[43] Marshall's approach was much the same.

Williams first saw the footage that Marshall was using for her *News at 5.45* report as it was being uploaded to the satellite for transmission to London. As the video was playing he saw the image of a skeletal inmate from Trnopolje looking through a fence that was a mix of barbed wire and chicken wire. The man's name was Fikret Alić, and his 'xylophone ribs', as Ed Vulliamy later described them, caught Williams's eye. He felt it was 'a very good shot' and asked to use that footage alongside his own team's images from Trnopolje for his *Channel 4 News* story. He had just an hour or so for the footage to be cut into his story, so he and his editor would have to work fast if they were to meet their own uploading deadline.[44]

When the ITN reports were broadcast, on 6 August 1992, and Vulliamy's report published the following morning, the reaction was spectacular: the story made the lead in most of the national newspapers; and it was also picked up as a major story worldwide. It also had political repercussions. Within twenty minutes of seeing it in the White House on television, President George H. Bush reacted immediately. He 'pledged that the United States "will not rest" until international organizations, such as the Red Cross, can inspect camps',[45] but, according to the *New York Times*, his calls had opened a 'three-way split at the United Nations over the role of its peacekeeping forces in the region'.[46] Two days after the reports made the front pages, British Foreign Secretary Douglas Hurd said on BBC Radio 4, 'I hope that there will be a Security Council resolution in the next few days which will put the emphasis on the escorting, the protection, of humanitarian help.' But, he continued, 'it may well involve the use of force'.[47] However, neither he, President Bush nor French President François Mitterrand were willing to send forces to stop the conflict, responsibility for which, in their view, was due largely 'but not exclusively, to Serbian nationalist forces'.[48] This reluctance prompted Paddy Ashdown, after returning from his visit to Republika Srpska, to write to Prime Minister John Major expressing his outrage at what he had seen and heard and pressing for speedy action. Ashdown said, 'I do not think that we have done ourselves any favours by our failures both of will and of action in the Yugoslav conflicts.'[49] In Belgrade, 'moderate but by then redundant Yugoslav President Dobrica Ćosić demanded that the camps be closed within thirty days'.[50] They were.[51] On 18 August, John Major had summoned his Cabinet back from holiday for an emergency meeting about the civil war and shortly afterwards announced that he would be despatching 1,800 troops to Bosnia.[52]

Vulliamy filed his report, which was published in *The Guardian* on 7 August. But he immediately 'shied from calling them concentration camps', he later wrote, 'because of the inevitable association with the bestial policies of the Third Reich'.[53] However, on reflection he later decided that 'concentration camp' was 'exactly the right term for what we uncovered that day'.[54] Eight months after Vulliamy and the ITN teams first visited the camps, the UN's Human Rights Committee also decided that they were concentration camps.[55] A year later so did the UN's Independent Commission of Experts.[56] But, when their report was published on 27 May 1994, they reflected the ICRC's comments of 3 August 1992: the reality had been that all sides had operated camps of varying descriptions, but it had taken two years to assemble a corroborated analysis.[57]

Over the months following the ITN footage broadcast on ITV and Channel 4 and the *Guardian* reports, many other stories were published about the camps, and the image of Fikret Alić was widely used, often juxtaposed with photographs of the Third Reich's concentration camps. The three reporters' stories had stimulated some short-term political action and it raised public awareness about what was going on in Bosnia, which heaped pressure on the politicians to act.

The impact of the reports had been such that all three journalists received awards: Penny Marshall and Ian Williams shared the 1992 British Academy of Film and Television Arts (BAFTA) award for Best News/Actuality Coverage and from the Royal Television Society (RTS) its International News Award for 1992. In the United States they jointly won an Emmy for Outstanding Investigative Journalism; Ed Vulliamy received several awards, including the 1992 British Press Awards International Reporter of the Year.[58] And there the story might have ended. Save for one of those unpredictable twists of fate. In this case the arrest of one man in Munich.

Hague trial

After the civil war in Bosnia ended, the long process of establishing the peace began. The United Nations set up a commission of experts under a Security Council resolution which took detailed evidence on all the camps in Bosnia operated by Serbs, Croats and Muslims. The commission concluded that 'all information all information available about Logor [*Serbo-Croat meaning camp*] Omarska seems to indicate that it was more than anything else a death camp'.[59] Of Trnopolje the commission concluded that it was not a death camp in the same sense as Omarska, but 'the label "concentration camp" is none the less justified for Logor Trnopolje due to the regime prevailing in the camp'.[60] One of the other crucial components for establishing peace was bringing to justice at least some of those who were accused of committing war crimes and/or crimes against humanity. A special court, the International Criminal Tribunal for the Former Yugoslavia (ICTY), was set up in The Hague to try those who had been arrested. In the years since the war finished ICTY has been hearing cases – as soon as suspects have been apprehended and taken into custody in the Netherlands. In some cases justice was relatively swift because suspects were quickly apprehended. But in other cases suspects were fugitives for years and bringing them to justice was a protracted and complicated process, as the cases against Slobodan Milošević, Radovan Karadžić and Ratko Mladić show.[61]

One suspect brought to justice at the outset was a minor military commander, a former café-owner and electrician called Duško Tadić. Tadić was accused of 'crimes against humanity', 'grave breaches of the 1949 Geneva Conventions' and 'violations of the laws or customs of war'. The charges related to his participation in the ethnic cleansing of Bosniak Muslims from parts of the Prijedor region of northern Bosnia – including Keraterm, Omarska and Trnopolje camps.[62] He was arrested in Munich early in 1994 by 'a plain-clothes special commando unit of the Bavarian police'.[63] His trial was initially going to be held in Germany, but with ICTY set up he was transferred to the tribunal's jurisdiction in April 1995. Tadić was one of many figures in the conflict, but he was 'alleged to have been part of a cruel plan, and he's a symbol of why this tribunal was created'.[64] His trial opened in May 1996 and he was ultimately convicted and sentenced to twenty years' imprisonment (April 1997).

In making its preparations for the trial the prosecution had asked ITN to supply copies of the uncut video material of the camps at Omarska and Trnopolje, which had been taken by Penny Marshall's and Ian Williams's cameramen. ITN agreed but this was a decision which was to earn it criticism and enemies.

At the opening of the trial Ed Vulliamy wrote in *The Guardian* that 'the core of the case is the Omarska concentration camp for Muslim and Croat prisoners, uncovered by *The Guardian* and ITN in August 1992'. The prosecutor, Grant Niemann, alleged that Tadić had been 'one of the perpetrators of ... the most horrific Serbian violence'.[65] Vulliamy said that Tadić, who had 'pleaded not guilty to a litany of killings, torture, sexual assaults,

and other physical and psychological abuse and to persecution'
was accused of 'playing a pivotal role in the ethnic cleansing
that swept across north-western Bosnia during 1992'. When
the video material was shown in open court Vulliamy wrote in
The Guardian,

> I had not seen ITN's 'rushes' – the untransmitted footage – of
> that day, with which the court accompanied my account. I have
> described the scene a thousand times but it never fades and here
> it was in vivid detail. The yard drill, the canteen, those spindly
> fingers, lantern jaws and burning eyes, the guards swinging
> their guns...[66]

The still images of beatings at Trnopolje taken on a camera owned
by Dr Azra Blazević, who was called as a prosecution witness,
lent considerable weight to the case.

Given the importance of the video material in the proceedings,
Tadić's defence team decided to engage the services of a media
expert, Thomas Deichmann, who would help it understand the
news coverage that had identified Tadić and establish any weak-
nesses that would help refute the prosecution's case. Deichmann
was editor-in-chief of a bi-monthly small-circulation journal called
Novo, and his journalism had been published in Europe and the
United States.[67] He 'specialised in German foreign politics and as
a result of that also on the Bosnian war, the crisis in Yugoslavia
and the Balkans'. The topics were 'intensively connected' because
'Germany was the first country to recognise Croatia and Slovenia'
and there had been public debate about it.[68]

In the words of one academic, Professor David Campbell, it
was 'Deichmann's views' that 'were the probable reason that
led him to be hired as a media expert' by Tadić's defence team.
Tadić's lawyers had 'sought to discredit' the news media's work in
identifying their client by arguing that it was really 'the extensive
media coverage in Germany, rather than first-hand experience
in Bosnia' – that is eyewitness testimony – which had firmly

identified him and his alleged activities. In other words without the press evidence there would be little else upon which to base a prosecution. Campbell said that 'Deichmann's content analysis of the German media provided the empirical basis' for the argument which had apparently impressed the judges, but ultimately had not prevented Tadić from being found guilty.[69] It was while Deichmann was evaluating the evidence that he gained access to ITN's camp footage, via the defence team. He took a copy of the video.

Deichmann studied the rushes in detail and thought that he saw something that to him was very interesting. He compared the uncut material with the footage used in the broadcast television news reports and concluded that the latter was misleading. He considered that the images used in both Penny Marshall's and Ian Williams's reports had given a very different view of Omarska and Trnopolje from that which he saw in the uncut rushes; and in particular, the barbed wire and chicken wire through which Fikret Alić had been filmed was not what he thought it seemed. Rather than Alić being behind the fencing, Deichmann thought he detected that the journalists were the ones who were behind the fence – he calculated that they were in a compound filming outwards – and that the area where the inmates had gathered was not bounded by fences at all, but rather was open to the countryside. He thought what he had seen would be a story worth publishing, because he considered that what he had seen amounted to a misrepresentation of the visual evidence.

When he returned to Germany from The Hague, he contacted the editor of a magazine whose articles *Novo* had sometimes published in translation, *Living Marxism*, or *LM* as it would later be called, along with a number of editors of other European publications. He put all on notice that he might be able to provide a story for them sometime in the future about 'this question of Trnopolje camp and the location of barbed wire'.[70] *LM*'s editor, Mick Hume, recalled that Deichmann had told him that he 'had something very interesting, and he sent me the transcript of an interview that he had done with Professor Mischa Wladimiroff', who had been the leading member of Tadić's defence team. Deichmann told Hume that Wladimiroff had appointed him as an expert to help with the defence case.[71] Hume told Deichmann that he was indeed interested in publishing the story because 'I knew him as a very reliable researcher, a good journalist'.[72] Hume read an edited version of the Wladimiroff interview in which the professor 'had some very interesting things to say about the famous barbed wire fence at Trnopolje'. Hume eventually published 'a shortened version' of the interview in *LM*.[73]

Press release

Ultimately, Deichmann completed his research – including a visit to the Trnopolje camp's site four years after it had closed – and readied his article for publication in *LM*. Before it was published, *LM* put out a press release to draw attention to it, which was distributed by Two-Ten Communications, a wire service. When ITN management saw it they were horrified. The press release was promoting an article that not only accused two of the company's leading journalists of misrepresenting what they had seen in the camps, but also that they had deliberately distorted the facts. By doing so the article in effect alleged that ITN had contravened its statutory obligation to broadcast balanced, impartial and objective news stories. This was serious stuff: it impugned ITN and its reporters and damaged its credibility and standing worldwide. If sustained it would be difficult to shrug off those allegations and it would have damaging repercussions with its overseas customers, destroying a reputation it had carefully and conscientiously built up over more than forty years. ITN decided it had no choice but to reject the allegations and fight to set the record straight.

Through its lawyers ITN managed to get hold of a pre-publication copy of the magazine from the BBC, which had been contacted by Deichmann and offered a copy of ITN's rushes. There they read that Fikret Alić's picture, which had 'for many … become a symbol of the horrors of the Bosnian war', was 'misleading'. Deichmann's article went on to say that the inmates at Trnopolje 'were not imprisoned behind a barbed wire fence' because it wasn't surrounding the camp at all. 'Trnopolje camp ... was not a prison, and certainly not a "concentration camp", but a collection centre for refugees, many of whom went there seeking safety and could leave again if they wished.'[74]

ITN discovered that the BBC's media correspondent, Nick Higham, was already working on the story, and they suspected that he was taking a perspective that *LM*'s allegations might just be true. ITN's editor-in-chief, Richard Tait, who had been the editor of *Channel 4 News* when Ian Williams's story had originally been broadcast, interviewed all of the people involved in bringing the reports back from Bosnia, viewed the broadcast items and the rushes and researched *LM*'s background and motives. He concluded that it was clear that *LM*'s story 'was a wicked lie from a weird fringe organisation with a track record of supporting the Bosnian Serbs and of vilifying the previous reporting of the camps by Roy Gutman'. He decided that 'we [ITN] had to defend ourselves and our teams'.[75]

At that stage there was more than just professional pride at stake. *LM* magazine had been in touch not only with the BBC but ITN's customers, like CNN, who had transmitted the original stories around the world. Understandably CNN told ITN of their concerns. As Richard Tait was 'fielding calls from ITN's customers and friends' he got wind that the BBC and a number of newspapers were planning imminent coverage of the allegations.

I had been the editor-in-chief of ITN who approved the transmission of the original reports. Now, having been promoted to chief executive of the company, I supported the new editor-in-chief's recommendation that ITN should be prepared to take legal action. It was to prove a controversial decision. On 24 January ITN sent a 'letter before action' telling *LM* that the story was untrue and that they should withdraw it and apologise.

However, according to Tait, '*LM* continued its campaign of vilification' and the company had to reassure its customers (ITV and Channel 4), its main regulator (the Independent Television Commission, later absorbed into Ofcom), and those that had given it awards (BAFTA and the RTS), that the allegations were completely unfounded. Meanwhile, the editor of *LM*, Mick Hume, called on ITN's awards to be withdrawn and made claims that the BBC and *The Times* thought *LM* had a great story on its hands.

Writ

In the light of these developments ITN decided that it had no alternative other than to issue a writ for libel, which it did on 31 January 1997. However, the magazine continued to attack. On 10 February it demanded that RTS, BAFTA, *Broadcast* and two international awards bodies should strip ITN of its prizes.

Mick Hume was described by BBC reporter Martin Bell as 'a professional contrarian',[76]and, according to *The Guardian*'s Luke Harding, the magazine's supporters were a 'surprisingly soigné army of students and media studies lecturers' who appeared undeterred by the writs that were flying around, and were 'turning the issue into a wider ideological crusade'.[77] In an article Harding said a *Living Marxism* fundraising event in March 1997 heard from 'a heavily-accented Serbian' speaker who 'announced blithely from the audience: "We have investigated the question of rape. There have only been eight documented cases in the former Yugoslavia."'

Harding wondered why 'a small left-wing revolutionary group, whose cadres appear to come largely from the former polytechnic sector' was 'making common cause with a bunch of unreconstructed Serbian nationalists'. He said *LM* argued that the causes of the Bosnian civil war lay not in 'resurgent Balkan nationalism' but in the Western powers' self-interest.[78] The magazine was also against gun control.[79]

In response Hume wrote to *The Guardian* declaring that 'Luke Harding doesn't like *Living Marxism*, me or Thomas Deichmann. But it might have been more useful for your readers if he had bothered to deal with the actual evidence that Deichmann has presented … Instead, on this central issue, there is a resounding silence.'[80]

At various times the magazine's supporters included the former Conservative MP George Walden, who had written 'an article praising *LM* in the *London Evening Standard*', and its advertisements included 'admiring quotes from Fay Weldon and J. G. Ballard'.[81]

But in an article headlined 'I Stand by My Story' Ed Vulliamy vigorously rejected Deichmann's arguments. He wrote, 'I was interviewing Fikret Alić while he was filmed. He had arrived from another camp, Keraterm, where he had witnessed the massacre of 200 prisoners in a single night – a crime confirmed by subsequent investigations.' He rejected Deichmann's claim 'that ITN "cooked" the picture, eager to show Alic behind the fence to give the impression that he was a captive' because they had been under pressure to come back with a concentration camps story. In his view Deichmann's contention was 'poison in the water supply of history, contaminating the reservoir of truth'.[82] But it went deeper than what might have been dismissed as personal pride. Vulliamy continued, 'One of the many things that this poison does is to very seriously defame ITN, *The Guardian* (for whom I wrote the story), Penny, Ian, the crew and myself.' However, Deichmann's article also suggested that Vulliamy 'wilfully misled The Hague war crimes tribunal by bringing our alleged conspiracy into my evidence'.

Vulliamy noted in passing another possible dimension – that it was 'especially scandalous since the [*LM*] article emerges just as the judges in … the trial of Duško Tadić … are due to give their verdict'. Vulliamy then reminded readers that 'unsurprisingly' Deichmann had been one of Tadić's defence witnesses.

In the meantime, ITN had launched an action as well against Two-Ten Communications, which was owned by the Press Association. In the High Court on 17 April 1997 the company apologised through its solicitor, Karen Mason, and said that it distributed press releases supplied by its clients without making any editorial input or amendment. ITN accepted the apology.[83]

As to its dispute with *LM* itself, ITN felt it had to take the case to trial. But by issuing a writ for libel the company committed itself to a court hearing unless *LM* apologised. ITN could hardly drop the action without receiving an apology and an admission of fault on *LM*'s part because doing this would have implied to the outside world that there must have been a germ of truth in the allegations.

ITN concluded that *LM* did not have any evidence to back up its allegations and hoped for an out-of-court settlement, which would have saved everyone the expense of a full trial hearing. But *LM*'s editor and publishers declined to offer a full apology and retraction.

However, it was becoming increasingly clear to ITN that, despite the lack of any evidence supporting *LM*'s allegations, the idea that there was something wrong with its story was being fairly widely discussed in journalistic and official circles. ITN's chairman, Mark Wood, had had a meeting with BBC executives who told him of their presumption that there was something in the coverage that was faked. ITN also discovered that a senior UN official had spoken disparagingly of its reporting. Those undercurrents determined ITN's course of action: if ITN's good reputation was to be preserved it would be down to a libel jury to do it.

It took three years for the action to get to the High Court in London. Richard Tait admitted that with the benefit of hindsight, 'ITN would have been better to press on with the court action earlier, but journalists are rightly reluctant to sue other journalists.'[84] Among the sceptics about ITN's decision to sue was Martin Bell, who himself had 'been a target for Mr Hume's verbal assault force'. He wrote that the libel action 'should never have been brought; in a free society, if not a Marxist one, journalists should refrain from suing each other'.[85]

But some went further than Bell and didn't just dispute ITN's decision, they challenged ITN's journalism, suggesting an anti-Serb bias. In October 1998, the future Conservative Education Secretary Michael Gove, then a journalist on *The Times*, wrote about the libel action, which then was still over a year away. In an article headlined 'Speaking Up for the Serbs' he told his readers that *LM* faced 'possible extinction at the hands of a powerful organisation it dared to criticise. Independent Television News has been so stung by an article in the magazine that it is using its formidable resources to pursue a libel writ against *LM*.' Gove saw it as a struggle between *LM*'s David and the ITN Goliath. He argued that *LM* were 'libertarians of the Left who now regard consensus as the enemy, not capitalism'. This seemed to strike a chord with Gove, who was from the libertarian right. He acknowledged that ITN's powerful images had a great influence on Western attitudes, but he believed that 'Trnopolje was not an extermination camp like Auschwitz, but a transit camp for prisoners-of-war'. Gove opined that while ethnic cleansing may have been dreadfully evil it was not comparable to the Holocaust. The problem was that 'ITN may not have wanted to equate Serb actions in Bosnia with the Holocaust. But their pictures allowed others to.'

Gove added to his charge sheet against ITN by citing a potential new Balkan tragedy: the Kosovo conflict, in which the NATO countries where lining up against Serbia. ITN's pictures, he argued, had also allowed the skewing of 'perceptions of a nation against whom we may be about to wage war ... confusion about the enemy can lead us into a no man's land'.

Gove's article drew a response from Richard Tait in which he defended ITN's staff. He made the point that,

> far from this being a rich company pursuing a poor, this is a case of ITN defending two honest and courageous journalists against vilification by a glossy and apparently well-funded magazine. We made clear to *LM* last year that we sought an apology and costs and would forgo damages. If they choose to run the risk of paying the price for what they said about us, that is their responsibility.[86]

ITN pressed ahead with their legal action and both sides prepared to do battle in the High Court in early 2000. It was at this point that John Simpson entered the story. He had started his BBC career as a sub-editor in the radio newsroom, which he 'hated', before realising his ambition to become a reporter and then a foreign correspondent. After ventures into political reporting where he felt 'utterly, utterly shackled' and TV news presenting, 'I was a crap newsreader,' he returned to foreign reporting.[87]

Strange Places, Questionable People was the title of a book he wrote in 1999 about his life as a foreign correspondent. He made a brief reference to ITN's coverage of the Bosnian camps. He wrote that it had been 'British television which gave a powerful impetus to the idea that the Bosnian war was the present-day Holocaust. By some clever planning a team from ITN managed to get to the camps run by the Bosnian Serbs at Omarska and Trnopolje.' He said that the 'pictures were quite unforgettable', had spread around the world but, 'somehow along the way, though, the reservations of the ITN team which filmed them were ignored. The ITN team was careful not to make the analogy with Nazi concentration camps. Others did.' This was very similar to the line Michael Gove had taken.

But then Simpson went on to publicly sign up to the Deichmann interpretation of the pictures. 'The skeletal figures weren't inside the barbed wire, for instance, they were *outside* it. The wire was old and ran round a small enclosure. The cameraman got behind the wire to film the scene.'[88]

Just weeks before the trial opened the news broke that Simpson had gone even further and had offered his services to *LM*'s defence team. Eddie Gibb, a journalist writing for the Scottish Sunday newspaper the *Sunday Herald*, wrote, 'The BBC and ITN are preparing for a head-to-head court battle over the reporting of the war in Bosnia. Veteran BBC foreign editor John Simpson has been lined up as an expert witness for *LM* magazine, which is being sued over an article it published in 1997 about ITN's reporting of Bosnia's "death camps".'[89]

In another, longer report in the same issue Gibb wrote that the 'case will raise fascinating questions about the limits of press freedom – and the fact *LM* is calling BBC foreign editor John Simpson as a defence witness offers the intriguing prospect of representatives from Britain's two biggest news broadcasters duking it out in court'.[90]

Behind the scenes Simpson's offer of help to *LM* had led to him preparing a witness statement which, like all such court documents, had to be disclosed to the other side, in this case ITN. At the company's headquarters in Gray's Inn Road, the senior executives and their legal advisers were shocked by what they read. Simpson's statement was a direct attack on the integrity of the company and its journalists. The contents of John Simpson's statement are revealed here for the first time.

The BBC correspondent pointed out that he had done long tours of duty in Sarajevo and elsewhere in Bosnia, and had 'acquired a very clear understanding of what the Bosnian Serbs did to their prisoners'. He admitted that 'I have not been to either Omarska or Trnopolje camps' but reported that he'd had long conversations with an investigator for the International War Crimes Tribunal at The Hague who had examined the circumstances in the camps in the light of ITN's report. His view was that it was not an accurate reflection of conditions in Trnopolje.[91]

He went on to dispute ITN's technical evidence, essentially on the basis that the BBC didn't do things that way. Simpson looked at ITN's evidence and the tapes, and in his view the barbed wire issue was as Deichmann had described it.

Simpson then expressed his opinion that

> the ITN team presumably realised this; but when the pictures were edited and presented these two points [that Fikret Alić was no longer threatened and that there was no barbed wire to keep him in], so essential to an understanding of what was going on at Trnopolje, were not made. They edited out altogether an interview they had recorded with a prisoner who seemed intelligent and not speaking out of fear, who told them that Trnopolje was not too bad. The commentary on the report as broadcast reflected this to

some extent, but the report was edited in such a way that it was dominated by pictures of an apparently starving man apparently imprisoned behind barbed wire. This image dominated everything. It reminded us all so much of the Nazi death camps that we assumed that we were seeing.

Later Simpson said bluntly that

ITN's reporting of Trnopolje was, I believe, profoundly mislead-ing. They should not have edited out the interview with the man who told them that the camp was not too bad. They should have explained about Fikret Alić and the barbed wire. If I had allowed elements as misleading as these to enter one of my reports, I would have regarded it as a matter of professional duty to put the record straight as quickly as possible. And if I found out that a BBC report by someone else had contained elements as misleading as this, especially in a matter of such importance, I would insist that the report should be changed and the wrongful impression corrected; no matter how awkward and embarrassing it might be.

His concluding remarks delivered an even wider judgement:

in my view it is not enough to say that even if the pictures weren't what they seemed to be, it doesn't matter because the Serbs were doing bad things elsewhere. Our reporting has to be as honest and as literally true as we can make it. As a result of ITN's report, people were given a false impression about one of the major events of the decade. And when *LM* pointed this out, ITN tried to silence it.

A few days before the trial began, a pre-trial review was held by the judge chosen to preside, Mr Justice Morland. He had joined the bench in 1989 and in 1993 had presided over the trial of the two boys accused of killing Liverpool toddler James Bulger. He also heard two high-profile libel cases in the 1990s, Naomi Campbell's action against the *Daily Mirror* and Neil Hamilton's case against Mohamed Al Fayed, the owner of Harrods.

Before him was the witness statement of John Simpson. Mr Justice Morland ruled that it was not admissible as evidence. The legal problem was that the statement was opinion not fact. It was what Simpson thought might have happened and what other people had told him they thought had happened rather than hard evidence of what had happened. Part of it was clearly hearsay. It was an interesting piece of journalism but Simpson had not actually been a 'witness' to any of it. The judge also ruled that statements by the journalist and writer Phillip Knightley and by 'a leading QC' were similarly inadmissible.

Trial

The libel hearing began on 28 February 2000. Elsewhere in the High Court in London's Strand, American academic Deborah Lipstadt was fighting David Irving in a libel action about the Holocaust that was billed by some as 'History on trial'.[92]

ITN's legal team and its leading counsel, Tom Shields QC, had decided that the best way of demonstrating that there was nothing to hide was to place every member of the teams that had gone into the camps, plus their editorial chains, on the stand where they could tell their own stories in their own words and from where they could be cross-examined by *LM*'s lawyers. It was a bold tactic. None of the ITN witnesses, including me, had ever appeared in a High Court libel case before. Who was to know if there wouldn't be some wrinkle in their evidence that might be seized upon by the other side. ITN really was putting its reputation on the line. The tactic drew some criticism from *LM*'s editor, Mick Hume. At one stage he professed surprise that Nik Gowing, the reporter who helped to get the original invitation from Bosnian Serb leader Radovan Karadžić, had not been called. Hume described him as 'about the only person, apart from the tea lady, we have not heard from in the last two weeks'.[93]

By contrast, with *LM*'s expert witness statements ruled inadmissible, Hume later claimed 'there were eighteen ITN witnesses versus me and Thomas Deichmann ... Presumably that is what the law means by "a level playing field".'[94]

The trial's opening day drew considerable media interest, probably because there was a latent expectation that perhaps ITN had really fallen down on the job and that all would be exposed. But as the days wore on and the journalists, cameramen and sound recordists, editors and executives gave their evidence it became clear to many that the journalists' and their team's modus operandi was transparent and comparable with other media organisations' practices. It was established that the ITV and *Channel 4 News* journalists, team members and editorial staff had all been acutely conscious of the heavy loading of the term 'concentration camp' and all decided not to use it for that reason.

On the matter of the fence the trial spent hours looking at a diagram that Deichmann had compiled when he visited the site of the Trnopolje camp four years after it had been closed. It had accompanied his article and *LM*'s lawyer took the court through the video evidence in 'excruciating detail' to show from where each shot had been taken.[95] *LM* had argued that because it was not complete and there was no contiguous boundary around what had been called Trnopolje camp, inmates were there for their own protection (according to the magazine) and were free to come and go. Moreover, Deichmann had argued, the area into which the journalists, cameramen, sound recordists and their minders had strayed was partially fenced and it was that fence through which the pictures of Fikret Alić had been taken.

However, during the various testimonies it became clear that the journalists, who were shepherded by Serb minders and only at Trnopolje and Omarska for approximately one hour each, had not noticed the exact orientation of fences. There was a telling exchange between Penny Marshall and *LM*'s barrister, Gavin Millar. When he asked her about the shot of Fikret Alić through the fence and the fact that it 'had assumed some significance as far as other media commentators and newspapers were concerned', she agreed: 'the image had become important because people were appalled by his condition'. But then she added, 'But you look at the picture and see barbed wire; I look at the picture and see Fikret. That is the difference between us.'[96]

The video evidence made available to the court was what had survived: in his opening remarks ITN's counsel had told the court that one of the camera tapes, which had contained closing footage taken at Omarska and the opening footage of Trnopolje, had been lost from ITN's archive several years before. The loss had only been discovered when ITN had been asked by the International Court, ICTY, to provide copies of all their footage to the court in 1995–96 for the Tadić trial. However, the missing footage was not considered to be a key and *LM*'s barrister did not make an issue of it, taking the view that what was available was sufficient for establishing the magazine's defence. But the loss led some observers to see something suspicious.[97]

The witness whose evidence appeared to observers to have the greatest impact came not from ITN or *LM* but from one of the camps. He was the Trnopolje camp doctor, who had been interviewed on film during the journalists' visit nearly eight years previously. Providing first-hand witness testimony, Dr Idriz Merdžanić, told the court that he had not been taken to Trnopolje camp of his own free will.[98] He said that he had nothing but the floor on which to sleep[99] and that the camp doctors were told that they would be held responsible for anyone who went missing from the camp.[100] He said that the medical laboratory was used for prisoner beatings and that screams were 'regularly' heard coming from inside.[101] He told how he had received the camera with which he took the still photographs of the beating victims, and passed on the film to Marshall, from Dr Azra Blažević.[102] Dr Merdžanić told the court that one of the people that he had photographed had subsequently died from his injuries.[103] He also said that one of the doctors, Dr Jusuf Pašić, had been transferred to Omarska where he had been killed.[104] Dr Merdžanić also told the court that there had been women at the camp, some of whom had been raped – 'particularly at night'.[105] When asked about food, the doctor said that it had first been brought into the camp by locals, although after they were 'sent away from their houses' the inmates had been allowed into the surrounding fields to dig potatoes and prepare meals, but that afterwards the ICRC had come to the camp and distributed food.[106] Medicine had been non-existent at the camp and lice rife, according to Dr Merdžanić.[107]

Dr Merdžanić told the court that preparations were made before the journalists visited the camp:

> A few days before they came we felt different. There were differences … Azra Blažević was the first one to find out that the journalists were coming … she found that out from a guard a day before … We decided to give them that film because we didn't know at the time whether that would be the last chance.[108]

But after the journalists left, Dr Merdžanić sensed real change for the better: 'Things were changing really fast. Other journalists started to arrive. Some people were coming from some international organisations, so then they ordered the wire to be taken down. People were allowed to go behind wire…'[109] Prisoners were registered, and that gave them a degree of protection. However, Dr Merdžanić also recounted the story of five prisoners brought to the camp while the Red Cross was absent. They had been beaten and eventually killed.[110]

At the end of the doctor's questioning by ITN's barrister, the court turned to *LM*'s counsel, Gavin Millar, expecting him to rise and challenge the evidence. Millar told the judge that he did not wish to question Dr Merdžanić. It was a crucial moment. This was first-hand testimony from a man who had seen what really happened at Trnopolje and *LM* had decided not to lay a glove on him. If John Simpson had been called as a witness later it would have been interesting to hear his response to Dr Merdžanić's evidence.

For *LM* Mick Hume and Thomas Deichmann were questioned and cross-examined for just over a day and made robust defences of their case. The trial has been analysed in detail by Professor David Campbell of Durham University and he also looked into some of the broader issues of the case, in particular some of the wider aspects of the fence and the description of Omarska and Trnopolje. Professor Campbell has noted that *LM*'s witnesses 'conceded the central point of their case against ITN'. They had acknowledged that 'the nature of the fence at Trnopolje had *nothing* to do with the issue of whether Alic and others were imprisoned in a camp'.[111] Both men had admitted that conditions at Trnopolje were severe and that killings, rapes and other brutal acts had occurred often. Moreover, the continuing presence of armed guards effectively meant that the inmates could not leave: they were imprisoned if not by a visible fence, then by an invisible one. The consequences of crossing either could be equally lethal.

After the closing statements and the judge's summing up, Mr Justice Morland advised the jury about the maximum damages, including aggravated damages, that could be made if it found for the plaintiffs.[112] The jury then retired and considered its verdict. After asking to review some of the video[113] it returned and announced to the court that it found that Penny Marshall, Ian Williams and ITN had been libelled by *LM* and awarded substantial damages to each (£150,000 each to Penny Marshall and Ian Williams for the damage that they had suffered, and £75,000 to ITN).[114]

Aftermath

Almost as soon as the jury made its award BBC reporter Nick Higham, who had been interested in the *LM* story from the start, reported the verdict on the BBC's *Six O'Clock News*. When he came to describing the judge's summing up he conflated the remarks. Higham said on air, 'In his summing up, the judge, Mr Justice Morland, told the jury *LM*'s facts might have been right but he asked, "Did that matter?"' It certainly mattered to ITN, who immediately contacted the BBC and asked for an apology.[115] ITN said that nowhere in his summing up had the judge used the words '*LM*'s facts might have been right'. Although he had used the words 'but does it matter', this had been in connection with another issue, namely whether the ITN team had been mistaken in thinking that they were not enclosed by an old barbed wire fence.[116]

BBC News acknowledged that their 6 p.m. summary of the judge's wording had been 'too condensed'.[117] Later that evening they broadcast a different and more accurate version of the story in the *Nine O'Clock News*. But they did not broadcast any retraction or apology for the earlier story. ITN made a formal complaint to one of the television regulators, the Broadcasting Standards Commission. The BSC examined the matter thoroughly and took representations from both parties. It considered Higham's draft script, 'which had been more precise about the role of the fence', but noted that Higham had 'been asked about 10 minutes before the start of the bulletin to shorten his report by at least 20 seconds'. In that time he 'over-condensed' his story. The BSC's verdict was that

> it was clear from the report as a whole that ITN had won the case. However ... the BBC's paraphrase of the judge's summing up could have left viewers with the false impression that ITN had got its facts wrong and won its case on a technicality. The Commission finds that this was unfair to ITN and to Ms Marshall and Mr Williams.

The BBC had to broadcast the BSC's finding.

LM and its supporters were more focused on the court's verdict rather than the BSC's finding and Mick Hume wrote a short piece in *The Times*. He complained about the trial's limits and that

> we could not win because the law demanded that we prove the unprovable – what was going on in the ITN journalists' minds eight years ago. We have apologised for nothing but we are not

going to appeal. Life is too short to waste any more time in the bizarre world of the libel courts.[118]

Twelve years later Hume was still smarting, at least a little, when in a book about free speech, he explained how 'my publisher and I were left with a personal bill of around a million quid in costs and damages'. He told his readers that 'the only thing this case has proved beyond reasonable doubt is that the libel laws are a menace to a free press and a disgrace to a democracy'.[119]

In 2000, John Simpson published another volume of memoirs in which he included a chapter of miscellanies, which he entitled 'Absurdities'. One issue on which he dwelt over two pages was ITN's duel with *LM*. He did not disclose what he had said in his witness statement about ITN 'misleading' the world. But nor was there any sense of regret about his support for *LM* – almost the opposite. He referred to 'the clever, iconoclastic magazine *LM*' and mentioned that it had been sued by ITN 'for alleging that some of its pictures had been misleading (ITN's boss said, with I presume a very unintended irony, that the case had been brought in order to defend freedom of speech)'.[120]

In Simpson's view, the main point remained about the 'heart of the problem with television news, which is the interpretation of pictures'. He said that 'everything depends on the impression that they are allowed to give the viewer who saw these pictures'.

Simpson did not mention the doctor's evidence of what had actually happened at Trnopolje but offered his own analysis that

> it was essentially a transit camp where people like the skeletal figure they filmed were taken before being released or moved onto other, or worse camps. Unpleasant things could certainly happen to prisoners there; no Muslim in the hands of Bosnian Serb captors during that evil war was entirely safe. But that didn't make Trnopolje what most viewers assumed it was.

On the role of the barbed wire, 'unfortunately the videotape "rushes" which might have proved this one way or the other could not be found'. He concluded: '*LM* lost the case, and was driven out of business by huge damages. Thus was the cause of free speech defended.'[121]

And the story might have finished there in 2000. But for the other reporter who had been there with the ITN teams at Trnopolje and Omarska back in 1992. Through all the years of controversy Ed Vulliamy of *The Guardian* never doubted that what he and the ITN journalists had reported was true and was not misleading. He believed it with a passion and made it almost a personal mission to bear witness to the truth of what he had seen. He kept in touch with the victims and gave evidence at the International Court. Although his own newspaper had not joined the legal battle with *LM*, Vulliamy had never sought to distance himself from those who did. He praised the editor-in-chief of ITN, Richard Tait, 'who realised two things had to be reclaimed: the reputation of his correspondents and the establishment of the truth about what had happened in the camps'.[122]

In 2012 he wrote a powerful and personal book, *The War is Dead, Long Live the War: Bosnia: the Reckoning. The Observer* newspaper had the bright idea of inviting John Simpson to review it.

A decade on from his allegation of 'profoundly misleading' reporting, the BBC's world affairs editor had been having second thoughts. He wrote of 'the overwhelming evil of Omarska, Trnopolje and Srebrenica' and 'the siege of Sarajevo'. He confessed that

> Vulliamy's account of what happened in the camps is completely unanswerable; and I'm sorry now that I supported the small post-Marxist magazine *Living Marxism* when it was sued by ITN for questioning its reporting of the camps. It seemed to me at the time that big, well-funded organisations should not put small magazines out of business; but it's clear that there were much bigger questions involved.

But what of Michael Gove, then of *The Times* and now the Education Secretary in Her Majesty's government? We wrote to his special adviser, putting these questions for Mr Gove:

1. Mr Gove said Trnopolje was 'a transit camp for prisoners-of-war'. What does he now believe happened at Trnopolje?
2. In the light of John Simpson's statement that he is now 'sorry' does Mr Gove have any regrets about the position which he, Mr Gove, took? If so what are they?
3. With hindsight how happy is he that – in the words of the *Times* headline – he was 'speaking up for the Serbs' over allegations of 'ethnic cleansing'?

His special adviser, Henry de Zoete, emailed back, 'I will pass on to Michael and let you know asap.' Mr de Zoete did not get back to us. We sent him two further emails asking for Mr Gove's response, but received no reply.[123]

When John Simpson summarised the Bosnian conflict twenty years on he wrote, 'Few people – journalists, politicians, soldiers – came out of the Bosnian war with much credit.'[124]

Some readers drew the conclusion that Simpson was accepting that he wasn't among the few. But maybe Dr Idriz Merdžanić, who risked his life to establish the truth about what he had seen as a camp doctor, was one of those few people who did emerge with credit.

2

W. N. EWER

Long before there was television news in Britain, before there was even regular radio news, the reporters who helped the public understand international events, the John Simpsons of their day, were the diplomatic correspondents of the national newspapers.

It was common practice for them to be by-lined by their initials rather than their Christian names. So it was that W. N. Ewer, while never a household name in the way that TV reporters such as Simpson would become, was a highly respected journalist for decades, not just in Fleet Street, the heart of the British newspaper industry, but also in Whitehall, the centre of British political power.

Yet the full story of W. N. Ewer was known only to those working elsewhere in London, in the various buildings that made up what the British civil service called 'Box 500' – the postal address of MI5, the British counter-espionage agency. MI5 kept an eye on Ewer throughout his career and from their files we have been able to piece together his story.

The extraordinary life and times of W. N. Ewer were symbolised on 22 September 1964 when a spry and distinguished-looking gentleman stepped out of a car at No. 1 Carlton Gardens, knowing that inside they were going to make a real fuss of him. He knew the place well, having been there before on business, but this time he was to be the guest at a particularly special lunch being held in his honour at the Foreign Secretary's official London residence.

There to greet him was not just the current Foreign Secretary, R. A. 'Rab' Butler, but also one of Butler's predecessors, Selwyn Lloyd. It was an unusually grand welcoming party for a reporter.

At seventy-eight years of age W. N. Ewer had been, for some time, the doyen of his particular trade – London's leading diplomatic correspondent. He had spent most of his career working on the *Daily Herald*, but had also made broadcasts for the BBC, written articles for other publications and penned the occasional political pamphlet. He had also been to Buckingham Palace five years earlier in morning suit and top hat to receive a CBE for his services to journalism.

William Norman Ewer – he rarely used his first name – was known to many of the assembled guests as 'Trilby' after the eponymous George du Maurier character. His friends gave him the nickname when he was young because, like Trilby, he used to walk around barefoot. He didn't do that anymore – at least not when he was 'on duty'.

Norman Ewer had been invited to lunch because afterwards he was to be given a very special gift, which marked the twilight of a distinguished career. He had just officially retired from the *Herald* after fifty-two years. The paper had closed down.

After a short speech Rab Butler presented him with an engraved pass. It was a pass that would give W. N. Ewer, as he signed himself, access to the Foreign Office's News Department, effectively its press office. Such was the esteem in which Norman Ewer was held that he was presented with a pass that would give him access to all of the Foreign Office's press facilities in perpetuity.

It was ironic considering that four decades earlier, in the 1920s, Norman Ewer was a Communist Party member committed to destroying everything that No. 1 Carlton Gardens and the Foreign Office press facilities stood for. In pursuit of that ambition he had run a brilliant network of reporters, Russian spies and former and serving Special Branch policemen. Their aim was to find out everything MI5 knew about the Communist Party of Great Britain. So they spied on the spy-catchers. And so successful were they that even MI5 had to admit that sometimes Ewer and his network knew what MI5 had discovered before they realised it themselves.

Getting started

Norman Ewer's journey through extremism to extremely respectable retirement began in a middle-class family in Hornsey, north London, in 1885. His father was a silk merchant. The son won scholarships to Merchant Taylors' School and to Trinity College, Cambridge, where he read Mathematics and History. After initially thinking of following a civil service career he began working for a prospective Liberal MP, Baron de Forest, who despite his Austrian title was a radical. De Forest won West Ham in a 1911 by-election. As a result of his work for de Forest, and the people that he met, Ewer became politically radicalised. He soon met George Lansbury, who represented the adjoining constituency. Ewer clearly impressed him because when Lansbury founded the *Daily Herald* in 1912 he recruited Ewer, along with other talented people such as G. D. H. Cole, Harold Laski and Francis Meynell, who would also go on to carve prominent careers for themselves. Collectively they would be known as 'Lansbury's Lambs'.

From the outset the daily paper had close links with the Labour Party and the TUC, and took radical positions, backing strikes and suffragette law-breaking; it also promoted syndicalism. Later, it enthused about the Russian Revolution.

The First World War provided an unexpected career break from journalism. Ewer registered as one of the conscientious objectors to the war. Some were assigned to non-combatant roles in the army, others to 'work of national importance' such as farming. Ewer ended up with a job as a swineherd on Lord Astor's estate at Cliveden and his first mention in MI5 files.

In July 1915 he gave what the files call 'a highly pacific and anti-British' speech. With Britain at war with Germany pacifism was a subject that aroused intense emotions. For some years before and after the war, membership of a range of organisations (some later considered as legitimately democratic bodies) was regarded with deep official suspicion and, in the case of activists, justification enough for further attention. Pacifists were of special interest to officials: were they pro-German? Were they cowards? Were they revolutionaries?

After the war Ewer returned to the *Daily Herald* and soon became its foreign editor. MI5 continued to keep an eye on him and they had the perfect way of doing it. Even though the war was over, any Briton who wanted to travel anywhere near Germany needed official permission in the form of a passport. Passports were at that time a relatively new-fangled concept: it wasn't just a matter of popping down to the local Post Office, passing over the forms and paying a fee. Official permission was required, and the process would not be regularised until later, under the auspices of the League of Nations. In February 1919, with the Armistice just three months old, the *Herald* wanted to send Ewer to find out what was going on inside Germany. He wouldn't be going to Germany, but he wanted to visit neighbouring Switzerland and Holland. So his editor wrote to the Acting Foreign Secretary, Lord Curzon, asking if he could kindly help get Ewer permission and a passport.

Before Curzon did, and because the letter came from the left-of-centre *Herald*, Curzon took soundings from other government departments. The Director of Military Intelligence (DMI), General Thwaites, advised that 'it is considered undesirable from a military point of view that he should be allowed to go to Switzerland or to Holland for the purpose of getting in touch with German and Austrian socialists'. MI5 provided extra detail and colour, telling the Foreign Secretary that Ewer 'preaches peace with Germany, followed by "revolution through bloodshed"'. His wife Monica, who was the daughter of the editor of the radical *Reynold's News* and, like Ewer, a journalist, was said to be 'equally rabid'. Ewer himself was also said to be 'a clever writer and fluent speaker' who had published poetry and was 'a dangerous and inflammatory agitator'. His card was clearly marked. MI5 had even spotted that he had put up £125 of his own money to fund a mass meeting at the Albert Hall and had lost it because the event was called off.

There is no copy in the files of Lord Curzon's reply to the *Herald* but we do know that nearly a year later, in January 1920, the *Herald* made another request for Ewer to travel, this time to Egypt. The Foreign Office had been unhappy about Ewer's reporting from the Paris Peace Conference, which had 'contained a number of carping criticisms directed against the policy of the Peace Conference from an extreme Labour standpoint'. But they realised that there was a bigger issue:

> unless some other substantial reason for refusing permission to leave is produced from authorities there, we are sure that such a refusal would only raise a storm of protest and lay us open to the suspicion of pursuing a policy which would not stand criticism.[125]

The Foreign Office seemed to realise that what they would like to do would not be defensible. If the same tactic was applied to all journalists writing stories that governments or officials did not like a large proportion of Fleet Street would have been instantly refused the right to travel.

Marked man

What Norman Ewer did next made him a marked man. On 31 July 1920, at the Cannon Street Hotel, in the heart of the City of London, a meeting of around 160 revolutionary socialists founded the Communist Party of Great Britain (CPGB). Soon afterwards Norman Ewer became one of its members.

The British state devoted considerable resources to keeping this fledgling party under surveillance. During the inter-war years there were periodic police raids. At various times its King Street offices in London were bugged, its telephones tapped and its post intercepted. Agents were placed inside its offices with the aim of collecting incriminating evidence. Membership lists were copied

UNIVERSITY OF CHESTER, WARRINGTON CAMPUS

and some of the members and their families were kept under surveillance.

Historians of the British Communist movement agree that Ewer was a key linkman between the *Daily Herald*, which had supported the Russian Revolution, and the Communist Party headquarters in London. In fact he was also a link between the *Herald*, the CPGB and the wider Communist movement, the Communist International.

In 1922 he went to Moscow. The main reason was to try to get help for the *Herald*. Ever since its creation the paper had been short of funds and at the beginning of the 1920s it lurched from one financial crisis to the next. With a circulation of less than 250,000 and failing to attract advertisers, partly due to its political stance, it was constantly on the look-out for financial support.

But this time, it was not just MI5 and Special Branch who were interested in what Ewer was up to; it was also a rather exclusive group of politicians: the men who were running the country. Lloyd George's Cabinet was told about Ewer's travelling arrangements in one of a series of weekly reports under the title 'Report on Revolutionary Organisations in the United Kingdom'.

Report number 137, dated 5 January 1922, informed the Cabinet: 'Norman Ewer has gone to Russia, ostensibly to make arrangements in connection with the *Daily Herald* Russian News Service. Interesting information regarding the crisis in the affairs of the *Daily Herald* is given in this report.' There was no explanation of who Norman Ewer was; presumably everyone around the Cabinet table knew that already. The government's interest in the foreign editor of the *Daily Herald* grew.

It is clear from the files that at least some of Ewer's (or possibly the *Herald*'s) letters were being read by the security services and his travelling companions were being noted:

Norman Ewer, to whom reference was made in last week's report, passed through Berlin on his way to Russia on January 3rd: it is interesting to note that he was travelling with Klishko, of the

Russian Trading Delegation, who figured in connection with the offer of £75,000 by the Third International to the *Daily Herald* last summer.[126]

The next year, 1923, Ewer was back in Moscow. The Comintern, the Soviet government organisation responsible for international propaganda and other matters, had just completed an evaluation of the CPGB and its relations with journalists at the *Herald*. According to some, Ewer was there 'to discuss possible arrangements for the transfer of the paper to the Comintern's control'.[127] One tangible thing emerged from this visit. Shortly afterwards the *Herald* serialised a pamphlet by Leon Trotsky, then a senior member of the Politburo, that justified Bolshevik rule in Georgia.

By the end of 1923 Ewer had attracted attention because he was a journalist on a left-wing newspaper, had criticised government policy, was a pacifist and conscientious objector, had helped to found the Communist Party in Britain, had travelled to Moscow, fundraised for his paper and printed Communist propaganda in it. But none of those was illegal.

Advert
It is what happened next that changed the game. Ewer probably knew that he was being spied on by MI5, so he decided to spy on them. To get started he put an advert in the paper – his paper, the *Daily Herald* – in November 1924. Headed 'Secret Service', the advertisement sought assistance for 'the Labour group', which, it said, was investigating undercover work. The advertiser said it 'would be glad to receive information and details from anyone who has ever had any association with any secret service department or operation' and it gave a *Daily Herald* box number for reply.

The advert worked. Someone was soon in touch. It was MI5: they had 'information and details' that the Labour group would be interested in, but they certainly weren't planning to hand it over. Instead they saw this as another opportunity to add to their information. They got one of their agents to contact the *Herald* undercover and offer to meet up. The agent was given a rendez-vous so off he set. What he didn't know was that the advertiser, the so-called 'Labour group', had worked out that he had a connec-tion with MI5 and was watching him from a distance. MI5 itself had the whole scene under surveillance and was watching their man being watched by this other man. It was time to call it off.

Far from disheartened, MI5 managed to arrange another undercover meeting with the people trying to spy on them. This time the person from the 'Labour group' who met the MI5 agent posing as a helpful soul was positively identified as Norman Ewer himself. He asked the agent how the security system worked and how it kept the Labour group under surveillance. Ewer appar-ently said that the group had been contemplating setting up its own security operation as a means of defending itself.

MI5's biggest lead came not from Ewer but from the man they'd spotted at that first, unconsummated, meeting. He was identified as Walter Dale and traced to a left-wing news agency.[128] By reading the agency's post and tapping its phones MI5 uncov-ered documents, some of which they eventually traced back to the French foreign office. But also in an early foretaste of what would later come to be known as the phone-hacking scandal, which gave rise to Lord Justice Leveson's inquiry, the news organisation was discovered to have links to a detective agency: the Vigilance Detective Agency (VDA). It was run by someone called Jack Hayes. He turned out to be a former police sergeant.

Hayes was a union activist who had resigned from the Metropolitan Police and become the head of the National Union of Police and Prison Officers (NUPPO). Back in August 1918 the London police had gone on strike over pay, union recogni-tion and the reinstatement of a union agitator who had been sacked. At its height almost 12,000 police walked out. Fears were expressed that the capital was being left to 'any evilly disposed person who cared to take advantage of it'. Coming soon after the Russian Revolution, and while Britain was still at war, nerves in

Westminster were tense. The strike was soon settled, but a number of militant policemen were sacked. In following months there were other police strikes, in Birmingham and Liverpool. There, as in London, police officers were sacked. Some found employment with the Vigilance Detective Agency and, MI5 concluded, became part of Ewer's enlarged circle. It appeared that the foreign editor of the *Daily Herald* effectively had his own private force of former policemen.

But, extraordinarily, Ewer's network went further than that, beyond former policemen to two serving Special Branch detectives, a sergeant, Charles Jane, and an inspector, Hubertus van Ginhoven. The three men met regularly at a Lyons café in Walbrook in the City of London with Walter Dale from the left-wing news agency. Dale kept a diary of this and similar meetings.

On 11 April 1929 the three men were arrested. MI5 had been tipped off by yet another former policeman who had been sacked after the police strike and who had now also been fired by Dale. Offered money by MI5, this man told them what they wanted to know about Norman Ewer. Ewer's days of spying on the spy-catchers were over.

MI5 had puzzled over how Ewer's 'network' operated and what it had done. Apart from acting as a courier service, passing documents to Russian contacts, MI5 discovered that the Special Branch men at the Lyons café were the key. Inspector van Ginhoven, who had been involved in the arrest of some leading members of the CPGB four years before, and his colleague Sergeant Jane passed on Special Branch and MI5 information about planned actions against either the British Communist Party or people closely associated with it.

However, Ewer's network carried out another activity: its team of ex-policemen kept MI5, MI6 and the Government Code & Cipher School (the forerunner of GCHQ) buildings and key staff under surveillance, reporting where their targets lived, their car registration plates and so forth.

MI5's conclusion was that 'it became abundantly clear that for the past 10 years [the 1920s], any information regarding subversive organisations and individuals supplied to Scotland Yard by SIS [Secret Intelligence Service, more commonly known as MI6] or MI5, which had become the subject of Special Branch enquiry, would have to be regarded as having been betrayed to Ewer's group'.[129] This was a tribute of a kind to a man who also held down a day job at the *Daily Herald*. It was also quite an operation by MI5 to put all the pieces of Ewer's jigsaw together.

With the ring rounded up, what happened next? The answer, which may appear surprising, is nothing. No one was ever prosecuted and no one was ever sent to prison for what they had done. Norman Ewer just carried on at the *Daily Herald*. The Attorney-General decided against charging anyone. In the case of the serving Special Branch men, van Ginhoven and Jane, a file note records that 'although ample evidence was obtained … it was decided that this would not be a suitable case for prosecution and Ginhoven and Jane were dismissed from the force on 25.4.29'.[130]

Some have suggested that the case came at an unwelcome time for the leader of the Labour Party, Ramsay MacDonald. His first ever Labour government had left office back in November 1924, after less than a year in power and in the wake of allegations about its connections with Soviet Russia. These had come to a head with the scandal over the so-called Zinoviev letter, which purported to urge the Labour Party 'to stir up the proletariat of Great Britain in support of … recently concluded Anglo-Soviet treaties, in preparation for eventual armed insurrection and class war'. It had been published in the press just before the 1924 general election and caused the party severe embarrassment. Only decades later was it confirmed as a fake and a dirty trick by MI6. Now, in 1929, Ramsay MacDonald was on the cusp of re-entering office and, in the light of the Zinoviev letter scandal, probably would have had little stomach for another damaging Russian case – particularly one that could be traced back to a newspaper that had been controlled by Labour and the TUC since 1922.

But there is also another possible reason, which the historian of the intelligence services Christopher Andrew has mentioned. One of Ewer's network, Jack Hayes of the Vigilant Detective Agency, had gone on to become a Labour MP, a junior member of Ramsay MacDonald's first government, and a member of Labour's national executive. MI5 knew that Hayes had introduced the serving policemen into Ewer's circle and even provided help in the shape of his constituency agent in shadowing a suspected Scotland Yard agent. Arresting him might just have been too politically explosive. This was appreciated by at least some in MI5.

A prosecution might also have led to disclosures about the extent of MI5's surveillance activities and the embarrassing disclosure that Special Branch had been a source of the leaks. Perhaps it was judged that the country wouldn't be ready for the news that some former and serving policemen could betray their country and, for a long time, outwit MI5 and MI6.

Or could it just have been that despite MI5's 'ample evidence' against two of the men there might not have been enough real and hard material on which to convict?

Speaking to MI5's Maxwell Knight much later in life, Norman Ewer justified what he had done by saying that it was 'purely counter' and that 'they did not touch espionage'. His aim was 'to obtain information as to what the British authorities were doing, and what steps they were taking against Russian and Communist activities in this country'. Knight didn't record whether Ewer ever argued that it was journalistic endeavour to find out what the security service was doing. If he did, it seems Ewer would have had difficulty pointing to any journalistic output which resulted from his very active research. But there was one other factor that neither discussed: the postal intercepts that had revealed the French foreign office documents, which Ewer's team had obtained. MI5 believed they had ultimately been forwarded to the Russians. Their source had been traced back to the *Daily Herald*'s Paris correspondent, George Slocombe, who purchased the documents from corrupt officials in the French foreign ministry. MI5 had lacked cast iron evidence, but in their view that had been espionage, pure and simple.[131]

A change of course

Back in 1929 Norman Ewer wisely decided it might be a good time to go abroad for a bit; he went to Poland. MI5's surmise was that he had gone to tell Russian intelligence what had taken place 'and to get fresh instructions'. But he soon returned to the *Daily Herald* and slowly began a full 180-degree about-turn in his political affiliations; having once been a supporter of Stalin he became a fierce critic.

Following an article he published late in 1929 he fell out with the CPGB and eventually resigned from the party, never to return. But during the 1930s some were still wary of Ewer's old pro-Communist leanings. The TUC's General Secretary, Walter Citrine, argued that he was giving foreign news 'a heavy pro-Soviet slant'. Ewer seemed to cool towards Communism and toward Stalin's Soviet Russia. It might have been a bluff. Soviet agents were sometimes ordered to create covers by rejecting former Communist sympathies. But, it is also possible that Ewer's break was more genuine, like that of many of his near-contemporaries, in response to news that emerged of what life was really like in Soviet Russia.

A scan through *The Times* court circular shows that he and his wife Monica, who by this time was carving out a success-ful career as a writer, were now having their very own version of the Roaring Twenties. They were fairly frequent regulars at gatherings of the great and the good. Throughout this period he continued to be a regular visitor to the Foreign Office News Department. MI5 records show that he had been an intimate of each successive head since the early 1920s, which would be the ambition of most diplomatic correspondents. Ewer was watched intermittently, but at the end of 1929 MI5 was forced to admit that it just didn't know whether or not he had closed down that part of his career for good.

During the 1930s the *Daily Herald*, which had gained a circu-lation of around two million, 'was unfailingly supportive of the Labour Party or the TUC line of the moment'. It was in favour of re-armament, and supported both Clement Attlee, the new Labour leader, and Prime Minister Stanley Baldwin during the abdication crisis. Nazism was a different matter, however. Writing later, the paper's then editor, Francis Williams, said,

> I was a good deal more suspicious of National Socialism from its very beginning than was Ewer who, whatever his private doubts, could hardly avoid reflecting in his news contributions a certain amount of the professional optimism of the Foreign Office – although he abandoned it long before the Foreign Office itself did.[132]

Later in the decade the *Herald* was a supporter of Neville Chamberlain's appeasement policy. Ewer was by then not only 'an unrelenting anti-Communist in reaction to his earlier views', but was also leaning towards Chamberlain's policy, whereas Williams was a critic. It was a state of affairs that seemed to reflect the confusion that was at the heart of the Labour Party's own views at the time of the 1938 Munich crisis. During that time one Home Secretary complained to the head of the Foreign Office that Ewer was one of the three 'darlings of the news department', all of them, by implication, representing trouble. Only when Germany seized the rump of Czechoslovakia the following spring did the paper's stance change.

A year later and still shocked by the signing of the Molotov–Ribbentrop Pact and the outbreak of war, Ewer wrote an article in which he referred to Stalin as a twentieth-century Genghis Khan. It was strong stuff and hardly a way of endearing himself to his former CPGB colleagues. Weeks later, and while things were going badly for Stalin's armies in the Russo-Finnish war, Ewer and others – including left-wingers such as Kingsley Martin and Fenner Brockway – were publicly attacked by the CPGB as 'people who had always been anti-Soviet' because they had not been prepared to follow the faith without question or reservation.

During the war Ewer helped to deliver the *Herald*'s 'crisp, concise war and diplomatic coverage'. As the end of the war approached it was becoming clear to many that the alliance between the Big Three – in which America and Britain had joined with Russia – would soon end in tears. The Soviet Union's territorial gains in eastern Europe were not going to be surrendered lightly, but reinforced. The chilly winds of the Cold War began to blow across Europe within months of Hitler's death. It was at this stage that Norman Ewer's career took yet another twist, and just as his early pro-Soviet activities had been partly secret, so too were his new anti-Soviet ones.

A general election was called and Churchill, his party worn out by years in office, lost to Clement Attlee's Labour Party. But the Labour Party entering office had a large majority and experience of government, having shared in the wartime coalition. It was no longer seen as a sop to the Soviet Union; Foreign Secretary Ernest Bevin was distinctly cool, if not hostile. A former trade unionist, he had spent much of his earlier life battling against Communist agitators and was under no illusions about their nature or their methods.

New opportunities

Government focus shifted onto the Soviet Union as a potential adversary. With ministerial support, Foreign Office officials established what was called the Russia Committee, whose objective was to co-ordinate policy towards Russia, to evaluate intelligence and deal with Russian propaganda.

The Foreign Office proposed to 'expose totalitarianism and communism in all their forms and wherever they may be found' but argued that 'no direct attack should be made on the Soviet government'.[133] Government accepted the diagnosis and what emerged over the next two years was a new and very shadowy Foreign Office outfit called the Information Research Department (IRD). It was set up officially in 1948, with much of the political spadework performed by a young Labour junior Foreign Office minister, Christopher Mayhew. For almost its entire life – it was closed down by Dr David Owen in 1977 – it operated as a covert propaganda and information organisation, producing anti-Communist literature, films and rebuttals of Communist campaigns. Its products were designed for use worldwide. It worked closely with MI6, diplomats, selected politicians, and carefully chosen journalists and academics. At its peak in the 1960s its staff numbered hundreds. One of its heads went on to lead MI6; another became a Conservative MP.[134] It had no public profile and was largely unheard of among the British public, although its activities were known to the Soviet Union almost from its inception – an early staff member was Guy Burgess (*Chapter 4*).

The IRD was run by the Foreign Office but it operated anywhere – overseas as well as domestically, including in Northern Ireland. It briefed MPs and decision-makers and helped to support small specialist overseas news agencies, some of which had been set up by MI6.[135] The IRD recruited a band of 'safe' journalists who received privileged access to secret factual background materials, which undoubtedly helped their careers. In return some wrote articles, books and pamphlets which 'tame' publishers then brought to the market. It is said that a few less assiduous journalists were presented with finished articles to which they had only to append their name. Academics were not entirely immune. The acknowledged scholar Robert Conquest, who helped to expose the details of Stalin's Terror and the Ukrainian famine, worked for the IRD from 1948 to 1956 (*see Chapter 3*). Some journalists later claimed that they knew the origin of the information they received and treated it just as they would any other source, but some sounded more convincing than others when deploying the argument.

By the time the IRD was created, Norman Ewer was positively hostile towards the Soviet Union and Communism. While he was still at the *Herald*, the IRD recruited him as one of its select band of journalists who would spread the word and fight Communist propaganda. The poacher had indeed turned gamekeeper.

In May 1947 Ewer wrote a critical series of articles about life in Russia. He also debated what life was like in Soviet Russia with a leading Communist, D. N. Pritt, KC, MP, an unrepentant Stalinist who had been expelled from the Labour Party seven years earlier. Ewer joined the Fabian Society's International Advisory Committee where, with Denis Healey, he represented 'the right of the spectrum'.

It has been said that the *Daily Herald* 'cheerfully adopted the nascent Cold War attitudes of the time'. The paper reported in July 1948 that the TUC had issued a circular against 'the Communist menace' and just in case readers didn't receive it in their workplaces, reprinted it almost in its entirety. Norman Ewer, diplomatic correspondent and emerging Cold War hawk, played his part, helped by the IRD. However, his task was made more difficult by the paper's steady decline, which it proved impossible to stop. Ewer survived and continued to work far beyond retirement age, but the resources available to him were diminishing.

It was at this time that Ewer became better known to radio audiences as a guest foreign policy expert on discussion programmes. He also broadcast for the BBC Overseas Service, where his relatively slow speech rate was well suited to audiences whose first language often was not English.

It was during the early 1950s that the IRD began publishing books – in an arrangement with several publishers. It launched a series of 'background books', which were 'rather simple anti-Communist propaganda'. Authors published included Leonard Schapiro, Sir Robert Bruce Lockhart, Bickham Sweet-Escott (who had been involved in wartime propaganda and intelligence operations), Bertrand Russell, trade unionist Vic Feather, Christopher Mayhew and, of course, Norman Ewer.

In the words of one historian, 'the IRD's hardest working and most dependable client soon became *Daily Herald* diplomatic correspondent W. N. Ewer'. It was also in the second half of the 1940s that Ewer began writing 'a weekly diplomatic commentary for LPS [London Press Service], appeared on innumerable BBC talk shows, and wrote prolifically for the COI [Central Office of Information] and the IRD'. Interestingly, Ewer was considered by some Foreign Office diplomats as 'ready ... to take direction as to the lines on which he should write'.[136]

In 1959 Norman Ewer received the summons to attend Buckingham Palace to receive a CBE. It can only be surmised that the services he had performed for the IRD, for Labour and for Britain in the Cold War had expunged his actions of thirty years earlier. Equally possible, although far less likely, is that his chequered past had been forgotten.

In the years after Ewer retired he continued to write, but contented himself with occasional letters to *The Times*. He died in 1977, aged ninety-one.

The National Archives later released MI5 files that told some of Ewer's story – at least from MI5's perspective. With the records so incomplete (a continuing problem faced by all historians), the action led to some serious academic discourse between Ewer's defenders and critics.

But it seems reasonably clear that he had been mixed up in things that went far beyond reporting. Even if it was not espionage, as Ewer had contended to Maxwell Knight, it certainly was not mere journalism. Rather than remaining an observer, Norman Ewer became a player in a political game, and he did it not once but twice – in different ways, at different times and for opposing sides.

When Ewer stepped forward to receive his perpetual press pass in 1964 it symbolised recognition that, in the end, after some meanderings along the line along the way, he had survived. Those former colleagues who are still alive are forgiving. As one, Geoffrey Goodman, told us, 'Ewer was a chap that had interviewed Trotsky ... you had to regard that with respect.'

3

WALTER DURANTY

In March 1933 several British reporters were at work in Stalin's Russia. One was the doyen of the foreign press corps, the correspondent of one of the world's great newspapers, but another was an outsider, a freelance uncertain of where his next commission would come from.

They were about to do battle over the coverage of a man-made disaster of epic proportions, maybe second only to the Holocaust in its scale and horror in the twentieth century.

One journalist would help to uncover the details, the other would deny them. It was a precursor of Holocaust denial. One man received accolades, the other was murdered. It took many years before the truth finally became known. But the story of the two men, which of them succeeded and which failed, is not a predictable tale of good prevailing over evil. It is much more complicated than that.

We now know that the 1932 famine in the Ukraine was a major catastrophe, a tragedy in which millions suffered and died, although it took decades for information to become available. For many years the Cold War kept Soviet archives closed to all comers – not only to Western historians, but also to Russians. Even now the scale of the disaster can only be guessed at, as figures are not accurate enough to be relied upon. Russian estimates, which broadly agree with those of Western historians, suggest that '5 million or more' people died, although records are neither detailed nor reliable enough to establish this as a certainty.[137] The famine was man-made and was the result of Stalin's first Five Year Plan, which was intended to propel the Soviet Union into an advanced industrial age. The plan was implemented between 1928 and 1932, and the brutal methods used to overcome resistance from the countryside only made things worse.[138]

One journalist was called Walter Duranty. He was a Briton who worked for the *New York Times*. He liked living well. He enjoyed good food, drink and women. He liked chauffeur-driven Buicks and was used to getting what he wanted. Even in Moscow. And he managed to do all this while Lenin and Stalin were running the country, and at a time when there were no formal diplomatic relations between the USSR and the USA.

He was showered with praise from politicians, friends and colleagues and by the time he left the country he was a celebrity, hailed as the doyen of foreign correspondents. Any sneers from those who disapproved were dismissed as envy or inexperience.

Newspapermen's reports were censored in Moscow in those days. But Duranty prided himself on knowing exactly what he could get past foreign ministry censors. So he wrote his stories close to the deadline, dropped them by the censors with little time to spare, and was then driven off to the cable office by his chauffeur, where he sent them to New York. And then he went off to enjoy whatever the good life had to offer that day. Remarkably, it was a lifestyle he kept up for what were thirteen of the most turbulent years in Russian history. By the time he left he had received plaudits from the leaders of both the Soviet Union and the United States. Who was Walter Duranty and what did he do to deserve such praise?

Duranty was an improbable figure. He aspired to be a writer rather than a journalist. But he admitted that he found it difficult to make up his mind about anything: 'I generally see too many sides of a question to be quite sure which of them is true.'[139] He worked full time for the *New York Times* for twenty-one years, the greater part of his working life. Former *New York Times* Moscow correspondent and the paper's historian, Harrison Salisbury, said that Duranty 'romanticised' that he was a Manxman, but he actually came from an upper-middle-class Liverpool merchant family.[140] He wrote that his family had died in a rail accident and that he was orphaned at the tender age of ten.[141] It was untrue.

In the words of his biographer, Sally Taylor, Duranty was 'short, balding, and unprepossessing in appearance, his one outstanding characteristic was a limp ... that and his keen gray eyes were what saved him from commonplace'.[142] He lost part of his left leg following a rail accident in France when he was in his late thirties. But he encouraged people to think it was a war wound. He had a 'thick-lipped, sensual mouth' and a nose that was 'finely-chiselled, but a shade too large, that bit too flat'.[143]

Born in 1884, Duranty went to Harrow until he was fifteen, when failing family fortunes saw him moved to Bedford Grammar School, where he proved to be one of the better pupils. He won an open classical scholarship to Emmanuel College, Cambridge, where he rowed for the college. He was a contemporary of the novelist Hugh Walpole.

Some critics implied that Duranty was a bit of a fraud, aping the modes of behaviour and dress of his 'betters', but he was the real McCoy: 'Duranty was indeed a Harrow boy, complete with top hat on Sunday, straw hat during the week; ample Latin, more Greek and the "steady drill in accidence and syntax, the acquisition of vocabulary..."'[144] He came easily to languages, was good with words; these skills later impressed journalist colleagues.

After Cambridge he spent several years travelling between Europe and the United States before finally deciding on a career in journalism. He came to the profession late: he was nearly thirty when he got his first job. He had hustled his way in to see the head of the *New York Times* bureau in Paris – Wythe Williams. Indeed Williams almost *was* the bureau. Duranty persisted every day until he finally wore Williams's resistance down and was offered a job. It was December 1913.

Duranty's life in Paris was a mixture. He was clubbable, well liked – even by many of his detractors – and was a great teller of tales. He had an eye for women, and many seem to have been attracted to him in return. In 1913 the earnest new journalist was a member of Left Bank café society, and had interesting friends. He shared one of these, his lover Jane Chéron, with the self-proclaimed 'wickedest man in the world', Aleister Crowley, who introduced him to *Magick*.[145] Jane introduced him to opium. It was a case of 'sex with the one partner, drugs with the other, a little magic on the side'.[146] He continued to use the drug periodically for some years, although he never became addicted. He practised satanic rituals with Crowley, but gradually distanced himself because he saw no results. But he kept in touch with Crowley into the 1930s.[147]

Walter Duranty never fought in the First World War, although he was early in predicting it.[148] During the hostilities Duranty worked for the *New York Times* as a journalist, first pounding the Paris beat while he learned his trade then serving as a war correspondent, where he witnessed terrible events and saw widespread carnage on the battlefield that allegedly affected his views about humanity ever after. Under pressure from his paper he faked at least one story, which he confessed in his autobiography twenty years later.[149]

After the war he soon became bored with peacetime Paris, fell out with colleagues and was grateful to be sent on foreign assignments. He covered episodes in the Russian Revolutionary Civil War and the Kapp Putsch in Germany.[150] While in Latvia he scored what he considered to be his biggest scoop: a Russian courier en route to the United States had been caught red handed carrying instructions for organising unrest. The courier was laden with jewels, cash and gold, and Duranty was given the exclusive story. Revealing a delight for the discomfort of others, he managed to persuade British diplomats not to tell an American diplomat, with whom he had fallen out over a woman.[151] The story broke on Christmas Day 1919 and was a hit in the US as it melded neatly into a contemporary 'Red Scare' then gripping the country; and it earned him a bonus. Afterwards, he filed stories from Paris about the Russian–Polish war; these he later admitted were wrong and based solely on one-sided French government hand-outs.[152]

How did all this lead to Duranty ending up in Moscow and becoming a star correspondent? It is here that fate lent a hand. He was the right person in the right place at the right time.

In 1920 the integrity of reporting by the *New York Times* came under the critical spotlight from two writers, Walter Lippmann and Charles Merz. Concerned by the paper's reports about Russia they studied its output from March 1917. They did not like what they found. Covering about 1,000 issues and 3,000 to 4,000 news stories, they concluded that the *New York Times*' reports were biased, misleading and in some cases completely false. Duranty – seven mentions – was among those whose work was singled out. The reportage was a case of selective perception, Lipmann and Merz concluded.[153] 'In the large', they wrote, 'the news about Russia is a case of seeing not what was, but what men wished to see.'[154] In terms that do not seem far removed from Lord Justice Leveson's inquiry into the standards of the British press they concluded, 'Where is the power to be found which can define the standards of journalism and enforce them? Primarily within the profession itself. We do not believe that the press can be regulated by law. Our fundamental reliance must be on the corporate tradition and discipline of the newspaper guild.'[155]

Their report made waves in the *New York Times* offices, although the paper never commented publicly. However, its editor, Carr Van Anda, knew that to avoid repeats he would have to post a permanent correspondent to Russia. It was then that chance played a leading hand for Duranty.

In summer 1921 a major famine broke out in Russia in the wake of a bloody civil war. Bearing Lippmann's strictures in mind, Van Anda decided that the paper needed a reporter on the spot to report events accurately. He chose 36-year-old Duranty. It was to be his big break. Duranty later wrote, 'at last in July 1921 luck came my way in the shape of the great Russian Famine, which then threatened to cost about 30,000,000 lives, and probably did cost 5,000,000 to 6,000,000 including deaths from disease.'[156] He faced some difficulty in getting into the country as Maxim Litvinov, the foreign affairs commissar, had been unhappy with his civil war reports, just like Lippmann and Merz. But Duranty soon won this opposition over. He would remain in Moscow as the paper's resident correspondent for the next thirteen years.

Once in Moscow he quickly set about getting himself well connected. His sociable nature helped. He soon got to know almost everyone who was worth knowing, including the resident Western press correspondents. A bon viveur, he kept a good table; his Russian housekeeper and mistress, Katya, who later bore him a son, was by all accounts a very good cook, which undoubtedly helped. Duranty quickly got to know how things worked, which levers to pull and which to leave alone. He was a regular guest of foreign embassies, although records show that the British, for one, were suspicious of him: some thought him clever, others mediocre.[157]

Within eighteen months of getting to Moscow Duranty had already acquired a reputation for accepting official news without question. Harrison Salisbury wrote that 'by 1923 Duranty was being called a "pro-Bolshevik correspondent" by an ad hoc committee on Soviet propaganda' that was working inside the *New York Times* editorial offices. Salisbury continued, 'Whatever the case ... Duranty's dispatches through the 1920s and into the 1930s saw Soviet Russia through lenses which, if not rosy, were certainly soft focus ... He was quick to defend Stalin and to provide a rationale for the food measures...'[158] Salisbury's verdict, however, was that Duranty was less than politically committed, and was rather a 'cynical man on the make'. One of Duranty's contemporaries, William H. Stoneman, saw Duranty as 'simply amoral about the rights and wrongs of Communism'. Another Moscow correspondent and contemporary, William Henry Chamberlin, thought Duranty had 'decided that the Communists were going to survive ... and that it was the job of a correspondent to back them, especially since he had no scruples about the dirty things they were doing'.[159] Maybe remarkably, there was an anti-Duranty lobby operating in the *New York Times* offices which saw him 'as little more than a press agent not only for the Bolsheviks but for the worst Bolshevik of all, Stalin'.[160] But it did not seem to have much effect: his editors still approved his stories and ran them with by-lines.

Duranty was no slouch. The record shows that he regularly filed stories: he filed over 150 by-lined stories in 1932 alone, and they covered topics as diverse as the Soviet economy, political murder, how Moscow was uninterested in the Lindbergh kidnapping, a woman who sold her husband for 100 roubles, freedom of speech, defence, foreign affairs, progress with the first Five Year Plan, peasants and the question of food, and the birth of the Union of Soviet Writers. The despatches also included stories about action against speculators, prospects for opening up diplomatic relations between the USSR and the USA, poor grain production – particularly in the Ukraine, the discovery of 'immensely important' iron deposits, decrees about Soviet food difficulties, educational reform, the expulsion of Lev Kamenev and Grigory Zinoviev from the Communist Party, food problems and their links to housing and industrial production, food and goods shortages, Moscow's view of Franklin Delano Roosevelt's election, and 'cleansing' of agricultural organisations in the north Caucasus which led to slow grain collection. In November 1932 he wrote a series of stories about 'growing food shortages' which he got out of the country using means which by-passed the censors. His editors were highly satisfied with that series.[161] But Moscow was not.

It is likely that some of the stories were re-written from official hand-outs, but then most of the Moscow correspondents would have done some of that. Duranty would check the facts to see if they made sense, and might add his own analysis, but sometimes he might also have gone out looking for stories. But he did not as a matter of course dig around for news in the way that, say, an investigative journalist might. He and many of his contemporaries did not hail from a tradition that as a matter of habit went and found stories that foreign governments would have preferred not to appear.

Duranty's experience in wartime Paris had taught him not to challenge what he was told by 'official' sources too persistently.[162] Where he scored with his bosses and many of his readers was that he sought to explain and interpret what he saw going on in the Soviet Union. He wrote despatches as a supporter, rather than a critic. He explained and justified rather than providing his readers with objective analysis. His editors in New York seemed to be satisfied and kept running his stories.

Duranty supported Lenin's New Economic Policy, which was an attempt to kick-start agricultural production after the bloody civil-war years by introducing small-scale capitalism. He did not question whether the Communist project was justified.[163] He endorsed Stalin's first Five Year Plan, despite its likely high cost in human misery. He told his readers in a 1931 despatch, filed from Paris while he was on holiday, that Stalin was giving his people 'what they really want namely, joint effort, communal effort. And communal life is as acceptable to them as it is repugnant to a Westerner.'[164] 'The whole purpose of the plan', he wrote, 'is to get the Russians going – that is, to make a nation of eager, conscious workers out of a nation that was a lump of sodden, driven slaves.' Some in America were equally enthusiastic observers.[165]

In 1932, and unusually for a journalist, Duranty wrote a poem called *Red Square* which the *New York Times* published and illustrated with photographs. He mentioned Lenin's vision of 'nothing short of world dominion under one Red Flag', and drew contrasts between the old and the new: 'New and vast, utilitarian, ugly, like the Soviet State'. But the poem also contained a particular phrase that his critics have since seized upon as revealing his attitude about sacrifice and change: 'Russians may be hungry and short of clothes or comfort. But you can't make an omelette without breaking eggs.'[166]

Duranty's 1931 articles had not only captivated his readers. They also caught the attention of the Pulitzer Prize Committee. In 1932 it awarded him the prize for correspondence, for 'his series of dispatches on Russia especially the working out of the Five

Year Plan'.[167] The citation said that his reports were 'marked by scholarship, profundity, impartiality, sound judgment and exceptional clarity'. In contrast, the *New York Times*' anti-Duranty lobby was highly critical and condemned them.[168] But no one took much notice of them.

British diplomats believed that Duranty knew more than he told his readers. One noted in early December 1932 that 'he has been waking up to the truth for some time ... but he has not hitherto let the great American public into the secret'.[169] The diplomat, William Strang, recounted that Duranty had sent a despatch 'by safe hand via Paris' from where it was cabled to New York and the paper had 'made a great play of it'. This was the six-part series about increasing food shortages. Duranty told Strang in confidence that the article had created waves: he had received a visit from 'higher spheres' – not the Soviet censors. His visitors accused him of stabbing the country in the back, and delivered a warning of dire consequences as relations between the USSR and USA were balanced on a knife edge. Duranty's concerns grew: if he left the country, as was scheduled, would he be allowed back? Clearly rattled he hung around to see if the trouble would pass. But the visit from the Soviet heavy mob did not stop Duranty from speaking about the increasingly serious food shortage and problems with establishing the scheme of collective farms to the Travellers Club in Paris less than a fortnight later.[170]

But Duranty was not alone in giving the Soviet Union generally positive coverage. Other Moscow correspondents did likewise. David Engerman, who in 2003 made a special study of American attitudes to the Soviet Union at that time, has written that the four leading Moscow correspondents – Walter Duranty, Louis Fischer (*The Nation*), Eugene Lyons (*United Press*) and William Henry Chamberlin (*Christian Science Monitor* and the *Manchester Guardian*) all shared basic assumptions about the Soviet Union. Like many Americans at the time, they were broadly enthusiastic about the rapid pace of change taking place in the country. They knew it would have costs in human terms, but that was the price paid for progress. And, like many observers, they had a low opinion of the Russian people, much like Duranty himself. Engerman noted, 'The journalists' calculations of these costs were discounted by their low estimation of Russian national character. Western journalists disparaged the peasantry almost as much as Soviet officials did.'[171]

Chamberlin wrote that the peasants' old lifestyle and values, including their religious faith and customs, which they were reluctant to give up on, were impediments to change. The creation of more efficient collective farms was a step forward from the 'backward', pre-revolutionary farming system. He wrote dispassionately about the 'liquidation [of the kulaks] as a class', which he defined as peasants who were 'formerly somewhat better off' and who 'were therefore regarded by the Soviet as exploiters'. He explained that the use of food – or rather lack of it – was a way of restoring the 'peasants' will to work'; and that some of the consequences were due to the destruction of crops and animals by the peasants themselves.[172] He told the Royal Institute of International Affairs in London early in 1933 that while the Soviet policies were succeeding in drawing the mass of the peasants into the new collective farms, more needed to be done. Mechanisation of the new collectives alone could not solve production problems if the peasants were not at the same time given 'sufficient incentive to work as hard in the collective farm as in [their] own individual holding'.[173]

Louis Fischer, before leaving for a six-month trip to the United States in December 1932, also wrote about the food shortages for *The Nation*, but said that they were due to 'bad organisation' and 'insufficient loyalty to Moscow's instructions', terms that were, in Engerman's view, 'cryptic phrases' and 'gross understatements'.[174]

Taking a benevolent view of the Soviet project undoubtedly helped: Lyons was the first foreign correspondent to be granted an interview with Stalin, but not to be outdone, days later Duranty schemed and followed in his footsteps and secured the first of what would be two exclusive interviews, eclipsing Lyons in the process.[175]

But what of the other British journalist, the freelance? His name was Gareth Jones. He was a man on a mission. Passionate, a prolific writer, fluent in Russian, he was acutely concerned for the human condition. He was Welsh and, like Duranty, a Cambridge scholar. He had studied Russian and German. Contemporary photographs show him to have been thin, but looking energetically fit, bespectacled and with a high forehead. He looked as though he had boundless energy. Jones was earnest and a man of conviction. He was politically aware and possessed humanitarian concerns. He was a prolific writer and saw that as his future profession.

For a short time he had worked in the United States and written about the Great Depression. He had also travelled to the Soviet Union before – in 1930 and 1931, the latter occasion accompanying the American food magnate H. J. Heinz II. After that visit, which also took in the Ukraine, Jones published an account of his visit anonymously, *Experiences in Russia 1931 – A Diary*.[176] He visited the Soviet Union three times in total, and would finally be banned from going back.

He arrived in Moscow in March 1933 with plans for a walking tour. But he was not a tourist. While in London, where he was assisting former Prime Minister David Lloyd George with his war memoirs, Jones heard stories about a man-made famine in the Ukraine where millions were dying and he wanted to do something about it. At the beginning of 1933 Jones had gone to Germany to witness the elections that would bring Hitler to power. While in Berlin he heard more stories, some from Polish diplomats. He planned to gather information about what was going on and write about it once he was back in the West. He little knew that the next months would be explosive, and little appreciated what their outcome would be.

Famine

It would not have been a great surprise to the foreign journalists in Moscow that the food shortages and agricultural problems that they had written about in late 1932 would get worse. Rumours circulated that conditions were bad in the Ukraine, among other places. Details were scant, but the news had already spread beyond the Soviet Union's borders.

Duranty had heard that the news was bad from freelance journalist Maurice Hindus and others, as he told British diplomats late in 1932.[177] But in public he was dismissive. He had already told his readers in November 1932 that the costs would be high. But rather than investigate further he chose to remain in Moscow and report what he knew would interest his readers the most: a dramatic spy story. One of the major news stories developing in Moscow at the beginning of 1933 was that of six Englishmen, employed by the British engineering firm Metro-Vickers, who were accused of spying and sabotage. They were to be put on public trial, and might face the death penalty.

But with news of the trial creating so much interest, the stories that Duranty and others heard about starvation in the Ukraine, Kazakhstan and other grain-producing areas assumed less importance. There were said to be vast numbers of expulsions, deaths and executions. Whole communities were transported to forced labour camps, animals had disappeared and there were reports of cannibalism.

Stalin's policy was that agriculture was to be collectivised and made efficient. Its produce would be sold abroad to earn foreign currency that would buy the machinery needed to help the country industrialise and modernise. Opposition would be crushed. Peasants were despised. Some Bolsheviks saw them as little better than animals.[178] Kulaks were seen as opponents of Communism and vilified.[179] A lethal mix of incompetence and the Soviet leadership's indifference to suffering combined to leave many millions of lives devastated. People died of hunger, disease, sorrow. Whole communities ceased to exist.[180]

Not long after Duranty had collected his Pulitzer Prize, Eugene Lyons picked up a report from a Soviet newspaper, *Molot* (Hammer), which was published in Rostov-on-Don. He realised that one of its stories amounted to an official confirmation of the famine. Unable to investigate himself, he passed it onto two colleagues, Ralph Barnes and William H. Stoneman.[181] The pair spent two weeks travelling through the affected areas, witnessing the famine first-hand. Arrested by the secret police, the OGPU (a forerunner of the KGB), they were returned to Moscow, but by then they had already written their stories and arranged for them to be smuggled out of the country via a German fur trader. They were published in the *Chicago Daily News* and the *New York Herald Tribune*. After publication the Soviet authorities banned the press from travelling to the affected areas. But Barnes and Stoneman suffered no retributions. However, to stop more news spreading Stalin introduced a system of internal passports which restricted peasants' movements, stopping them in particular from going to the towns. The measures only disappeared in the late 1970s.

Meanwhile, yet another British journalist resident in Moscow was taking an interest in the famine story. Malcolm Muggeridge had arrived the previous September with his wife Kitty, a niece of the leading Fabian Beatrice Webb, to report for the *Manchester Guardian*. Muggeridge admitted being sympathetic to the Soviet Union – as was his paper at the time.[182]

Muggeridge travelled to the Ukraine to see for himself what was happening. He later said, 'It was a big story in all our talks in Moscow. Everybody knew about it ... that there was a terrible famine going on.'[183] He set off at the end of January, travelling via Rostov-on-Don. He posted his stories to England without first showing them to the censors.[184] They were published anonymously by the *Manchester Guardian* on three consecutive days, beginning on Saturday 25 March 1933. Recognising that he would not be able to stay in the country once the reports came out, Muggeridge left Moscow in early spring, helped by the fact that Chamberlin, the paper's regular correspondent, had come back earlier than expected from an overseas trip.

Muggeridge had travelled through three regions. In the Ukraine he saw 'the same story – cattle and horses dead; fields, neglected: meagre harvest despite moderately good climatic conditions; all the grain that was produced taken by the government; now no bread at all, no bread anywhere, nothing much else either; despair and bewilderment.'[185] In the next report he wrote, 'To say there is famine in some of the most fertile parts of Russia is to say much less than the truth: there is not only famine, but – in the case of the North Caucasus at least – a state of war, a military occupation.'[186]

Muggeridge was later furious that the articles had been 'heavily sub-edited' and placed in a less prominent position in the paper, which he thought was intended to soften their impact.[187]

When Gareth Jones arrived in Moscow he met Malcolm Muggeridge. He arranged a walking tour into the affected area. He was well prepared and had a supply of pocket diaries in which he planned to record what he saw.[188] When finished he returned to Moscow, where he spent a few days meeting people before travelling home via Berlin. On 19 March 1933 he met the Foreign Minister, Maxim Litvinov, whom he had met during his previous visit, and Walter Duranty. He noted in his diary, 'March 19. Moscow. 1) Met Litvinoff [sic]. 2) I don't trust Duranty. He still believes in Collectivisation.'[189]

What Jones did next would set him against Walter Duranty and caused a controversy that still lingers on. Jones wanted to tell the world about the famine and get help for the starving masses; Duranty did not.[190]

The story breaks

Shocked at what he had seen, when Jones reached Berlin he decided to hold a press conference. The billing must have been dramatic because it drew newspapers and news agencies from both sides of the Atlantic. The *Manchester Guardian* carried Reuters' report on 30 March – two days after Muggeridge's final despatch had appeared. Jones, the report said, had 'walked alone through villages and twelve collective farms. Everywhere was the cry, "There is no bread. We are dying." This cry came from every part of Russia, from the Volga, Siberia, White Russia, the North Caucasus, and Central Asia.' It quoted Jones's account of a train journey: 'A Communist denied to me that there was a famine. I flung a crust of bread which I had been eating from my own supply into a spittoon. A peasant fellow passenger fished it out and ravenously ate it.' But, directly below this story *The Guardian* placed a report of a talk given to the Workers' Education League. The speaker, P. A. Sloan, had said that 'starvation had existed with far greater severity in pre-revolutionary days and peasants now tended to complain a lot more because they were so much better off under the new regime'. Sloan criticised reporters in the USSR for failing to make contact with workers or students.[191]

In America reports appeared on 29 March. Edgar Ansel Mowrer wrote in the *Chicago Daily News* that 'Jones saw famine on a huge scale and the revival of a murderous terror. The Russians are thoroughly alarmed over this situation and, he explains the arrest of British engineers recently as a maniac measure following the shooting by the government of thirty-five prominent agricultural workers.'[192]

In London, the *Daily Express* also printed the Reuters report on 30 March, concluding, 'In short, said Mr Jones, the government's policy of collectivisation and the peasants' resistance to it, had brought Russia to the worst catastrophe since the famine of 1921 swept away the population of whole districts.'[193] Below that was a short piece about the Soviet ambassador, Ivan Maisky, who had said that the Metro-Vickers engineers would be given a 'just and fair trial' and that 'we must not allow ourselves to be carried away by the passion of the moment'.[194] On 1 April the paper published a trailer for a series of articles by Gareth Jones that were due to appear the following week.

The backlash begins

Two days after Jones's press conference, and possibly pressed by his editors, Walter Duranty filed a report. In an article entitled 'Russians Hungry, but Not Starving', he wrote, 'In the middle of the diplomatic duel between Great Britain and the Soviet Union over the accused British engineers there appears from a British source a big scare story in the American press about famine in the Soviet Union, with "thousands already dead and millions menaced by death and starvation."'[195] He continued,

> Mr Jones is a man of a keen and active mind, and he has taken the trouble to learn Russian, which he speaks with considerable fluency, but the writer thought Mr Jones's judgment was somewhat hasty and asked him on what it was based. It appeared that he had made a forty-mile walk through villages in the neighbourhood of Kharkov and had found conditions bad.

He went on, 'I suggested that that was a rather inadequate cross-section of a big country but nothing could shake his conviction of impending doom.' Duranty then mentioned other stories that, when originally published, were supposed to have been based on eyewitness accounts but were subsequently found to be untrue – 'all bunk, of course'.

Duranty said Jones had told him about the hunger, which he knew 'to be correct not only of some parts of the Ukraine but of sections of the North Caucasus and lower Volga regions and, for that matter, Kazakstan [sic]'. But he said it was a consequence of attempts to drag biblical-times Soviet agriculture into the twentieth century. Farmers had delivered 'the most deplorable results'. He acknowledged that collectivisation had been mismanaged and that food production was a mess.[196] But then, in a chillingly familiar phrase,

> But – to put it brutally – you can't make an omelette without breaking eggs, and the Bolshevist leaders are just as indifferent to the casualties that may be involved in their drive toward socialisation as any General during the World War who ordered a costly attack in order to show his superiors that he and his division possessed the proper soldierly spirit.

Duranty said that after talking to Jones he had made official enquiries about the 'alleged' famine. His researches had found that there was a serious food shortage in the country, and malnutrition, which led to disease and death. However, using tortuous logic, 'there is no actual starvation or deaths from starvation'. He concluded that the situation was definitely bad, 'but there is no famine'.

A week later, in another piece, and in a sentence that could easily have come from George Orwell's *1984*, he wrote,

> In the excitement over the Spring sowing campaign and the reports of an increased food shortage, a fact that has been almost overlooked is that the production of coal, pig iron, steel, oil, automobiles, tractors, automotive parts, locomotives and machine tools has increased by 20 to 35 per cent during recent months.

He continued, 'That is the most effective proof that the food shortage as a whole is less grave than was believed – or, if not, at least distribution has greatly improved, which comes to the same thing for practical purposes.'[197] This was Duranty writing more like a Soviet public relations officer and less like the critical foreign correspondent he was supposed to be.

It took nearly a month for Jones's reply to Duranty's reports to get into the *New York Times*. In a passionate letter, published on 1 May 1933, Jones thanked Duranty for his kindness and helpfulness, but, he said, 'I stand by my statement that Soviet Russia is suffering from a severe famine.' He then listed his sources: 'foreign observers', private conversations with nearly thirty diplomats, peasants, German colonists and journalists. The latter, he said, had been turned 'into masters of euphemism and understatement' by Russian censorship. 'Hence they give "famine" the polite name of "food shortage" and "starving to death" is softened down to read as "widespread mortality from diseases due to malnutrition".' He mentioned that Muggeridge's articles supported him. He had not seen, he said, 'dead human beings nor animals' in villages, 'but one does not need a particularly nimble brain to grasp that even in the Russian famine districts the dead are buried and that there the dead animals are devoured'. He ended by remarking how successful the Soviet Foreign Office had been in 'concealing the true situation in the USSR'.

Other Moscow-based foreign correspondents also cast doubt on Jones's story. Meanwhile in Britain Muggeridge faced criticism from those who believed strongly in the great strides that Moscow was making in modernising its agriculture. He was called a liar, or labelled naive. His attackers included George Bernard Shaw and the historian A. J. P. Taylor, as well as his in-laws, the Webbs.

There was a strand of opinion in Europe that was dismissive of such stories. A month before Muggeridge's articles had appeared, the *Manchester Guardian* published a letter signed by George Bernard Shaw and twenty others saying how 'particularly offensive and ridiculous is the revival of the old attempts to represent the condition of Russian workers as one of slavery and starvation'.[198] Muggeridge noted that a group of admirers, including the Webbs, were in denial about unpalatable Russian news. 'It's true that in the USSR people *disappear...*' Muggeridge later recalled Beatrice Webb saying to him before he left for Moscow.

He later felt that such people secretly admired Stalin's power. 'Though they professed admiration for Stalin's economic and industrial achievements, it was ultimately his immense power that commanded their respect and even reverence.'[199] Others believed that the detractors 'avoided exposure to the famine' and were 'shown only what the Russians wanted them to see'.[200]

Reviewing the issue over sixty years later Muggeridge's biographer, Richard Ingrams, said:

> If not actually contradicting the Muggeridge/Jones account, Duranty and the *New York Times* had succeeded in creating a smokescreen of doubt. And in the meantime, editors had focused their attention, as far as Russia was concerned, on the trial of the Metro-Vickers engineers. The fate of six British citizens was

considered more newsworthy than that of 6 million or so Russian peasants.[201]

But why was Jones singled out for criticism? There were probably several reasons. He was committed, earnest and plausible. His very independence and obvious sincerity made him dangerous, from Moscow's point of view. He had independently validated other published reports about the famine – some, such as Muggeridge's, based on eyewitness testimony, others published by correspondents resident outside the Soviet Union. The *New York Times*, for instance, also printed stories about the famine – using the word *famine* that Duranty could not bring himself to use – written by its Vienna correspondent. But, of course, they were not direct eyewitness accounts.

But Jones's independence also meant that he was unable to count on support from powerful backers. Engerman argues that because Jones was not a regular Moscow correspondent who might be persuaded by the news censors to tone down what they considered to be unhelpful news, he needed to be rubbished because little other pressure could be brought to bear. To help them the press censors 'drafted in the Moscow regulars' to undermine Jones's credibility.

But Duranty was not entirely alone in denying what Gareth Jones had said. All four of the leading Moscow correspondents bore their share of the blame, although some later recanted.

Louis Fischer had denied the story even though at the time of Jones' press conference he was on a lecture tour in the United States.

Eugene Lyons went back to New York less than a year after the famine story first broke.[202] He later admitted that on his return to America he had written hesitantly phrased stories about the famine because, he said, US-based 'Soviet sympathizers and liberals treated him as a renegade' and that his early descriptions of the scale of the famine 'fell far short of the horrible conditions that he knew had existed'.[203] He later lost faith in the Soviet project and ultimately became a hawk in his attitudes towards the USSR. Writing in 1937 about his and others' performance in reporting the story, Lyons said, 'The dividing line between "heavy loss of life" through food shortage and "famine" is rather tenuous. Such verbal finessing made little difference to the millions of dead and dying, to the refugees who knocked at our doors begging bread…'[204]

Of Jones's story, Lyons observed,

> …on emerging from Russia, Jones made a statement which, startling though it sounded, was little more than a summary of what the correspondents and foreign diplomats had told him. To protect us, and perhaps with some idea of heightening the authenticity of his reports, he emphasized his Ukrainian foray rather than our conversation as the chief source of his information.[205]

He continued by saying that the Moscow correspondents had collectively complied with the Soviet authorities' wish to kill the story.

> Throwing down Jones was as unpleasant a chore as fell to any of us in years of juggling facts to please dictatorial regimes – but throw him down we did, unanimously and in almost identical formulas of equivocation. Poor Gareth Jones must have been the most surprised human being alive when the facts he so painstakingly garnered from our mouths were snowed under by our denials.[206]

The revelation hardly caused ripples.

A US Congressional Commission into the Ukrainian famine was established in the 1980s. It reported in April 1988, concluding that Duranty and Fischer had taken the lead in the denials.[207]

To many observers Fischer's part in the cover-up was based on a view that 'the truth could only damage Soviet efforts to gain diplomatic recognition, stall Litvinov's anti-Fascist initiatives, and, most important, set back the Five Year Plan'.[208] Some of Duranty's critics charged that he had received money and favours from the Soviets, but this was dismissed by James Crowl, who made a study of the case. Crowl wrote that 'for years [Duranty] had admired the Soviets and had been convinced that they were doing what was best for Russia, even though the cost in lives and suffering was high'.[209]

So what explains Duranty's actions? Was he a mouthpiece or did he genuinely believe, as Stalin did, that the price was worth it and that peasants had brought it on themselves by resisting collectivisation? Muggeridge thought that Duranty was simply seduced by power and those who wielded it.

But it is also important to consider the atmosphere in which the Moscow correspondents worked. Soviet news management should not be underrated. Aware that news of the famine could prove very damaging for Russia's interests abroad, the Soviet government arranged for the Foreign Office Press Department, the NKID, to apply pressure to silence the Western correspondents. The department was headed by Konstantin Oumansky, and a small team of multilingual censors kept the foreign correspondents under control. The pressure – and sometimes blackmail – included threats not to renew visas, to bar correspondents from the Metro-Vickers trial and presumably some things more personal. Richard Ingrams found the threat of being kept from the Metro-Vickers trial a credible reason for correspondents' compliance.

Even though Oumansky's team was small it approved every telegram before it was sent and reports were rejected, sometimes amidst threats and abuse from both sides.[210] The team received feedback from Soviet embassies abroad, giving it a reasonable idea about what was leaking out of the country. Overseas, Soviet diplomats approached foreign editors and journalists offering corrective steers about the news and suggesting angles they might pursue. Fifty years later, the 1980s Congressional Commission noted that 'censorship made many journalists far more circum-spect than Jones'.[211] Some correspondents like Walter Duranty appear to have understood what they could get passed and did not push at the boundaries. But that was just a step away from becoming complicit; and it was far removed from Duranty's experience in wartime France twenty years earlier.[212]

In 1934 Malcolm Muggeridge published a novel based on his experiences in Moscow. In the preface he gave a frank description of the pressures under which journalists worked.

> There is stiff censorship, of course; but it is not generally known that foreign journalists work under perpetual threat of losing their visas, and therefore their jobs. Unless they consent (and most of them do) to limit their news to what will not be displeasing ... they are subjected to continuous persecution...[213]

He added that Russian friends or relatives might also be targeted if other methods did not work. 'The result is that news from Russia is a joke, being either provided by men whom long residence in Moscow has made docile, or whose particular relationship with the Dictatorship of the Proletariat puts its words into their mouths...' He may well have had Duranty in his sights with that description – one of the novel's characters, Jefferson, is loosely based on him.

A glimpse of other dynamics at work is also provided by a memorandum written by a Berlin-based American diplomat. He met Duranty in June 1931. A. W. Kliefoth told Washington what Duranty had said: 'In agreement with the *New York Times* and the Soviet authorities, his official despatches always reflect the official opinion of the Soviet regime, not his own.'[214]

Like William Strang's observation that Duranty held back on telling his readers what he knew, the Congressional Commission accepted there were occasions when Duranty had privately conceded the scale of the Ukrainian famine might be ten million deaths, but had refrained from sharing that information with his readers. 'But they're only Russians,' he is said to have remarked privately.[215]

Were there other possible explanations? There is the valid question why in 1921 Lenin's government had been prepared to reveal how bad the famine was, and to accept international aid, whereas in 1933 Stalin was not. It is possible that in Stalin's desire to beat the last of the resistance out of the peasants and to complete collectivisation, the Soviets could not very well admit to there being a famine and then refuse any aid that followed. National pride and not wanting to lose face is another possible explanation. Some have asked whether Stalin 'preferred to sacrifice millions of lives rather than Soviet prestige'.[216]

The 1980s Congressional Commission thought that Duranty had 'been taken by surprise'.[217] Maybe Duranty had been caught out, just like the American diplomat he caught out with his Latvian scoop. Or did he panic to conceal his lack of enterprise and smug laziness?

More reports about the famine appeared in the West over the summer of 1933 and Duranty came under pressure from the paper's editors to investigate. The Metro-Vickers trial was over and New York knew that he was free to go and see for himself.

He filed reports in August that implied that censorship was taking its toll on the news coming out of the country. But what he told British diplomats did not leach into his reports. In a minute dated 26 September 1933, William Strang reported to the British Foreign Office in London that he had spoken to Duranty, who had just returned from a visit to the famine areas with 'Mr Richardson of the Associated Press'. Passing the report on to 'The King, Cabinet, Dominions', Strang's colleague, T. A. Shone, noted, 'Mr Duranty considers it possible that 10 million people have died, directly or indirectly, for lack of food, during the last year, & I think this estimate exceeds any that we have yet had.'[218] What Duranty had seen and heard revealed to him the scale of the events that Jones, Muggeridge and the others had written about. Did that 'understanding' between the *New York Times* and the Soviet government that he had mentioned to Kliefoth two years earlier figure in downplaying the story?

Duranty retired from Moscow in March 1934, but not before he had received one more accolade. He was a firm believer that

Russia and the United States should establish firm diplomatic relations. It seemed peculiar to many that after fifteen years official ties between the two countries still had not been restored. 'Duranty strongly believed that US recognition of Russia was essential to counter the growing military strength of Nazi Germany and Fascist Italy.'[219] Acknowledging his growing stature as a foreign correspondent he had been summoned to meet the Governor of New York in the summer of 1932. Governor Franklin Delano Roosevelt was campaigning for the Presidency. The meeting had gone well and lasted several hours. 'I asked all the questions,' Roosevelt said, 'it was fascinating.'[220]

Within months of his election as President Roosevelt achieved one of his policy goals: the restoration of diplomatic relations between the two countries. In the months leading up to the announcement, and as news of the famine emerged, Ukrainian groups in the United States did their best to focus attention on the famine and pressed Roosevelt to ask for an investigation of conditions in the Ukraine before granting recognition. But it came to naught. In November 1933 Duranty accompanied Soviet Foreign Minister Litvinov to the United States, securing an interview en route. At a dinner held in New York to mark the announcement a few days later President Roosevelt was generous in his praise for Duranty, whom he called 'one of the great foreign correspondents of modern times'. On his return to Moscow Duranty was granted a second and final exclusive interview with Stalin. It took place on Christmas Day 1933.

Stories about the famine continued to appear periodically over following months, but Duranty was now no longer keeper of the sacred flame of famine denial, so to speak. He continued to cover Russian stories – including some of the big Moscow show trials held during Stalin's purges, and there, according to academic analysis, his performance was also less than satisfactory. Again he was shown to have delivered the official version of events without question. His Moscow replacement, Harold Denny, fared no better.[221]

Duranty left Moscow in 1934 after nearly fourteen years, but continued to produce occasional articles about the Soviet Union for the *New York Times* for several more years, kept on an annual retainer. He published several books and was active on the lucrative American lecture circuit until the late 1940s, by which time his career was entering its twilight years. He died in 1957, at the age of seventy-three. On his deathbed he married the American woman Anna Enwright, who had been his companion for the last eight years of his life. She died in 1971 and, following her request, his ashes were placed inside her casket and they were buried together.

The future was not dazzling for Gareth Jones. He continued his travelling and writing, publishing articles about Stalin's Russia and other places he visited. While in the Far East in 1935 he was kidnapped by Chinese bandits along with a German fellow traveller, whom some believe to have been a Soviet agent. While the German was released after two days, Jones was not and, in circumstances still unclear, was murdered two weeks later, some suspect on Stalin's orders.[222] He was on the eve of his thirtieth birthday.

There are many unanswered questions about the famine cover-up. Had Duranty played another role – had he been a go-between who tried to keep in check opposition to what Roosevelt was trying to do in opening up diplomatic relations with Russia? Was the *New York Times* involved too? Was it a case of downplaying the unpleasant in order to achieve a greater prize? Was it a case of not being able to make an omelette without smashing eggs? He was not alone in holding this view. After all, Louis Fischer had published a book in 1931, titled *Why Recognize Russia?*[223]

We now know that in the Second World War Roosevelt was concerned enough to downplay bad news about its ally the USSR. Documents recently released by the US National Archives show how far his administration went to cover up news of the Katyn massacre.[224] Is it plausible that FDR had been just as concerned about the famine? Had the pressure from Ukrainian groups in the United States – which was ignored – been a factor? Did their unhelpful arguments need to be undermined in order to weaken them and keep the policy of diplomatic recognition on track?

When the Congressional Commission studied the events in the 1980s – America and 'the evil empire' were then in the final stages of the Cold War – it concluded, 'The American government had ample and timely information about the Famine but failed to take any steps which might have ameliorated the situation. Instead, the Administration extended diplomatic recognition to the Soviet government in November 1933, immediately after the Famine.' Summarising its reasoning it continued, 'The Commission has found no evidence that this knowledge played any role in the decision to normalize relations with the Soviet Union.'[225] But it was a carefully crafted phrase that left room for doubt.

The Commission also found that 'a number of the members of the press actively denied in public what they confirmed in private about the famine.'[226] Moreover, it concluded, 'during the Famine certain members of the American press corps cooperated with the Soviet government to deny the existence of the Ukrainian Famine'. Harsh words indeed. An accusation of line-crossing on a mass scale.

To Muggeridge, interviewed in 1983, 'Duranty was the villain of the whole thing … It is difficult for me to see how it could have been otherwise that in some sense he was not in the regime's power.'[227]

The story of Walter Duranty and his lead in denying what he and his Moscow colleagues privately knew to be going on is a sorry tale. It undermines his other journalism, because it focuses attention away from it, but it also illustrates how easy it is to cross the line between being an impartial observer and becoming a protagonist, a cheerleader, a propagandist. Duranty was all three. It is clear that Duranty increasingly boxed himself in as the unintended consequences of his denials became manifest. Trying to maintain a position that was increasingly impossible to hold eventually became too much.

When, in March 1934, he suggested to his editors that he retire, they readily accepted – perhaps with indecent haste. Engerman suggests that they were pleased because Duranty had been spending increasingly more time on leave away from the USSR and was becoming less effective.[228] He struck a deal with his bosses at the *New York Times* that, for an annual retainer of $5,000, he would travel the Soviet Union for three months a year, writing articles for the paper. The rest of his time was his to use how he pleased. He continued to file reports from Russia for the rest of the decade, wrote books and had some fun. When he sometimes ran out of money his wide circle of faithful friends bailed him out. He never made a career as a writer; his books – apart from a few short stories – were all either memoirs or about current affairs or Russia. He continued to be treated as a star foreign correspondent for many years.

It took nearly twenty years after his death for the studies of his role in the famine to emerge. In his final syndicated column, the veteran American political columnist and Cold War hawk Joe Alsop wrote about the condition of the Fourth Estate from which he was retiring. He wrote,

> Duranty, an agreeable man who was a friend of mine, was the foreign correspondent most admired in his time, except by those who had some real ideas of the horrors Joseph Stalin was perpetrating in Russia. Those who seriously reported the horrors, as William Stoneman reported the hideous government-created famine in the Ukraine, did not last very long in Moscow.
>
> Duranty instead covered up the horrors and deluded an entire generation by prettifying Soviet realities. Hence he was showered with the adulation of American intellectuals who did not want the truth. He was given a Pulitzer Prize. He lived uncommonly comfortably in Moscow, too, by courtesy of the KGB. By deluding an entire American generation, Duranty also did much harm. It makes me angry to remember him, although I liked him.[229]

Alsop later remarked to Harrison Salisbury, 'Duranty was a great KGB agent and lying like a trooper.'[230]

Periodically, Duranty's story has resurfaced, each time with a slightly different angle, and as more information emerged from archives after the fall of the Berlin Wall.[231] It has been kept alive by Ukrainian émigré groups which focused attention on the famine; many arguing that it was in fact a genocide, or *Holodomor*. The story may also have played a part in undermining the evil empire, by focusing attention on past Soviet misdeeds, and showing its leaders' capacity for ruthless policies and wilful disregard for human suffering.[232]

Duranty never completely recanted.

Is it possible that Soviet officials had a hold over him that ensured his compliance for years afterwards, as some have wondered? Were Katya and their son that pressure point? This seems unlikely as Duranty is not known to have had any contact with either beyond the 1940s; and he was no doting father, by all accounts.

Or was it simply that he didn't like being upstaged by a young upstart? Did Jones simply upset the great doyen because he got the story that Duranty missed? It was probably not so simple, as we have seen.

Yet was the famine cover-up or denial really so unusual? Was it a peculiar creature of its time and circumstances? Many critics would say it was. After all, American journalism prides itself on fearlessly battling for the truth and has uncovered stories like My Lai, Watergate, Iran–Contra and many others that prove it. Its practitioners will not hesitate to reveal stories that are as uncomfortable for US administrations as the Ukrainian famine story would have been for Stalin. Even allowing for the qualifications sometimes made by *Project Censored*, which claims to be 'the oldest media watchdog research group in the US with a specific focus on education and media literacy' and aims to 'tell the News That Didn't Make the News and Why', it is how US journalism likes to see itself.[233] But in early February 2013 news broke that the CIA was running a drone base in Saudi Arabia from where it mounted operations against targets in the Arabian Peninsula including Yemen. The news was not so much about the base; after all a base was widely suspected to be located somewhere in the region. Rather the news was that it had been kept secret for two years in a willing collusion between the US media and the US government.[234] That came soon after former President Jimmy Carter revealed in the short feature accompanying the DVD release of the Oscar-winning film *Argo* how he had 'prevailed' on editors not to reveal the story of how several American diplomats were rescued from Iran by the CIA.[235] The story only became known when President Bill Clinton declassified the files eighteen years later. So, eight decades later the US media may sometimes not report stories which it knows to be accurate, just like Walter Duranty did from Moscow in spring 1933.

Around the Millennium moves were made to have Duranty posthumously stripped of his Pulitzer Prize, but the prize's management committee declined, because it said the award had been made for the quality of his 1931 journalism, which predated his famine denials. In November 2006 the Ukrainian Parliament passed a resolution declaring the famine to have been an act of genocide against its people.[236] In 2010 the Parliamentary Assembly of the Council of Europe passed a draft resolution that acknowledged that the famine had been man-made, but did not consider that it was an act of genocide.

There is a postscript to this story. The West, in 1933 still suffering itself from the effects of the Great Depression – high unemployment, poverty, hunger – had its own problems and they were closer to home; the story was forgotten. But it is the case that Western mouths ate some of the grain that had been taken from the Ukraine, Kazakhstan and elsewhere and exported by Stalin's Russia – grain that had been sold to earn the precious foreign currency that was needed to buy the machines that would drive forward Russia's industrial modernisation. To that extent the West was a part of the problem, not just an impartial observer.[237]

4

GUY BURGESS

For several weeks in May 1944 Guy Burgess set something of a gold standard for conflicts of interest. For most of each working day he was a producer for the BBC, but for two hours a day he was a propagandist for the Foreign Office and he also spied for the Soviet Union.

The man described by his BBC boss as 'lazy' and 'slipshod', but with a 'fertile' brain, had three different roles and three different employers.

Two of the employers did at least know about each other. The BBC and the Foreign Office agreed to this unusual combination of journalism and propaganda as part of his transfer from one to the other. Our new research reveals that Burgess got his new job because of his time at the BBC and with the help of a BBC governor who knew about Burgess's Russian connections and was probably also one of his lovers. Burgess was always living with the risk of arrest for having sex with male friends and strangers. He was also a prodigiously heavy drinker. Yet this was a man whose friends, contacts and sexual partners included some of the most powerful people in the land. Once he settled in at the Foreign Office Burgess would be taking home as many secret documents as he could carry and arranging for them to be photographed for the Russians.

On 1 May 1944 – the first day of Burgess's unusual transition – the weather was sunny in London so he would probably have walked from his flat at 5 Bentinck Street to Broadcasting

House, a journey of seven minutes. The flat was owned by Victor (later Lord) Rothschild and Burgess shared it with his lover Jack Hewit and his friend and fellow spy Anthony Blunt.[238] Victor Rothschild's future wife Tess, who was also living there when Burgess moved in, had expressed the hope that he wouldn't 'bring pick-ups back' but that was too much to hope.

As Burgess walked to Broadcasting House passers-by might have noticed a rather 'dirty and unkempt' figure and an aroma that combined yesterday's sweat, last night's alcohol and this morning's chewed garlic cloves. At just a shade under six foot and weighing in at twelve stone he would have stood out a little above the average Londoner.

John Green, one of Burgess's BBC colleagues, later recalled that he often looked like an eccentric university don or a 'dirty don' with 'filthy habits'. Occasionally taken to task about this, more than once he had agreed to 'grow up' and keep his workplace clean, but never seemed to manage it. Something always got in the way.

Burgess's time as a journalist is often overlooked and his years at the BBC can appear to be a small career step on the road from Cambridge University to the Foreign Office. But research in the BBC and government files suggests it was much more than that; and information released to us under the Freedom of Information Act shows how. The BBC was his entry point into networks of British society as varied as the political class and the gay underground. It was his invitation to important parties, his passport to official events, his safe haven when other jobs didn't work out and ultimately the Foreign Office's rationale for hiring him. Put simply, it was a great way of meeting useful people; and Burgess was good – very good – at meeting useful people.

It was his time at the BBC which allowed him access to senior politicians such as Winston Churchill and Anthony Eden. Some MPs, such as Harold Nicolson and Tom Driberg, became close friends, and many others became close acquaintances. And his circle also included senior civil servants and diplomats, security and intelligence service officials, academics, bankers and journalists. In short, he knew nearly everyone who was 'anyone'.

They became key people in his journalism, his espionage and his life. They helped provide insights into official thinking, corroboration of information gained elsewhere, or simply interesting tittle-tattle, much of which he passed around. While this would undoubtedly have been useful for Guy Burgess in developing his career, it would also have been useful for his colleagues in Moscow, who were trying to understand what threat Britain posed to them and their international interests. While some of Guy Burgess's friends would later desert him after he had defected, a surprising number would remain loyal.

Guy Francis de Moncy Burgess spent a lifetime making contacts. Born in 1911, the son of a naval commander, he got a head start by being educated with the privileged at the Royal Naval College Dartmouth and later at Eton College before winning a scholarship to read History at Trinity College, Cambridge.

In 1934, while at Cambridge, Burgess was recruited by the Soviet NKVD – the People's Commissariat for Internal Affairs – which later became the KGB. Burgess, and his fellow spies Donald Maclean, Kim Philby, Anthony Blunt and John Cairncross, became known as the five 'Cambridge Spies'.

The five all came from privileged backgrounds, having attended the best public schools and Cambridge University. All were recruited by the Russians in the mid-1930s and all went on to work within the very heart of the British government machine. Maclean was a high-flying Foreign Office diplomat, Philby became a senior MI6 officer, Cairncross worked first for the Foreign Office and then the Treasury, and Blunt worked for MI5 before becoming the Surveyor of the King's Pictures and an internationally acclaimed art expert. None of the five men was ever arrested or punished; and many of the government's files on them are still closed.

The damage which they did lay partly in the sheer volume of secret documents and information that they passed to their friends in Moscow, for their spying careers spanned decades. But part of their significance also lay in the fact that they shook the very foundations of the British Establishment by showing that simply being a member of a socially exclusive class did not mean embracing its values and keeping its secrets. They betrayed not only their country, but also their class.

In 1951 the deception ended when Burgess, by then a junior British diplomat, and his colleague Donald Maclean fled to Moscow to avoid being arrested as Russian spies. The legacy of those stressful and personally chaotic years was the alcoholism which killed Burgess at the age of fifty-three.

Dying to volunteer

Most accounts say that back at Cambridge in 1934, the KGB's recruiting sergeant at the university had been Dr Arnold Deutsch, a London-based academic who doubled as a Soviet spy. He recruited Philby and, allegedly, twenty-seven other agents in the UK.

The intelligence historian Christopher Andrew put it rather differently. He wrote that Burgess and his colleagues 'weren't so much recruited as dying to volunteer'. In Burgess's case the eagerness and excitement seems to have been particularly acute.

Ill health prevented Burgess from taking his final exams and he was awarded what's known as an *aegrotat* – an honours degree without classification. So although Burgess's reputation as a 'brilliant' student nearly always preceded him it was never actually tested in an examination. However, Burgess did carry out several months of postgraduate research at Cambridge and this helped to establish his academic reputation.

Of other work he did after his degree, he was at Conservative Central Office for a time, gave some financial advice to his friend Victor Rothschild's mother and spent a short period writing articles and practising sub-editing for *The Times*, for which they thanked him but offered no prospects. In between he worked for an MP, Captain Jack Macnamara, which helped throw up a smokescreen around Burgess's real politics. The right-wing Conservative MP had good contacts in Nazi Germany and one of Burgess's friends described him as 'so far to the right of the Conservative Party that it was quite reasonable to call him a fascist'.[239] Working for Macnamara gave Burgess the opportunity to see parliamentary and political papers – including confidential ones – that passed across his desk. It is not difficult to imagine where some of them would end up.

To say Burgess set about leading a double life in these early years hardly does justice to the multiple layers he created around his persona.

He worked for the secret service of the Soviet Union, but also ran errands for the secret services of Great Britain, MI5 and MI6. At times he appeared to be a left-winger who visited Russia, and he attended at least one rally in Paris organised by a Communist front. At other times he was a right-winger who had joined the pro-Nazi group the Anglo-German Fellowship, as did his friend Kim Philby.[240] The bottom line was that these networks gave him opportunities to meet useful and powerful people who were at the heart of British and European society; and in the process to sparkle.

Of the many official and unofficial networks he belonged to, two of the most secretive took priority in his life. One was the Comintern, an organisation originally set up in an effort to co-ordinate the activities of Communist parties worldwide and in the process to sustain the Bolshevik revolution. It used a range of aggressive propaganda and espionage activities to achieve its ends.

The other was what became known as the 'Homintern', a nick-name given by Sir Maurice Bowra to a homosexual subculture whose members during the 1920s and 1930s were drawn from the rich and powerful of Europe and whose politics embraced all shades of opinion from the far right to the far left.[241] Burgess and Captain Macnamara MP were active members of the Homintern. The members developed a lingua franca that enabled them quickly to identify themselves, and were experienced in furtiveness, because their sexual encounters were at that time illegal and, if exposed, completely ruinous to themselves and their families.

The historian and former diplomat Robert Cecil knew four of the Cambridge spies. Of Burgess he wrote,

> He had been a homosexual, of course, ever since his years at Eton; but he had no feeling of being an outcast, because he lacked all sense of shame. He had no particular wish to change the law on homosexuality; so long as he succeeded in defying it, the risk involved gave an added frisson to his exploits. He fitted excellently into the interlocking circles on the fringes of politics, art, letters and intellectual debate, in which as a younger man he had shone.[242]

None of these intriguing activities amounted to a proper job with career prospects.

In the year or so after leaving Cambridge Burgess's career had, to say the least, lacked direction, and was hardly what someone with his intellectual gifts might have expected. Whereas some of his contemporaries had seen the great offices of state as suitable targets for their future careers, he seems to have realised that a career in the media would be more fitting to his talents. In November 1935 he got help from the Cambridge University Appointments Board, which recommended him for a job in the BBC Talks Department. Burgess was a man of 'quite first-rate ability' who had been 'through the communist phase'. One of the board's staff wrote, 'I do not think he has any particular politics now but I expect they are rather towards the left ... He is a somewhat highly-strung fellow, too, but gets on uncommonly well with people, including being notably successful with a number of stupid pupils whom he supervised for his College.'[243]

The next month the renowned Cambridge historian G. M. Trevelyan followed up with a letter to Sir Cecil G. Graves (then the BBC's controller of programmes), recommending someone who he said 'would be a great addition to your staff'.

'I believe a young friend of mine, Guy Burgess, late a scholar of Trinity, is applying for a post at the BBC.' He explained that Burgess had been in the running to become a fellow in History but had decided instead, correctly in Trevelyan's view, that 'his bent was for the great world – politics, journalism etc etc'.

Trevelyan's letter went on, 'He is a first-rate man, and I advise you if you can to try him. He has passed through the communist measles that so many of our clever young men go through, and is well out of it.'[244]

When the BBC took up a reference from Burgess's tutor at Trinity, J. Barnaby, he too thought Burgess had travelled through Communism to what he called 'a form of left-wing conservatism', but significantly, he added, 'How long that will last I should be sorry to predict'. He found Burgess exceptionally able but high-lighted character defects as 'the faults of a nervy and mercurial temperament'. He concluded that by hiring Burgess the BBC 'would be taking risks' but 'if I were in your place I should think it was worth taking them'.

Professor George Macaulay Trevelyan may have been the Regius Professor of Modern History but he and his colleagues' judgement on Burgess's recovery from an outbreak of 'communist measles' could not have been more wrong. Burgess had been a left-wing activist in his final undergraduate year, but his left-wing activism was not some passing student fad.[245]

It was to be a year, however, before Burgess would finally enter through the hallowed portals of Broadcasting House. The Cambridge letter-writing campaign finally seemed to have worked.

BBC recruit

Burgess joined the BBC's training reserve at the beginning of October 1936.[246] His friend Denis Proctor, a principal at the Treasury, and Captain Macnamara vouchsafed for him. For the next three months Burgess would learn basic studio and production skills.

On 1 January 1937 he became an assistant in the Talks Department, earning £260 per year, but he would not do any talks himself. He was consigned to production rather than presentation or announcing because the BBC had noticed that his diction was bad. He would be firmly positioned on the other side of the microphone.

Burgess was to spend two spells at the BBC: 1937–38, in which he helped to produce talks, and 1940–44, when he returned for a second stint in a similar role on programmes such as *The Week in Westminster*.

'Talks' was an important department in the BBC, accounting for much of the factual programming on the corporation's only domestic radio station, the BBC National Programme. It was to be a perfect home for Burgess and there to make him feel at home was the senior producer George Barnes, who Burgess just happened to know from his time in Cambridge when he lodged at Barnes's home. The new recruit seemed to start well. He was asked to help produce programmes such as *Keep Fit with Miss Quigley* and *How Things are Made*.

'Brilliantly able, widely-read and with a keen sense of humour he's delightful company,' said one of his first appraisals. 'Has produced some admirable programmes and is always likely to do so when interested.'

Guy Burgess worked hard on behalf of his various masters. His first year at the BBC provided him with ample opportunities to produce programmes which would expand his circle of influential friends and acquaintances. He produced talks on art given by his friend Anthony Blunt and by personalities such as Professor Hugh Seton-Watson, who taught Russian History at London University, E. H. Carr, the Marxist historian and former diplomat, and Lord Elton, the Oxford historian.

But, in March 1938 Guy Burgess's BBC career came to a sudden, if temporary halt when a medical certificate arrived from a doctor in Mayfair.

'Mr Guy Burgess has been to see me this afternoon and I suggest he should have a holiday considering the state of his nerves.' A BBC official added the note, 'Mr Burgess is away today. It is not known when he will return.'[247]

Three weeks later the same doctor wrote to the BBC requesting a further week off for Burgess. He reported a visit from Burgess's mother, who had been looking after him in the south of France. 'She informs me that he is better, but that she did not think him well enough to return just yet. He is still in a very nervous state and suffering from insomnia.'

Significantly Burgess's mother wanted to reassure the doctor that 'he is very sensible and does not go out or touch any alcohol'.

Burgess's drinking caused increasing concern to his friends as the years passed. One was Harold Nicolson, a former Foreign Office diplomat, an MP, a writer, a broadcaster and a noted expert on foreign affairs. He was married to the writer Vita Sackville-West.

Nicolson later confided to his diary, 'I dined with Guy Burgess. Oh my dear, what a sad, sad thing this constant drinking is! Guy used to have one of the most rapid and active minds I knew.'

Nicolson knew of Burgess's active and presumably more sober mind from the time when they first met in the mid-1930s – they were already dining companions by March 1936 when they had shared a dinner with John Maynard Keynes. A study of Nicolson's unpublished diaries reveals the extent to which the two men enjoyed one another's company. It paints a very different picture to the infrequent meetings and social occasions hinted at by the published ones. Some friends believed the Burgess–Nicolson relationship was also sexual – it was even suggested that Burgess 'procured friends' for Nicolson. Hints from the unpublished diaries suggest that they were correct.

There are other accounts of gay gatherings in Whitehall, some of them hosted by Tom Wylie, the private secretary to the Minister at the War Office, that show their close social acquaintance. In what seem to have been remarkably risky circumstances, Burgess and Nicolson attended one of these on the night in 1936 when

Burgess first met the person who would soon become his most regular lover, Jack Hewit.

Professional relationship

The professional relationship between Harold Nicolson and Guy Burgess began to develop at the BBC in 1938, when they worked closely together on a series of weekly talks called *The Past Week*.

For the month of September 1938, which led up to the Munich agreement between Chamberlain and Hitler, the programme was to be the cause of a polite but nonetheless intense battle between the BBC and Nicolson, as they tried to agree on what should and could be said on the air about Hitler, Nazi Germany and the prospects of war. The BBC, aware that the government was keeping a very close eye on its programmes, reflected the dominant media mood of the time, which was that war with Germany was to be avoided at all cost.[248] Nicolson was one of the MPs arguing for a more resolute response to Hitler. Burgess seems to have stayed out of it, leaving his BBC boss and former landlord George Barnes to do battle with his friend and 'lover' Harold Nicolson over the broadcast of *The Past Week*. The talk scheduled for 5 September 1938 was particularly problematic. The Foreign Office were not happy with what Nicolson was proposing to say.

George Barnes decided that the script which Nicolson had submitted should be passed on to a senior official at the Foreign Office, the head of its News Department, Rex Leeper. He was so concerned about what happened next that he wrote a note for the file, setting out an hour-by-hour account. An extract from the note gives a flavour of what transpired:

> 3.30 p.m. Mr Leaper [*sic*] telephoned to say that 'the Foreign Office cannot take any responsibility for Mr Nicolson's script as submitted and that in the view of the gravity of the situation, and of the pace at which it is changing, the Foreign Office would prefer no talk at all on that subject was broadcast tonight'. I asked if this was an instruction. He replied that the Foreign Office could not

instruct the BBC on a matter like this, but that the recommendation was very strong.[249]

Nicolson himself was angry at the cuts Barnes was suggesting
under pressure from the Foreign Secretary, Lord Halifax. He
initially suggested the whole talk be cancelled, which alarmed
Barnes. But then he agreed to re-write it.

Barnes's note for the file recorded, 'I returned to Broadcasting
House and arranged with the announcer and Mr Lidell, who was
on duty, to be ready to fade out Mr Nicolson's talk if in my opinion, he departed too far from his script.

'I met Mr Nicolson at 9.30 and he produced a third script
which was, in my opinion, innocuous. As he did not wish me to
remain I left him at 9.55 p.m.'

Modern-day producers handling a sensitive programme would
find it extraordinary that a producer would not be present for a
live broadcast because the presenter 'did not wish me to remain'.
Perhaps even more extraordinary is that at one point the producer
planned to leave it to an announcer, even one as experienced as
Alvar Lidell, to fade out the speaker if he didn't keep to the script.

The broadcast went ahead, but BBC executives later admitted
to themselves that it sounded as if it had been censored. However,
like true English gentlemen Barnes and Nicolson set about trying
to restore relations in time for the next programme.

Nicolson wrote, 'My dear Barnes, I feel I owe you an apology
for having been so ill-tempered last night. The fact is that I had
been working on that beastly talk all afternoon and that I was
appalled at the thought of having to do it all over again.'

For Guy Burgess it must have been something of a relief that
this battle between his two friends seemed to have been resolved
so politely without *The Past Week* ever going off the air. But soon
he was involved in a new row at Broadcasting House.

At the end of November 1938 he told Nicolson that he
was incensed that following a request from the Chamberlain
government the BBC had cancelled a talk due to be given by a

serving admiral in a series which Burgess was producing about
the Mediterranean. When Burgess told Nicolson that he was
going to resign from the BBC, Nicolson tried to calm him down
and advocated reflection, but Burgess went ahead and resigned
anyway.

Career change
However, the reason given for his departure from the BBC in the
corporation's files is that 'MI', Military Intelligence, had asked
for Burgess to be seconded to work on propaganda at the War
Office but the BBC refused so he resigned and left the corporation. This looks to be the more likely explanation. Working at the
BBC Talks Department had been a good career move for Burgess
and an opportunity to meet a range of important people across
public life and gather information that was of potential use to
both the programme-makers at the BBC and the spymasters at
the KGB, as well as his informal contacts at MI5 and MI6.

Just before he left the BBC he had met Winston Churchill for the
first time to ask him to do a talk for the Mediterranean series.[250]
Churchill was then a Conservative backbencher and the leading
opponent of Chamberlain's appeasement policy. He told Burgess
he had been 'muzzled' by the BBC before and he imagined he
would be even more muzzled as the BBC seemed to be under the
control of the government. Burgess sought to reassure him that
the Foreign Office merely saw the scripts in advance.[251] Nothing
came of Burgess's programme proposal but he committed brief
details to a BBC memorandum soon afterwards.[252]

The meeting was one that clearly made an impact on him, as
he later made a tape recording about it, of which a transcript
was finally released a few years ago. It reveals that an intellectu-
ally restless Burgess could occasionally jump ahead of his own
narrative:

Anyhow, having finished discussing Munich Week with Mr
Churchill I left his house and got into my car outside, and I have

forgotten to mention that before doing that he had trotted out of the room and he said: 'I'll leave you but I'll return', and he did return in about a minute and a half bearing a volume, and he said, 'Mr Burgess ... before you leave me I would wish that you accept this – my speeches.'[253]

But useful as his work at the BBC had been in providing opportunities for Burgess to meet leading politicians like Churchill and collect books of their speeches, his Soviet controllers must have thought that as the prospect of war between Britain and Germany grew there must be organisations that would be even more fruitful places of work.

Coming at such a crucial time in international politics, and undoubtedly helped by his efforts on behalf of the British intelligence services, a move to 'MI' (Military Intelligence) could be his entry into a network of much greater interest to Burgess's colleagues in Moscow than the BBC. It was his – and their – reader's ticket to secret official documents and his passport to gatherings at which important secret information would be exchanged.

The KGB files record that from December 1938 Burgess had managed to get himself into Section D of the Secret Intelligence Service (SIS), also known as MI6, which is confirmed by files in the National Archives.[254] Section D had been established early in 1938 by a military swashbuckling type, Major Lawrence Grand, to devise dirty tricks and to develop psychological warfare.[255] An internal history says that recruitment 'was on a personal basis ... and was not altogether inappropriate for a small organisation working in extreme secrecy'.[256]

Some sources say that Burgess was recruited by MI6 via one of its senior officers, David Footman. Again it appeared that a BBC connection had been useful. The two men had first met in 1937 when Burgess produced a talk on Albania given by Footman, who was then the deputy head of MI6's political intelligence department. It has also been suggested that Burgess had performed some clandestine intelligence work for Footman while still working for the BBC during the months leading up to the 1938 Munich crisis;[257] and at the same time KGB files reveal that he was also performing valuable clandestine work for his friends in Moscow.

One of Section D's great wartime successes came during the German invasion on the Netherlands in 1940 when its operatives managed to seize 'the bulk of Amsterdam's industrial diamond stocks' and spirit them to England.[258]

During Burgess's time in Section D he acted as an MI6 representative on something called the Joint Broadcasting Committee (JBC), which was based at 71 Chester Square in London. This was conveniently located since it was a matter of yards from the flat in which he was living at the time. Here in rather tense meetings BBC executives, jealously protecting their role as the nation's only broadcaster, met the MI6 officials who were transmitting their own anti-Hitler broadcasts to Germany from radio stations in mainland Europe, including Radio Luxembourg, which the British government secretly owned. They were aiming to extend their network of radio stations into Liechtenstein and former BBC producer Guy Burgess now found himself involved in trying to set this up. And there at the JBC to offer advice was its director, the former BBC director of talks Hilda Matheson, and among the other board members, the ubiquitous Harold Nicolson.

In the symmetry which seems such a constant characteristic of the whole Burgess saga, Matheson had been instrumental in launching Harold Nicolson's career as a broadcaster in 1930 and went on to have a lesbian relationship with his wife Vita Sackville-West. So it is just possible that two JBC board members, Burgess and Nicolson, were sleeping together, while another, Hilda Matheson, was sleeping with Nicolson's wife.

Among Burgess's other work he devised and ran a course at a training establishment at Brickendonbury in Hertfordshire, where sabotage was taught.

Burgess had also been involved in abortive sabotage plans against the Germans. He was told to travel to Moscow to organise things with Soviet organisations. As a cover the Foreign Office and MI6 organised for him and an Oxford friend, the philosopher Isaiah Berlin, to travel as couriers carrying diplomatic bags. Foreign Office diplomat Gladwyn Jebb and Harold Nicolson, who was by then a junior minister in the Ministry of Information, had helped with the arrangements. The safer long way round via America and Japan had been advised. But Berlin and Burgess never got to Russia. They got as far as Washington when the plan was scrapped and Burgess was ordered home. Berlin was left to make his own way back. Berlin 'later believed that someone in British Intelligence, perhaps Victor Rothschild, decided that Burgess was too unreliable ... to be trusted and had him recalled'. But apparently it was Victor's sister, Miriam Rothschild, then in Washington, horrified to find Burgess on such a mission, who warned Frederick Hoyer Millar, a senior diplomat at the British embassy. He cabled London and Burgess was recalled.[259] A couple of weeks after returning Burgess saw Harold Nicolson, who recorded in his diary, 'He is still determined to get in touch with the Comintern and use them to create disorders in occupied territory.'[260]

But there was trouble ahead for Burgess in MI6.

In the autumn of 1940 Section D of MI6 was merged with SOE, the Special Operations Executive, which was created to conduct guerrilla operations against the enemy, often through local resistance fighters.

By the end of 1940 Burgess had apparently been sacked just a few months short of his thirtieth birthday for 'irreverence', or what is more likely to have been insubordination. Gladwyn Jebb (later, Lord Gladwyn) later took credit for weeding Burgess out, feeling 'he was quite extraordinarily dissolute and indiscreet and certainly unfitted for any kind of confidential work'.[261] But it did not appear to prevent Jebb and Burgess from meeting socially during the war.

Burgess's departure from Section D is confirmed by an oblique reference in an SOE file in the National Archives, which has been found by Jeff Hulbert. There is a list of people who had 'been given their conge [sic; the sack]'. It continues, 'There will be others to come – probably two or three more, including one BURGESS, who is now employed in the school.'[262]

Having got the *congé* from MI6 and with no regular remuneration from Moscow for his work for the KGB, and moreover no position that could be useful to them, Burgess desperately needed a job.

A new job...
He headed back to the only other place which had ever employed him, the BBC. But he needed a story to explain why he had suddenly become available. The BBC bureaucracy seemed to swallow it.

> I understand that there has been some re-organisation in the M.I. branch where he was employed, and that by agreement with his chief Burgess can be – in fact has been – released from his duties and is free to start work with the 'Corporation'.

Mr W. R. Baker of the BBC's 'General Establishment Office' could hardly believe his luck.

It seems that an experienced member of the BBC Talks Department in London had been transferred to the Midland Region and Baker had to help fill the vacancy 'at the first possible moment'. Burgess had

> considerable and successful experience with us previously on the preparation and production of Talks and it will be a very great advantage indeed to us to retain his services indefinitely on the same type of work.[263]

Once again he seems to have found an opening that he could exploit for the benefit of all of his masters. There was just the small problem of avoiding Burgess being called up for military service. Baker pulled out all the stops in a letter to the Ministry of Information.

We are extremely fortunate in finding that Burgess is available to resume his previous occupation with us, subject to our being able to secure his reservation from military service ... We shall be extremely grateful for any steps you can take to enable us to retain the services of Burgess.[264]

The authorities were soon to get another request that Burgess should not be called up. Burgess may have been let go by MI6 but he had friends in MI5, Britain's counter-espionage agency, and they gave him the code-name *VAUXHALL*.[265] MI5's recruiting sergeant was none other than Anthony Blunt, whom Burgess had helped recruit as a Soviet spy, whose broadcasting career Burgess had launched, and whose flatmate he was about to become. We are told that in the security service archives is a document in which Blunt wrote, 'Burgess has been working for us and has done extremely valuable work – principally the running of two very important agents who he discovered and took on. It would therefore be a great pity if he were called up.'[266] It is not hard to imagine that Burgess and Blunt had cooked up this request.

Given such unusual circumstances as the BBC and MI6 both applying to the War Office to keep Burgess in London, it is perhaps understandable that in Moscow Centre they sometimes wondered if all this was too good to be true. The information coming back from Burgess, Blunt and Philby was so voluminous, so good and so consistent that it seemed highly plausible that they were in fact double agents and the KGB was the victim of a massive plant by the British. It seems that Moscow's strong suspicions endured for a couple of years, although it is likely that the Cambridge Five themselves never realised that they were under suspicion. But whatever Moscow's suspicions the 'Cambridge Spies' carried on spying.[267]

When he re-joined BBC radio in 1940 Guy Burgess became a producer on the weekly political discussion programme *The Week in Westminster*. He was responsible for timing the scripts, editing them, nominating, preparing and evaluating speakers as well as being knowledgeable about parliamentary activities and issues.

He realised the broadcasting potential of politicians such as Douglas Houghton, John Strachey and Hector McNeil, for whom he was later to work at the FO. Sixty-five years later, Stella Rimington, a former head of MI5, described a list of the programme's participants while Burgess was the producer, with more than a hint of incredulity in her voice, as containing 'everyone under the sun'.

As a part of his work on *The Week in Westminster* Burgess was required to develop his political contacts within Parliament, part of which had decamped to Church House after the Palace of Westminster had been damaged by bombing. But it was not all his own work. Burgess was able to call on the support and assistance of his friend Harold Nicolson, particularly after the latter left the Ministry of Information and became a governor of the BBC.

Burgess produced over a hundred *Week in Westminster* programmes between 1941 and 1944. He drew on a relatively small pool of MPs, a number of who appeared several times. The MPs were selected in consultation with Burgess's bosses at the BBC, the party whips and the Ministry of Information. But Harold Nicolson's unpublished diaries reveal that the pair sometimes discussed the programme and potential speakers during Nicolson's visits to Broadcasting House for governors' meetings, or over a drink after they had finished.

For instance, Nicolson and Burgess discussed recommending the only Communist MP, Willie Gallacher, as a speaker.[268] When proposed, the other parties agreed because Gallacher was a good speaker, knew the rules and played the game.

Megan Lloyd George MP (Independent Liberal) topped the list with sixteen appearances and was considered to be one of the best performers. Lord Hailsham later recalled from his five appearances as Quintin Hogg MP that Burgess was 'a brisk, intelligent and professional producer. If he was a little given to drink and plying his customers with drink, well that was all right.'[269]

Lord Thorneycroft told the House of Lords in 1989 that during his four appearances as Captain Thorneycroft MP he got to know Burgess 'very well'. He said Burgess 'was employed to collect young men from both parties in Parliament ... He knew everyone very well ... He was considered ideal in that particular world.'[270]

But Burgess was not only a busy producer. Word got around that he was someone who had views that were worth hearing. In June 1942 the Leader of the House of Commons, Sir Stafford Cripps, who was an early advocate of planning for the post-war world, invited several BBC producers, MPs and others to dinner so that he could hear their views. Guy Burgess joined his BBC colleagues Eric Blair (George Orwell) and William Empson, together with Harold Nicolson, and Labour peer Lord Winster.

It may not have been quite the sparkling occasion that Burgess was used to, however. Orwell recorded in his diary: 'Spent a long evening with Cripps (who had expressed a desire to meet some literary people) ... About 2½ hours of it, with nothing to drink. The usual inconclusive discussion. Cripps, however, very human and willing to listen.'[271]

Burgess's gregarious nature helped him establish good relations with MPs. But there were other avenues open to him as well. Over three-quarters of the way through his stint on the programme he told the BBC that he had access to a private dining club and asked his boss and old friend, George Barnes, whether the BBC would foot the bill for him and his guests, who might be fellow producers: £2 a head, 10 shillings for food and 30 shillings for drink. Barnes managed to suppress his alarm and dampened it down by insisting on a drinks bill of a few shillings. Wine would be off the menu.[272]

As well as producing *The Week in Westminster* Burgess was responsible for around 250 other radio programmes, including one that was a prototype for a genre that became known as 'consumer affairs'. Called *Can I Help You?*, and fronted by Professor John Hilton, the weekly programme aired many public issues but also helped publicise government advice and

information campaigns including, crucially, how to fill out daunt-
ing and unfamiliar official forms. Its 'Kitchen Front' features were
presented by Aileen Furse, who went on to become the second
Mrs Kim Philby. Working on the programme seems to have given
Guy Burgess ready access to the many ministers and their civil
servants who were actively battling on the home front. But potentially just as significantly the programme attracted thousands of
letters from listeners seeking the solutions to problems in their
daily wartime lives. In the early days of opinion polls and mass
observation surveys it would have given Burgess and Moscow
an unrivalled independent insight into British civilian morale. A
sister programme for the armed forces prompted a similarly valuable postbag, this time from the military front line.

Sometimes Burgess's ideas would be intended to please both
his masters – the BBC and the KGB – and maybe his friends in
MI5 as well. David Graham, a BBC colleague, later recalled how
in 1941 Burgess proposed that the corporation should have

> an informed diplomatic correspondent who would have an office
> with, of course, a locked door in Broadcasting House; and the
> Foreign Office would then send diplomatic telegrams so that
> the diplomatic correspondent could be properly informed and
> tell the responsible news people and comments people within the
> BBC what was going on.

With hindsight Graham realised Burgess's real motives:

> The implication was quite clearly that Burgess would be the man.
> Now if, of course, he had been the diplomatic correspondent and
> had had a locked room inside Broadcasting House which he could
> have stayed in after office hours and maybe photographed (if he
> had been taught how) or certainly written down the words of tran-
> scribed cipher telegrams, this, as we now know, would have been
> of first class use to some other people he was in touch with outside
> office hours at the Soviet embassy.[273]

Nothing came of this proposal from Burgess but other ideas were embraced enthusiastically.

In June 1941 Nazi Germany invaded the Soviet Union and within days the British Empire and the USSR were allies. Sir Richard Maconachie, the director of talks, invited suggestions from talks producers for programmes that would support the new alliance. Soon afterwards Burgess wrote a memo entitled 'Draft Suggestions for Talks on Russia'. In it he recommended Dr Anthony Blunt for talks on Soviet art, noting that he was not a Communist, but also suggested talks by Dr Christopher Hill, the expert on Russian history, who, he acknowledged, was a Communist.

Helpfully, Burgess knew Peter Smollett, the head of the Ministry of Information's Soviet Department and an occasional BBC broadcaster himself. During the war Smollett's team at the ministry helped to organise official British government pro-Russia rallies – including one in the Royal Albert Hall. They also had a hand in BBC radio programmes about Russian themes. Thirty such programmes were broadcast to British listeners in October 1943 alone.

Burgess and Smollett seemed to work well together in the cause of promoting partnership with the Soviets, which may partly be explained by the fact that Smollett was later revealed to be a Soviet spy as well.[274] He had been watched by Special Branch since the late 1930s but was never prosecuted and continued to work for the Ministry of Information as the head of its Russian Department until mid-1945, when he returned to journalism.

The Smollett connection may also have been involved in helping with what sounds like an unusual challenge which Burgess had been set by his Moscow masters. According to Anthony Blunt, Moscow had at one time tasked Burgess with wooing Clarissa Churchill, the Prime Minister's niece, so that he could get close to Winston Churchill. As Blunt told it, Burgess was initially horrified, but then declared himself ready for the challenge.[275]

Jeff Hulbert has discovered that for a time Clarissa Churchill worked as a research assistant for Smollett at the Ministry of Information. Each month Smollett's department produced a glossy newsletter for Russia called *Britanskiy Soyuznik*. One very brief memorandum, dated 2 August 1942, refers to the departure of a member of the staff: 'Miss Clarissa Churchill will not come back and we shall therefore be grateful if you can recommend another research assistant to work in Britanskiy Soyuznik,' Smollett wrote.[276] There is no mention of this episode in Clarissa Churchill's memoirs.

According to intelligence historian Christopher Andrew, probably Burgess's most remarkable coup within the BBC, on behalf of the NKVD, was to arrange for a talk on the Eastern Front in January 1942 by a man called Ernst Henri, who was later revealed as another Soviet spy. Henri told listeners that the Soviet armed forces would triumph and used the occasion to reassure everyone, including Soviet moles, that the Soviet intelligence services were 'among the best in the world'.[277]

Warning signs

Burgess was clearly having some success on both fronts – the BBC and the KGB. But, perhaps inevitably given Burgess's complicated life, the staff files at Broadcasting House in London and KGB headquarters in Moscow began to fill up with warning signs.

The first followed an incident just across the road from Broadcasting House at the Langham Hotel. Burgess had wanted to collect some papers from his room, but had found the way barred by a locked door. So he tried to smash it open. In May 1941 a security official wrote,

> I found that the door of Room 316 had been damaged in an attempt to force it open by using a fire extinguisher, the contents of which were spread all over the carpet outside ... The whole incident was most unsatisfactory, and I must add uncalled for.

Burgess was, perhaps, a little the worse for wear and had the distinct scent of alcohol on his breath. He had become angry with the security staff, had been arrogant and somewhat abusive.

Four days later Burgess wrote a fulsome, if pompous and sarcastic, report about the incident. 'I am extremely sorry that any individual should feel injured by the manner in which I raised the question of getting into my room at the Langham Hotel to remove some urgently necessary papers last Thursday. Also that the Department should in any way be injured by this.'[278]

In January 1943 it was his expenses that began to catch the eye of BBC administrators. A Mr O. Thompson felt unable to certify Burgess's expenses sheet. 'His office hours are very flexible – he is rarely here before 10.45 a.m. since he reads his papers and Hansards at home and spends most of the day out of the office making contacts.'

Then it was the issue of why Burgess always travelled first class. He argued he had 'successfully established the principle' and saw no reason why he 'should alter my practice when on BBC business particularly when I am in my best clothes to attend a Service'. Dragged into the row the head of the department, his old friend the long-suffering George Barnes, decided 'there is no case for Mr Burgess travelling first class'.

On 20 April 1943 the administrative officer (Home) at the BBC, G. J. B. Allport, wrote a memo to the controller of the Home Service headed 'Guy Burgess and the Week in Westminster'. His main concern was the money Burgess was spending in the parliamentary bar and his practice of lending out BBC secretaries to do typing for MPs. 'We shall soon get a bad name at the Treasury.'

> I cannot believe that it is not possible to do business with responsible MPs except at the bar. You will notice that the same names crop up fairly frequently, Quintin Hogg, D R Grenfell etc., while there is almost continual entertaining to Lobby correspondents.

Allport concluded, 'I do not know whether it is my business to say this, but I feel someone will be asking before long whether it would be better to have a rather older person in charge of this series.'[279]

Meanwhile the KGB's files show the pressure getting to Burgess in increasingly alarming ways, culminating in his plan to become Burgess the assassin.

Sometime in 1938 he had been instrumental in recruiting a friend, a former Oxford fellow and author, Goronwy Rees. According to records later released by the KGB Rees was a relatively short-lived agent. However, Rees knew that Burgess had been a KGB agent and also knew, through Burgess, about one of the other members of the Cambridge Five, Anthony Blunt. In Burgess's view this made Rees a serious risk to him. Over succeeding years Rees – by then serving in Military Intelligence – and Burgess remained good friends. But suspicion seems to have continued to gnaw at Burgess. Four years later – 1943 – Burgess twice raised the issue with his KGB controller, on one occasion asking for permission to have Rees assassinated; and on another, offering to do the job himself as he had been responsible for the predicament in the first place. Moscow sought to calm Burgess's anxieties and concluded that an assassination was not necessary.[280] Rees, a wartime intelligence officer, only confided his knowledge about Burgess to MI5 after Burgess had fled in 1951.[281] Rees never knew that his friend had wanted to have him assassinated and continued to see Burgess socially until the latter's defection. The assassination plans didn't prevent Burgess enjoying dinner with Rees and Harold Nicolson one evening in January 1944.[282]

Even though Burgess was working six days a week, twelve hours a day in his day job, he still managed to find such opportunities to relax with friends in convivial company when not engaged in spare-time MI5 work. Apart from dinners with Harold Nicolson in fashionable places such as the Café Royal he also met friends in less salubrious places, the West End clubs and drinking dens. One favourite haunt was the Gargoyle Club, described by the art collector and aesthete Harold Acton as 'a dinner and dance-club with paintings by Matisse hung on the walls'. The habitués included Acton, Noel Coward, Augustus John, Harold Nicolson and Guy Burgess. Several times in the summer of 1942 Harold Nicolson, Guy Burgess and others went on to the club after first dining elsewhere. One evening, so the club's historian records, Burgess asked the painter John Craxton if he would like to go back with him to his flat. 'Would you like to be whipped – a wild thrashing? Wine thrown in?' The painter, reportedly terrified, was saved by the writer Philip Toynbee.[283] Acton wrote waspishly about Burgess, whom he loosely described as one of the 'parlour pinks who talked as if nothing could be worse than the freedom they enjoyed to damn the government and the old order who had given them that freedom'. Of these he singled out Burgess:

> The most vindictive of these was Guy Burgess ... though nobody could have been less diplomatic. Brian [Howard][284] confided to me that his equipment was gargantuan – 'what is known as a whopper, my dear' – which might account for his success in certain ambiguous quarters.[285]

Recruitment

27 March 1944 must have been a busy time in the office of the Permanent Under-Secretary of the Foreign Office, Sir Alexander Cadogan. Apart from running the Foreign Office, which was at full stretch with a global war, he was a highly regarded diplomat who travelled with Churchill to meet Stalin and President Franklin D. Roosevelt. But on the 27th Sir Alexander found time to write to the director-general of the BBC, R.W. Foot, with a request for the transfer of a relatively junior member of the BBC's staff.

> Dear Foot,
> I am writing to ask if you would be good enough to consider the release from employment in your Corporation of Mr Guy Burgess, for service in our News Department.

Cadogan explained that the calls on this department were becoming extremely heavy, that they'd recently had to release two members to other work and he wanted to fill the vacancies.

I understand that Mr Burgess of your Talks Department is interested in this vacancy and from our point of view he would be well
qualified to fill it. I fully appreciate that he is doing most valuable
work with the British Broadcasting Corporation and I fear that his
release may inconvenience you. But as I have said our own need
is great, and we should therefore be most grateful if you could see
your way to facilitate his transfer to us.

This was the letter that set in train a series of events that culminated in one of the most embarrassing episodes in the history of
the British Foreign Office. As Lady Bracknell might have observed
in an Oscar Wilde play, 'To lose one diplomat defecting to the
Russians may be regarded as a misfortune; to lose two looks like
carelessness.'

Cadogan's letter seemed to us to merit further investigation.
For instance, given that Burgess was not a senior figure in the
BBC hierarchy and Sir Alexander Cadogan was very senior in
the Foreign Office, was it really necessary to make such a high
level intervention as a personal letter to the director-general of the
BBC? By contrast we found other examples of transfers between
the two organisations resolved at a much lower level.

We drew up a list of questions and Jeff Hulbert set to work in
the archives.

Why the hurry to hire Burgess?
Why did it require a request from 'Perm Sec F.O' to 'D.G. B.B.C'?
And perhaps, most significantly, why Burgess in particular?

It was relatively easy to establish why someone extra was needed
in the Foreign Office News Department. With a war waging in
Europe and the Far East there were incessant enquiries from
the world's press who were eager for news and keen to check
facts. As Cadogan explained in the letter, the News Department
were two people down because of transfers out, and so needed
replacements.

Documents in the BBC's Written Archive and others released to us by the Foreign Office under the Freedom of Information Act show that Burgess was on three months' notice and the Foreign Office badly wanted him to begin working for them sooner. Cadogan said as much to Foot when he wrote about staff shortages; and he was a big enough gun to convince Foot that he really meant business.

But why Burgess? How did Cadogan even know he existed? This is where the story gets more interesting and intriguing. Not surprisingly, the Foreign Office has never been very keen to reveal why they were so eager to hire a Russian spy from the BBC. They have told us that their file on Cadogan's letter and related matters can no longer be found and may have been lost or destroyed at some point.

So we took a twin-track approach, searching archives which were already in the public domain, but also requesting the release of other secret Foreign Office papers under the Freedom of Information Act.

The first route took Jeff Hulbert to the private papers of the then Foreign Secretary, Anthony Eden. There he found that the name Guy Burgess cropped up within the innermost circles of the Foreign Office. So too did Harold Nicolson's. In addition, the head of the Foreign Office News Department, by then William Ridsdale, was familiar because he had been a member of the small team since 1919.

What lay behind these documents in the Eden archive was a debate which his officials were already having in 1943 with an eye to a post-war world. One area that was considered especially important was a future strategy for Britain's public relations and propaganda needs. Sir Alexander Cadogan asked his senior staff for ideas and William Ridsdale put forward some first thoughts.[286] A while later he wrote to his bosses that 'the BBC feel – quite properly in my view – that they are not catering adequately in the Home Service for that large section of their public who are interested in international affairs...'[287] He suggested that the BBC should broadcast regular talks on foreign affairs using a small panel of 'expert' speakers who would prepare the British and Empire audiences for the return to peacetime politics and international diplomacy. Among the names he suggested was W. N. Ewer of the *Daily Herald* (*see Chapter 2*).

Two days after his memo was sent, a handwritten comment appeared on the manuscript: 'I think this is a good plan. But see the marginal notes and please speak.' It is initialled AE (Anthony Eden) and dated 9 May 1943. Soon afterwards Eden's principal private secretary, Oliver Harvey, added a comment about ensuring a fair balance between the political right and left.

A few days later Ridsdale wrote back to Harvey, revealing that Eden's office had suggested that Harold Nicolson would be an ideal figure for handling the job.[288] However, Ridsdale told Harvey there was a slight problem: namely that BBC governors didn't broadcast, under what he termed a 'self-denying ordinance'. But moves were soon made to get the BBC's wartime boss, Minister of Information Brendan Bracken, to agree to waive the restriction.

Harold Nicolson must have seemed an obvious name for Eden's office to put forward. He was essentially an insider who was a safe pair of hands: a former Foreign Office diplomat, an MP, a former junior minister, a writer, a broadcaster and a noted expert on foreign affairs. But he was also an insider known to Eden himself. Nicolson's wartime diaries record how closely he worked and associated with Eden's inner circle and in April 1943, at Eden's behest, he agreed to help reduce the department's workload and later became one-third of a Foreign Office retirement board that was tasked with helping rid the department of unwanted diplomats. So Nicolson had all the qualities that Ridsdale's plan required. Between May and November little more seems to have happened to take the proposal forward, but late in December 1943 Ridsdale wrote a memorandum suggesting that with the end of the war now looking a little more certain, perhaps it was time to dust off his plan and move it forward. At the turn of the year, and with Cadogan's approval, Ridsdale invited the BBC to lunch to discuss how the proposal could be brought back to life. His note of that meeting, which is dated 10 January 1944, includes the sentence 'I saw Mr George Barnes, Director of Talks, and his colleague Mr Guy Burgess.'[289]

'I like these ideas'

A manuscript note initialled by Cadogan shows that he read it on 11 January 1944 and Eden wrote, 'I like these ideas,' signing off Ridsdale's note, with its mention of Guy Burgess, on 15 January.[290]

On 26 January 1944 Ridsdale had telephoned Nicolson about the proposal for him to begin educating the British public about post-war foreign affairs. A week later, on 2 February 1944, Nicolson's unpublished diary records that Ridsdale and Nicolson met over lunch at the Moulin d'Or restaurant to discuss the proposal in more detail.[291]

Crucially, Guy Burgess was also at the lunch. We know from Nicolson's unpublished diaries that in the eighteen months before Burgess started working at the Foreign Office the pair had met at least twenty-six times socially – either for drinks after BBC meetings, or for lunch or dinner.

Reviewing the evidence so far showed that it was Eden's office that had suggested Nicolson for a job; was it now Nicolson who in turn suggested Burgess for a job over lunch with the F.O?

Nicolson's role in Burgess's appointment was indeed confirmed by files released to us by the Foreign Office in the spring of 2013. One secret internal document says:

> In March 1944, Burgess was invited by Mr Ridsdale, then head of the News Department in the Foreign Office, to fill a vacancy in that department. He had apparently been recommended to Mr Ridsdale by Mr Harold Nicolson, among others.[292]

So when Sir Alexander Cadogan wrote to the BBC asking for Burgess it was not just some letter that he had been asked to sign as Permanent Secretary. It was a request for someone whose name and potential usefulness he already knew about from internal documents. After all the man had been recommended by someone close to the Foreign Secretary himself.

It is not easy to overstate the importance of the decision to recruit Burgess, given what is now known about the scale of damage that Burgess the spy wreaked once he got into the Foreign Office. One of Cadogan's successors later compounded that mistake by engineering a permanent post for Burgess.[293] There was no attempt to vet him. At least two very senior diplomats, Frederick Hoyer Millar and Gladwyn Jebb, had previously acted to get rid of Burgess in 1940: once when he was stopped from travelling to Moscow, and the other when he was sacked from Section D. Yet when he got into the Foreign Office in 1944 they kept quiet about him. Vetting might have revealed that Burgess had also applied for a job with MI5, but had been turned down. That service was at least suspicious of his reliability but the reservations do not seem to have been passed on to the Foreign Office. This was a pity, because at the time MI5 reported personally to Anthony Eden, the minister responsible for the organisation.[294]

Having received Burgess's resignation from the BBC, his boss there, George Barnes, tried to persuade him to stay by offering him the chance to produce a new Foreign Affairs series.[295] This didn't work and the BBC formally accepted his resignation with one small note of protest from an official who handwrote, 'If he has resigned there is nothing more to be done but FO ought not to have offered him a post without our agreement.'

There then began a negotiation about when Burgess could leave. Burgess came up with the idea that 'it should be possible for me to continue to do work for both departments while I am learning my job at the Foreign Office'. How convenient.

So on 1 May 1944, with both parties agreed, Guy Burgess stepped out of his flat and into the London sunshine to make his way to the BBC, to do a morning's work, secure in the knowledge that he would be able to keep every one of his many employers happy.

Within weeks of arriving in Whitehall Burgess 'regularly filled a large holdall with Foreign Office documents, some of them highly classified, and took them to be photographed by the NKVD', according to one Russian archive. One KGB officer, Yuri Modin, complained that there were only three KGB officers available to handle the top-secret intelligence that was 'pouring in' from the Cambridge spies and other agents in Britain.

It would ultimately have been either Ridsdale or his boss, Ivo Mallet, who gave Burgess permission to take Foreign Office documents home just a few weeks after he joined the staff. Ostensibly intended to help him cope with his new and heavy burden, the decision led to a vast increase in the KGB's workload. But it was not entirely secret because on at least one occasion Harold Nicolson's diary records that he was shown a number of confidential Foreign Office telegrams 'exchanged with Moscow' while having dinner with Guy Burgess. Nicolson never raised an eyebrow.[296]

The KGB's files reveal that within eighteen months of joining the Foreign Office Burgess had passed over 4,400 files to his Soviet colleagues. Memoirs also record the newest recruit to the News Department 'gazing dreamily out of the window across the Horse Guards Parade...'

The first chill winds of the Cold War were making themselves felt and it was the start of a lacklustre career inside the Foreign Office which culminated in his appointment in 1950 as a temporary second secretary at the British embassy in Washington.

In 1951 Burgess was sacked for drunkenness and insulting behaviour. One final straw was his involvement in a chain of driving incidents in Virginia in which he claimed diplomatic immunity both for himself and his American companion. Once the state Governor had reported the details to the British ambassador, Burgess was sent home to London in disgrace, although he found time to spend almost two weeks in farewell visits and then sailing home on the *Queen Mary*. Within a matter of days of his return he and fellow Cambridge spy Donald Maclean had absconded to Moscow fearing arrest as Russian spies.

Five years later, in February 1956, Burgess and Maclean made their first public appearance in Moscow, confirming that they had been in Russia since their disappearance. They issued a joint statement which denied in remarkably bald and unconvincing terms that they had ever been spies. Specifically it said of Burgess that 'neither in the BBC nor in the Foreign Office nor during the period that he was associated with the secret service did he make any secret from his friends or his colleagues either of his views or of the fact that he had been a Communist'.[297]

The statement prompted letters from MPs to the Foreign Office about how they had recruited him from the BBC if he was such an open Communist. One MP asked, 'Was he taken on by the Foreign Office without reference or recommendation from the BBC?'

Civil servants were put to work drafting a reply.

We now know from the files that the honest answer to that question was that Burgess was never checked out by the Foreign Office. The drafters could hardly say that, so they tried to pass some of the blame to the BBC. The men from the F.O. talked on the phone to the men from the BBC and said they were 'anxious to include' in their statement a line from the BBC director-general's reply to the request for Burgess. This said that the release of the producer 'would be a serious loss' to the corporation. Including this line in a Foreign Office statement would clearly imply there had been a BBC endorsement of Burgess's character. The BBC was resistant but the two sides compromised by agreeing that the DG had 'made it clear that in the circumstances then obtaining his [Burgess's] departure would be a loss to the Talks Department'.[298]

What the BBC really thought about the 'loss' of Burgess is probably best set out in a note which George Barnes wrote at the time.

He is very clever, full of ideas, well informed, with a large circle of acquaintances and is good at getting up a subject quickly. His office work is slipshod and he needs a good secretary to be efficient. He is lazy and has not learned to express himself exactly when writing; he is not conscientious and takes a very liberal view of his duties.[299]

'Burgess', wrote Barnes, 'does not suffer fools.'

There's another interesting footnote to Burgess's time at the BBC. When he absconded with Maclean on 25 May 1951 no one was quite sure where they had gone, although the assumption was always that they were in Russia.

In September 1951 a BBC official reported a most unusual event. Several years before Burgess had borrowed a number of books from the BBC library. In classic Burgess style he had never returned them.

But at four o'clock on the afternoon of Saturday 15 September someone handed the books in to the commissionaire at the reception desk at Broadcasting House.

The report didn't say who the 'someone' was. Surely it couldn't have been Burgess himself; maybe it was a friend. It concluded, 'You may wish to pursue this as I understand that the Foreign Office are anxious to ascertain the whereabouts of Mr Burgess and it might be helpful to them.'

5

JOHN PEET

As the Berlin press corps arrived at a news conference given by the East German government on Monday 12 June 1950 only one of them knew in advance why they had been invited and what the story would be. There was a simple reason for that. The story would be him.

Berlin had been Hitler's capital and the pride of Nazi Germany until just five years before but now it was divided up into four sectors, all under foreign occupation. The victorious wartime allies, America, the Soviet Union and Britain plus France, divided up not just the country into their own zones but its capital into their own sectors. The border lines between the three Western sectors in the west of the city and the Soviet sector in the east symbolised the divisions within Germany and the wider division of Europe between Western democracies and Soviet satellite states. It made Berlin the de facto capital of the Cold War. Armies that had once fought together in a common cause now faced each other across barbed wire and barricades representing the colliding ideologies of capitalism and communism.

In this city of symbolic boundaries, a British journalist was about to make a very personal crossing of a line. It was to happen in a building which had once housed Hitler's Propaganda Ministry but had, rather appropriately, become the Government Information Office of the Soviet Union's fledgling East German state, the German Democratic Republic (GDR).[300] The room where Josef Goebbels had once briefed the Nazi press was full of reporters. They had been invited to this news conference a few days before but had not been told what it would be about. Some of the journalists were from the GDR or other countries in the Soviet bloc. Others were correspondents from the Western media who, before the Berlin Wall was built in 1961, regularly crossed in and out of the Russian sector to attend events.

'I am standing here today...'
The head of the GDR Information Department was a veteran German Communist called Gerhart Eisler who had spent the Second World War in America and had then returned to Germany as a propagandist for the new Communist state. He opened the press conference in his usual way but told the reporters that on this occasion it would be one of them who would be speaking from the podium.

To the surprise of the Western media, the reporter who stepped forward to speak did not come from the Communist press corps in the room but was one of their very own, the much-respected and well-connected chief correspondent of the Reuters international news agency in Berlin.

John Peet, aged thirty-four, was tall and very thin. His first job at Reuters had been as a correspondent in post-war Vienna where he had been congratulated by the agency on his 'excellent news file'. He was then posted to Germany and such was Reuters' confidence in him that Peet was soon promoted to bureau chief.[301]

Now his colleagues in the Berlin press corps watched as he rose from his seat among them, walked forward a few yards to the GDR podium and turned to face them.[302] In those few steps Peet had crossed a symbolic line.

He spoke to the assembled journalists in fluent German with an upper-class English accent. 'I am standing here today because I am no longer willing to serve those who propagate war. As a Western journalist, chief correspondent in Berlin for Reuters News Agency, I have become, without wanting to, a tool for the war machinery directed by America.'[303]

He set out his argument in more detail and then declared, 'This is why I have decided to leave my position in the west and move to East Berlin, whatever the personal consequences for me may be.'[304]

The correspondent of the *New York Times*, Kathleen McLaughlin, wrote of the reaction among Western journalists: 'His action stunned not only his British and United States colleagues, but also German correspondents who had worked with him on news coverage in Berlin.' She explained that Peet had become widely known for his 'frequent and disgusted criticisms following press conferences staged by Herr Eisler', the very man who was now stage-managing Peet's presentation to the world as a supporter of the East Germans.[305]

The correspondent of the Soviet newspaper *Pravda* (meaning Truth) also observed the shock among Peet's former colleagues. Yuri Korolkov wrote, 'The correspondents of the Western papers remained dejectedly in their seats, stunned by the exposures of John Peet.' In contrast, 'the correspondents of the democratic press greeted this statement with storms of approving applause'. Peet's statement had 'made an immense impression on all those present at the press conference'.[306] Korolkov reported that the Western press 'were so confused that at first they could not even ask a single question. Then someone asked, "When did Mr John Peet join the Communist Party?" The reply caused still greater confusion – "John Peet was never a member of the Communist Party and is now non-party."'

The questions continued: was Peet seeking asylum in the GDR? No, just moving there for the time being. What would his future job be? No idea.[307]

Peet hadn't forgotten his own instincts as a Reuters man. After answering questions he went to a phone and filed a despatch about what he had just done. It was the first Reuters heard about it.

He dictated his story:

By John Peet, Reuters correspondent, Berlin, June 12 – Reuters chief correspondent in Berlin, 34-year-old John Peet, today made a public declaration that he 'could no longer serve the Anglo-American war-mongers'. Mr Peet made the declaration to more than 200 German and foreign correspondents at a press conference in the East German Information Department.[308]

When he finished dictating Peet told the Reuters office that if they needed to call him back with any messages they could contact him in Eisler's office.[309] His colleague in the Berlin bureau who took down Peet's despatch could barely believe what he was typing about his own boss.[310] When he sent the story back to the Reuters news desk in London the story was 'sat on' while executives tried to decide what on earth to do with it.[311]

Over at the rival Associated Press (AP) news agency, the Peet story was already old news. While the Reuters man had been up on his feet making news the AP man rushed outside to report it, sending out the first few words of a breaking story that agencies call a 'snap'.[312]

Peet later had to admit, 'I was scooped on my own story.' Even more ironic, his own story of what had happened in Berlin that day never appeared anywhere. 'Reuters in London decided that my nicely rounded "obituary" was not suitable for publication and they spiked it.'[313] But Reuters did follow up his suggestion that they call him at Eisner's office with any questions. The executive who called him had just two questions: 'Is that John Peet?' and 'What have you done with the safe keys?'[314]

Peet had already anticipated his employers' obsession with proper accountancy and had handed the safe keys to one of the Western reporters at the press conference. He had also calculated that Reuters owed him £46 7s. 6d. in salary.[315] So before he left the Berlin bureau for the last time he had taken out £40 from the office petty cash. Reuters sent him a cheque covering the remaining amount, plus his pension contributions.[316]

'*What a shock...*'
It was the symbolic end of John Peet's career as a Reuters foreign correspondent. And it almost brought about the end of his brother Stephen's career at the BBC. British intelligence, through its connections with the BBC, stopped Stephen, a distinguished film-maker, from getting a staff job at the BBC because of his brother's defection. But the decision to blacklist Stephen Peet was later overturned and he went on to great career success.[317] The same cannot be said of John Peet.

He later wrote that he had,

> at the age of thirty-four, abandoned the moderate security, the congenial work and the fair prospects as Head of the Reuters Bureau in West Berlin to plunge into the uncertainties of a very different life in the young German Democratic Republic, which was at the time regarded by most of the world as a ramshackle nonentity, likely to disappear at almost any moment.[318]

But at the time, John Peet didn't convey any of this uncertainty in a letter to his parents: 'As you probably heard chose peace. Writing new address. Love. John Peet.'

His father, Hubert Peet, sent a postcard from Devon to the Reuters management: 'What a shock. As I told your Mr Mason, it was a complete surprise. My wife and I would like to express to you our regret for the dis-organisation and trouble our son's sudden action must have caused Reuters.'[319]

If John Peet had ever seen this letter, his father's apologetic attitude might have surprised him because he had modelled his early life on his father's radical views.

Hubert Peet was a journalist and a socialist. He worked in Fleet Street on the *Daily Sketch* and *Daily News* and is believed to have covered the 'Siege of Sidney Street' when Winston Churchill, then Home Secretary, took personal command as police with shotguns surrounded anarchists in a tenement in east London.[320]

But Hubert Peet was also a Quaker and this was to have a significant effect on his life. In 1916 he was conscripted into the British Army to serve in the First World War. He refused to be a combatant soldier and was court-martialled for refusing to obey an order to parade. As a CO, 'conscientious objector', he told the court:

> I am a Quaker and a Socialist, and I believe that the teaching of Jesus means that I must confront violence with gentleness, anger with reason, hatred with goodwill. Though I may be technically a soldier I cannot be one actually and morally, and therefore I cannot recognise any military order.[321]

Hubert Peet was sentenced to 112 days' hard labour and then was court-martialled a second time for refusing to obey orders. In total he spent two and a half years in prison. His son John was just one year old. When Hubert Peet was finally released from jail a Quaker journal, which he had previously helped to edit, reported that 'the long period of isolation, poor food, cold and confinement has its inevitable effect on his physique'.[322]

Just after his release in 1919 came a moment that was to become John Peet's first memory of his father. Peet junior was three years old as he sat with 'the total stranger who was said to be my father' watching him make a cardboard model of his prison cell.[323] Hubert Peet was never able to get work on a Fleet Street paper again and instead had to fall back on helping to publicise the work of missionary societies.[324]

Testimony to the significance of his father's imprisonment on his life came when he was asked to introduce himself at the start of an oral history interview.

'My name is John Peet. I'm a Londoner from a fairly normal middle-class family, slightly different from many middle-class families in that my father had been a conscientious objector in World War One, a Christian Socialist.'[325]

Of the four themes in his father's life – journalism, socialism, Christianity and pacifism – Peet embraced the first two and rejected the second.

He helped to publish a newspaper while still a schoolboy and immediately he left school he joined a local paper in Kent as a cub reporter. Socialism came as easily as journalism. At the age of eight he told friends, 'I'm Labour.'[326] He was brought up in what he called 'rather a strange ILP sort of an atmosphere', a reference to the Independent Labour Party, a socialist party which had grown up separately from the main Labour Party but at this time was affiliated to Labour.

But in his teenage years his socialism became more Marxist. What he called his 'very Liberal Quaker boarding school' at Saffron Walden in Essex allowed him to take out a postal subscription to the Communist Party newspaper, the *Daily Worker*.[327] In 1931 he filled in a coupon in the paper which urged readers to enrol in the Communist Party and got back a confirmation that he had been duly enrolled. He heard nothing from the party until nine months later when got another letter saying 'the first duty of a Communist is to pay party dues' and demanding three shillings in back contributions.[328]

When Peet moved to another Quaker school he came out as what he called a 'public school Red' by standing as the Communist candidate in a mock election. He came last but proudly sent the result to the *Daily Worker*, who printed it.[329]

Weapons training

So Peet became a journalist and a socialist with Marxist sympathies, but he decided that, unlike his father, he was not a Christian. Then, when he left school, he rejected the Quaker belief in pacifism and did it in the most dramatic way possible, by joining the army.

Feeling myself that anybody who felt that he was a revolutionary ought to have some knowledge of the weapons which at that time seemed necessary to fight a revolution with, I joined the Grenadier Guards, which seems a rather obscure way of preparing to be a revolutionary.[330]

Within two years this decision was to prove, in Peet's words, 'quite useful'. Having bought himself out of the army as soon as he'd had enough training in handling weapons, and having seen the Nazis at first hand as he travelled in pre-war Germany and Austria, he signed up for the anti-Fascist Republican side in the Spanish Civil War.

As he fought alongside a senior commander in the British battalion, a former IRA man called Paddy O'Daire, Peet was shot in the ankle by Fascist troops. A wounded colleague died alongside him in an ambulance but Peet recovered.

When the Republican side decided to withdraw non-Spanish troops from the war, Peet and the rest of the British battalion returned to London. He had gone to Spain because he believed 'that the whole world was heading towards a world war'.[331] Now he was even more convinced of the coming conflict but he found the British public uninterested.

'That made people who had come back from Spain extremely cross, that people's minds seemed to be closed totally. And looking back ... I would eternally regret it if I had not had the privilege of being able to go to Spain and take part of the struggle.'[332]

When Peet's forecast proved accurate and the Second World War broke out he applied to be an RAF pilot but was rejected. He concluded that Special Branch at Scotland Yard was screening applications and keeping out those who had fought for the Republican side in Spain.[333]

Whatever the reason for his rejection it meant that Peet was not among the pilots who fought and won the Battle of Britain, and who, on a statistical basis, were more likely to die than to survive. Instead he spent the war working for the British authorities in Palestine initially as a policeman but then as a journalist on

British-controlled Jerusalem Radio and in the Public Information Office there. Peet not only survived the war but added some middle-ranking editorial posts to a CV that helped him get a significant post-war job in Fleet Street.

It may sound surprising that in August 1945 John Peet walked into the Reuters headquarters in London and walked out with a contract as a sub-editor. And that after a trial period in the role he was made Vienna correspondent without Reuters even testing his fluency in German.[334] But the agency was very short of journalists who had the languages and the experience to report from areas of central Europe that were under Allied control.[335]

Peet was later transferred to Warsaw and ultimately to Berlin. By 1949 he was bureau chief of one of the world's most trusted news-suppliers in one of the world's most important news centres. He was in charge of four full-time British correspondents, three German journalists plus typists, teleprinter-operators and drivers.[336] He had a large and comfortable flat where Germans of various political persuasions would welcome the chance to get warm, have a cup of coffee, have something to eat and maybe secretly use the telephone to call abroad, which they weren't allowed to do by the Allied occupiers. Among the visitors was the playwright Bertolt Brecht, who had left Germany during the rise of Hitler and had only just returned from spending much of the war in America.[337]

But outside the Peet home and its informal mix of visitors, Germany was dividing more and more as every month passed. In 1949 the three zones of the country occupied by the Western powers were joined together to formally establish the Federal Republic of Germany (FRG), soon followed by the Soviet zone titling itself the German Democratic Republic. It seemed that Germany would never return to being a unified, independent state.

The Reuters bureau chief in Berlin took stock of the situation:

Professionally I was doing very nicely, and apparently giving full satisfaction, but I began to anticipate difficult times ahead. Ever since my schooldays I had regarded myself, despite my somewhat erratic course, as a committed Marxist, agreeing in general with the political line of the international Communist movement, though I was reluctant to become a card-carrying Red.[338]

Peet said he was 'faced with a decision'. In various accounts he has mentioned different factors which played a part in this decision – one of them, slightly bizarrely, was something someone told him over cocktails one day.

The commander of the British Army of the Rhine, General Sir Charles Keightley, went to lunch at the British Press Club in Berlin. Peet had been disturbed by rumours that the Western allies were going to re-establish German armed forces in their sectors. He quoted Keightley as saying over drinks, 'I recently talked about the whole thing with Monty – Field Marshal Montgomery – and we totally agreed that a German army had to be created as soon as possible. Some stupid politicians are still opposed to any such step, but it won't take long before we can proceed.'[339]

Doubt has been cast on this by the Headquarters of the British Army of the Rhine, who said that General Keightley was at the Press Club that day but 'did not attend the cocktail party and made no such statement'.[340]

Apart from the prospect of German rearmament, Peet also cited as a factor the contrast between the speed with which the East had 'de-nazified', eliminating former Nazis from public posts, compared to the West. He believed the Western powers were deliberately slow in trying and sentencing them. Peet always wrote about 'nazis' rather than 'Nazis', believing that it would be wrong on a point of principle to bestow a capital letter upon them.[341]

Decision

Only Peet knew which of these different factors weighed most heavily in his decision and whether there were other, perhaps personal, reasons that played a part. But in his mind the time for debate was over. 'It seemed only logical for me to line up with the young German Democratic Republic, which against great odds appeared to be making a good start in constructing a new-style state on a Socialist basis on German soil. So I crossed the dividing line.'[342]

The decision having been made in his mind he 'contacted the proper quarters' in East Berlin to organise how he would cross that dividing line. They came up with a plan. First he should go to a lot of trouble to give colleagues the impression that he had long-term plans in the West. He should then await a call saying that 'Primrose has a message for Daffodil'. This would include a coded reference to the time at which he should drive east. [343]

The 'Primrose' message duly arrived and at 15.00 on Sunday 11 June 1950 he set off in his car through the Brandenburg Gate, and made his way to an address he had been given. Once he got there he drove into a garage, the garage door closed behind him and an East German official was waiting there for him.[344] There was no going back now.

The next day Reuters executives read Peet's dramatic last despatch reporting his own news and tried to decide what to do next. They drafted a statement which said his action had come as a 'complete surprise'. 'None of his British or American colleagues in West Germany had any knowledge of the fact that he had particular political views. His reports were always exact, impartial and irreproachable.'[345]

Reuters didn't offer any public explanation for his decision. But in private they speculated. 'There can be no doubt that continued ill health and nervous strain' had played a part, according to one colleague. 'Bear in mind extraordinary tension Berlin situation and effect this can have upon sensitive and nervous temperaments,' cabled back another.[346]

Peet's direct boss, Alfred Geiringer, searched for any clues that, in hindsight, should have marked Peet out to them but the best he could come up with was a memory that their Berlin bureau chief 'liked to wear loud ties and coloured waistcoats and suede shoes' to be 'non-conforming'.

In conversations in nearby bars they wondered if somehow a woman had been involved. Peet had a complicated private life. He was married four times and reading his autobiography it is difficult to keep track of who he was married to at any one time. In later life he opened a suitcase one day and found that his then wife, who he was just about to abandon for another woman, had taken her revenge by slashing to pieces one of his smartest suits.[347]

For Reuters the company there were bigger issues. Its authorised history by Donald Read later captured the dilemma:

> The reputation of Reuters was now at risk. One of its leading correspondents had been revealed as a covert left-wing activist. Could Peet be represented as curiously naïve? But, if naïve, why had the agency selected such a man for one of its top postings? And had he been acting alone, or was Reuters widely infiltrated by covert reds?[348]

The last question was not some exaggerated fantasy. The Peet affair coincided with another threat to Reuters' reputation. The agency's management had discovered that about a dozen of its journalists, Communist Party members and 'fellow travellers', had formed what some called a 'cell'. It seems to have been an informal group who discussed tactics in advance of meetings of the National Union of Journalists.[349]

One of the members was Derek Jameson, a newsroom journalist who went on to become a Fleet Street editor and a popular broadcaster. According to Jameson the members of the cell had decided that they would never allow their political views to influence their work.

> At Reuters we had taken a conscious decision that we would not try to doctor the Reuters file. We would stand by their principles of objectivity, fairness, independence and not show any bias at all. So it was all very fair and balanced and worked very well until one

of our sympathisers – a young lady – was editing a keynote speech by President Harry Truman and cut out all his references to Stalin, Russia, Communism – these attacks on her beloved Soviet Union.[350]

The authorised history of Reuters named the journalist as Frances Wheeler, who was a sub-editor, and said that she was found to have omitted an important long reference to the Cold War in Truman's speech.[351]

Derek Jameson was caught up in the aftermath.

> There was a terrible outcry, one of the clients noticed, she was hauled over the coals, broke down and blew the whistle – she named us and so a great purge began. Nobody actually got the chop, 'you're fired', but a word in their ear, 'I'm afraid your career won't go anywhere here, old boy'.[352]

Most of the journalists she named were moved on by Reuters in one way or another and some ended up working for the Soviet news agency or other Communist news organisations.[353] Jamieson himself survived what he called a 'blacklist' by getting himself called up for National Service and later threatening action against Reuters if they failed in their legal duty to re-hire staff after such service.[354]

With the discovery of a Communist 'cell' in their Fleet Street office and the revelation that a major bureau chief was a Communist sympathiser, the Reuters general manager, Christopher Chancellor, wrote to one of his duty editors, who had been uncovered as 'the leading spirit' of the 'cell'.[355]

He told Lawrence Kirwan that working for Reuters involved its staff 'in a form of self-discipline and self-abnegation. Those of you who feel strongly on political matters must be doubly careful in the position of trust which working for Reuters involves.'[356]

A new employer

John Peet, having resolved any problems about trust by leaving

Reuters in a very sudden and public way, set about finding new employment. He went from being a paid correspondent for a news agency to being a paid propagandist for a government.

His first task was to write about his experiences at his old employer for his new employer, the government of the German Democratic Republic (GDR). His articles for their newspaper, *Neues Deutschland*, also appeared in a left-wing French newspaper. But they didn't appear in the British *Daily Worker*, his favourite read in his schoolboy days, because, according to Peet, the paper said that British libel laws would make publication impossible.[357] He also wrote a booklet in German, 'I Choose Peace'.[358]

The other part of his work was addressing public meetings around East Germany. He spent six months addressing up to three meetings a day for the German Peace Council, part of the Soviet 'World Peace Council'. He said his travel amounted to '40,000 kilometres by car and train to every corner of the Republic'.[359]

But reports in the archive of the East German secret service, the Stasi, seen by British academics Stefan Berger and Norman LaPorte, 'showed little enthusiasm about Peet and his message'.[360] A photograph of one of the meetings, printed in his autobiography, shows Peet standing on a platform in a rather crumpled suit reading out his speech to some rather bored-looking East Germans standing below.[361]

When his appeal to East German audiences began to dwindle, Peet and his employers decided to turn their attention to the audience in Peet's homeland, with some surprising success.

The *Democratic German Report*, the *DGR*, is thought to have been the only foreign-language newspaper in Communist Europe produced almost single-handedly by a Westerner. According to Berger and LaPorte's study of Peet's life in the GDR, the *DGR* appeared every fortnight as an eight-page newsletter. The articles were by-lined by 'John Peet', 'Eustace Gordon' or 'Frederick Ford'. In reality they were all written by John Peet.

Of the 38,000 copies, half were posted to Britain, targeting trade union activists, teachers, journalists and particularly MPs. For a time the *DGR* had a feature called 'Our Hansard' which reprinted questions which MPs had asked based on information which Peet had provided.[362]

Peet knew that an audience existed among left-wing Labour Party members who wished the GDR well and were suspicious of developments in the rival Federal Republic of Germany (FRG). First and foremost the *Democratic German Report* was an anti-Fascist publication highlighting where former Nazis had been accepted back into public life in West Germany. Peet said that the thriller writer Frederick Forsyth first learned of the 'Odessa' network of former Nazis from the pages of the *DGR*.

Coupled with this focus, Peet emphasised what he saw as the threat to world peace that the re-armament of West Germany posed. His other task as a 'critical friend' of the GDR was to present a positive picture of developments, which he did while expressing a few concerns in order to try to maintain some semblance of independence.[363] As one might expect from a former news agency man, the magazine was well written. But those like Berger and LaPorte who have studied all Peet's articles have concluded that 'the regularly held belief that Peet regularly poked fun at Communist jargon and the regime's sullen lack of humour is a myth'. In their judgement, the degree of direct criticism of the East Berlin regime was marginal.[364]

At the time of his defection, the *New York Times* reported, 'In the same coolly rational tone in which he had delivered his indictment of the British and Americans, Mr Peet retorted that many things in Eastern Berlin had roused his criticisms and that he hoped to be able to voice critical as well as commenda-tory views.'[365] That was to turn out to be a touch naive. Stasi files reveal that privately Peet was critical of events such as the Soviet invasion of Hungary and the suppression of the Prague Spring of 1968.[366] But in public he was fiercely loyal to the Soviet bloc, especially on the big issues.

No issue came bigger than the construction of the Berlin Wall in 1961. In his autobiography Peet repeated the GDR line that the wall had to be built to protect the East's economy from 'not just a brain drain, but a muscles drain and a skills drain'.[367] He further argued that a subsequent recovery in the economy and standard of living was 'not the only satisfactory result of a painful decision'. The division of the city had, in his mind, prepared the way for the treaties a decade later which formalised the creation of the two states, the GDR and the FRG.

He forecast that

> the division of the old Germany into two separate and distinct states today looks as permanent as anything else in a world largely divided between two power blocks. As long as the balance of power rules the world scene, any reversal appears inconceivable.[368]

Free to come and go

What of Peet the person as opposed to Peet the polemicist? Unlike those who, like Philby, Burgess and Maclean, had defected to the Eastern bloc after working for the Russians from within the British secret service, John Peet had committed no offence under British law. He was free to return to his homeland, which he did every second year to visit relatives. He gave lecture tours and, on one trip, he sat down with an interviewer from the Imperial War Museum and recorded his memories for an oral history of the Spanish Civil War. In his autobiography he said he was 'very happy with my fourth – and presumably last – wife, a GDR girl who does not even remember the Second World War'. He also socialised with former colleagues, gave interviews to visiting British television crews and even attended the opening of the new Reuters office in East Berlin in June 1987.[369]

To those who would wonder 'yes, but was he happy?' his relatives maintain that he lived a good life. But Sandy Gall, a Reuters man turned ITN anchorman, continued to meet Peet at press conferences in East Berlin and formed a different view. 'I would say rather a sad person because once he'd defected they lost interest in him because you know he'd given them their propaganda coup and he had a rather miserable time, probably didn't have much money.'[370]

John Peet contracted bowel cancer and died in East Berlin on 29 June 1988. He was seventy-two. His autobiography was published posthumously the next year. The publisher titled it *The Long Engagement: Memoirs of a Cold War Legend*.

In November 1989 the Berlin Wall fell and the two Germanys, which Peet had predicted would stay as permanent 'separate and distinct states', began to reunify. The German Democratic Republic, to which Peet had crossed an enormous line and for which he had dedicated half his life, ceased to exist.

'Do you like Spanish watches?'

In the final chapter of his autobiography he recalled how in the 1930s 'when party members or fellow travellers were upset or mystified by inexplicable events in the Soviet Union, they were often assuaged with the glib phrase that you could not make an omelette without breaking eggs'. In an echo of Duranty's earlier use of the term (*Chapter 3*) he put a new spin by asking some extra questions. The final words of his book were: 'But where is the omelette?' One friend has said that Peet's original plan was to call the book 'But Where Is the Omelette? I Am Still Looking'. It seemed to confirm the conventional wisdom that Peet was a naive but honest man, a reporter who'd sacrificed his career for his politics but had always been straight about it. His only proven dishonesty was that at his press conference in Berlin he denied that he had ever been a member of the Communist Party although he had, in fact, signed up as a schoolboy.

But elsewhere in the book there was a sting in the tail to Peet's story which suggested a wholly new and very different side to him. The publisher's sleeve note explained that 'John Peet died in East Germany in 1988. He had already drafted a vivid and entertaining autobiography, but when he learnt that his cancer was incurable he decided to add to this an account of his links with Russian intelligence.'[371]

The 'Long Engagement' of the book's title now appeared to be not just between Peet and Communism but Peet and the KGB. He revealed that he'd had a 'commitment to the Soviet Union' which went 'well beyond the normal manifestations of support and sympathy'. He told how while in Spain in 1938 with the International Brigades he had been taken to meet 'a thick-set middle-aged man in khaki uniform without insignia or badges of rank' who spoke with a heavy German accent.[372]

This man stressed to him how important it was that 'the popular front should be fully informed about developments in every country, including confidential developments, and at this point I finally realised what he was getting at'. Peet said he replied, 'If I understand you rightly, you are asking if I would be willing to be a Soviet spy.'

Peet had apparently been waiting for this moment and was ready to commit. 'For many months I had been fighting against Fascism with rifle and machine gun, intelligence work for the Soviet Union, the only power which had effectively aided the Spanish republic, and apparently the only reliable anti-Fascist bastion, was obviously a continuation of the struggle in a different field.'[373]

His orders were that when he returned to Britain he should slowly sever any links with Communists, establish himself as a normal member of society, be patient and wait to be contacted. Under no circumstances should he take the initiative and make contact with any Soviet agency.

He was given a code by which his first Soviet contact would identify himself. Nine months later, back in London a 'very normal middle-class Englishman' with tweeds, moustache and pipe asked Peet, 'Do you like Spanish watches?'[374] These were the code words. Peet was now talking to the Soviet secret service.

However, according to Peet, it would be a full fourteen years before they contacted him again using the code. By then he was working as what he called 'a public relations man (or paid propagandist if you prefer) for the GDR' in East Berlin. Still believing that the Soviet Union appeared to be the 'only hope for mankind', he said he had agreed to meet Soviet officials and they reminded him of the commitment he had made back in Spain. Peet said an agent put to him 'a series of preposterous suggestions, all of which I turned down'. First of all, they wanted him to make the acquaintance of a particular Western correspondent working in West Berlin. This could be done by taking the correspondent on a motoring tour, staging a breakdown at a specific time and place where the Soviet agent would suddenly appear as a friend. Next came the idea of what Peet christened a 'fancydress kidnap' in which Peet would dress as a British officer, drive to West Berlin, and 'arrest' a German whom the Soviets suspected of spying in the East. Having rejected these and other ideas, he said he agreed instead to transmit back 'a certain amount of West Berlin journalistic scuttlebutt'.[375]

He also described how later, while he was working for a time in Geneva, the Soviets asked him to get to know female staff at the UN agencies in the city. He said he had told them 'that the seduction of prospective spies was not definitely not my line'. He had then told his minders, 'I could see no future in any further collaboration.' [376]

The revelations in his book confounded his immediate family. His brother Stephen told academics Stefan Berger and Norman LaPorte that John only came up with this story after he had been asked by his publisher to rework the manuscript of his biography. Berger and LaPorte found no sign of Peet the spy in the files of the East German Stasi or the Comintern in Moscow.[377]

Reuters' own investigations into Peet at the time of his departure brought conflicting feedback from British intelligence. An initial message from the Berlin bureau to the London news desk said 'hushhush boys equally surprised'. But in a more considered eight-page letter to Reuters head office from the agency's head of operations in Germany, Alfred Geiringer, he reported that, 'British intelligence in Berlin say that because he joined the International Brigade during the Spanish Civil War and still a member of the IB Association in London, they had a Peet dossier'. According to Geiringer, British intelligence claimed that they had 'forwarded a report on Mr Peet to the Foreign Office with a request to inform Reuters'. There is no mention any such report reaching Reuters but it is fair to assume that if British intelligence ever informed Reuters that their chief correspondent was a Soviet spy they might have done something about it.[378]

There is a similar conflict of emphasis in the files in the National Archives in London. A Foreign Office telegram from Berlin to London on the day of Peet's defection recorded that he 'has been known, both to his colleagues and to ourselves, as not being unsympathetic towards communism in general, but we had no evidence hitherto that he allowed these sympathies to influence his work as a correspondent'. This telegram focused on Peet's private life, reporting that his wife had left him for personal reasons which had caused him to give 'the appearance of being mentally unbalanced'. It also says that he 'has been, for some time, a very sick man' 'suffering from duodenal ulcers'.

The telegram concludes, 'We are taking the line to press enquiries here that he has been a sick man for some time and suffered also from the strain of overwork and family troubles.' A Foreign Office man on the desk in London wrote on the file that this line 'is the best they can do'.[379]

But two years later when no less a person than the Prime Minister, Winston Churchill, showed an interest in the Peet case, British intelligence were keen to project that they knew a lot about him. Writing to 10 Downing Street from Box No. 500, Parliament Street B.O., London SW1, the postal address used by MI5, an official immediately pointed out that 'John Scott Peet, born in London on 27 November 1915, has been known to us for some considerable time'. It chronicled how, for instance, in 1936 he 'had already established a connection with the *Daily*

Worker'. It also recorded that in 1939 he was again reported as a member of the Communist Party and in consequence was turned down for a commission in the RAF. Peet's suspicion at the time was that his spell in the International Brigade in Spain had cost him the commission so he had been on the right lines. MI5's letter to Downing Street demonstrated the depth of their scrutiny of Communists in Britain but made no mention of him spying for anybody.

Churchill had been alerted to the Peet case by someone who sent the Prime Minister a copy of the *Democratic German Report*. MI5 were able to tell Churchill how many copies had been ordered from Berlin after an advertisement appeared in the *Daily Worker* (100), how many copies (381) of one edition in 1952 were posted from Berlin to 'provincial addresses in the UK', how many of another edition to London addresses (575) and how many (ten) were sent to Collets bookshop in London, 'one of the principal sellers of Communist literature in this country'.

'In addition to the above we have spotted 213 back numbers going to various UK addresses.' So the Prime Minister is to be assured that 'the measures taken have been such that not many copies can have got to addresses unnoticed'.[380] These secret documents were not released until 1994, forty-two years later.

MI5's hardworking team, busy counting copies of obscure German magazines, seem to have been matched in zeal by their counterparts over in MI6. They appear to have made their own contact with Peet, inviting the defector to defect back to the West. The Stasi files show him regularly reporting back to his East German masters on these approaches.[381] Peet claimed in his book that an American journalist, apparently acting for the CIA, offered him twenty thousand dollars in cash to come back.[382] But no one ever says Peet spied for them.

So what are we to make of John Peet the committed Communist who apparently signed up as a Soviet spy but never got to do much real spying? Was this a much more serious crossing of journalistic ethical lines than going from reporter to propagandist or was it a fantasy dreamed up on his death bed under pressure from his publisher to sell a few more books?

Undoubtedly John Peet liked reading about spies and liked helping people write about them. The master espionage novelist Len Deighton has acknowledged Peet's advice on the detail of life in East Berlin. Deighton wrote the foreword to Peet's book, calling him 'one of the most intriguing men I ever met'. Deighton wrote of Peet, 'His life is a puzzle, but then to some extent everyone's life is a puzzle.'[383]

There is one particularly interesting part of that puzzle. To believe Peet's account that he was recruited as a spy but was an inactive one we would have to accept that the KGB would sit quietly for fourteen years with a man of Peet's calibre on their books as he worked as a journalist in three hotbeds of espionage: wartime Palestine, post-war Vienna and Cold War Berlin, and only activated him after he had already broken cover as a Communist sympathiser by which time he was useless to them as a spy. If true it reads as if someone at KGB HQ fell asleep on the case of the long-term sleeper.

This leaves two possibilities. One is that he was much more active as a spy than he chose to reveal but didn't want to give away too much detail. He had demonstrated his care about such matters when he left West Berlin. He went to enormous trouble to destroy documents in his flat such as address books and Christmas card lists to avoid friends and acquaintances being 'harried to some degree by the spooks of various nations'. Maybe on his death bed he didn't want too many spy files being re-opened and old contacts questioned.

The other possibility is that he crossed a different ethical line and made up the story of John Peet the Soviet Spy.

Eighteen days before he died Peet provided a further twist to the story – one which he had not mentioned in his book. In a letter to Paul Moor, an American journalist based in Germany, Peet said that the same intelligence unit which had recruited him to the Soviet cause during the Spanish Civil War had hired another soldier in the Republican Army for what he called 'a real job'.

The man was to assume the identity of a fallen colleague in the International Brigade, find his way into what Peet called 'Trot circles', make his way to Mexico and get to work with an ice axe.

The details match the story of Ramón Mercader, the man who killed Leon Trotsky in Mexico in 1940.

Peet told Moor that he had been asking himself a hypothetical question: if he had been asked to do that job, would he have agreed? He concluded, 'Sometimes, in the middle of the night, the terrible thought comes over me that I would have done it.'[384]

6

REG FOSTER AND BRENDAN MULHOLLAND

In 1963 two newspaper reporters became legends of Fleet Street for upholding one of the principles of their craft: never reveal the sources of a story. But according to the whispers in Fleet Street the real story was rather different, that the two men couldn't reveal their sources because they didn't have any – they had made their stories up. Fifty years later the whispers became public and appeared for the first time on the record, triggering howls of outrage among their former colleagues.

This became the latest chapter in the legend of 'Foster and Mulholland', an already extraordinary saga embracing everything from the arrest of a very British civil servant as a Soviet spy in the heart of Whitehall to the fate of a Prime Minister and the curious connection with a widow and her army officer husband. It was also a trial of Fleet Street and its ways of doing business.

In the most detailed re-examination of the legend for many years we have tried to find out what happened and why it still matters to some people so much later. We have discovered evidence that was heard in secret and kept secret until now, but also that official files have inexplicably gone missing. Alongside a debate about whether these reporters crossed any ethical lines, there are important questions about whether the state crossed a line in its pursuit of the two men.

The Foster of 'Foster and Mulholland' was Reg Foster, known as 'Fireman Foster', an old Fleet Street hand. As a crime reporter he knew the ropes: hang around the smoky press room in Old

Scotland Yard, keep close to the telephone just in case a story broke and be first phoning the news of it back to the office. If he knew which detectives were on the case he'd try to talk things over with them in the pub, especially if they were all out of town together on a big murder story.

He was used to working on his own; he was his own boss. Usually he only went to the office 'once a week, late at night. And only to pick up my expenses.'[385] 'We ran our own show – we were left alone ... The offices of the papers I worked for,' he said, 'why, they hadn't changed since Charles Dickens was around. Desks full of banged-out Royal typewriters with worn ribbons, dim and knee deep in junked copy paper, smoke and noise and sub-editors still wearing eye shades.'

Foster had followed that routine for much of his working life: looking for scoops and exclusives, following up leads from the police and witnesses. Before the war he'd worked for the *Daily Mail*, where in 1936 he'd scooped everyone with his story about the Crystal Palace fire. It was said that a relative working for the fire service had tipped him off. By all accounts the relative continued passing fire stories to him. Some colleagues thought his reports revealed his enthusiasm for fire detail. So much so that someone nicknamed him 'Fireman Foster' and the name just stuck. Colleagues regarded him as a safe pair of hands, one who would never betray a confidence;[386] 'it meant the coppers trusted us,' he said.[387]

September 1962 saw 58-year-old Reg Foster still pounding the crime reporter's beat. After working on the *Daily Mail* and doing war service (he served in an Army Security Branch and then worked on a service newspaper in India[388]) he had served on the *Daily Herald* and then moved to the *News Chronicle*, where he was its chief crime correspondent. When that paper folded he moved across Fleet Street and became 'the number two crime man at the *Daily Sketch*'.

A tall, grey-haired Londoner – he had gone to Alleyn's School in Dulwich – he often wore a trilby hat, like many of his generation, and a jacket and tie; and when the weather demanded it a knitted jumper. It was almost a press corps uniform.

Brendan Mulholland was from a different generation and background. Around half Foster's age, he hailed from Dublin and was making a name for himself as a general reporter on the *Daily Mail*, where he regularly got his stories by-lined. He had started as a copy assistant with the *London Morning Advertiser* and, after working for several other titles, moved to the *Daily Herald* and then on to the *Mail*. He was dark haired, tall and muscular, with features that were described as 'kindly but somewhat lugubrious'. He was gregarious and colleagues and friends liked his company. In the words of one obituary he was 'one of Fleet Street's most popular journalists'.[389] The cut of his clothes was just that little bit sharper than Foster's.

Reg Foster and Brendan Mulholland were not colleagues, although the *Mail* – then a broadsheet – and the *Sketch* – a tabloid until its closure in 1971 – were owned by the same group. Yet a story that erupted in late summer 1962 would link them and turn them briefly into *causes célèbres*.

A spy story

On 12 September 1962 William John Christopher Vassall, a junior civil servant, turned up to his office in the Admiralty building in London's Whitehall and was arrested by two Special Branch detectives. He was a clerical officer in the Civil Lord of the Admiralty's office, later merged into the Ministry of Defence. He was searched by Superintendent George Smith and Chief Inspector Ferguson Smith and taken to Scotland Yard. Afterwards the detectives searched his flat in fashionable Dolphin Square, Pimlico. Vassall confessed to them that he was a Soviet spy.

September was usually a month when the country was just getting back into gear after the summer holidays and, from a number of perspectives, Vassall's arrest probably couldn't have come at a worse time. The party conference season was in the offing, and there were prospects of impending industrial unrest and economic gloom.

It was a tense time for Prime Minister Harold Macmillan's government. Throughout the year his government had been doing badly in the public opinion polls and, with a general election no more than two years away, he had acted in spectacular fashion to reverse the trend. In the wake of a particularly disastrous by-election result in Orpington only weeks before, he had sacked one-third of his Cabinet. What he had hoped would be seen as a revitalisation and renewal was instead dubbed 'the night of the long knives', an altogether unflattering analogy with Hitler's vicious 1934 power struggle with the Brownshirts. Liberal MP Jeremy Thorpe famously said, 'Greater love hath no man than this, that he lay down his friends for his life.'[390]

When news about Vassall broke, a day after his arrest, there was intense interest from Fleet Street. Spy stories were big in the British press and had the potential to become epic, often aided by governments' addiction to official secrecy and their reluctance to reveal or admit anything unless they absolutely had to. This addiction frequently fuelled suspicions that keeping silent was more to protect governments from political embarrassment and incompetent officials from exposure than to keep everyone safe in their beds. Macmillan knew this. The world was living under the shadow of the Bomb and spy stories played on widespread anxieties that the West was becoming increasingly vulnerable, rather than safer.

Vassall's arrest followed two major spy exposures just over a year before: the Portland Spy Ring, which had seen several people jailed in March 1961 for passing naval secrets,[391] and the arrest and jailing of MI6 spy George Blake two months later.[392] From Macmillan's point of view Vassall just made things a lot worse.

In August 1961 the Berlin Wall had gone up, then in October there had been a tense stand-off in Berlin between Soviet and Western tanks where, for several hours, the opposing sides waited to see who would fire first – neither did, but it was close.[393]

Vassall's arrest underlined for everyone how security could not be absolute. Security may have been tightened following previous spy exposures, but Macmillan accepted occasional security failure as a necessary price to pay for living in a relatively open society: it would be possible to have a watertight security system, but totalitarian methods would have to be used and he found that 'distasteful to our national sentiment and contrary to our long traditions'.[394]

When told about Vassall's arrest Macmillan was far from pleased.[395] He said, 'You can't just shoot a spy as you did in the war. You have to try him ... better to discover him and control him, but never catch him...'[396] He was concerned that there 'would be a great trial ... an enquiry ... a terrible row in the press ... a debate in the House of Commons and the government will probably fall. Why the devil did you "catch" him?' he asked the head of MI5.[397]

Fleet Street readied its army of reporters for battle with the authorities and with each other. All of the nationals, the Sundays, radio and television news, regional and some local newspapers were on the case. Several dozen reporters are known to have covered the Vassall story. Foster and Mulholland were just two.

There were minimal facts on the record. *The Times* reported on 14 September that a 38-year-old Admiralty civil servant had appeared before the Chief Metropolitan Magistrate, Sir Robert Blundell, at Bow Street Magistrates' Court, charged with Official Secrets offences and that he had recorded 'secret information at the Admiralty and elsewhere'. Vassall's address was given as 'Hood House, Dolphin Square, Pimlico, SW'. The offences had been committed between 18 August 1962 and 11 September 1962 and the criminal intention had been 'prejudicial to the safety or interest of the state'. The hearing lasted three minutes.

Fleet Street mobilises

Editors wanted to know much more. Who exactly was Vassall? What was his background? What did he do? How long had he been doing it? How did he escape detection? How was he caught?[398] What damage did he cause? What did it mean for the country's security? Who was to blame? What would be done to stop it happening again?

Vassall's Whitehall work, his neighbours, his local shops, pubs, restaurants, taxi firms, all became fair game in a feeding frenzy.

As a crime reporter Reg Foster had many years' experience of gathering just this sort of background 'colour' about criminals. He had covered a number of major cases; some, like 'The Camden Town Blazing Shed Murder', were given titles that could easily have been cited by Horace Rumpole, John Mortimer's fictional crumpled barrister. Reg Foster is said to have become so close to the wife of a murder victim that he even helped her to fill out insurance claim forms. 'She was later uncovered as a poisoner who had doctored her spouse's cornflakes.'[399]

Foster and Mulholland had to work fast on Vassall. Normally the legal process grinds slowly, which also gives the press time to research the kind of personal details which cannot be revealed during a trial but make for multi-page end-of-trial reports. However, where national security matters were concerned it seems justice could be lightning fast. Vassall was arrested on 12 September and on 22 October he appeared at the Old Bailey, pleaded guilty, and the same day was sentenced to eighteen years' imprisonment.[400] A total of forty-one days from start to finish.

The Old Bailey had heard from the Attorney-General, Sir John Hobson QC, how Vassall, while posted to the British embassy in Moscow, had been enticed into taking part in 'certain compromising sexual actions' with men; and that Vassall had recalled 'photographs being taken'. Homosexual acts were illegal in Britain and Russia, and Vassall had been blackmailed, threatened with imprisonment in Moscow, then with exposure in the British embassy and finally, slightly bizarrely, he was told that he would be responsible for a serious international incident if he did not succumb. Vassall had caved in and spied for the Russians for up to seven years. Now his punishment for that was to face eighteen years in a British jail.

The morning after he was sentenced the newspapers were free to publish the background stories they had worked on. The *Daily Sketch* proudly announced 'the whole fantastic Vassall story compiled by *Daily Sketch* reporting team Peter Duffy, Desmond Clough, Peter Burden, Reg Foster, Liam Regan, and led by Louis Kirby'.[401]

One part of the 'fantastic' story was printed on the front page of the *Sketch*'s first edition, but ended up inside the paper in later editions. It was about an inquiry which the Prime Minister had ordered.

Three major questions will be posed in the inquiry:
- Why did the spy-catchers fail to notice Vassall who sometimes wore women's clothes on West End trips?
- Just how safe are Whitehall's morals?
- Are there any more such highly vulnerable men in secret jobs?

In the *Daily Mail*, Brendan Mulholland was given the lead by-line in their coverage. It included a story headlined 'Spy Who Guarded Secrets' about Vassall's trips to Scotland taking secret documents to the Ayrshire home of his minister, the Civil Lord of the Admiralty, Thomas 'Tam' Galbraith. Much had been written in the press about their relationship with the clear implication that it was a homosexual one. Galbraith later resigned under the pressure of the publicity, although he was eventually cleared of all suspicions and returned to public office within months.

But immediately after the post-trial surge of Vassall coverage, Fleet Street was almost immediately diverted to other more important stories. The trial had closed just hours before the world first learned from US President John F. Kennedy that the Soviet Union had been installing nuclear missiles in Cuba. Around midnight London time, as Vassall spent his first uneasy night in jail, Kennedy spoke on television live from the White House. He demanded that the sites be removed and threatened to take action if they were not. Worldwide he placed US forces on high alert.

And for the next week the world nervously eyed developments in the Caribbean as the superpowers teetered on the brink of all-out nuclear war.

The Vassall story seemed to be over for Foster, Mulholland and the crime reporters. The spy story became a political one, covered by their colleagues in the Westminster lobby. Harold Macmillan sensed that his political opponents were already preparing their weapons, sharpening their blades. He would later record in his memoirs, 'Yet even with some experience I could not anticipate the full malignity of some of the attacks which were to be delivered on Ministers and others of the highest reputation. Yet so it was to prove.'[402]

Tribunal

Admiralty security lapses had been at the heart of the Portland spy case eighteen months earlier and a security review carried out by Sir Charles Romer had identified what needed to be done.[403] Macmillan had also set up a wide-ranging review of official security under a judge, Lord Radcliffe, who reported in April 1962.[404]

Now, after Vassall's conviction, Macmillan decided to establish a new committee of inquiry under a senior civil servant, Sir Charles Cunningham, to try to prevent a repetition of the previous year's painful security debate. And this quick, almost knee-jerk decision backfired and rather than decrease the pressures on the Prime Minister it created new ones.

Over the next two weeks Macmillan faced repeated calls in Parliament for him to look again at the committee's terms of reference, extend its membership, increase its powers. It was a short but highly effective war of attrition.[405]

Cunningham's committee first met on 25 October 1962. It was charged with looking into Vassall's career and 'the general oversight in the Admiralty of his behaviour'.[406] However, Macmillan acknowledged in his diary, 'I had to admit ... that a Committee of Civil Servants would not do.' After some discussions the idea of setting up a tribunal emerged, 'over which Lord Radcliffe had agreed to preside'.[407] Born in 1899, Viscount Radcliffe was a barrister who became a Law Lord in his early fifties without ever having been a judge. During the Second World War he was successively the Assistant Director-General of the Press and Censorship Bureau, the Chief Censor, and Director-General of the Ministry of Information, its chief executive while Brendan Bracken was minister. Radcliffe also chaired two pre-Indian independence boundary commissions (Punjab and Bengal), an inquiry into the future of the film industry and others. His 'combination of *gravitas* and imagination' made him, in Peter Hennessy's words, 'formidable in committee'.[408] Radcliffe was a Reith lecturer and it was considered he had 'one of the most distinguished minds of his time'.[409]

Meanwhile, Macmillan complained in his memoirs that he had other things on his plate: 'While these events were boiling up, I had been engaged in what seemed the opening phase of a Third World War...'[410] and he was sleeping barely two hours a night.

So, in the face of the parliamentary clamour, Cunningham's committee was quickly wound up and Radcliffe's tribunal immediately set to work.

It was at this point that the die was cast. For within the terms of reference, which were wider than Cunningham's, was a sting. The government, taking notice of issues raised during the parliamentary shenanigans, charged Radcliffe with looking into allegations made in the press about security lapses and whether Vassall should have been spotted sooner. In Radcliffe's own words, the tribunal decided to 'ascertain and test the truth of certain allegations arising out of the Vassall case'.[411] And because Radcliffe was a tribunal it would operate like a court and had powers to subpoena witnesses and to compel them to answer its questions, and punish them if they didn't.

Over the next three months Radcliffe would sit for almost thirty complete days – in a mixture of full- and half-day sessions. Around two-thirds of the sittings would be held in camera. Leading counsel would represent several major newspapers, a couple of journalists, Lord Carrington (First Lord of the Admiralty), Peter Tapsell MP and ex-minister Tam Galbraith MP.[412]

A browse through the Radcliffe tribunal's files, held in the National Archives at Kew, is enlightening. There are witness statements and affidavits, details of allegations (including sexual), transcripts, lists of the issues to be probed as well as the usual administrative minutiae.

Quite simply Radcliffe wanted to know where the details reported in the press – some of which were lurid – had come from, and what evidence there was to substantiate them. In a different context those same questions might well have been asked in dozens of Fleet Street editorial offices, as well as in many journalists' watering holes after hours.

The difference was, however, that editors might be prepared to print allegations if they helped to help move the story along, and there was a defensible chance that they were accurate. For Radcliffe, it was a matter of national security and full standards of legal proof were needed. Moreover, the press had clearly found out things that the officers of MI5 and Special Branch either had not or, if they had, did not want to become public knowledge or could not be proven. The allegations had caused government considerable difficulty, had already damaged one ministerial career and could harm others. For Radcliffe, bluntly, the press had to put up or shut up.

Over the following two months the tribunal interviewed dozens of witnesses. A six-page internal document named around two dozen journalists whose stories were of interest to the Radcliffe team. They all had to give statements and were placed on standby to give oral evidence. There was no escape.

The late autumn and winter of 1962–63 were bitter for Macmillan's government. It faced repeated allegations of incompetence and ineptitude. The shine had gone off Supermac's image in the three years since his general election victory. Perhaps in some cruel joke played by the weather gods it was also bitterly cold in the country too. The UK was experiencing its longest cold spell in decades: snow had fallen and was, weeks later, still lurking as dirty ice in the gutters around the building where the tribunal was holding its hearings. As the journalists trooped in to give their evidence the press was, in one of those rare occasions, not only reporting the story, but *was* the story.

Radcliffe's style was taciturn. There was no real repartee of the sort that sometimes erupted in Lord Justice Leveson's equally serious inquiry five decades later. There were no Paxman-esque ripostes. Radcliffe was looking into very serious matters and it showed from the questioning. Journalists were asked about their facts, how they got them, how they interpreted what they got, and what validated them. In its own way Radcliffe was questioning the journalists' methods and modus operandi, just like Leveson. It was not so much press ethics that concerned Radcliffe, but rather the facts and whether there had been leakage from official sources. Had civil servants, service personnel and others spoken too freely; had the press somehow been complicit in infringing the Official Secrets Act?

Reg Foster was called into Lord Radcliffe's court mid-afternoon on 15 January, 1963, and returned the next day to complete his evidence. He had come to the Vassall story late, he said, only becoming involved a week before Vassall's trial. He had written material that ended up in a background piece about Vassall.

His written statement said that his information 'that Vassall was known to have bought women's clothing in the West End came from sources outside the office. I am unable to reveal the sources of this information.'[413]

Looking back all these decades later it is interesting to note that Foster said his information was that Vassall 'bought women's clothing in the West End', whereas the *Daily Sketch* article had said Vassall 'sometimes wore women's clothes on West End trips'.

It is not possible to read all of Reg Foster's opening verbal testimony because it has been lost. The file containing the relevant transcript, long thought to have been retained by the Treasury Solicitor's department for some legal reason, is now known never to have been released to the National Archives, unlike the other transcripts. Working with TNA archivists, Jeff Hulbert established that the file had been lost, and the catalogue has now been amended. Sadly, part of Vassall's testimony was also in the same file, along with three other days' transcripts.[414]

The transcripts that do survive show that on the next morning the session opened with a series of submissions made by his and other lawyers, arguing why he should and should not refuse to name his source. R. V. Cusack QC, for Foster and his newspaper group, argued that journalists should not name their sources, the Attorney-General argued the opposite. Ultimately, Radcliffe said that the tribunal was required to act like a court, journalists had no special privileges, and he had no flexibility. It was a case of revealing the sources or facing the consequences for contempt.

Counsel for the tribunal, John Donaldson QC, asked where Foster's information came from.[415] Details pieced together from what survives in the archive show that he said he didn't know the name or names of his source(s). That was not a problem, came back the reply, because if you could tell us what they did, or describe them for us, we might just be able to find them for ourselves and ask them. But crucially, when asked for this help he refused: 'Could you help us by telling us the type of source from which it came?' Foster replied, 'No, Mr Donaldson, I could not.'[416]

In a further one-and-a-half pages of tribunal transcript Foster was taken step by step through a series of questions that highlighted the fate that awaited him if he continued to refuse. Radcliffe wanted to make sure that he fully understood the implications. In reply Foster cited his professional and personal ethics – values which he shared with many Fleet Street colleagues. Some of them had given their lives fighting in the last war to preserve those very ethics that Radcliffe was now challenging, he said. He refused and would take the consequences.[417] In order to let those consequences sink in, Radcliff instructed Foster to go home and sleep on it and to come back the following morning to say whether he had changed his mind. Foster replied that it would be a waste of time as he would not have a change of heart. But Radcliffe assured him that it really would be necessary.[418]

Journalists were trained to respect their sources, but equally to beware the consequences if they did not. 'The journalist who blabs ... will soon find he is trusted by no one. His sources will dry up and he will be useless in the job;' so said a contemporary legal handbook for journalists.[419]

One of Foster's *Sketch* colleagues, Desmond Clough, then took the stand and was asked where he got a story that, as a result of Vassall's spying, Soviet 'trawlers' bristling with aerials and radar – aka electronic surveillance ships – had tracked NATO ships on manoeuvres. He also refused to name his source. He was then taken through a familiar series of questions by the Donaldson–Radcliffe duo and arrived at exactly the same point as had Foster earlier: he too would take the consequences, he said.[420]

The next day Foster duly appeared bright and early and told Radcliffe that he had not changed his mind. So, rather than prolong the agony Radcliffe stiffly informed him that a report would be sent to the High Court. There would be consequences. Next, Clough told Radcliffe the same and was given the same curt response.

Later it was Percy Hoskins's turn. *Daily Express* chief crime reporter Hoskins had made allegations about Lord Carrington knowing of another anonymous Admiralty spy as a result of the Portland case, but doing nothing about it. That amounted to accusing Carrington of treason. Hoskins's story of 8 November 1962 said that that conclusion had been reached when a document found in the possession of the Portland Spies' KGB controller, Gordon Lonsdale, after his arrest could not be traced to the Portland naval establishment.[421] The *Express*'s political editor and chief lobby correspondent, Douglas Clark, had repeated the allegation the following day, adding detail that Carrington had been summoned by Macmillan and asked why he had not told him. The allegations also appeared elsewhere. Radcliffe eventually tracked down the source of all the reports to Percy Hoskins's original story. So where did he get it from?

It is tempting to picture the rotund Percy Hoskins, standing before the judge very much like the little Cavalier boy who was asked by the Roundhead, 'And when did you last see your father?' Was he going to face the same consequences? He endured a long, searching cross-examination by some legal toughs, including Lord Carrington's QC, Helenus 'Buster' Milmo. Milmo had a reputation for being more than a little pugnacious. Asked where he got his facts, Hoskins told the tribunal that he had simply done his research: the details had all been published before, mostly in his own paper. He 'had not regarded it as making any sensational revelations; and that, although he had said in the article that he was making new disclosures, this was inaccurate as he was only seeking to put previously published material into proper perspective'.[422] So, it wasn't new, it was just the way he'd written it. In terms that would come to acquire a very different meaning in another judicial tribunal forty years later, he'd 'sexed it up'. Made the old seem fresh and exciting; had aroused his readers' interest and curiosity.

He took the tribunal through his sources and there indeed were all the relevant facts, published up to eighteen months before. He had got some from stories published in other newspapers. Had he checked those in particular? 'No, I am afraid that does not happen in Fleet Street,' he said, probably with a slight air of resignation. He also pointed out that his stories had been dictated and that while he had corrected the errors they were never re-set because the stories were printed on 'features' pages and so all editions had carried the errors. Only news pages were re-set and corrected, he told the tribunal.[423]

Hoskins admitted having a secret 'official source' who confirmed his spy story for him, but Lord Radcliffe did not press him to reveal the identity. The source had been used solely to confirm that Hoskins was on the right track, much as Deep Throat had done in the Hollywood film *All the President's Men* when in one dramatic scene not hanging up the telephone indicated that the reporters were on the right track.[424] Only in Hoskins's case it probably would have happened over a pint, or a cup of tea, and if there was any music it would have been a juke box rumbling in the background. Dismissing the reporter Radcliffe said, 'Well, Mr Hoskins, that is all, unless it becomes necessary to recall you at a later date with regard to the name of the person you spoke to.'[425] But Hoskins was never called back to collect a ball and chain.

The next day it was Brendan Mulholland's turn. He had published several facts of interest to the tribunal, including that 'Vassall had keys to all kinds of cupboards and doors in the Admiralty. His colleagues wondered, but nobody asked.'[426] He had written that Vassall had, in his £10-a-week Dolphin Square apartment, nineteen suits, over 100 ties, twelve pairs of shoes and over three dozen shirts, but that did not interest Radcliffe. But other background facts did: Mulholland had written some 'colour' material about Vassall, including his school career, his indifferent performance while in the wartime RAF, an office nick-name ('Auntie'), his plans to transfer from the Admiralty to the Foreign Office, and that Vassall's biggest coups were passing on information about submarine detection, radar and radio warfare. Mulholland had also written about Vassall's visits to deliver papers to the home in the Scottish Highlands of his minister, Thomas Galbraith. Mulholland had also published an interview with Galbraith.

Where did all of this come from? Mulholland was cross-examined by Ramsay Willis QC for Galbraith and the Attorney-General, Sir John Hobson QC. The questioning was hostile. Willis first sought to establish that Mulholland had not interviewed Galbraith at all, but instead had simply had a conver-sation. He and Mulholland argued the semantics but were unable to agree exactly what the difference was. They also could not agree how long the meeting had lasted: Willis said five to ten minutes, Mulholland thirty minutes to an hour. One or two inaccuracies, Mulholland said, were down to transcription errors made when the stories were typeset and they were never corrected; and some of the words used were those of the *Daily Mail*'s sub-editors, not his. Evidence submitted shows this was accurate.

Mulholland irked Radcliffe and his interrogators because he could not show his near-contemporaneous notes: he had lost them. But Mulholland's meeting with Galbraith had been conducted together with the *Daily Telegraph* reporter Harry Miller, who in later evidence supported much of what Mulholland said.

However, Willis did establish that some of Mulholland's interview story had included material that was either 'journalistic licence' or taken from material supplied by *Daily Sketch* reporter Louis Kirby. Kirby had spoken to Galbraith by telephone from London at roughly the same time that Mulholland and Miller went to Scotland. But, in what had clearly been an unusual arrangement, the editors of the Associated Newspapers stablemates, the *Daily Mail* and the *Daily Sketch*, had agreed to tell their reporters Mulholland and Kirby to compare notes about their discussions with Galbraith before going into print. The reporters spoke over the lunch recess during the Vassall trial.[427] *Daily Sketch* assistant editor Donald Todhunter and Louis Kirby both confirmed this to Radcliffe.[428]

However, when pressed to name the sources of some of the information about Vassall's visits to Galbraith's home in Scotland, Mulholland refused. He said some had come from anonymous local estate workers – he did not even know, he told Radcliffe, if they worked on Galbraith's estate or that of his neighbour, Lord Strathclyde. Other information came from anonymous local pub customers and residents.

The Attorney-General cross-examined Mulholland about Vassall's background, his spying activities, the nickname, allegations that Vassall had 'sponsors', or protectors in the Admiralty, and the transfer to the Foreign Office. Mulholland passed to Radcliffe a piece of paper naming the source of details about Vassall's school career: it was the *Daily Mail*'s Cardiff correspondent. But as regards his other sources, his lips remained firmly sealed.

In all, Mulholland's testimony came to over fifty pages of tran-script, which probably equates to around three to four hours in total. It was split over two days. His testimony was just about the longest given by any of the journalists called. He made one more appearance: just after lunch that day he was told that his refusals meant he would be visiting the High Court in the company of Reg Foster and Desmond Clough.

So what were the consequences for Clough, Foster and Mulholland? Unlike Hoskins, and a couple of other journalists who had also declined to name their sources but got away with it,[429] Lord Radcliffe wrote a note and passed it to the tribunal's secretary. The journalists, who would later be dubbed 'the silent men', were to be sent to the High Court, charged with contempt.

A few days later each was brought before a judge. Desmond Clough was first. His judge was Lord Parker, the Lord Chief Justice. He was asked if he would consider naming his official source, but he declined. Lord Parker considered that there was no option other than to threaten a prison sentence. Six months was the term he pronounced. However, he thought it best if the defendant was given ten days to mull it over. He also hoped that Clough's source would do the honourable thing and come forward. It is also just possible that the thought was going through Parker's mind that the threat, like most forms of torture, might actually have the desired effect without the need to carry it out and get messy.[430] Moreover, it might also influence Reg Foster and Brendan Mulholland. So while Clough was allowed time the proceedings against the others were adjourned, just in case.

In the intervening period two things happened. The first concerned Reg Foster, and the second Desmond Clough.

Colonel's widow

Mrs Ivy Pugh-Pugh (née Popple) was a 61-year-old widow living in Herne Bay, Kent. She preferred to be known as Jeanne. Widowed in 1938, she had married Colonel Thomas Pugh-Pugh two years later. He had actually been born Thomas Pugh Pugh (without the hyphen). He was around eight years her senior and, she said, involved in the theatrical business.

When she read in the *Sketch* that Foster was threatened with prison she was outraged. She believed she had evidence that could keep him out of jail.

She called the paper straight away and managed to speak to Foster personally. Intrigued by what she told him he sent a colleague, John Austin, to see her. She told how during the war her husband had introduced her to a young man called John Vassall.

As Brendan Mulholland was finishing his own testimony to Radcliffe she repeated her story to the *Sketch*'s assistant editor, Donald Todhunter, reporter Louis Kirby and another person whom she believed to be a lawyer.

Having heard her story the journalists contacted the publisher's QC, Mr Cusack, who quickly told Radcliffe in open session that a new witness had come forward. Radcliffe decided to hear her evidence in secret, and a special 'in camera' session was hastily arranged for 30 January 1963.

With only the tribunal members, the lawyers and John Vassall present, Mrs Pugh-Pugh took the stand. Radcliffe warned her *never* to discuss with the press what happened during the session.

The lawyers took her through her written evidence. The file, which Jeff Hulbert discovered in the National Archives marked 'secret', consists of three statements and typed lists of clothes with their sizes and prices. At the bottom in handwriting were six names, and one of them said 'John Vassall £5'. There was also part of a handwritten letter to her daughter, Mrs Cook, from a gentleman with a Bude address.[431]

During the next hour or so she confirmed that she had not been offered any money by the *Sketch*.[432]

The lawyers cut to the chase: 'Shortly after your wedding [to the Colonel] did you discover something about your husband's character?' 'Yes,' she answered, telling how, arriving back home early one day she saw in the hall a 'beautiful coat and some gloves'. At first she thought that her husband was entertaining, but no one was in the house apart from him. So where did they come from?

It took a little time until the Colonel reluctantly admitted that the clothes were his. She told the tribunal: 'After the first sort of revulsion I took a philosophical view of it, and thought whatever I do, whatever I say, he is still going to dress like this.' The Colonel told her there 'was nothing in it. I just dress up like other girls wear trousers, I just wear this. There is no harm in it...'[433] But the thought of it made her ill.

The couple often held cocktail parties. She remembered one where 'four ladies' attended: 'One was Brenda ... Another gentleman was known as Dolores, one as Carrie and one Suzanne.'[434] It is tempting to picture the reactions in the room as the stiff and sober lawyers heard these revelations.

There had been no other guests because her husband had later told her that he had wanted 'to test my reactions'. She added that they were 'frightfully well educated ... and very retiring, shy'.

Just to make quite sure that everyone understood what Mrs Pugh-Pugh had said, counsel for the tribunal asked her, 'You say they were, in fact, ladies?' 'No,' she replied, 'they were gentlemen but dressed as ladies.' Asked how she knew she replied, 'Because at one time my husband said to one of them, "My wife does not normally see eye to eye with this, old boy."'[435] That had fixed it in her mind.

She was asked if she had met any of the guests before. She had: 'One night I was in and my husband brought a gentleman in and he went straight into his study. My husband was very nice, mind you, but he was very difficult, I would say that.' Shortly after he called her in 'and he introduced me to Mr John Vassall. We went into the lounge. We had a brandy and a coffee...' and afterwards Vassall left.

Between a year and eighteen months later at another party she 'recognised, after a lot of hilarity, that one [guest] was Mr Vassall'.[436] She revealed that his name was 'Brenda'. 'I thought what an awfully ugly name it was. They usually took beautiful names, like Suzanne and Dolores, but Brenda was such an ugly name.'[437] That would have been either in 1944 or 1945. She never knew the names of other guests.

During her testimony Mrs Pugh-Pugh revealed herself to be bad with dates.

In December 1955 the Colonel died. But it was only in 1958 that Mrs Pugh-Pugh decided to sell his effects and to use the proceeds to pay for a holiday in the south of France for herself and her daughter. That was when she came to meet Vassall again.

She remembered placing a classified advertisement in *The Times*, in June or July 1958. She remembered the wording: 'Theatrical boots and shoes for sale, extra high heels, large sizes'. She used a pseudonym, Major Duval, to avoid embarrassment.

She remembered receiving a letter of interest from John Vassall, as well as a letter from Bude. The tribunal did not trouble itself looking for the advert that she claimed to have placed.

Mrs Pugh-Pugh told Radcliffe that she sold 'a pink satin corset' to the man she recognised as Vassall, as well as a book. He had called to look at the stock in person, but they did not talk over old times, as there was not time. He spent £5.

She also sold two albums containing erotic photographs to a 'well-known' gentleman who lived in Widemouth Bay, Bude. They included one or two photographs in which Vassall was dressed as Brenda.[438] At one stage Radcliffe thought about trying to recover the albums to see whether the photos were still inside, but never pursued it.[439]

Vassall's counsel, Kenneth Richardson, emphasised that Vassall denied ever having bought women's clothing from her. He fired off a series of questions which rattled Jeanne Pugh-Pugh. She showed that she couldn't remember dates very well, nor could she tell people's ages. How then could she ever be sure – or persuade the tribunal – that she had ever sold women's clothing to Vassall? The strain began to tell.[440]

When his turn came to cross-examine her Foster's QC declined, saying, 'I had hoped at one time it might help Mr Foster, but I must concede it seems to go to quite different matters.' He added, 'Even if Your Lordship were kind enough to allow me to put questions, I do not think I should desire to do so.'[441] His surprise witness had lost credibility and everyone knew it.

It was left to the Attorney-General to administer the *coup de grâce*. He challenged her handwritten sale notes, which included John Vassall's £5 purchase. They could have been written at any time he said: they were all in the same hand and ink colour; there was no way of determining whether they were contemporaneous with the sale. They were not credible evidence.

Radcliffe delivered his view of her testimony:

I think Mrs Pugh-Pugh's evidence, which I would assume was well intended, leads us nowhere. It does not help us with regard to Mr Foster's source, and it does not in any way suggest that Mr Vassall's activities, whatever they may have been, were such that they were before the public eye. But if you wish to call Mr Vassall, you may do so.[442]

If the tribunal had made any attempt to find the *Times* advert it would have struggled. A search through the newspaper has failed to find it. But, intriguingly, Jeff Hulbert has found that an advert with wording suspiciously close to Mrs Pugh-Pugh's was published in the classified section of the paper on 8 July 1947, eleven years before the date that Mrs Pugh-Pugh had remembered. It read, 'THEATRICAL SHOES, mostly large: extra high heels; no coupons, write PO Box B 448, Willing's, 352 Gray's Inn Rd, WC1'.[443] If the sale had been conducted at that time it would have been so much closer to her claimed meetings with Vassall and his appearance would have been fresher in her mind, making her ability to identify Vassall after all those years less of an issue.

But Willing's was the publisher of press directories, it was not

Major Duval. The ad cannot be directly linked with Mrs Pugh-Pugh and shall have to remain a coincidence.

So as Mrs Pugh-Pugh's evidence was dismissed Foster's last chance to escape a stay in jail evaporated.

The day before Mrs Pugh-Pugh's testimony Vassall had admitted purchasing women's underclothes – but not in the open in the West End – instead by post. He said he sometimes wore them in his Dolphin Square flat, but never in public.[444] Of course, he could have worn them under his suit in public, but no one would ever have known. In his witness statement Foster had only said that Vassall had bought women's clothing in the West End, it was his newspaper that had said that Vassall 'sometimes wore women's clothing on West End trips', but it was Radcliffe who added the layer of meaning that Vassall's activities 'were such that they were before the public eye'.

More witnesses

It was now Desmond Clough's turn, and over the last weekend of January 1963 another surprise witness came forward. This time it was credible: an Admiralty press officer who might have been Clough's source, although he had not realised it at the time. With undoubted sighs of relief in Fleet Street and in Radcliffe Desmond Clough was freed from the threat of prison.

On 31 January Foster made one more appearance before Radcliffe. He was recalled to answer more questions, but was not asked to name any sources and did not refuse to answer anything.

The next day, Friday 1 February 1963, Reg Foster stood with Brendan Mulholland in the High Court before Mr Justice Gorman. A High Court judge since 1950 and a lifelong bachelor, Sir William Gorman had heard some noteworthy cases, including one of Viscount Stansgate's actions that would see him becoming plain Mr Anthony Wedgwood Benn.[445] At the beginning of the year he had sentenced James Hanratty to death for the A6 murder. At its end, sandwiched between Vassall and Radcliffe, he had sentenced a female civil servant, Barbara

Fell OBE, [446] to two years' imprisonment for passing Foreign Office files to a Yugoslav press attaché.[447] To make way for the contempt hearings Gorman broke off from a libel case involving Odhams press.

In both their cases Mr Justice Gorman satisfied himself that the tribunal's request was proper and then cut to the chase. Would they name names? No they would not, both said. Well, in that case, he would move on to the second task, which was to punish them for their refusal. The judge declared with regret it was his solemn duty to commit each to prison. They would have a short period of reflection, but if they both persisted they would serve three months and six months respectively.[448] There never was any reflection. Both stuck to their guns and remained tight lipped and went first to Brixton prison and then to an open prison. But there was one final act. On 8 February the Radcliffe tribunal held a surprise 45-minute public session. Three witnesses had been identified who might be able to help Brendan Mulholland. Radcliffe told the assembly that he wanted to hear the evidence 'in full in case it should assist Mr Mulholland to assist us in the inquiry…'[449]

The witnesses had evidence about the claim that Vassall had been nicknamed 'Auntie'. Of the three, one was a clerical officer colleague of Vassall, Patrick Delahunty. The others were Delahunty's acquaintances. They had spoken to him outside a pub shortly after Vassall's arrest. The other two remembered Delahunty telling them that in the office Vassall was known as 'Miss Vassall' on account of his effeminate appearance. Pressed by Mulholland's counsel, Delahunty admitted that occasionally he had referred to Vassall as 'Miss'. But that was as far as it went. Delahunty was probably fearful of disciplinary action for speaking about his work. Mulholland's QC was invited by Radcliffe to ponder whether the testimony would be helpful to Mulholland. But he considered it would not help because it 'did not deal with his sources of information' and there was no evidence that he had ever met any of the three. So all hope for Mulholland flickered out, too.

When Foster and Mulholland went to prison there was an

outcry. This was in contrast to five years earlier, when reactions had been muted after two student reporters had been jailed for Official Secrets Act offences. The pair had published an article about British eavesdropping on the Russians in *Isis*, the Oxford University journal.[450]

Foster and Mulholland's union, the National Union of Journalists, lobbied for their release. In Parliament questions were asked by the opposition. The journalists, who were driven separately to prison – in Foster's case by a Sheriff of London's officer in a Renault Dauphine saloon – began their first night behind bars where, one newspaper report had it, the inmates got extra sugar in their cocoa before lights out. Both launched appeals which were rejected by the Court of Appeal and permission to appeal to the House of Lords was refused.[451] At the open prison Reg Foster played in the football team (in goal) and tended the garden. They both got full remission, although for a time that was touch-and-go. Reg was released on 7 May 1963 after sixty-one days. Brendan Mulholland was freed on 6 July. In his case his experience gave him the material for his first novel, *Almost a Holiday*, which maybe with a degree of unintentional irony, was published by the Prime Minister's family firm in 1966.[452]

Report

While the two men were in prison Lord Radcliffe published his report to Parliament. The report said, '(Mr Mulholland) refused to give the names of ... two different persons.'[453] Over the space of several pages it detailed Mulholland's failure to deliver 'the name of the person from whom he said he obtained his information about'[454] Vassall's alleged sponsors, or protectors, within the Admiralty. It also noted he was 'unable to tell the name of the second alleged sponsor or to establish that he existed'.[455] The first sponsor Mulholland had identified as Vassall's former public school headmaster. He had subsequently become an Admiralty civil servant and denied the accusation, which Radcliffe accepted.

When it came to Mulholland's claims about Vassall's activities while visiting Galbraith's Scottish home, Radcliffe said, 'We regard his conclusion of fact as altogether unfounded; and we must add that, after hearing Mr Mulholland, we were far from satisfied that he had ever obtained any significant information at all from the informants he spoke of.'[456] Of Foster's reporting he said that 'vague and unsupported suggestions that it was his practice to wear women's clothing in the West End remained wholly without substantiation'.[457] Mrs Pugh-Pugh's secret evidence was not mentioned in any way.

When Foster was released from prison, the *Sketch* covered his return to civilian life. But it also printed an editorial that delivered a stinging attack on Radcliffe, whose report was being debated in Parliament as Foster walked through the prison gates. The paper accused Radcliffe of dismissing evidence that, it said, would have kept Reg out of prison. The paper said that 'many people have forgotten why he was there'. He was in prison 'because Mr Foster refused to say "what type of source" told him Vassall bought women's clothes'. The fact that Vassall wore women's clothes had been confirmed by Radcliffe.

But the paper also said that it had been 'confirmed too by a Colonel's widow, Mrs Jeanne Pugh-Pugh'. She had told Radcliffe how 'she herself sold women's clothes to Vassall', the paper said. Mrs Pugh-Pugh, an unlikely defender of press freedom, came out into the open. 'On Monday she came forward and revealed her name ... "to put right the wrong done to Mr Foster",' the paper said.

But Radcliffe's report had rejected Foster's and Mulholland's allegations because they 'were not backed by "any other acceptable evidence"'.[458] The paper told its readers that neither she nor her evidence were even mentioned in Radcliffe's report. But it added that Radcliffe had no difficulty in accepting Vassall's words alone 'on much weightier issues'.

This emphasis on Mrs Pugh-Pugh and her evidence rather contrasted with the downbeat tone of Foster's counsel at the secret hearing when he, perhaps unwisely, conceded, 'I had hoped at one time it [her evidence] might help Mr Foster.'

The *Sketch* sternly warned its readers: 'Remember, Lord Radcliffe and his colleagues are not infallible.' There were, it said, 'a number of assertions in their report which are open to serious question'. It concluded: 'They made a mistake about the authenticity of Mr Foster's report.' He had emerged as 'a journalist whose professional accuracy has been doubly confirmed'.

But as the dust settled the story was quickly forgotten because it was overtaken by other events and, indeed, a bigger scandal. There was no cry of 'foul!' The politicians debating the report focused on other targets. Reg settled back into handling crime stories.

There is no evidence that coming out into the open caused Mrs Pugh-Pugh to suffer any legal sanction, which is surprising given Radcliffe's uncompromising warning to her. But then neither the paper nor she revealed any of the specific details and so were probably safe enough. She lived for another twenty-seven years secure in the knowledge that she had played a small but significant part in those events. She died in 1990 aged eighty-eight.

Brendan Mulholland left Fleet Street just around the time that his first novel hit the bookshelves and went to work in a newly created news agency in Plymouth, which had been set up by a former leading Fleet Street crime reporter, Rodney Hallworth. He died in 1992 aged fifty-eight. Reg carried on working as a freelance crime reporter until he was well into his seventies, but he never completely put away his notepad and pencil. He died in 1999 aged ninety-five.

Fifty years after Mulholland and Foster left jail what are the hindsight verdicts on the two men and the judge who effectively tried and sentenced them? Even while the two men were still alive rumours about the credibility of their reporting were given some substance by Lord Denning, the Master of the Rolls. He was one of the judges who heard Foster's and Mulholland's appeals. He implied that for all anyone knew they might have made their stories up and because they wouldn't let anyone know their sources they themselves could never be checked. In one of those flurries of logic for which Denning was both loved and hated in roughly equal amounts he had put his finger on one of the crucial points.[459] It was a point seized upon by government supporters who repeated it under the cloak of parliamentary privilege when Vassall and Foster and Mulholland were debated.

Macmillan's unofficial biographer D. R. Thorpe quoted correspondence with veteran Fleet Street columnist Anthony Howard: 'An opinion widely held in Fleet Street was that Mulholland and Foster were in an impossible position, as they had no sources to reveal.'[460] Over the succeeding years, veteran Fleet Street crime reporter Rodney Hallworth, who later worked with Brendan Mulholland, came to the view that the two men had made up at least some of the facts.[461]

In Reg Foster's obituary in *The Guardian*, Matthew Engel put it more obliquely: 'He may have had a genuine scoop, or may just have used his freedom of expression. I think we had better leave it like that.'[462]

The first person to go public in unequivocal terms was the author Richard Davenport-Hines, in his 2013 book on the Profumo affair. He said, 'The truth is that they did not want to admit that they were liars who had invented their stories. Everyone knew it.'[463] But Davenport-Hines didn't name those who 'knew it'. *Daily Mail* columnist Geoffrey Levy wrote in reaction that Mulholland's daughter Katherine was shocked to discover her father branded a liar. Levy quoted a former *Mail* journalist and great friend of Mulholland's, Graham Lord: 'He's calling Brendan Mulholland a liar and a phoney martyr as a matter of cold fact without presenting evidence, chapter and verse, to back it up. And I know he is wrong.'[464] But equally he offered no evidence; and that is the nub of the problem: there is no conclusive evidence.

But there are important issues arising. The first is why Mulholland and Foster were selected for prison out of all the reporters who appeared before Radcliffe.

Several other reporters escaped jailing because either their sources or their information could be verified by other means: Percy Hoskins (*Daily Express*), Sidney Williams (*Daily Herald*),

Tom Tullett, Hugh Saker and Barry Stanley (all Mirror Group newspapers), and Ian Waller (*Sunday Telegraph*). Most of them had felt at the time that they came close to sharing Foster and Mulholland's fate.

Mulholland had not revealed his source for saying that Vassall was known as 'Auntie' among civil service colleagues. He could not produce hard evidence for that nickname but Radcliffe was told by a last-minute witness that Vassall had been called 'Miss'.[465] But Mulholland had not revealed other sources, which bothered Radcliffe more: the person who told him that Vassall had protective sponsors within the Admiralty, or indeed who the second sponsor was. And there were also those details about what Vassall did when he travelled to Galbraith's Scottish home to deliver papers, and who told him.

Similarly Foster could not prove the line in the *Sketch* that said Vassall had worn women's clothes in the West End, but the inquiry heard that Vassall admitted buying and wearing women's clothes. Mrs Pugh-Pugh's evidence of Vassall wearing women's clothes at parties in Central London was dismissed unmentioned, but why would the widow of an army officer in Herne Bay make up such a story, revealing her late husband's transvestism, and why would she risk imprisonment by faking documents?

There was a case for reasonable doubt either way on both stories so why in the great scheme of things was it so essential to uncover the sources of the stories? Was this a search for truth or a search for leakers and whistle-blowers? Could it also be a way of discrediting those who embarrassed the security services by implying they missed obvious clues?

It is worth remembering that during the time of Radcliffe's public sessions the Attorney-General, Sir John Hobson, was also wrestling with what he saw as disturbing aspects about the emerging Profumo scandal. Government would have a motive for making an example of the press to keep it in line. Keep it cowed and under control and when the big one happened – in this case Profumo – as everyone knew it would eventually, press coverage would be less cavalier. The press would be careful not to print facts it could not verify. That would help to keep a lid on it and limit the damage. If this was the policy it clearly didn't work because the press coverage was widespread and unforgiving.

What of the Prime Minister, Harold Macmillan, 'Supermac'? His actions in setting up the Radcliffe Inquiry, rather than dampening down the Vassall affair, had the opposite effect. They had inflamed passions and, with a new Leader of the Opposition emerging in the shape of Harold Wilson, he had to face a younger and a more formidable opponent. The stories about Vassall continued and, with two of their own put behind bars, the press turned up the heat on his government. In one of those twists that sometimes happens in politics one miscalculation leads to another. By refusing to do anything to help spring Foster and Mulholland, the government was targeted by several opposition MPs who also happened to be journalists. They forced a debate in the House of Commons on 21 March 1963. During it several members of the opposition tossed verbal hand-grenades into the proceedings. Close to 11 p.m. George Wigg, followed by Barbara Castle, Richard Crossman and others, under the cloak of parliamentary privilege, repeated rumours they had heard about a certain minister and his involvement with a young lady who had disappeared while involved as a witness in a criminal trial. They demanded a statement. The next day they got it, for the girl in question was called Christine Keeler, and the minister was the Secretary of State for War, John Profumo.

The debate about Reg Foster and Brendan Mulholland had, in fact, no longer been solely about their imprisonment – to which government remained deaf. It helped prepare the way for the biggest scandal of Macmillan's government, one which neither Profumo nor Macmillan would survive. Within seven months, and claiming ill health, Macmillan would resign; and within eighteen months Wilson would be sitting inside No. 10, where he too would soon be fretting about security, spies and journalists.

7

CHARLES WHEELER

At one microphone sat Charles Wheeler, 'the finest reporter in the BBC's history' according to one of its directors-general.[466] At another, ready to interview him, was the BBC's 'Grand Inquisitor', Jeremy Paxman. Wheeler and Paxman had worked together for many years on BBC2's news analysis programme *Newsnight*, most famously when Berlin celebrated German reunification in 1990. Wheeler interrupted Paxman's attempt to present the programme live from the Berlin Wall to declare, 'Jeremy, this is pure Monty Python, having a serious political discussion in the middle of a firework display.'[467]

In 2003 they met again in the comparative calm of a BBC radio studio in London to record an interview for a programme to mark Wheeler's forthcoming eightieth birthday.[468] Old colleagues they might have been but Paxman wasn't about to sacrifice his reputation for tough interviewing. He gave Wheeler a vigorous cross-examination, especially about his time as one of the BBC's Washington correspondents.

Paxman: You know, I've heard right-wing Americans describe you as being anti-American ... What do you say to the anti-American charge?
Wheeler: I think I was pro-American. What I've often felt is that they were so often mis-governed because their system throws up such really awful people.
Paxman: Who are you to say that?

Wheeler: Why should I not say it?

Paxman: Well, he's the elected President of the United States.

Wheeler: Jeremy, come off it.

Paxman: You were a reporter.

Wheeler: Yeah, sure.

Paxman: That's all you are.

Wheeler: Yes.

Paxman: Well, what are you doing making those sort of observations about the President?

Wheeler: Because you're asking me questions and I'm answering them honestly. I think that a reporter should be able to say what he thinks – about his leaders and other people's leaders.

Paxman: What...

Wheeler: Jeremy, you're in a weak position here.

Paxman: What he thinks or what he sees? There's a big difference here. And people say you cross this line.

Wheeler: Which line did I cross? Did I see too much or did I think too much?

That final exchange crystallises the debate about the journalism of Sir Selwyn Charles Cornelius-Wheeler, 'absolutely the greatest' according to BBC colleague John Simpson and committed supporter of the underdog over many decades of reporting from around the world.[469]

Charles Wheeler never toed any Establishment line. In his eighties he was knighted at Buckingham Palace but in his youth he was once declared by royal courtiers to be 'persona non grata' there. This happened after an incident when, towards the end of a long overseas tour by the Queen, Wheeler had been overheard in a pub complaining, 'I wish that bloody woman would go home, I'm bored with this trip.'

About the same time in the 1950s he caused a row by telling British listeners that Ceylon, as it was then called, was being governed 'by an inexperienced eccentric at the head of a Cabinet of mediocrities'.[470]

And not a lot had changed five decades later when in a radio interview he said that the trouble with the American political system was that it 'throws up such really awful people'. For example, Vice-President Dan Quayle had been 'a featherweight and an unattractive one at that'.[471]

The more the BBC lionised him in later life the more radical and outspoken he became. In one tribute programme he talked about his coverage of the American urban riots in the 1960s. 'I don't think we should have tried to be dispassionate. I came to believe that violence was justified in a riot because it made white America listen.'

No wonder that in one tribute programme another colleague, John Humphrys, said of him: 'He never sought celebrity but neither did he walk away from controversy or confrontation.'

Opinions

Reporters like Charles Wheeler have always presented a challenge to a system of broadcasting which by law requires 'due impartiality and due accuracy' in news from all licensed TV and radio broadcasters in the UK. The statutory requirement for 'due impartiality' makes broadcast journalism different from all other kinds of media in the UK. There is no equivalent for newspapers or online news. In the United States the nearest equivalent, the fairness doctrine, ended in 1987. In Britain the BBC and ITV are under an obligation to be impartial whereas the *Daily Telegraph*, *The Guardian*, *The Sun* and *Daily Mirror* are not.

To be very precise, when Charles Wheeler joined the BBC in 1947 the due impartiality rule wasn't yet in place. As a later BBC study of the concept revealed, 'The strange thing is that the BBC was never told to be impartial. People often assume it was there on its birth certificate – the first Wireless Broadcasting licence of 1923. It was not.'[472] Nor did the first Royal Charter of 1926 mention it.

In 1927 a rule was laid down that 'the BBC must not express in broadcasts its own opinion on current affairs or matters of public policy'.[473] But the first requirement to be impartial in reporting other people's opinions came as late as 1952, after Wheeler joined, when the BBC agreed to broadcast 'an impartial account day by day prepared by professional reporters of the proceedings in both Houses of the United Kingdom Parliament'. But this seems to relate only to parliamentary reporting, a role which Wheeler sadly never performed.[474] In fact it was as late as 1996 before the BBC had a formal requirement to treat 'controversial subjects with due accuracy and impartiality'.

However, the bottom line is that for much of Wheeler's BBC career his employers were either required to be impartial or said they were anyway regardless of any formal obligation. There are three episodes in Wheeler's long career that illustrate the ethical challenges this created.

The first, appropriately, was in the country where Wheeler was later to enjoy his 'Monty Python' night of celebration at German reunification.

Berlin and Budapest

Wheeler was born in Germany in 1923. His father, a former RAF officer, was an agent for a shipping company and was based in Hamburg.[475] As an adolescent, young Charles used to take bread to Jewish neighbours hiding from the Nazis in the woods. With the prospect of war he was sent back to Britain to attend Cranbrook School in Kent, where his geography teacher recorded that 'he has done little but what he has done is fair' and his general knowledge teacher observed that he needed 'more intellectual humility'.[476] His first job after school was tearing agency copy off teleprinters and handing it out around the *Daily Sketch* newsroom in London. But then in 1942 he joined a secret naval intelligence unit directed by Ian Fleming, creator of James Bond, and took part in the D-Day landings in Normandy. At the end of the Second World War he used his fluent German to break the news of Hitler's suicide to a group of German prisoners of war, who applauded in relief.[477]

After the war he hoped to find a job back in newspapers but had to settle for the BBC's External Services and a post as a sub-editor, not in the German service where his fluency would have been invaluable, but in the Spanish language service to Latin America. Wheeler did not speak Spanish so he wrote news bulletins in English and someone else translated them. He was moved to the main newsroom to help cover the 1948 London Olympic Games. Then in 1950 came a big break in his career when he returned to Germany as the BBC German service's representative in Berlin to cover the post-war division of the country.[478]

Wheeler was, according to one colleague,

> as English as they come but he was totally at home in Berlin and in Germany. I'm sure the fact that he'd been there when young made this his patch and he carried this enthusiasm, this commitment to what was going on not just to Eastern Germany but Eastern Europe generally for most of his working, journalistic life.[479]

Three years into his assignment Wheeler witnessed an event which was to symbolise that commitment. Such was the impact it had on him that he later took the trouble to translate into English and adapt a German book by Stefan Brant, with the title *The East German Rising: 17 June 1953*, which described itself as 'the first full story of this remarkable and quite unprecedented rising of the working people and peasants of a totalitarian country against their oppressors'.[480]

It was no exaggeration when the book called the uprising 'astonishing'. The story began with a strike by building workers in Berlin on 16 June 1953. By the next day it had turned into a widespread uprising across East Germany against the government, which the Russians had installed in the Soviet zones they occupied after the Second World War. Here was the working class rising up against the very people who claimed that they were the vanguard of the proletariat. Clearly from the Russian point of view this was a dangerous development that might infect the working classes of other countries in the Soviet bloc. The demonstrations were promptly suppressed by Soviet tanks.

Much later Wheeler looked back on the uprising with almost

calm detachment: 'There was a lot of talk about free elections, the word spread and the next day every single town in the zone rose up but by evening the Russians had the thing in hand by using tanks and that was the end of the rising.'[481]

But one of those who worked with him at the BBC remembered rather more passion. Michael Peacock, later to become controller of both BBC One and BBC Two, recalled a Wheeler who was 'really, really committed to telling the world what was going on in Eastern Berlin and every other minute he seemed to be talking about the workers rising, workers' revolution'.

In an interview in his later years, Wheeler talked about his coverage of the East German uprising, and what he said raised a different set of ethical issues. His interviewer was Michael Nelson, general manager of the Reuters news agency from 1976 to 1989 and one of the principal architects of its global expansion into financial news. In 1997 he published a book called *War of the Black Heavens* about the role of Western broadcasters during the Cold War. As part of his research he talked to Wheeler about his time as a correspondent in Berlin in the early 1950s. Specifically, Nelson talked to Wheeler about his relationship with a Foreign Office unit called IRD (Information Research Department) which was secretly funded by the British government, was linked to the British Secret Intelligence Service, SIS or MI6, and was tasked with generating anti-Communist propaganda in the Cold War. It was the same unit as the one W. N. Ewer (*see Chapter 2*) worked for.

Wheeler told Nelson that on 16 June 1953, as the uprising developed, he was walking along the street in Berlin when a car drew up alongside him. In the car was a man called Peter Seckelmann, who he believed to be from the IRD. 'Get over to East Berlin,' Seckelmann told Wheeler. This tip-off allowed Wheeler and the BBC to beat their competitors in the coverage of the workers' uprising. Wheeler believed Seckelmann got his information because the IRD had access to clandestine British intercepts of domestic East German communications.[482]

But the connection between the BBC and the IRD in Berlin

went deeper than useful tip-offs to reporters. It was a two-way relationship. Michael Nelson discovered that the BBC job to which Wheeler had been appointed had previously been titled not as a 'correspondent' for the BBC External Services but 'BBC European Service liaison officer'. It had been based inside the British military headquarters, at no cost to the BBC. By the time Wheeler took up the job the BBC had moved out of the military HQ but the close relationship with the military and the security services remained.

Wheeler revealed to Nelson that one of the two IRD men in Berlin would visit him in his office armed with sheets of information. According to Nelson, Wheeler told him he 'was not allowed to look at them but the IRD man paraphrased the contents. They were gossipy news items about East Germany, which Wheeler sent to London for use in German service programmes.' The IRD's access to the intercepts of East German communications meant 'it was not too difficult to find items that put the regime in a bad light or stories that made them look foolish'. In some ways it was the Western equivalent of the propaganda effort which John Peet (*Chapter 5*) was making for the Soviet side.

In 1954 the BBC–Foreign Office relationship was taken to a new level when the BBC agreed that all the mail that it received from eastern Europe would be passed on to a secret department in the Foreign Office. Any listener in a Communist country who wrote to praise or complain about a BBC programme would have their details passed to British intelligence and into their files. The BBC was under orders that wherever possible the letters should be provided with the original envelopes. Presumably this was to help identify addresses and it is possible that some of the letter-writers were then contacted by British intelligence. In return the BBC – and its External Services at Bush House – was given privileged access to confidential Foreign Office cables, an arrangement that was still going strong in the late 1970s.

Wheeler told Nelson that he received eight or ten visitors a day who would give him information. Sometimes he would persuade them to write to the BBC, effectively getting them into the system.

He recalled only one occasion when he had knowingly passed information to MI6, which he had done at the request of the informant.[483]

In 1997, *The Times* summarised what was going to be in Nelson's book: 'BBC correspondents in Eastern Europe in the 1950s, including the veteran broadcaster Charles Wheeler, were fed classified material gleaned from covert intercepts of Soviet bloc communications in a secret government operation to generate anti-Communist propaganda broadcasts during the Cold War.'[484]

Michael Nelson said the article caused great concern at the BBC because nobody had previously admitted that such a relationship existed between the corporation and British intelligence. In a later book he said, 'It was typical of the honesty of Charles Wheeler that he should acknowledge that such a give-and-take relationship existed as an essential part of the work of a BBC correspondent at the height of the Cold War.'[485]

Three years after the Berlin workers' revolt, Wheeler was again an eyewitness when the Soviet Union suppressed another uprising with chilling military efficiency, this time on the streets of the Hungarian capital, Budapest, in 1956. By now he was working as a producer on BBC television's *Panorama*, carrying the programme's only portable camera, which he'd been expressly forbidden to take with him. With typical Wheeler disdain for authority he ignored the instruction and filmed interviews with Hungarians who believed, at that moment in the uprising, that they had succeeded in asserting their national independence. Wheeler asked an English-speaking woman in the street who was now running Budapest. She replied, 'The revolutionary committee is governing the town, the revolutionary committee was elected by several other committees which were elected in every factory and in every working place and the university.' He asked her what she expected from the future and what she hoped would happen now. She replied, 'We hope that our country will be entirely free.'

When Wheeler got back to London and started editing the film for transmission, news came through that Russian tanks had crushed the uprising. Wheeler found the news 'devastating'. He said, 'I got as close to weeping as I'd ever got about anything.'[486] 'Most shattering of all was having to listen to the BBC re-broadcast those despairing appeals to the West for help.'[487]

The production team wondered what to do about the film they had shot, which in many ways was now out of date, because the Russians had taken over. But they soon realised that showing those few days of 'freedom' would be an even more powerful record of what it had been like when Hungarians appeared to be in charge of their own destiny again.

Washington

If Germany and central Europe was Wheeler's first great love and his first big career break, the United States was to be his second. His profile was raised when he started to appear regularly on British television screens as one of the BBC's two Washington correspondents. He and fellow reporter Gerald Priestland covered all the big stories of the '60s from the Vietnam War to the civil rights movement. It was, in the words of a later BBC Washington correspondent, Martin Bell, 'always an uneasy partnership' because the two men saw America through very different eyes.[488]

As an example, Bell highlighted Wheeler's reporting of the civil rights movement:

> He broke away from the 'on the one hand this and on the other hand that' tradition of BBC reporting. If he felt that something was wrong, he found a way of saying so. I was told that some of his work drew sharp intakes of breath from the senior managers of the time, for they had no taste for controversial journalism, but to their credit they let him get on with it.

The most striking example of this was Wheeler's reporting for BBC radio and television of the riots in the Watts area of Los Angeles in 1965. In one BBC TV news report he spoke directly to camera about what the black rioters had told him.

They talk about police brutality in these terms – they push us around, they arrest us for nothing, they call us niggers, they say we stink, they insult our women, we've had this for years, as long as we can remember and the point finally came when somebody decided he wouldn't take it any more ... It boils down to this, they say, we are treated as second-class citizens, we're even treated as animals, we have been behaving like second-class citizens, we have been behaving like animals, we know it, we can't help it, it is going to go on until something is done.[489]

Wheeler never actually said then that he thought the violence was justified, but he did confirm years later, in a BBC interview, that this was indeed what he thought at the time: 'I came to believe in those two years when these riots were going on ... that violence was justified in a riot because it made white America listen.' He said of the rioters:

They were really the victims because they were burning down their own ghetto and I used to go around saying this at Washington dinner parties and people would be absolutely horrified at the idea that a journalist would think that burning down buildings was a justified form of protest. I believe it was.[490]

As a predominantly foreign correspondent, Charles Wheeler rarely covered the disturbances on the UK's streets from Londonderry to Toxteth and Brixton and so we will never know what would have happened if he had used the same reporting techniques and displayed the same sympathies with rioters. I suspect the response from his editors and from politicians would have been very different.

Newsnight
In 1980 Wheeler joined BBC *Newsnight* as a presenter then a reporter. And so began the third great career episode as he enjoyed the freedom to travel around the world. In the Middle East after the first Gulf War in 1991 he stood on a storm-swept hillside in the Kurdish area of Iraq and reported on the desperate state of the Kurdish refugees trying to escape from Saddam Hussein's

retribution. Mostly he let the pictures speak for themselves and one English-speaking refugee speak for herself. Then, standing cold and slightly dishevelled amidst a line of vehicles, he offered a calm and considered view on what he was witnessing:

> You spend five or ten minutes in this area and no matter what clothes you are wearing you are soaked and you are wet and you are miserable. These people have been here two weeks, two weeks since they left these Kurdish towns. The road is closed and what these people cannot understand is why they are still sitting here and why so little aid is coming from outside.[491]

The British Foreign Secretary, Douglas Hurd, was later to talk of 'something must be done' journalism (*see Chapter 9*). Wheeler was too elegant a writer to reach for such clichés as 'something must be done'; he got his message across in more subtle ways.

Despite the power of Wheeler's reporting from Kurdish Iraq and similar images in the rival ITN bulletins, the then Prime Minister, John Major, effectively responded that nothing could be done: 'What is happening in Iraq at the present time is very distressing, and it is malignant, I agree entirely with that thought. But it is also wholly within the borders of Iraq, and we have no international authority to interfere with that.'[492]

Within a week the impact of the coverage by Wheeler and others was such that this policy was reversed and something was done. Major and Hurd announced their proposal to create 'safe havens' inside Iraq to protect the Kurds from Saddam.

Wheeler later said of his reporting of the plight of the Kurdish refugees in Iraq: 'All right, I wasn't dispassionate ... but I was terribly angry and objectivity flies out of the window on these occasions. What do you want me to do, do an interview with somebody who thinks this [situation] is good to balance the story?'[493]

Wheeler believed that as a foreign correspondent, 'you've got to remember that you have access to more than just the bare facts. You've got access to people, you've seen things that the viewer and listener don't have so you have to do more interpretation.' He also wondered, perhaps remembering that the first BBC impartiality rules were limited to trying to get a balance in the reporting of Westminster politics, that a BBC foreign correspondent may have 'more licence than you get as a domestic political reporter for example where you have lots and lots of people sensitive to what you are saying and watching your back'.

Another example of classic Wheeler reporting from this period showed his focus on the underdog, in this case an underdog that most viewers would probably never have known existed. After American, British and Saudi troops had driven Iraqi troops from Kuwait most correspondents were occupied with covering joyful liberated Kuwaitis and the oilfields set on fire by Saddam's departing, defeated troops. But 'dogged, determined and bloody minded' as Jeremy Paxman called him, Wheeler sought out a different angle and investigated claims that Palestinians, who the Kuwaitis regarded as collaborators with Saddam, were being tortured in a Kuwaiti hospital.[494] In a head-to-head confrontation with a Kuwaiti doctor who denied the allegations, Wheeler stood his ground until the doctor finally and unwisely said of the Palestinians, 'If they were treated badly, they deserve it.' Wheeler responded with icy calm, 'Are you speaking as a doctor?' 'As a Kuwaiti citizen, not a doctor,' came the reply. Wheeler knew he had won the argument. He politely thanked the doctor and ended the interview.[495]

Wheeler spent his sixty-eighth birthday in a war-damaged hotel in Kuwait City and apparently said, 'I can't believe how lucky I am to be here. Something awful might have happened to me – like retirement.' In 2001, unusually for a journalist, the government appointed him a CMG – Companion of the Order of St Michael and St George – which, according to the official website of the British monarchy, is awarded to those 'who render extraordinary or important non-military service in a foreign country'. In 2006 he was knighted.

Charles Wheeler never really stopped reporting and because he left the BBC staff in 1976 to work freelance, no one could retire him against his will. He was making television programmes well into his eighties on subjects as varied as the British soldiers shot for desertion in the First World War and the forcible migration of thousands of children from Britain in the first half of the twentieth century. In 2008 he was working on a radio programme about the Dalai Lama, whose flight from Tibet in 1959 he had covered as the BBC's Delhi correspondent, when he died aged eighty-five. The cause of death was lung cancer. He had been a lifelong smoker.

Two years before he died I had the chance to talk to him about his career. I interviewed him for the Royal Television Society (RTS) to mark his knighthood and the next morning we were interviewed together on Radio 4's *Today* programme. Before the RTS event he was very touchy about the fact that I had mentioned his knighthood in a preview article in *The Guardian*. I put that down to humility but I also wondered if he regretted accepting the honour.

In *The Guardian* I had said that 'the journalism of one man poses intriguing and sometimes awkward questions' about the rules on impartiality. I asked when 'engagement' (then a BBC buzzword) with people caught up in news events became commitment to their cause. On *Today* I wondered when a 'professional judgement' (allowed by BBC guidelines) became a 'personal view' (not allowed).

As befitted a knight of the realm looking back on half a century of journalism, Sir Charles Wheeler was wonderfully relaxed about debating these issues. He had once said that 'the trouble with the quest for a statutory definition of impartiality is that it will create incoherent journalism, a Tower of Babel, truth smothered by sheer words'.[496] Now he declared with pride rather than any embarrassment, 'You mention something called the BBC guidelines. I have been working for the BBC for more than fifty years and I've never seen them in my life.'

Instead he offered an alternative to official BBC rules:

One guideline that has always stuck in my mind – this came up after I said something rather unusual about the then Prime Minister of Ceylon – I'd called him an inexperienced eccentric running a cabinet of mediocrities – there was a big row about that and about three months later Hugh Carleton Greene, BBC's then Director-General who was himself a journalist, raised this with me ... and he said, look, as a foreign correspondent this is what you should do – sail as close to the wind as you can, but get it right. And that's been my guideline. And if you get it right there is no problem.

8

FREDERICK FORSYTH

THE FORSYTH SAGA - AN AFRICAN TRILOGY

Prologue

It is such an intriguing story that it could come from the pages of a thriller.

A young foreign correspondent is sent to an African civil war but gets into a row with his employers in a battle between truth and censorship. Called home and banned from the front line he decides to return to the war at his own cost. Telling the story the way he wants involves risking his life. He is ready to shoot himself rather than be captured and tortured by enemy troops. He also makes enemies among the troops he is with. Our hero emerges unscathed but ghosts from his past reoccur with strange regularity for the rest of his life.

In fact this is the real life story of the bestselling novelist Frederick Forsyth. As with many of his thrillers there are unpredictable twists in this tale.

Forsyth was sent to Nigeria by the BBC in 1967 to cover the conflict caused by the eastern region, Biafra, breaking away from the federal state. At the time it seemed a relatively normal assignment for a reporter with the job title 'Foreign Correspondent, London-based'. Forsyth's desk was at the BBC but he regularly was sent on foreign trips.

Why was it that this visit, and his subsequent ones to Nigeria, ended with his journalistic contemporaries so divided on whether or not Freddie (as they knew him) had taken the Biafran side?

Why do so many of them think that when the BBC pulled him out he went back to work for the Biafrans as a propagandist?

And how did he later get caught up not just in one attempted coup in west Africa but two?

No BBC correspondent, not even Charles Wheeler, has ever been involved in such controversy about alleged partisanship. And no correspondent accused of breaking the impartiality rules that Forsyth and Wheeler and all other BBC journalists worked under has ever turned the tables so publicly, declaring that it was not them that were taking sides but the BBC.

When I joined the BBC as a news trainee in 1969 it was after Forsyth had left in controversial circumstances, but the story of what he had done in Nigeria as a foreign correspondent, and what he'd been doing since, was a regular talking point in the BBC Club bar across the road from Broadcasting House.

The conventional in-house view was best summarised by John Simpson, now the BBC's world affairs editor but then a junior journalist, who wrote, 'As an extremely lowly sub-editor in the BBC radio newsroom I had to put Mr Forsyth's Biafran dispatches on the air. Even at the age of twenty-three I could see that he had accepted the Biafran line entirely. He was reporting propaganda as fact.'

Former ITN correspondent Michael Nicholson, who also covered the Biafran war, recalled seeing Forsyth in what he said was the uniform of the rebel army and armed with a revolver. From these and other sources, including the BBC, the National Archives and interview comments from Forsyth himself, Jeff Hulbert and I have put together a record of those events. A popular TV series of the time was called *The Forsyte Saga*, based on three novels of the Edwardian writer John Galsworthy, and a diplomat caught up in the Biafran controversy was to label it 'The Forsyth Saga'. As with Galsworthy's work, ours is a trilogy.

Volume One: Nigeria divides and Frederick is sent to the front
Even after Nigeria became independent from Britain in 1960 the
influence of the former colonial power was still strong on its politics (British experts had helped write its federal constitution) and
its trade (British Petroleum was the dominant oil-producer). Harold
Wilson's government was very much on the side of the federal forces
trying to crush the Biafran secession. Undoubtedly, as in so many
wars, concern about control of oil supplies was never far away.[497]

Martin Bell, whose reporting from Nigeria for the BBC
helped make his reputation as a leading foreign correspondent,
remembers:

> My recollection of that war was that it was hugely controversial at
> home – actually more so even than the Vietnam War, with which
> it was of course concurrent – because the British were actively
> involved. We weren't in Vietnam, but my goodness, we were fund-
> ing, we were arming the federal Nigerians and the people were
> suffering on the ground.

The BBC agreed with the British government that the first mention
of the conflict in any news story would never refer to 'Biafra',
which might imply some recognition of it as a sovereign state,
but a form of words such as 'the breakaway south-eastern region
which calls itself Biafra'. This didn't exactly trip off the tongue.

All the BBC's written archives are kept in a small building on the
outskirts of Reading. In the files on Nigeria there are many examples
of the tension between broadcaster and government throughout the
Biafran conflict from 1967 to 1970. The most regular complainant
was the British High Commissioner in Nigeria, Sir David Hunt,
better known a few years later as a winner of the BBC's *Mastermind*
competition. But at this point his preoccupation with the BBC
was the output of its overseas radio services. He concluded one
complaint letter to the BBC with this comment on those services:
'They announced last week that the Duke of Edinburgh was going

to visit West Africa. The news roused great excitement here as you can well imagine. When people discover that it is quite false it will be another nail in the coffin of the BBC's credibility.'[498]

Into this kind of stressful atmosphere in July 1967 stepped 29-year-old Frederick Forsyth. He had joined the BBC in 1965 after four years as a Reuters foreign correspondent, including a period as the Reuters man in France and East Germany. The BBC files report his promotion in January 1967 to 'Foreign Correspondent, London-based'.[499] In the summer of that year the BBC decided that in addition to having its correspondent in the federal capital, Lagos, it needed to send a reporter to cover the area controlled by the Biafrans. Forsyth was chosen and before he was sent it was decided that he needed a proper briefing about Biafra, its people (who were mostly from the Ibo tribe) and its controversial leader, Colonel, later General, Ojukwu.

Forsyth later recalled, 'The briefing basically was that the secession of Biafra – the eastern region – from Nigeria was being forced upon the people by the ruthlessly ambitious Ojukwu.' He says he was told 'that they were perfectly happy under the Nigerian dictatorship and the prediction was that the magnificent and British-trained, largely Hausa, Nigerian army would invade and sweep through'.

Forsyth's initial experiences in Biafra were rather different:

What I got there to find was that the people were massively in favour of secession, that the restraining influence had been Ojukwu and far from sweeping through, there was absolutely no military movement whatever.

I discovered absolutely everything I had been told was rubbish. Being naive (not about reporting, I had been four years with a far better outfit called Reuters, but about the BBC mindset) I reported this. Outrage, horror, he must be biased. Asked to recant, I repeated what I was seeing – no federal victories.[500]

Starting with our High Commissioner in Lagos and moving up through the Commonwealth Office, the Wilson government

adopted a passionately pro-Lagos view and imparted this to the
BBC. The High Commissioner and the senior BBC West Africa
man were 400 miles away in Lagos but they knew far better than
the man in the thick of it.

The BBC's man in Lagos was veteran foreign correspondent
Angus McDermid, who became a legendary figure when he side-
stepped Nigerian censors, sending back an exclusive story on the
assassination of an army general by dictating it in Welsh.

But soon Forsyth was offering a rather different perspective
on the Biafran conflict from the BBC's man in the federal capital:

> He [McDermid] began filing these reports from the Nigerian
> propaganda ministry, putting the attribution perhaps at paragraph
> three or four, so it sounded as if the BBC was making flat state-
> ments. Then Broadcasting House began bombarding me – it wasn't
> the other way round – will you please tell us about all these things
> seen from the Biafran side – the rebel side as they called it. And I
> had no choice but to file back and say, they're not happening.

But Forsyth didn't just report what he saw with his own eyes, he
also reported the claims which the Biafrans made. In his mind
this was no different from McDermid reporting the claims which
the federal side made from Lagos. But Lagos didn't see it that way
and trouble began brewing.

First the Nigerian federal government complained to the BBC
that he was 'working illegally in Eastern Nigeria'. As they didn't
accept the secession of Biafra they resented a BBC man entering
what they still regarded as their territory without their permission. Forsyth was using neighbouring Cameroons as his crossing
point and a British diplomat there, Nicol Morton, tracked him
down. Like many British diplomats around the world his role was
partly to debrief correspondents on what they had seen on the
front line and report back to Whitehall. His cable to colleagues
had a patronising tone:

I formed the impression that Forsyth did not see more nor learn more than what the Biafrans wanted him to know. And whereas I would not wish to misjudge him, I imagine his reporting objectivity was coloured by his lack of experience in unsophisticated places.[501]

Mr Morton got an enthusiastic reply from fellow diplomat G. D. Anderson in Lagos. He seems to have been the first to draw the literary allusion with Galsworthy's novels, and headed his memo 'The Forsyth Saga'.

The Forsyth Saga
Your letter ... of 4 August about Forsyth, the BBC's ex-man in Enugu/Douala was read here with the closest interest as ... [a] contribution to lengthy exchanges we have had with London about the BBC's (in our view!) inept and unintelligent reporting generally on the civil war in Nigeria – and about Forsyth's part in it in particular. ... You may however get a little quiet amusement from reading the enclosed sheaf of telegrams about BBC/Forsyth ... You may see a little more of Forsyth, perhaps on his way out of Eastern Nigeria again for the second – and we hope the last time.
I should perhaps explain that our grouse against Forsyth/BBC is not so much that the tenor of their broadcasts is pro-Biafran ... but that they have tended to retail as BBC news the undigested and unattributed Biafran news hand-outs, thereby, in many eyes, lending fictitious authenticity to Biafran reports and thus coming close to the point of being Biafran propagandists.[502]

The diplomatic cables from August 1967 in the National Archives reveal how the Forsyth Saga escalated from grumbles between diplomats in west Africa to direct contact in London between the Commonwealth Office and the BBC. One cable reports a success in getting the BBC to back down and stop transmitting one of Forsyth's reports.

CONFIDENTIAL

IMMEDIATE COMMONWEALTH OFFICE TO HIGH COMMISSION LAGOS

BBC told us this morning they had received cable from Forsyth reporting claims made to him by Eastern authorities in Enugu that RAF had taken over Kano Airport.

We confirmed to BBC that there was absolutely no truth in this story. BBC said they would not use it on African services even with denial and after discussion agreed to recommend internally that it should not be used on any services even though coupled with denial.[503]

Inside the BBC the best guide to corporate thinking about news and current affairs traditionally came from the so-called 'ENCA minutes'.

Each week for many decades the editor, News and Current Affairs (ENCA) would bring together his (and it always was a 'his' in those days) senior executives for a mixture of departmental housekeeping, service messages and editorial guideline-setting. The minutes were distributed to middle management and avidly read for any clues about what was really going on. During the late '60s the main sport on the night shift in the BBC radio newsroom was going through managers' filing cabinets trying to find copies.

The ENCA minutes about Forsyth for the next few months of 1967 were typically gnomic but in hindsight very significant.

On 18 August 1967, just two days after the telegram from Lagos had been received in the Foreign and Commonwealth Office, the ENCA minutes recorded that

FNE [foreign news editor] said it had been decided to suppress a report from Frederick Forsyth reporting Biafran rumours of the closing of Kano airport because it had been alleged that the closing was intended to hide the stationing there of RAF fighter squadrons. But once this report had been denied by the Commonwealth Office, some parts of Forsyth's despatch had been used.[504]

However, this was not to be Forsyth's last appearance in the ENCA minutes. In early September 1967, ENCA was told that the Nigerian federal government had been threatening to expel a BBC TV reporter in Lagos, David Tindall. The minutes say:

> It was not clear whether this was because they were dissatisfied with Tindall's reporting or simply annoyed because Frederick Forsyth had been reporting from Biafra ... Senior Foreign Duty Editor asked whether Forsyth should be withdrawn. Editor News and Current Affairs favoured keeping Forsyth on the spot for the time being. ACOS [Assistant Controller Overseas Services] drew attention to a recent dispatch from Forsyth which he described as 'extraordinary'; the External Services had not used it.[505]

There's no explanation of which despatch this was. But it could have been the kind of Forsyth report which John Simpson later recalled: 'He announced, without any qualification, that Biafra had shot down (as far as I remember) sixteen federal Nigerian aircraft. The newsroom copy of *Jane's All the World's Aircraft* said that the federal air force possessed only twelve.'[506]

Whatever the specific details of the despatch, five days later the ENCA minutes record that 'Frederick Forsyth was returning to London now that the Nigerian story was no longer in the forefront of the news'.[507]

Two months later another single sentence, but this time in the minutes of a different meeting, records: 'ENCA confirmed that Freddie Forsyth would be reverting to his previous role as a reporter.'[508]

His days as a BBC foreign correspondent were over, at least for the foreseeable future. He was grounded to a more domestic agenda.

The reason for this is never explained in any available BBC archive document. And what of the reason he was withdrawn from Biafra in the first place? Was it because of what he'd filed, or because of Nigeria's threat to expel a BBC man in Lagos or because 'the Nigerian story was no longer in the forefront of the news' – probably the least likely explanation as Biafra continued to be a major news story for some time.

A year later the head of BBC External Services, Charles Curran, came up with yet another version in a letter to Sir David Hunt. The British High Commissioner in Lagos believed that Forsyth had been 'an ardent Ibo partisan and spread the most alarming and exaggerated report of their progress'.[509] Curran, presumably trying to avoid giving Hunt the satisfaction of knowing that his complaints might have worked, explained that Forsyth was withdrawn 'when it became impossible for him to transmit his reports, either for television or radio. There would clearly have been no point in retaining a correspondent in a place without communications.'[510] Another unlikely story: communications from the front were a problem throughout the Biafran conflict and reporters didn't give up in frustration.

Martin Bell's view four decades later is very direct and very different from that of BBC colleague John Simpson:

> I had the sense that the BBC was – in a sense that would be unthinkable now – in the government's pocket. The British High Commissioner didn't like Freddie Forsyth's reporting and Freddie was withdrawn for no good reason.
>
> I think he was an incredibly brave guy. But if that happened today, there should be more resistance now – I hope – to Foreign Office pressure. He was scapegoated. I found nothing wrong with his work at all. It was brave. He might have made a map-reading error here or there, but it was vivid, first-hand reportage. What did the British High Commissioner think? That we were supposed to report this war from one side only? No, he was scapegoated.

Forsyth's own, shorter-form, explanation is: 'They said I was biased because I contradicted the High Commissioner.'

Having read all the available files I don't believe the BBC sent Forsyth to Biafra to get the Biafran point of view but to witness what they expected to be the fall of Ojukwu's regime. One of ITN's correspondents in Biafra, Sandy Gall, later wrote in his memoirs that Forsyth's reports for the BBC 'had quite truthfully depicted a string of successes for Ojukwu'. This was not what the BBC in London or Sir David Hunt in Lagos had expected, nor was it what Harold Wilson's government wanted to hear broadcast.

Two of Forsyth's television reports that I have been able to view are energetic, vivid reportage. I could see no obvious bias in them, no breach of the principle of 'due impartiality'. On the issue of his reporting of Biafran claims, the BBC may have overlooked his experience as the Reuters man in Communist East Germany when, in Forsyth's words, 'everything that came out of the Information Ministry was propaganda, you reported it as it was, I always started my reports with the source of the claim, I never crossed the line'.

Nowadays experienced broadcasters are expected to go further than just repeating claims, especially ones that they suspect may be dubious, and even to point out when people in the news make factual mistakes. But back in 1967 rather than highlight where, say, the Biafrans might have got their facts wrong on the number of federal Nigerian jets shot down, the BBC dropped the story altogether under pressure from Lagos and London. Possibly the threat from the Nigerians to the BBC's important Lagos bureau, and with it all the BBC's coverage of the story, may well have tipped them over the edge into withdrawing Forsyth. Sitting in his high commission office in Lagos, Sir David Hunt probably took some credit for the outcome.

But, for Forsyth, the result was demotion to the ranks and a personal and professional crisis.

Volume Two: Biafra: what Frederick did next
This volume begins in a café in London in the autumn of 1967 where Forsyth sits alone over dinner. He'd discovered that British media organisations were going on a trip to Biafra organised by a Geneva-based PR company called Markpress which had won a

contract with the Biafrans to promote their cause.[511] Forsyth had proposed to his BBC news editor that he should join the trip but the idea had been rejected by senior executives. Over dinner in the café, Forsyth pondered his future:

> That was the point at which I said quite bluntly, is the BBC an independent newsgathering organisation or is it an instrument of British government?
>
> Shall I now blow quite a good career to pieces on a point of principle or shall I knuckle under and go back to the Beeb and serve out my time until I'm old and grey, with a pension and deputy head of some department inside Broadcasting House. And I sat for three hours mulling it and finally said, no. This you have bloody well got to cover or you will never be in your own eyes, in the shaving mirror, a journalist again. So I paid the bill and got a cab to Heathrow.

It's what Forsyth did when he got back to Biafra that has created the most debate among his contemporaries. Having resigned from the BBC he was no longer bound by the statutory duty to remain impartial. Like any British newspaper reporter he was free to be partial if his editors back in London agreed with his line of argument. But just how far can any journalist go in his or her commitment to a cause without losing their credibility?

Forsyth says he was primarily a 'stringer' for various British newspapers. Stringers are freelances sometimes on retainers, sometimes paid by the day. They send back copy and provide logistical support when staff reporters, often known as firemen, turn up on their patch. Forsyth and the Biafrans saw an opportunity for each other. He could cover a story which he was strongly involved in and from which he could make a living, they could use him to get their case across.

A BBC *Timewatch* programme about Biafra made in the 1990s included an interview with Patrick 'Paddy' Davies, a Nigerian Ibo who worked in the Biafran Propaganda Directorate.[512]

He told *Timewatch* that

> Biafra welcomed the foreign press because it knew these were the
> people who were supposed to help disseminate Biafran propa-
> ganda. And so, even though Biafra had only one telex line to the
> outside world, and it was very much in demand by everybody,
> Frederick Forsyth was given access to this telex line. He was given
> a Volkswagen car, which was a rare thing in Biafra, and he was
> given petrol vouchers by Ojukwu. This enhanced his work, and
> Frederick Forsyth became very, very useful as a friend of Biafra.

Michael Nicholson, who covered Biafra for ITN and, along with
Sunday Times photographer Don McCullin, brought back the
starkest images of starving children, says Forsyth was seduced by
the suffering endured by the Biafrans. He tells of encountering a
man who looked like a 'model mercenary':

> There was this guy in a tiger suit, camouflage suit, with a beret and
> dark glasses. I think he had a kerchief around his neck – very debo-
> nair – and he had a pistol, he had a revolver. And he introduced
> himself as Freddie Forsyth, which was a bit of a shock because
> that's the last thing I expected an ex-BBC man to look like. But he
> introduced himself as General Ojukwu's PR man, liaison man, the
> man between the visiting international press and General Ojukwu
> himself.[513]

On the issue of his dress code, Forsyth's response to this allegation is that Biafran officers at the front would not let anybody go
there in civilian clothes because in a jungle environment, anyone
who was 'not in a camouflage uniform' would 'stand out like a
sore thumb and attract bullets'.

On the matter of the revolver, Michael Nicholson says Forsyth
was worried about a plot to get rid of him because 'he had made
some dangerous enemies and without Ojukwu's protection they
could kill him and nobody would know how or when or where'.

I had this quote in my mind as I sat across the table from Frederick Forsyth in a BBC radio studio in November 2011 to record an interview for a Radio 4 programme, *When Reporters Cross the Line*. I asked him why he carried a gun in Biafra back in 1967. I was not expecting his answer:

'I was going to blow my own brains out rather than be taken alive by the Hausa.'

Shocked at this reply I paused for a moment to gather my thoughts before continuing.

Purvis: But that shows the extraordinary danger that you were in. And you were doing this as a freelance correspondent without any commitment to a cause?

Forsyth: If you want to cover a war, you can't just sit in a hotel. If you look at the list of dead war correspondents, it's big.

Purvis: Well, I sent some of those people to the front – including some who died, I'm sad to say – but if one of them had said to me, I'm carrying a gun because I might need to kill myself rather than be captured, I'd suspect that was time to bring them home.

Forsyth: Well, possibly you're right, but I don't think you've ever seen a body the Hausa have finished with – I have.

Then I put to him perhaps another extraordinary claim about his time in Biafra. Jeff Hulbert had found in the National Archives a previously unpublished letter in 1967 from a Mr Arbuthnott of the British high commission in Lagos to diplomats back in London. I handed it to Forsyth, who had never seen it before, and he read it out:

From Mr Arbuthnott – British High Commission in Lagos

To Mr Lewis at the Foreign and Commonwealth Office in London

Forsyth's personal support for the Biafran cause and personal affection for Odgers – his pet name for Ojukwu – are well known. He was indeed reported as having written the Biafran story in a caravan in the well-guarded grounds of Ojukwu's Umuahia home, and world press and television have both said that he holds the rank of major in the 'Biafran' army under the name Atkinson.[514]

So I put directly to the now world famous novelist: had he once been Major Atkinson of the Biafran army?

> Forsyth: No, I was not. I was never Major Atkinson. It's Tommy Atkins [laughs].
> Purvis: Meaning?
> Forsyth: Well, Tommy Atkins was a name given to a British soldier by Kipling. Private Tommy Atkins. So he, Ojukwu, mockingly called me Private Tommy Atkins. It was never Atkinson, it was never Major – it was Private Tommy Atkins.
> Purvis: Odgers, as it says he was known to you. Is that right?
> Forsyth: I may have called him that, yes. But not to his face.

So Forsyth is clear that he was never a member of the Biafran army. The term he prefers is that he was 'embedded' with them. The concept of reporters living alongside soldiers goes back to the coverage of the Crimean War in the 1850s and possibly earlier than that. In return reporters agree not to give away the soldiers' position, tactics or other military intelligence.

The word 'embedded' entered the journalistic lexicon after the Iraq War of 2003 when both the British and American armies invited reporters from countries inside the 'Coalition', though noticeably not from countries outside, to join them on the battlefield against Saddam Hussein's troops. Undoubtedly the military commanders and their political masters believed that the reporters would become bonded with the soldiers and report events from their perspective.

But this version of embedding is different from Forsyth's. During the Iraq War the reporters were certainly dependent on the military, just as Forsyth was, for food and for transport. They had no freedom of movement, they either went where the army went or they were 'unembedded'.

But at all times they were accountable to their own news desks for maintaining their editorial independence. If at any time they felt that the conditions imposed by the military were unreasonable they would have had the support of their employers for breaching the military censorship or for opting out of the pact with the military. In fact one ITN reporter in Iraq in 2003, Romilly Weeks, disobeyed an instruction from a commanding officer and filed a report which she felt he was objecting to not because it endangered his troops but because it embarrassed him. She knew she would have the support and logistical resources of ITN if she needed it.

But Forsyth had no single employer happy to bring him back to London with a new job waiting. He had to file to a number of organisations as a freelance, and to continue to do that he needed the constant logistical support of the Biafrans. That inevitably limited his options. Colonel Ojukwu paid for his accommodation, his food, his car and his petrol vouchers. There are also Commonwealth Office documents claiming that Forsyth acted as an envoy for Ojukwu, taking a message from him to a senior British diplomat in London.[515]

Some of the British correspondents in Biafra – none of them necessarily critics of Forsyth – are in no doubt about his public relations role.

Walter Schwarz of *The Guardian* wrote in his memoirs that Forsyth 'had become one of Colonel Ojukwu's propagandists'.[516] Peter Sissons, then of ITN, wrote in his that Forysth 'walked out on the BBC, put on a uniform and did his best to help the Biafrans, principally by presenting their case to the world's media'.[517] Michael Leapman, then of *The Sun*, told me, 'He was always around and he was the man to go to if you wanted interviews and other facilities that the Biafran press people couldn't fix.' Sandy Gall of ITN wrote, 'He was the only means Ojukwu had of getting his views to the rest of the world.'[518]

But Gall is also one of those with a sneaking regard for Forsyth's commitment: 'I admired his devotion to what was obviously a lost cause.'

And Martin Bell, then of the BBC, believes: 'He was soldiering for a cause he believed is right. It's not a thing that I would do. But as an individual, I thought it was rather commendable that he should risk his life in a cause that he believed in.'

I read these quotes to Forsyth and put to him that the evidence suggested that he combined freelance reporting with being, in effect, a liaison officer for the media on behalf of the Biafran side. His first response was to emphasise his role as a 'stringer' but then he paused.

> Forsyth: Slow down just one second here, if we are talking now after May 1968 then we are looking at a situation now where we have a completely new story, the starving children, did I militate for them? Too bloody right. Oh yes, I was trying to get the world to sit up and take notice of a massive human emergency, a humanitarian disaster.
>
> Purvis: So were you a campaigner for the children of Biafra?
>
> Forsyth: As much as I could be, yes.
>
> Purvis: Was that done as a campaigning journalist or as a representative of the Biafran government?
>
> Forsyth: The former.[519]

It seems that in Biafra Forsyth was at various times – and sometimes simultaneously – an independent freelance stringer, a campaigning reporter, as well as a 'fixer' for the Biafrans, an adviser to their President and a lobbyist for their cause. As conflicts of interest go, it was a full menu.

The 21st-century view would be that a reporter couldn't be all those things at the same time, certainly without being transparent about it, and not seriously compromise himself. But the rules were much greyer then.

Volume Three: Frederick gets caught up in one coup too many
In January 1970, as Nigerian troops captured one Biafran town after another, Ojukwu fled into exile leaving his deputy to

surrender. One million people are estimated to have died in the fighting or the famine over the three years of the conflict.

Forsyth ended up back in London where he met *Guardian* correspondent Walter Schwarz in a pub near Regent's Park. Schwarz recalls in his memoirs:

> I felt sorry for him – a failed journalist – and as I left I asked in a patronising way what he was up to these days. He said he was writing a novel. Oh yes (still patronising) what about? 'It's about some people trying to kill De Gaulle.' I wished him luck.[520]

The next year *The Day of the Jackal* was published. It was fiction inspired by fact, in this case a real-life attempt in Paris in 1962 to shoot the French President by right-wing opponents of French withdrawal from Algeria. It sold a lot of books, formed the basis of a successful film of the same name and provided the media with a nickname for the international terrorist Illich Ramírez Sánchez, who became universally known as 'Carlos the Jackal'.

Forsyth had been a Reuters man in France at the time of the attempted shooting in Paris and one of his later books, *The Dogs of War*, similarly made into a successful film, was also based on his real-life experiences reporting the mercenaries in the Biafra war.

But in 1978 the *Sunday Times* Insight Team alleged that Forsyth's connection with mercenaries from his days in Biafra went much deeper than this. According to the newspaper, he had provided a quarter of a million dollars towards a plot to overthrow the then President of Equatorial Guinea in 1972. The *Sunday Times* named the organiser of the plot as a Scottish mercenary, Alexander Gay, who, it said, had met Forsyth in Biafra. Gay had allegedly ordered an arsenal of weapons – automatic rifles, light machine guns, mortars, bazookas and 40,000 rounds of ammunition – and recruited mercenaries and former Biafran soldiers. Forsyth's own objective, it was said, was to provide 'a

new homeland for the defeated Biafrans'. However, the mercenaries were arrested in a boat off the Canary Islands and the coup
never happened.[521]

There were similarities between this narrative and the plot of
The Dogs of War, published two years later, although in the novel
the coup actually happened and the motive was mineral wealth,
not helping Biafrans.

Forsyth denied the *Sunday Times* story and his former literary
agent, Bryan Hunt, said that Forsyth was too mean to have loaned
anybody a quarter of a million dollars: 'To imagine Freddie
giving anyone ten pence would be amazing.'

However a few years later, Forsyth was quoted as admitting
that he had indeed played a small part in the aborted coup
attempt, posing as a South African arms-dealer. It was said he
had done this to help gather research for a novel.

The twists in this tale continued into the next century.

In 2004 the former mercenary and British Army officer Simon
Mann organised an attempted coup in the very same country,
Equatorial Guinea. It bore a striking resemblance to what was
said to be Forsyth and Gay's plan. It ended the same way when
the mercenaries were arrested on their way to west Africa, though
this time it was in Zimbabwe.

Then in 2009 Forsyth happened to be in the west African state
of Guinea-Bissau, again to research a novel, when the President
was assassinated. Always a foreign correspondent, he telephoned
one thousand words of copy to a British newspaper about what
he had seen. 'Unfortunately the American intelligence services
listened to it and wasted my wife's computer screen.' He has no
proof of this unusual cyber-attack.[522]

The following year, in August 2010, when Forsyth sat down
to record a half-hour interview with Stephen Sackur for the BBC
programme *HARDtalk*, there was a lot to talk about.[523]

Sackur was well briefed. The programme's opening included the
line: 'Fact or fiction, has Frederick Forsyth sometimes blurred
the lines?' Sackur started this revealing encounter by raising the

allegations that Forsyth had once funded an attempted coup in
Equatorial Guinea:

> Sackur: The truth is, when you were researching *The Dogs of
> War*, about a bunch of mercenaries involved in a plot to topple a
> west African regime, you were actively in touch with a bunch of
> real-life mercenaries and you have said to respected journalists in
> the not so distant past that you gave that man money. The man
> we are talking about of course is Alexander Gay. Did you give
> him money?
> Forsyth: Yes.
> Sackur: You in a sense were financing him.
> Forsyth: Well, not that much.
> Sackur: How much did you give him?
> Forsyth: Never mind, it was information. I rarely, rarely buy infor-
> mation but this was necessary. I wanted to find out exactly what
> was going on in order to make a contribution, so I did.
> Sackur: There's an ethical problem here, isn't there?
> Forsyth: No.
> Sackur: You knew this man was plotting to bring down a govern-
> ment and you handed him money.
> Forsyth: I knew it wasn't going to happen.
> Sackur: How did you know that?
> Forsyth: Because it was impossible, it just wasn't going to happen.
> Sackur: In your books it's not impossible.
> Forsyth: In the book you can make it happen, but you look at
> something and say it's not going to happen, it's not going to go
> forward, so I watched and it didn't, it was discontinued.
> Sackur: It was discontinued because British intelligence got wind
> of it, and it was intercepted.

They then debated the rights and wrongs of Forsyth standing bail
for Alexander Gay when Gay was charged after depositing a case
at a left luggage office. 'I was prepared to believe that the man
was minding a suitcase for someone else but he shouldn't have

been, it was a stupid thing to do, he put it in a left luggage office, it was discovered, there was a live firearm inside it.'

Did he cross a line in that relationship? Forsyth explained it was a matter of loyalty: Gay had once 'pulled me out of a hole in a combat situation and I might not be here but for that'.

Forsyth pointed out thirty years after he had helped to fund Gay's planned coup in Equatorial Guinea there had been another failed coup, also penetrated by intelligence agencies which he called 'Mr Simon Mann's attempt to knock over the same island, funnily enough'.

And what of the strange events in the night in Guinea-Bissau in 2010 when Forsyth happened to be in the capital as the army killed the President because they thought he'd been behind the death of one of their generals?

Sackur wondered if some people thought there might be a connection between Forsyth's arrival and the fighting.

Forsyth denied any involvement but volunteered that he thought the Americans did believe there was a connection. He explained that he'd filed a report on the fighting to the London *Daily Express*, where he was a columnist. 'Everything up there in the ether is intercepted, probably by the National Security Agency in Fort Meade, Maryland.' When he got back to his farm in Berkshire he discovered his wife's computer had ceased to function, which he blamed on the Americans though he accepted he had no proof. He thought they were suspicious because of his 'bit of previous in west Africa'.

As one of the *HARDtalk* team, Bridget Osborne concluded in an article for the BBC website: 'To paraphrase Oscar Wilde badly, to be involved in one West African coup attempt and for that to be found out might be considered a misfortune, but to be caught up in what appears to be a second West African coup attempt looks like carelessness.'

By then Forsyth was no longer a practising journalist, but a very successful novelist, who was also politically active and vocal.[524] Some of his novels were inspired by real events but he was now unashamedly a man of fiction. Was the novelist researching plots for his latest book still governed by any of those values that influenced his earlier career? He didn't seem to think so. In fact the marketing of his books was probably helped by the speculation about what exactly he had been up to in Africa. But one thing is certain: this particular Forsyth Saga may be factually accurate, but it seems too far-fetched for any Edwardian novelist or any modern thriller-writer to have dreamed it up.

9

MARTIN BELL

He was one of the BBC's most famous and respected foreign correspondents and was at the high point of his career. Viewers noticed his distinctive 'lucky' white suit and admired his calmness under fire, especially when his luck ran out and he was wounded by shrapnel. One newspaper columnist wrote that he was 'one of the very few journalists employed to stand in front of television cameras who can properly and with pride be described as a reporter'.[525]

But when Martin Bell got a phone call in 1992 from the editor of *Panorama*, it was very much what he called 'the PBI' (poor bloody infantry) of television news being addressed by the 'officer class' of television current affairs.[526]

During his career Bell had already been on the battlefields of Biafra, Vietnam and Kuwait. Now he was in Bosnia where the biggest armed conflict in Europe since the Second World War was taking place. But he'd only ever made one film for *Panorama*, the BBC's flagship current affairs programme. By his own admission it was a failure.[527] Back in 1974 he'd been made a 'temporary member of the officer class' for a programme to mark the first five years of the 'Troubles' in Northern Ireland. He seemed a natural choice as the BBC news reporter who'd spent most time there reporting how the civil rights campaign of the late '60s, the arrival of British troops and the IRA bombing and shooting campaigns of the early '70s had evolved into what Bell called 'the closest thing to a civil war inside the UK'.[528]

That programme, in his own words, 'set out where we had

come from and where we stood' but 'when the final titles had
rolled, what had been the point of it? There wasn't one.' He
concluded that the fault had been his because his programme
'really had nothing to say'.

Now, eighteen years later, the latest editor of *Panorama* was
offering Bell another chance at current affairs. Glenwyn Benson
asked if he would 'do her a Bosnia'. The conflict in the former
Yugoslavia was a subject on which Bell would definitely have
something to say. He was excited: 'No conditions, no instructions,
no preconceived notions or prescriptive shadows falling across
my path. It was a journalistic blank cheque.'[529] What Martin Bell
wrote on that blank cheque was to start an ethical debate that
has lasted right up until the present day. It has stirred up strong
feelings among his closest colleagues and divided opinion among
other journalists. Most significantly it has revealed a confusion
about what one of the BBC's priorities, its commitment to 'due
impartiality', actually means. As recently as July 2012 one of
Bell's editors, who had subsequently become an academic, was to
write, with some understatement, 'There is much confusion over
terms.'[530]

The Bells were newspaper people. Martin's grandfather was
a news editor on *The Observer* and his father, Adrian, invented
the *Times* crossword, but Martin was a BBC journalist. He has
said that he got his first job, in the BBC newsroom in Norwich in
1962, because the editor there was the father of an ex-girlfriend.
It was like that in those days. Six years earlier the then director-
general of the BBC, Hugh Carleton Greene, who had a home
in East Anglia, watched the output and was so shocked that he
sent along a senior editor from London to instruct the Norwich
newsroom in the basics of television journalism.

The instructor would have had available the in-house guide to
journalism, 'The Radio Newsroom, News Guide'. The versions of
this pamphlet which were produced in the 1960s never provided
a clear definition of impartiality. Rather the reverse. The authors
believed that broadcast journalism was about what you selected

to transmit and that 'to couple the word selection with the word impartial would seem to be a paradox. Any selection must, of its nature, be to some degree partial.' [531]

But it did offer one helpful clarification to young journalists like Bell: 'Impartiality must not be confused with neutrality. We are not pallid neutrals in regard to matters which offend the national conscience. We are not neutral in regard to crime, and to the sins of cruelty and racial hatred.'

As Martin Bell's career moved on from Norwich to London, to Washington and the world's trouble spots, he learned that the BBC's independence wasn't always clear cut.

When in 1966 he was sent to his first armed conflict, the Nigerian Civil War between the breakaway Biafran state and the federal authorities in Lagos, he 'had the sense that the BBC was – in a sense that would be unthinkable now – in the government's pocket'. [532] Harold Wilson's government was on the federal side.

Going up to a line

By contrast, nearly three decades later the British government of John Major wasn't on any side in Bosnia. Instead this was a conflict which ministers preferred to stay as far away from as possible. In their minds, much greater events were going on. The Berlin Wall had just fallen, Germany was reuniting, Britain and America had just defeated Saddam Hussein's troops in Kuwait. Privately some recalled parallels with Neville Chamberlain's comment during the Munich crisis of 1938 that the dispute over the Sudetenland (part of Czechoslovakia) was 'a quarrel in a far-away country between people of whom we know nothing'.[533] Publicly the British Foreign Secretary, Douglas Hurd, said the British government rejected three policy options for Bosnia: sending in troops to impose a peace, sending material support to one side or another, and doing nothing. 'We made a fourth choice. We decided to save civilian lives by supporting the humanitarian aid effort. At the same time we mobilised ideas and pressures for a negotiated settlement.'[534]

The United Nations sent in a 'protection force' (UNPROFOR)

with priorities such as supplying humanitarian help for civilians and orders which avoided military confrontation with the rival factions. British troops joined UNPROFOR as part of Mr Hurd's 'fourth choice'.

If it had ever come to deciding which of the Serbs, the Croats, the Muslims and, for a brief bloody spell, the Slovenes were the villains of this almost tribal conflict then British public opinion would probably have picked out the Serbs.

In Martin Bell's view the Serbs 'started this war, they killed and they burned and they ethnically cleansed' but 'they didn't hold monopoly rights on evil'. He concluded that 'the Serbs were demonised by themselves as well as by others. But such is the nature of television that some of the coverage of the war was quite literally weighted against them.'[535]

To his credit Bell tried, at some personal risk, to resist this weighting. He said that he always made a habit of talking to the 'supposed bad guys' in conflicts he reported so he spent a lot of time with the Serbs.

During internal BBC debates about the shape of the *Panorama* programme he argued against 'constructing a charge sheet against the Serbs in the form of a forty-minute video-prosecution'.[536] Instead he would prepare a report which showed what was happening and heard from all sides. The climax would be what he called a final 'peroration'. He would put the case for a form of military intervention by the outside world that would go much beyond 'peacekeeping'.

Bell began by asking in a piece to camera, 'Is it time to cut and run or to intervene?' He seemed to answer his own question when in his final piece to camera, delivered in a ruined building, he concluded, 'The case for intervention is not to help one side against the other, but the weak against the strong, the unarmed against the armed, to champion the everyday victims of this war who until today have had no protection. It is fundamentally a question of whether we care.'[537]

His report, 'Forcing a Peace', shown to millions of primetime TV viewers, had an immediate impact in Britain.

Peter McKay of the *London Evening Standard* admitted he didn't see it 'but everyone is talking about it. Mr Bell's report – according to all I have spoken to who saw it – more or less said: "Right, let's go."'[538]

Andrew Marr in *The Independent* had seen it, called it 'the strongest, most harrowing piece of filmed journalism yet to come out of Bosnia' and was in no doubt about Bell's message: '"Peace-making has failed. Negotiation has failed. Diplomacy has failed…" Then he called for military intervention.'[539]

In *The Times*, columnist Simon Jenkins called it 'a ferocious plea by a brave reporter for the world to intervene' but believed Bell's conclusion was 'a tendentious assertion'. Jenkins thought Bell would say he was unbiased but in fact 'he was biased', 'he wanted to blot out thought'. Like Bell, Jenkins had a powerful conclusion:

> Mr Bell claims that intervening is a sign of caring. I disagree. It means in Bosnia asking soldiers to risk their lives and more Bosnian lives, merely to get a particular pile of corpses off the nation's screen. That is not caring. It is a way of trying not to care.[540]

This produced a counter-blast from John Naughton in *The Observer*, who supported 'an unforgettable film by Martin Bell' against Simon Jenkins, 'an egregious little swot who once edited *The Times*'.[541]

The editor of *Panorama*, Glenwyn Benson, wrote to *The Times* to respond to Jenkins's criticism of Bell and his way of getting the audience's attention. She said the 'saturation coverage of diplomatic and military details' could induce a different kind of bias against understanding: 'a sense of helplessness and even boredom among the public. Martin Bell's programme corrected that by reclaiming viewers' attention so dramatically to the subject. It is a legitimate function of current affairs to enable people to connect via the camera with what is really happening.'[542]

This was endorsement indeed for Bell from his masters in London.

Two decades later at the Frontline Club in London I sat down with Martin Bell to record an interview about impartiality. The years had not diminished his commitment that he was right to have said what he said back in 1993 in Sarajevo in the ruins of the city's main library.

Bell: It was a very critical time, it was the first winter of the war, Sarajevo was dying under bombardment, people were starving and I was later accused of crossing the line of calling for intervention. Well, if you actually look at the words, I never did. I said if we intervene, such and such are the consequences and if we don't, such and such are the consequences and it is a question fundamentally of whether we care. End of script.

Purvis: You started with a piece to camera that says, 'Is it time to cut and run or to intervene?' Those were the opening two options you set out. But I suppose there was a third option which you could characterise as muddling along. But by not including that option, you were in a sense ruling out that option, weren't you?

Bell: Because I didn't think the middle option was tenable. And if you look back, I mean this was a war in a small country in which we know that 98,000 people died and two million were driven from their homes. There was no middle option and it was folly to suppose there was under an inadequate mandate. I proposed what I thought were the two tenable options – either we got on or we got out. I suppose looking back I could have said we carry on as we are. But I'd showed so much of where we were at that particular time, it was obvious from the images that carrying on as we were was not an option.

Purvis: OK, I think it's worth quoting the final piece to camera: 'The case for intervention is not to help one side against the other, but the weak against the strong, the unarmed against the armed, to champion the everyday victims of this war who until today have had no protection. It is fundamentally, a question of whether we care.' Now I can't come to any other conclusion than that you support the case for intervention because you seem to be saying that if I don't support the case for intervention, I don't care.

Bell: Yeah, do we care or don't we? I think that goes up to a line, but it doesn't cross a line.[543]

I also interviewed one of Martin's BBC colleagues, Michael Buerk, and read him that final piece to camera.

Buerk: I would want to watch that programme and I wouldn't want to stop that programme going out. But it placed Martin in a position where he is not simply a reporter, he is an advocate. I have reservations about that anyway, but one of the reservations is that it is very difficult to scramble back into being a dispassionate reporter again.

I highlighted to Michael Buerk the use of the word 'care' in Martin Bell's last sentence, the implication being that if you care you must agree with intervention. He replied, 'Yes. That's verging on the manipulative ... It's you either agree with me or you're a heartless uncaring person.'

Martin Bell is still unapologetic, believing that he went 'up to a line' but didn't cross it. He told me, 'It was a considered analysis deriving from my experience in that war, week in week out, month in month out since the previous April. It was a considered and quite cool analysis – it's quite coolly delivered as well. No, I'd stand by every word of it – even now.'

In the early 1990s the British Foreign Secretary, Douglas Hurd, became a staple diet of British television news as he arrived for and departed from European Union meetings about Bosnia. He was facing increasing criticism in British newspapers over what was seen as his overcautious policy in the Balkans.

The Foreign Secretary decided on a fightback. He decided to launch it at an event at the Travellers Club in London, one of the oldest gentlemen's clubs in Pall Mall. It was founded in 1819 'to provide a meeting place for gentlemen who had travelled abroad' and the original rules included the restriction 'that no person be considered eligible who shall not have travelled out of the British

Islands to a distance of at least 500 miles from London in a direct line'.[544]

Hurd spoke to the club in private but to make sure his words got a wider audience the Foreign Office faxed his speech to news organisations.

Hurd told the Travellers Club that journalists had become the founder members of the 'something-must-be-done school', pushing for military intervention in Bosnia. 'We have not been, and are not, willing to begin some form of military intervention which we judge useless or worse, simply because of day-to-day pressures from the media.'[545]

In the text that was sent out in advance Hurd named the offenders: 'Most of those who report for the BBC, *The Times*, *The Independent*, *The Guardian*, have been in different ways enthusiasts for pushing military intervention in Bosnia, whether by air or on the ground.' But according to one media commentator, when Hurd actually made the speech, 'years of diplomatic training got the better of him and he left out the names of the guilty parties'.[546]

It didn't matter. Everyone who needed to know did know who he was talking about. A week later BBC correspondent John Simpson gave a lecture, Making News, to the Royal Television Society, in which he put the name of Martin Bell into the public debate. He recalled the *Panorama* film on Bosnia, which he said was 'quite intentionally a personal view'. Simpson went on, 'He indeed wanted something done. It was clearly labelled as his private opinion. The rest of his reporting, as with every other BBC correspondent who has been there, had been perfectly objective.'[547]

The next month Bell himself replied to Mr Hurd with customary gusto. 'We have been described by Mr Hurd as founder members of the "something-must-be-done school". Surrounded by so much misery and destruction, it is humanly difficult to be anything else, but to want to see an end to it.'

Bell said the journalists were certainly not out to 'get the government'. But he couldn't resist tweaking the Foreign Secretary's tail about British policy in Bosnia:

> I understand very well that the government, under many pressures, including those generated by television, is probably doing as much as it can: Britain has, after all, the largest of all the UN contingents now in Bosnia: or to put it another way, as little as it can get away with.[548]

Martin Bell's comments appeared to have no impact on Douglas Hurd's policy. More than a year later, in December 1994, the Foreign Secretary was still arguing in an article in *The Independent* that negotiation was still a better option in Bosnia than escalation of the war or a withdrawal by the West. Britain could, at least, still help save civilian lives. 'Something must be done is not a policy. I do not meet many people who want the British Army to go to war in the Balkans. There is no just outcome that we can be sure of achieving.'[549]

Yet within a year the British Army, with its allies, had gone to war in the Balkans. It turned out to be a very short war that achieved quite a lot.

While the Bosnia debate had raged in the policy salons of London, back on the streets of Sarajevo the killing had carried on. UNPROFOR did its best but mostly stood by and watched, and sometimes, as in the case of the Serb massacre of Muslims at Srebrenica in July 1995, even vacated a so-called 'safe zone' to the killers and their 'ethnic cleansing'. It was the worst massacre of the war and this seemed like a turning point. NATO finally bombed the Serb positions around Sarajevo, which allowed the Muslim and Croat troops to advance. The Serbs agreed to talks and by the end of the year all sides had signed the Dayton peace accord. Martin Bell would have been entitled to say 'I told you so two years ago.'

Attachment and impartiality

Instead he sat down 'to reflect more than usual on the life that I have lived'. The Bosnian war had 'mattered to me more than anything else I have lived through, and still does'. The result was a book, *In Harm's Way*, published in October 1995. Inevitably Bell's story from Bosnia took up most of the book but at the end of a paragraph on page 128 there was a brief but wider passing thought. 'In the news business it isn't involvement but indifference that makes for bad practice. Good journalism is the journalism of *attachment*. It is not only knowing, but also caring.'[550]

The term was never used again in the book and was never explained beyond that single sentence about knowing and caring. Yet deciding what exactly the journalism of attachment was and whether you were in favour of it or against it became a continuing thread in journalistic debate in Britain for many years. The lighting of the fuse for the debate came a year after the book's publication at Newsworld '96, a conference in Berlin attended by 500 international broadcasters. By now Bell had tendered his resignation to the BBC because he felt sidelined after leaving Bosnia. He planned to leave the corporation two months later.

As he spoke, I was sitting near the front of the hall taking notes. As the editor-in-chief of the BBC's rival, ITN, I was concerned by the attacks Martin Bell was making on the integrity of some of my reporters. I feared that this would become the major talking point of the conference. I needn't have worried. A bigger story was about to break.

Martin Bell turned his guns on what he called 'bystanders' journalism' which concerned itself 'more with the circumstances of war than with the people'. He did not believe reporters 'should stand neutrally between good and evil, right and wrong, aggressor and victim'.

Bell once wrote, 'Let me declare an interest; all the reporters who work regularly on the Bosnian beat are, at least privately, interventionist.'[551]

For some newspaper correspondents there was no problem in abandoning neutrality and making their private view public. That was what some of them were paid to do.

But these were broadcasters gathered in the conference hall in Berlin and the British ones were, like many of their international counterparts, required by law to remain 'impartial'.

When the session was opened up to questions from the floor, a young man to my left got up and identified himself as Lucian Hudson, a senior editor on the BBC's international 24-hour television channel, BBC World.

He attacked the 'journalism of attachment' as 'very risky'. Martin Bell sounded to him 'like a celibate priest who at a certain stage in his life has decided to go and bonk. The temptation to get engaged is just too great and he wants to get stuck in.'[552]

Bell responded, 'Now you know why I prefer to work in war zones rather than the BBC. In war zones I only have to watch my front.' He later wrote of the incident that he had been 'set upon from the floor by a middle-ranking BBC executive who clearly saw me as a heretic and backslider from long-established truths. He compared me to a priest who had grown weary of the long years of celibacy and had resolved to explore the carnal pleasures hitherto denied.'[553] Despite his views on middle-ranking BBC executives, a month later Bell withdrew his resignation when a new roving reporting role for him was agreed.

Bell's colleagues on the BBC's reporting front line were slow to come forward in support of 'the journalism of attachment'. Partly, one suspects, they weren't clear what exactly the journalism was attached to. Was it to one side or another, or was it simply to caring? As one media commentator, John Lloyd, later put it, 'To what do reporters decide to be attached?' [554]

Bell's concept even earned a place in a history of propaganda by the media academic Professor Philip Taylor. He interpreted Bell as 'effectively arguing for the media actively to serve a propagandist role: propaganda for peace'.[555] The 'journalism of attachment' certainly sounded like a journalism of advocacy. More like counsel for the prosecution or the defence rather than the court reporter or a judge's even-handed summing up.

John Simpson of the BBC, who had defended Bell over Douglas Hurd's attack, said that 'Martin Bell is talking nonsense and he knows it'.[556]

A former BBC correspondent, Robert Fox, later said, 'I am at deep difference with my colleague and friend, Martin Bell, because he coined the phrase "journalism of attachment".'[557]

In 2011 I asked former BBC foreign correspondent Michael Buerk what he thought the term meant: 'I haven't the faintest idea. I've never had the faintest idea about Martin and his journalism of attachment.'[558]

Martin Bell's most considered views on his craft came in a 1997 'FOOC' – an eight-minute audio essay for *From Our Own Correspondent*. He called it 'The Truth Is Our Currency'.

With hindsight, what is most striking about the essay is that Bell rejected some ethical concepts but then went on to embrace others which sounded very similar. He began:

> Let me start with a heresy. I was trained in a tradition of objective and dispassionate journalism. I believed in it. I don't believe in it any more. But from where I have been since and what I have seen I would describe it as a sort of bystanders' journalism, unequal to the challenges of the times.

It appeared that he rejected objectivity. 'Objective? I'm not sure what it means. I see nothing object-like in the relationship between the reporter and the event, rather I use my eyes and ears and mind and stored experience, which is surely the very essence of the subjective.'

So he rejected objectivity but then he appeared to go on to embrace impartiality: 'What I do believe in still and hold fast to more than ever is fairness and impartiality, and a scrupulous attention to the facts, and a determination to pay heed to the unpopular spokesmen of unfavoured causes.'

And just to be certain he reminded the listener of the BBC's statutory commitment to impartiality: 'Fairness and impartiality remain our abiding principles and besides in our coverage of domestic politics they are obligations laid on us quite properly by law.'[559]

So Bell believed he was definitely impartial but deliberately not objective. It was to be many years before anybody offered a clear way through this definitional maze.

In 2007, an 81-page report on impartiality produced for the BBC Trust said, 'Fortunately this report is not required to provide an elaborate definition.' Impartiality was 'an elusive, almost magical substance, which is often more evident in its absence than in its presence'.[560]

For a time the BBC College of Journalism website included a video, 'Introducing Impartiality', in which Evan Davis introduced a new concept called 'Impartiality with Attitude' in which reporters could demonstrate 'attitude' while remaining impartial. By 2012 the video no longer appeared on the site.[561]

The site did say in 2012 that 'impartiality is not the same as objectivity or balance or neutrality, although it contains elements of all three.' But the differences and similarities were not explained.[562]

Kevin Marsh, the former editor of one of the BBC's flagship programmes, *Today*, has cited examples of 'how the BBC's defining value of impartiality had, by the turn of this century, become so complex and differentially understood that even the BBC's governors didn't quite understand it and found it difficult to apply in practice'.[563]

It was Richard Sambrook who, as head of BBC Newsgathering, had been one of Bell's editors through the turbulent years in Bosnia, and who tried to bring some light to these confused proceedings. Sambrook had gone on to become the director of BBC News during what became known as 'Hutton' (*see Chapter 13*) and by 2012 was director of the Centre for Journalism at Cardiff University. He wrote a paper on impartiality and objectivity in the digital age in which he explained that 'impartiality' and 'objectivity' are used interchangeably, 'although they mean different things and are used differently in the US from the UK'.[564]

Sambrook offered two short-form definitions: impartiality was 'the removal of bias' whereas objectivity was 'a disciplined approach to isolate evidence and facts'. On that basis he politely concluded that 'there seems to be confusion' in Bell's conviction that he no longer believed in objectivity. In fact, rather than be against objectivity, 'the identification of facts and evidence seems to be exactly what Martin Bell supports'.

The former news editor, helping to clear up what one of his reporters really meant to say fifteen years earlier, then turned his attention to Bell's views on 'impartiality'. In his 'FOOC' Bell had said he was in favour of it. But Sambrook argued that in reality Bell was concerned about it because the absence of bias or opinion about facts 'produces a value-free moral equivalence between good and evil'. He quoted Bell's own reporting of a massacre in Bosnia which, he said, was 'a model of how to avoid moral equivalence in journalism that was still framed by objectivity and impartiality'. Bell had reported:

> It's hard to look at some of these pictures. Harder to tell the story of Ahmici without them. What happened here can frankly not be shown in any detail. But the room is full of charred remains of bodies and they died in the greatest agony. It's hard to imagine in our continent and in our time what kind of people could do this.[565]

If one accepts Richard Sambrook's 2012 definitions the logical conclusion is that Martin Bell was right in maintaining that his 1993 *Panorama* did not 'cross a line'. He had been both objective because his judgement was based on facts and evidence and impartial because he had not been biased. He had also avoided 'value-free moral equivalence'.

Echoing that conclusion the current BBC guideline on impartiality says that BBC staff 'may offer professional judgements rooted in evidence. However it is not normally appropriate for them to write or present personal view programmes ... on controversial subjects in any area.'[566] Bell's final piece to camera would appear to have been a 'professional judgement rooted in evidence' rather than a 'personal view' even if at the time his colleague John Simpson said it clearly was.

Martin Bell has, however, owned up to one crossing of a line and his admission came in a rather unlikely place, on an imaginary desert island, between listening to 'Rock of Ages' by the 'Queen of Gospel', Mahalia Jackson, and 'On the Road Again' by the

American country singer Willie Nelson. On *Desert Island Discs* in July 2001 Bell looked back on his career and explained how in 1980 he had been in El Salvador when fifty people were crushed to death after shots were fired at a crowd attending the funeral of the campaigning Catholic archbishop Oscar Romero. Bell said, 'I reproached myself afterwards, saying surely you could have done something to help people.'

So when in Bosnia he saw 20,000 people being driven from their homes,

> obviously I felt guilty that I was unable to help them. I was the only person there with a set of wheels, I convinced myself that it was important to get the story out and I was editing it and this UN official, Colm Doyle, who later became a very good friend of mine, an Irish army officer, arrived, checked in, I rushed down, I said look what's happening, you can't let it happen, go and see the Serbs, tell them to stop them doing it, and that's not really a journalistic function ... I crossed the line.[567]

Twenty years after his Bosnia *Panorama*, Martin Bell was still prepared to stand up for what he said. He was still proud to be a member of the 'something-must-be-done club'. He said, 'I find the company I keep there more honourable, and easier to live with, than those who associate with the opposing faction, the "Nothing Can Be Done Club".'[568] There was no mention of a 'Here's what's happening, I'll leave it to you to decide' club.

As for any longer-term legacy of his work, Bell light-heartedly and rather modestly offered this forecast in a book of his poems:

> When I'm gone I hope you'll pause a minute,
> And say, sadly not to my face,
> The world is a slightly less worse place because of my time in it,
> But just as probably you'll recall,
> I made no bloody difference at all.[569]

10

SIDNEY BERNSTEIN

On his way to a seat in the House of Lords, Baron Bernstein caused more trouble than anyone in the history of British commercial television. The evidence is in the files of past broadcasting regulators stored safely in the archive section of Bournemouth University.

To the staff of Granada Television Sidney Bernstein was the founder of their company, a giant of a figure in their creative lives. But the archives reveal that, to the authorities, 'all who work on Granada's current affairs seem to some extent to carry the Bernstein chip on their shoulders'. This was to be a constant issue for two decades.

An example is provided by a script for Granada's regional news for the north of England on 24 November 1965. What was transmitted on Granada's *Scene at Six Thirty* that day was out of the ordinary for a number of reasons.

The script, read by two presenters in a studio in Manchester, had nothing to do with the north of England. It was about the next day's elections in Northern Ireland.

To produce an item, any item, about Northern Ireland politics on British television in 1965 – before the civil rights protests and the subsequent IRA campaign made global news – was most unusual; certainly the BBC discouraged network producers from enquiring too much into the politics of the province.

Some of the terminology used in the script, such as references to Northern Ireland as the 'six counties', was that of the minority nationalist community.

Importantly, the item was probably the most devastating critique of the province's government ever broadcast at that time. It talked of the Unionist Party being 'the political arm of the Orange Movement ... which for forty-four years has ruled Ulster from Stormont'. Roman Catholics were described as being 'victims of a religious apartheid which stops them from getting the best jobs or adequate living conditions'.

An independent historian would probably conclude that, with hindsight, this was a fair analysis of the situation in Northern Ireland in 1965 as the leader of the Unionist Party, Captain Terence O'Neill, was making the very first tentative steps towards reform.

But history also records that the then regulator, the Independent Television Authority (ITA), 'concluded that the item failed to exercise due impartiality (Section 3 (1) (f) of the Television Act) and that it editorialised contrary to Section 3 (2)'. The broadcast had, after all, according to the ITA, 'given great offence to the Government of Northern Ireland'.[570]

Sidney Lewis Bernstein was never a reporter himself but as one of the major figures in the British media for three decades – from cinemas to TV and publishing – he fought a relentless battle with the authorities over what the journalists he employed could say on the air.

Ray Fitzwalter, one of Granada's most distinguished journalists, wrote that 'Sidney Bernstein was born with a silver screen in his mouth, having inherited a small cinema chain'.[571] It was 1922; Bernstein's father, a Jewish immigrant from Latvia, had died and Sidney, then aged just twenty-three, took control of the family's twenty cinemas around Britain. He started Saturday morning film shows for children. The name *Granada* was, according to company mythology, inspired by a walking tour which Bernstein made of southern Spain.[572]

Through the Film Society, which he founded in 1925, Bernstein got to know everyone who counted in the movie business and when war broke out he appeared to be a natural choice to become the film adviser to Winston Churchill and his coalition government. One of the roles was choosing films for Churchill to watch for relaxation at weekends. But the appointment was not so straightforward. MI5 was worried. A Security Service report from 1936 released from MI5 files in 2010 said, 'Sidney Bernstein is now reliably reported to be an active secret Communist ... He always cuts the news films in his cinemas so that Fascist scenes etc. which might make a favourable impression are removed. Items about Russia are given prominence.'[573]

The MI5 dossier said Bernstein had helped the Soviet embassy to vet journalists applying to go to Moscow and had provided funds for a Czech-German agitator named Otto Katz. Bernstein renounced any links with the Communist Party in 1939 when the Soviet Union signed the non-aggression pact with Germany but MI5 said, 'It would be unwise to accept this statement at face value.'[574]

Bernstein undoubtedly had Communist friends and was involved in projects that had Communist support but there is no hard evidence he was ever a party member. He did belong to the Labour Party and was a local councillor in London in the 1930s.

Despite MI5's concern he was confirmed in the wartime film adviser role, and set about it with real vigour. The British government through the Ministry of Information (MOI) and the Foreign Office wanted to influence American opinion in favour of Britain, but the view in New York was that the Germans were much more effective in sending their newsreels over by air than the British. The German newsreels also had better war coverage, partly because of what one British official called 'the German system of placing cameramen (and killing them off) in the front line of every advance'.[575] The British propagandists were very keen to monitor the output of their Nazi equivalents. Sidney Bernstein had the answer.

He arranged that German newsreels sent to America via neutral Portugal would be intercepted in Lisbon, flown back to Britain and copied, and the originals then flown back to Portugal and put back into the distribution chain without anybody noticing. The idea worked for six months until a film-handler in Portugal spotted that the film had been through British hands from notes in English which someone back in Britain had accidently left attached to the film.[576]

In 1945 Bernstein was with Allied troops who entered the Belsen concentration camp. He had been working with the Psychological Warfare Division of the Allied forces. He told his commanders, 'My personal opinion is that we need a first-class documentary record of these atrocities and we cannot be content with the rather crude and un-thought-out newsreel so far shown.' He wanted it to be shown to German civilians, who, in his view, were still in denial that they knew what had been happening in the camps. In the film he wanted, for example, to name the German companies who made the incinerators for the death camps. He called a friend, Alfred Hitchcock, for advice on the editing. No detail was overlooked, nothing was left to chance. But there was a problem ahead.

The British government was initially in support of the project. However, as time went on some officials argued that as the British wanted the Germans on their side in rebuilding the country, why denounce them to their faces? Bernstein pushed on with the film but he was told there was 'no hurry for it'. He 'didn't take kindly' to this. The British government finally shelved the production and never showed it publicly. This probably wasn't Sidney Bernstein's first battle with authority about what should be shown on a screen, but it wouldn't be his last.

We beg to differ

In 1948 Granada applied for a licence for a TV station but this was only 'to transmit films to our various Granada theatres' from a central control room. A clever idea, years ahead of its time and one which would have saved Granada a lot of money on prints and projectors, but not exactly a TV network as we know it. Nothing much came of it.

In 1949 when the Beveridge Committee on broadcasting was set up, Bernstein's politics overruled his business instincts. Instead of joining the growing campaign for a commercial, advertising-funded television network, Granada took the Labour Party line on the need for state control of broadcasting and argued that 'the right of access to the domestic sound and television receivers of millions of people carries with it such great propaganda power that it cannot be trusted to any persons or bodies other than a public corporation or a number of public corporations'.[577]

When in 1953 the Conservative government made it clear that it didn't agree and that commercial television would be allowed, based on regional franchises, Bernstein did an elegant about-turn: 'It seemed prudent to update our application for a licence, to keep it alive.' When Granada duly won the licence for the north of England part of the new ITV network and went on the air in May 1956, Bernstein made a gesture to his previous belief in solely public broadcasting by ensuring that one of the first Granada programmes shown was a tribute to the BBC.

Sidney Bernstein was now absolutely in his element. He had his own TV station with its own headquarters in the centre of Manchester. He talked as if he had his own country – 'Granadaland' – stretching from Liverpool to Hull. When in later years the franchise map was changed and the eastern half was hived off into a separate area from Granadaland, Bernstein observed, perhaps half-jokingly, that 'if the territory of Granada is interfered with in any way we shall go to the United Nations'.[578]

Not that the chairman of Granada needed to spend undue amounts of time in Granadaland. He would fly in on the Granada plane from Kent, spend two or three days in Manchester then fly home. For many years he refused to appoint any directors who lived locally in the region.

Ray Fitzwalter has written that working for Granada 'was like being employed by the Arts Council one week and a second-hand clothes shop the next'. Broadcasting was 'a moral and cultural imperative' delivered under rigid cost control. Bernstein would tell staff there was too much sand in the fire buckets and that pencils should be cut in half to get best value for money.[579]

But Bernstein reserved his main fire for what was known simply as 'the authority'. One colleague later reflected, 'In Sidney's view Granada was a sovereign state, proudly independent and morally at least the equal of any Broadcasting Authority.'

The Independent Television Authority files at Bournemouth University are littered with exchanges of fire between the two sides, mostly arising from the statute which the ITA judged Granada had breached, not for the first time, when it transmitted its analysis of Northern Ireland to the viewers of northern England.

The key clause was included in the first Television Act of 1954: 'All news given in the programmes, (in whatever form) is presented with due accuracy and impartiality.' This was the first time that such a requirement had been placed on any British broadcaster. Impartiality had to be observed on all programmes about 'matters of political or industrial controversy or relating to current public policy'.

The man in charge of enforcing this was the first director-general of the ITA, Sir Robert Fraser, an Australian who had come to Britain as a student at the LSE. Like Bernstein he had been a Labour supporter and had stood as a Labour candidate, in his case as an unsuccessful candidate for Parliament in 1935. He had also been a leader-writer on the *Daily Herald*. Like Bernstein he had worked for the Ministry of Information during the war, but whereas after the war Bernstein had gone back into private enterprise, Fraser had stayed firmly within the public sector. For the next decade and a half the two men were never to agree on what 'due impartiality' actually meant. As Bernstein once teased the ITA, if Granada made a programme on drunk drivers would there have to be one view in favour and one against?

In May 1956, only a year after Granada first went on the air, the two men met face to face and Fraser warned Bernstein that the ITA was anxious about 'an apparent overall bias to the left in Granada programmes'. Bernstein said 'Granada aimed to bring a fresh eye to social and political issues' but claimed this was not inconsistent with the Act and 'could not be taken as imparting a socialist bias'.[580]

Fraser said they would be watching carefully in the future but nothing much seems to have changed because two years later, on 18 March 1958, Fraser sat down and wrote a memo pouring out his troubles with Granada. He sent it to the ITA chairman, Sir Ivone Kirkpatrick, who had just taken the job after retiring as the top civil servant in the Foreign Office following the Suez crisis. The memo was headed 'The Politics of Granada'.

> I think the time has come when I must commit to writing my increasing anxiety about the general political tendency of Granada programmes.
>
> One must begin by admitting that the evidence is not very easy to assemble. There are very few cases on which it is possible to lay one's finger...
>
> The fact remains that no one watching Granada programmes over a long period could be left in any doubt that the company has its own political outlook and that this finds consistent expression in its programmes...
>
> Granada has lately had documentary and discussion programmes on the treatment of homosexuals, of murderers, and of coloured immigrants, and really one is left in no doubt that Granada is opposed to capital punishment, to the present laws about homosexuality, and to the way in which coloured people are treated...
>
> It is almost as if, while the rules of the road were generally observed, none the less the traffic always seems to come in the same direction.

Fraser then moved on to the two groups of people who he felt sure would agree with him. One was the other franchise-holders, who were becoming 'increasingly restless' about showing controversial Granada programmes on their regional stations. The other was the Conservative Party, whose members 'have lately let me know in no uncertain terms that their anxiety is beginning to change to anger'.

Having set out his views Fraser concluded by admitting, 'I am at a loss to know what to do about it.'

His chairman replied with a handwritten note at the bottom of the memo: 'I also don't know what to do.'

Fraser decided that the ITA could at least keep a 'consistent log of all Granada programmes with any kind of political content'. There is no sign of a log in the ITA files or further reference to it. But undoubtedly ITA executives were carefully monitoring Granada's programmes.

Tim Hewat first came across Granada folk in a bar in Manchester in the early hours of one spring day in 1957. An Australian, he was the northern editor of the *Daily Express* and when he finished work around midnight he would go to the Midland Hotel where Granada staff also liked to meet up after work. He was asked to meet Bernstein and hired to assist him on special projects.

One Granada veteran wrote of him, 'Tim liked to pose as a headlong ruffian of the Australian earth ... he presented himself as the dynamic newsman straight from Ben Hecht's *The Front Page* ... he liked to be the coarse, totally truth-telling, appalling, shocking, rough diamond hillbilly.'[581]

In 1961 Hewat went off to Cuba to shoot some films about the revolutionary government of Fidel Castro, which had overthrown a pro-American regime. When he returned he wrote a note to Sidney Bernstein: 'Cuba is a bastard and that's a fact.' He came back with the view that 'the revolution was long overdue, is a good thing, and is popular with most of the people. It is now a Marxist revolution and aims to be more so. Cuba probably needed a hefty dose of Marxism. The country had been outrageously and stupidly exploited by the Americans.'[582]

Bernstein's protégé then set about turning his footage into four programmes for the ITV network titled *Cuba Si* and his personal views were not exactly disguised. After transmission the usual channels swung into action. The ITA's deputy director-general, Bernard Sendall, gave Granada early warning that 'we cannot escape the conclusion that the four programmes taken together lacked impartiality and were in places slanted unfairly against the United States.' This judgement was confirmed in a chairman-to-chairman letter from Sir Ivone Kirkpatrick to Sidney Bernstein citing the 'due accuracy and impartiality' provisions of Section 3 of the Television Act, which *Cuba Si* had breached. Bernstein replied that 'we really cannot see that we have breached the sections to which you refer'. He suggested a meeting with the ITA members who had viewed the programmes.

A month later he was writing again to the ITA chairman, this time thanking him for a 'most pleasant and happy lunch with authority members'. The letter concluded: 'I have no further comment to make on our views on subsection (1) of Section 3(c) and (f) of the Television Act but it was very kind of you to give me the opportunity of explaining why – most respectfully – we beg to differ. Yours sincerely, Sidney.'

Proof that peace was nowhere near breaking out came the following year in an episode described by an ITA official as 'Granada and Cuba again'. With the world's eyes firmly focused on the Cuban missile crisis between the United States and the Soviet Union, Tim Hewat dusted down his *Cuba Si* films and edited them into a single one-off background documentary. He sent the ITA a draft script for 'an intimate look at the island in the centre of the world crisis'; it would be voiced by announcer Bob Holness, later better known as the presenter of the ITV quiz *Blockbusters*.

The script survives and is a mostly factual but also mostly uncritical view of Castro and his Cuba. The only negative note comes towards the end: 'The events of the last few weeks have shown that Castro's links with Communism have become a chain which has dragged his people into the centre of the East–West conflict.'

Hewat and his script got short shrift from the ITA. In their view his previous films were now 'condemned material and had earned the rare distinction of being classed by the Authority as a breach of the Act'. Recycling them with a new peg, even one as significant as the threat of global war, was not going to be allowed.

Hewat was not put off controversy by the sagas of *Cuba Si* and *Cuba Again*. If Hewat's mentor and patron was Bernstein, then the man who tried to steer him through the choppy waters was Denis Forman.

Like many pioneers of British television Forman had an interesting war, in his case the Battle of Monte Cassino when the Allies besieged German troops in a hilltop monastery and took heavy casualties on the slopes below. It cost Forman a leg. Like Bernstein he had contacts in the film industry and after the war he became director of the British Film Institute (BFI). It was through Bernstein's brother Cecil, who was a BFI director, that he got a job at Granada.

He set about making his own contribution to Granada's growing reputation for high quality programme-making and getting into trouble.

One of the principal battlegrounds was Granada's flagship weekly current affairs programme, *World in Action* (*WIA*).[583]

The programme's first editor was Tim Hewat, who loved to use metaphors that viewers could relate to. One of the most popular programmes of the time was *Sunday Night at the London Palladium*, a live variety show from the stage of the London theatre which included a quiz called 'Beat the Clock'. The familiar clock face provided a way to engage viewers in a 1963 *WIA* about the relatively dry subject of defence procurement.

The script read:

This, after Big Ben, is probably the most familiar clock in Britain – the clock that ticks out the big money prizes on Sundays at the Palladium.

Tonight we use this clock to signal its biggest money ever paid for by the taxpayers.

Tonight every full-circle sweep of the hand that takes exactly a second – and every flashing light stands for £1 – sixty pounds a second every second.

And that's the speed at which Britain is, this year, spending money on defence ... sixty pounds a second ... £3,600 a minute ... £216,000 an hour ... £5,180,000 a day, £1,838,000,000 in the year.

What does the customer get for the money?

The programme then went on to list examples of alleged waste in defence spending. The ITA previewed the programme and decided to ban it.

Forman and Hewat got the news at Granada's London offices. Forman later remembered Hewat's reaction to the decision. 'The fuckers,' said Tim, and again and again, 'the fuckers'.

But the two men came up with an extraordinary riposte.

Forman rang *World in Action*'s rival on the BBC, *Panorama*, and explained what had happened. Remarkably it was agreed that *Panorama* would show on the BBC the central ten minutes of Hewat's film that could not be shown on ITV. Just before that evening's *Panorama* went out Forman rang Sir Robert Fraser at the ITA and told him, 'I thought you should know, Bob, that part of our Defence *World in Action* is going out on *Panorama* tonight.'

There was a long pause before Fraser replied, 'Thank you for telling me, Denis.'

The authority was shocked; no one would have dreamed that two rival current affairs programmes would have co-operated to defeat censorship. Some time later Fraser wrote to Bernstein saying this 'stunt' had made him feel sick.[584] There was a smell of vengeance in the air. Every edition of *World in Action* would now have to be vetted by the authority in advance.

Trench warfare

On 28 February 1966 Tony Pragnell, a senior executive at the ITA, wrote to a partner at an external law firm:

Dear Geoffrey,

There is about to be a major confrontation with Granada about their lack of political impartiality. I have prepared a brief setting out our legal powers in this matter. I enclose a copy. Could you simply say whether you consider it correct and complete?

It was the start of what Forman was to call three years of 'trench warfare'. The internal ITA dossier on Granada read like a regulatory charge sheet. It set out the law – 'the requirements of the 1964 Act'. Then there was the evidence for the prosecution in the form of ITA reports on specific programmes. A *World in Action* on the BBC in 1965 had been 'quite irresponsible', 'nothing less than a sustained attack on the BBC'. In a programme on the drug industry 'the amount of time allowed for the industry to present its case was minimal'. A *WIA* on Vietnam had 'a minority view at its end' which 'appeared to be a summing up'. The script of the Granada view of the 'six counties' of Northern Ireland was there too.

Also in the file was a transcript of an interview in which Bernstein was formally questioned by the new chairman of the ITA, Lord Hill:

Lord Hill: The Act requires two things. Political impartiality and the absence of an editorial view. In your experience have you had difficulty in applying these two principles required by the Act?
Mr Sidney Bernstein: The first one, no. The second one, we think we have accepted the Authority's dictum in the matter but it has been with great restraint.
Lord Hill: Successful restraint?
Mr Sidney Bernstein: Yes we have. We have carried out our obligations in that respect with regret.

The file also contained a background brief on the man himself. 'There is a negative attitude on the part of Sidney Bernstein towards the requirement of the Act.' Further the ITA believed Granada 'is allergic to the concept of impartial presentation of all points of view in public affairs'. The ITA's starkest pre-trial judgement on the chairman of Granada was that 'all who work on Granada's current affairs seem to some extent to carry the Bernstein chip on their shoulders'.

As it turned out, the 'major confrontation' was, in Forman's words, 'a bit of a fiasco'. For all their detailed internal planning the ITA staff had failed to tell Granada that their meeting would be about a whole list of programmes. Granada thought it was about just one programme, on the pharmaceutical industry, and prepared accordingly. Neither side gave any ground.

In November 1969, Granada executives took up what they regarded as an invitation from the ITA to set out their own interpretation of the due impartiality clause in the Television Act. Forman produced twelve pages, apologising for its length and the fact that 'it reads a little like a lawyer's draft'. The document remains to this day one of the most considered pieces written on the concept of 'due impartiality', which is held so dear by British broadcasters but, as we have seen from the Martin Bell chapter, is rarely defined.

Forman set out what he understood to be the ITA's interpretation then contrasted it with Granada's. He cited the parallel with a court case:

> The Authority expects the person providing the programmes to act in matters of this kind as both counsel for the defence and counsel for the prosecution, and to pass on to the public the function of judge and jury ... Granada believes that it is the proper function of the persons providing the programmes to present a controversial issue to the public, not from the point of view of the prosecution or the defence, nor of both sides one after the other, but from the point of view of the judge in his summing up. In this he refers to the facts on both sides, but he exercises the function of judgment in giving less weight to the arguments of one and greater weight to the arguments of another.

The final section of Forman's paper was called 'Further outlook'. There was one peace offering: 'We recognise our editorial judgement must give way to that of the Authority.' But there were plenty of barbs with it. The debate between the two sides had become 'obsessive', the ITA's 'degree of consternation' was 'unmerited' and, in a final finger to authority, Granada hoped that 'the indirect pressures of censorship which have affected our team very seriously from time to time in the past can be removed'.

Forman's follow-up meeting with Fraser after the November 1969 paper found the director-general of the ITA in a belligerent mood. The Granada letter had revealed the width of the gap between the two sides. But Fraser had something to say that went beyond disputing the contents of the letter. In his view Granada's current affairs output showed a persistent left-wing bias and if he were a Communist he would have no doubt as to where to look for a job in television. It would be Granada.[585]

After the meeting Forman called Sidney Bernstein, or SLB as he sometimes called him, who was at his holiday home in Barbados. Forman found him angry but cool. Bernstein said, 'I have had to live with plenty of this kind of rubbish in my time. Do nothing until next week.'

Peace of a kind

Fraser and Forman were both unhappy with the way things had gone at their meeting and decided to have a follow-up. Mindful that what had appeared in the ITA's files might affect Granada's chances of having its licence renewed, Forman cleverly got Fraser to put on the record that Fraser wasn't accusing him or his senior executives of being 'Communist/Marxist/anti-democratic'. This compromise was peace of a kind.

There were to be more two more rows and both were about *World in Action*. In 'The Quiet Mutiny' in 1970 John Pilger visited Vietnam and spoke to American soldiers who reflected the disillusion with the war that was spreading throughout the American army and back home. The ITA found it to be 'outrageous left-wing propaganda' even though Granada claimed two members of the ITA's own staff had passed the programme in advance.

The second row was closer to home. John Poulson was an architect and property developer who seemed to have fingers in most of the pies in the north of England. 'The friends and influence of John L. Poulson' was a *WIA* special which was banned not under the Section 3 clauses about impartiality, but as 'a matter of broadcasting policy'. The regulator, by now called the Independent Broadcasting Authority (IBA) because it also oversaw commercial radio, never explained exactly what this meant. Instead of replacing *WIA* with another programme Granada left the screen blank as a protest. Then it was revealed that two members of the IBA board had business contacts with key players in the Poulson affair. The IBA effectively backed down, allowing the transmission of a revised version with only cosmetic changes from the original. Poulson was later found guilty of corruption and sent to prison for seven years, the judge calling him an 'incalculably evil man'. *World in Action* was completely vindicated. The IBA was not. This was a landmark moment when a broadcaster effectively overturned a regulator.

But there was to be a sting in the tail for Sidney Bernstein.

The IBA had a rule that all members of boards of ITV companies should retire at seventy. Granada asked for a five-year extension in his case. The IBA agreed he could stay as a director until seventy-five but would have to resign as chairman of Granada TV at seventy-one. His brother Cecil took over. Sidney could remain as chairman of the Granada Group, which was outside the IBA's control, but it wasn't the same. He and his colleagues took it as a personal snub from the IBA.

Perhaps the most bizarre moment of Bernstein's later years came when he took the company into a full-scale legal battle with the Ford car company because they wanted to call a car 'Granada'. He accepted that he'd borrowed the name from a Spanish city but claimed he'd added value to it. The TV company finally gave up. In 1979 Bernstein retired completely from the Granada business.

In 1985 Sidney Bernstein finally achieved closure on something that had frustrated him for thirty years. Granada made a film about the film which he had made about Belsen, but which had never been shown. It included long extracts from his original draft version and an interview with him. The programme was shown on television in Britain and also in America on the Discovery Channel under the title *A Painful Reminder: Evidence for All Mankind*. The synopsis reads:

> British soldiers came upon Belsen concentration camp in 1945. They could not believe what they saw. But army film cameramen were with the troops and filmed everything. With the camera unit was Sidney Bernstein, working as Head of Film for the Allies' Psychological Warfare Division. He resolved that the definitive factual film of the camps must be made, so that the world could be told the truth.[586]

Today Bernstein's film can be seen anywhere in the world via YouTube.

Five years after Bernstein died in 1993, *World in Action* died too, a victim of the new programme strategies brought about by the increased focus on profitability in commercial television. Then in 2004 at the conclusion of the inevitable consolidation of the many ITV licences into one company for England and Wales, the name 'Granada' began to disappear from the network, retained only for regional programmes in Bernstein's 'Granadaland'.

But in 2012 came evidence that perhaps the spirit of Bernstein, Forman, Hewat and others lived on. The last head of Current Affairs at Granada, Alexander Gardiner, in his new guise as an executive for factual programmes in what was now 'ITV Studios', oversaw a programme that contributed to what John Simpson called the BBC's 'worst crisis in fifty years'. An ITV documentary, *The Other Side of Jimmy Savile*, revealed the full extent of the allegations against the former BBC presenter. The work of Gardiner and his team triggered a flood of new allegations by victims of Savile and others who now felt free to speak out. The programme won multiple awards including the RTS award for 'Scoop of the Year'. The citation praised 'an investigative challenge which had defeated other media organisations over decades and had been achieved with commitment, skill and sensitivity. The programme-makers had given a voice to victims who had always been denied one, with unprecedented impact across many British institutions.'

Sidney Bernstein and the old Granada trouble-makers would have been proud.

To judge Bernstein's full legacy it is best to look back to that 1958 ITA memo, 'The Politics of Granada'. Sir Robert Fraser wrote that 'really one is left in no doubt that Granada is opposed to capital punishment, to the present laws about homosexuality, and to the way coloured people are treated'. Half a century on, capital punishment has gone, homosexuality is no longer illegal and there are laws to prohibit discrimination against ethnic minorities. Bernstein's Granada can't take all the credit for these changes in public policy but, uniquely for a British broadcaster, it can claim to have been an agent for social change. No regulator knew quite how to handle that. But no regulator ever fined or otherwise sanctioned Granada for breaches of the rules, nor threatened to take its licence away. Possibly their judgement was that, for all their frustrations with Granada's 'politics', taking off the air the company that made *Coronation Street*, the nation's most popular programme and the network's best commercial banker, would not have been a very smart 'political' move.

11

SANDY GALL

In 1980 two men sat across a lunch table in London – one was from the British television news company ITN, the other from British Intelligence, MI6.

It was a very British occasion. The location was Stone's Chop House, known for its traditional English food and as a meeting place for Establishment chaps. For many years women hadn't been admitted to Stone's. The food was roast beef and Yorkshire pudding. And the talk was of a country far away but one which Britain had invaded three times in colonial days for what it believed were the wider strategic interests of its empire. Each time Britain departed defeated.

Now Afghanistan was back on the British government's agenda because in 1979 the Russians, learning nothing from British history, had sent in their troops to try to maintain the country's place in the Soviet Union's own empire. They were fighting different guerrilla groups known collectively as 'the mujahideen', meaning 'a person who fights a jihad' or 'Muslims who struggle in the path of Allah'. One group was led by Osama bin Laden and funded by the Saudi and Pakistani governments. The British and American governments were supporting other groups.

What was discussed at that lunch and at subsequent lunches and meetings was to have a major effect on the way Afghanistan was to be reported in Britain for a decade and beyond. And it raised questions about who was using whom and whether in the relationship between news-gathering and intelligence-gathering any ethical lines are crossed.

The ITN man at the lunch was Henderson Alexander 'Sandy' Gall, once a veteran foreign correspondent for Reuters, who, since joining what was then Britain's most watched TV news service, had combined reporting with presenting the news.

The man from MI6 was paying for lunch because he had a question for Sandy Gall and it came from no less a person than the Foreign Secretary, Lord Carrington. How could the war in Afghanistan between the Russians and the Afghan mujahideen be kept 'in front of the British public'? Gall explained there was a shortage of TV pictures of the conflict and it appeared the only way that could change was if freelance cameramen thought there would be a financial return in going there. He offered his advice and left it at that.[587]

But two years later he and his contact were back at Stone's and this time Gall was paying because he was the one looking for advice. He was planning to visit Afghanistan and wanted suggestions about who to meet there. The man from MI6 volunteered a name that meant nothing to Gall – Ahmed Shah Massoud (sometimes spelt as *Masud*), a mujahideen leader still in his twenties and based in the Panjsher Valley, north-east of Kabul. 'We think he has all the makings of a second Tito,' said the man from MI6. For a man from British intelligence to make comparisons with the Yugoslav partisan leader who Britain had backed against the Nazis and who had united various factions into one nation was praise indeed.

Gall later recalled, 'As I walked back to the office I felt more excited than I had been for a very long time.' Gall had already collected a fair few exciting moments in his career. In 1965 he made a film for ITN about the IRA which showed gunmen being trained in handling weapons, practising throwing hand-grenades and in which he interviewed the IRA's chief of staff and other leaders. A decade later such a film would have caused major controversy and ended up with Gall being questioned by the police under anti-terrorism legislation.[588] At the time, no one seemed to notice. Later he spent time in one of Idi Amin's 'execution cells' in Uganda, and in Vietnam was an eyewitness as the Vietcong took over Saigon. A departing British embassy official left him the keys for safekeeping. Later, in 1991, Gall was the first correspondent to get back a report as coalition troops crossed into Kuwait to drive out Saddam Hussein's army.

But whenever Sandy Gall looked back on his years on the road one moment seemed to strike an especially emotional chord. In 1956 Reuters sent him to the Hungarian capital, Budapest, where the Russians were crushing an uprising led by the Prime Minister, Imre Nagy. This Communist had turned against Soviet Communism and wanted to take Hungary out of the Warsaw Pact, something the Russians were not prepared to tolerate. Nagy and his colleague General Pál Maléter sought asylum in the Yugoslav embassy. Nagy was tricked into leaving, believing that he was being offered safe conduct. Instead he was arrested and never seen again.

Sandy Gall later recalled:

> I was the only Western correspondent in Budapest when the news came over Moscow radio that Nagy and Pál Maléter and the rest had been tried in secret, found guilty, sentenced to death and executed, all done before anything was announced ... As a Reuter man you're supposed to be impartial and one was impartial in one's reporting but one's own private feelings were that this was a dreadful system that could behave in this sort of way.[589]

And he later wrote: 'In their crushing of the Hungarian Revolution the Russians displayed a callousness and a ruthlessness that even they would find hard to improve on.'[590]

Afghanistan
Gall has linked his time in eastern Europe to his decision, in 1982, to set off to Afghanistan with a documentary crew:

> I was interested initially because of the Russians being there,

the Soviet Union, after all I'd spent a lot of time in Germany, in Hungary where the Soviet Union was very much involved, and I had seen Soviet power at its worst, you might say, I wondered what was going to happen there.

In this first trip he set a style that was to become familiar over the next decade: a veteran foreign correspondent accompanied by mujahideen and pack-horses traverses steep mountainsides to meet and talk with a guerrilla leader. A documentary, a book and several promotional radio interviews later Gall was making clear the impact which 'the second Tito' – Ahmed Shah Massoud – had on him.

> He impressed from the very start, a quality of leadership and authority, he was only twenty-eight, he had achieved it himself because of his brains and his organisational skills, and his courage, he was a man apart ... I came away feeling that he was a very impressive character, very clever, very dedicated ... I think he's just a natural, and an organisational genius, almost a genius.[591]

Given this enthusiasm one radio interviewer wondered how unbiased Gall's view was: 'I think I have been long enough in the profession to know how to be impartial ... I went in with a completely open mind and anything I've said or written is what I saw and what I heard there.'[592]

Sandy Gall's reporting of Afghanistan was about to develop in a very significant way and again it would be with a little help from a friend.

He had first met Zia ul-Haq in the lobby of the Intercontinental Hotel in Amman. It was September 1970, known as 'Black September', when King Hussein of Jordan and his troops launched an all-out attack on the Palestine Liberation Organisation, the PLO. What became a civil war was sparked by the PLO using Jordan as a base for attacks against British and American airliners and other Western and Israeli targets.

Gall was reporting the crisis for ITN, Zia was a Pakistani brigadier advising the King of Jordan on how to defeat the PLO. He helped Gall get access to film Hussein's victory celebrations with his Bedouin troops.

Seven years later Gall was at his desk at ITN one night when the news broke that the Prime Minister of Pakistan, Zulfikar Ali Bhutto, had been overthrown by a military coup led by a general, a certain Zia ul-Haq. Gall put in a call to the new leader of Pakistan and a week later a familiar voice came on the line. 'Sandy? Zia here. How are you, how are the family?'[593] An invitation to visit Pakistan followed and for the next few months Gall regularly talked with Zia on and off camera, most noticeably in April 1979 when former Prime Minister Bhutto was hanged for the murder of a political rival following a trial which many believed to be unfair. The next day Zia told Gall on the phone that he had overruled pleas for clemency because 'I have tried to show that nobody, whether high or low, is above the law'.[594]

In another interview in that period Zia told Gall, 'We don't intend to stay for years,' instead it would be just 'months, certainly months' before free and fair elections.[595] But five years later, in 1984, Zia was still very much in charge and he had an idea about Afghanistan, an idea which he had discussed with the British Prime Minister, Margaret Thatcher.

Sandy Gall got to hear about it at another of his lunches with MI6, this time at a Soho restaurant. MI6 had been sent the minutes of a meeting between Zia and Thatcher. They showed that Zia had appealed to Thatcher for more media coverage of the war and mentioned Gall's documentary made two years before. He apparently had offered to support Gall if he made another trip.[596]

Zia was able to make that offer because he wasn't just an interested neighbour watching events across the border in Afghanistan. In many ways the Afghanistan war was Zia's war. He ran it as a proxy for America once they had decided that in this Cold War climate if the mujahideen were the Russians' enemy they must therefore be America's friend. Most of the military and financial aid which Washington sent was directed through one of the Pakistani intelligence agencies, the Inter-Services Intelligence Directorate, the ISI.

When Gall and an ITN team arrived in Pakistan they discovered that not only had Zia organised for them to go into Afghanistan with a group of Afghan mujahideen but that he would be sending four of his own Special Forces troops along to make sure they were safe. At a meeting Gall came up with an impromptu request to the Pakistani military leader: 'Could we take some SAM7s with us? It would make a brilliant picture if we filmed a Russian helicopter being shot down by a Russian missile.' Zia agreed and organised it through the ISI.[597] With hindsight, as a senior executive of ITN, I should probably have pointed out to Sandy that we were in the news business rather than the arms business.

As it turned out the mujahideen never did get to shoot down a Russian helicopter with a Russian missile, much to the relief of local villagers who pleaded that if they did the Russians would come and bomb their homes.

On his return to London Gall was invited to lunch with the head of MI6. 'It was very informal, the cook was off, so we had cold meat and salad, with plenty of wine,' Gall noted.[598] They talked missiles and Gall passed on the mujahideen's concern that they needed better ones than the Russian SAMs. MI6 made sure the CIA got a copy of Gall's latest TV documentary, which showed the problems the mujahideen were having with SAMs.

In the mid-1980s news reports and documentaries shot on location and then brought back to London to be edited still had an important place in British television but the appetite was growing for more live coverage using a new generation of lightweight satellite dishes. These could be transported to remote locations where they would be pointed up at the relevant passing satellite to feed pictures back to base.

During this period I had progressed up the ITN hierarchy partly through my interest in such technology. By 1988 I was a senior editor when Sandy Gall came to me with an intriguing idea. Again it had come about through his network of friends and contacts. On this occasion it was Lord Cranborne, whom Gall described as 'an ardent supporter of the mujahideen'.[599] Cranborne had persuaded General Zia to allow a satellite dish into Pakistan, where it would be taken to pieces and transported on the backs of horses into an area of Afghanistan controlled by the mujahideen. It could then provide live pictures from their camps. By luck and timing it looked as if this venture could come to fruition in time for the Russian withdrawal from Afghanistan in February 1989. How would ITN like to join and help organise the expedition to the outskirts of Jalalabad, which was about to fall to the mujahideen?

Mujahideen

It took less time for me to decide to go ahead than it probably should and on 15 February 1989, as the Russian ground forces finally departed, British, and then a few minutes later American, viewers watched the first ever live transmissions from inside Afghanistan. Sandy Gall sat, dressed in Afghan clothes, with the mujahideen in a camp where, since it was three o'clock in the morning there, nothing much was happening. Local villagers asked the ITN team and their Afghan and Pakistani minders to move on for fear of reprisals by the Russians. A few days later the village was bombed. ITN had been assured the Russians would not be able to detect the source of what, to them, was an illegal transmission inside Afghanistan but villagers suspected a spy in the village had passed back details of what had occurred that night. Sandy Gall returned to London, his reputation as the silver-haired gentleman bravely reporting from the Afghan front line further enhanced. Other reporters came and went but none made the impact of Gall.

A few months after the Russians gave up and went home Sandy Gall was back in the saddle crossing the mountains to visit Massoud again to see how he was progressing in his battle against the Communist government which the Russians had left behind.

In one of his reports he said:

This is one of the arms trails from Pakistan to Afghanistan. A few RPG rocket boosters and their white plastic cases went in with the convoy we joined, but this year the arms trail to the north – the stronghold of the most famous guerrilla commander of them all, Ahmad Shah Massoud – has been virtually empty. While other lesser commanders get regular shipments Massoud is reported to have received no fresh supplies at all through the American-financed and Pakistani-controlled arms pipeline.[600]

In November 2012 I interviewed Sandy Gall at the BBC, a new and slightly strange experience questioning on air a reporter who'd once been one of my team at ITN and asking him about decisions I had been involved in. I focused on his report about arms shipments and what lay behind it, especially his relationship with the most famous guerrilla commander of them all, Ahmad Shah Massoud.

Although the British and the Americans both supported the mujahideen they took very different sides. The British helped Massoud – their 'second Tito'. The Americans championed a leader called Gulbuddin Hekmatyar, believing that his fighters killed more Russians than anybody else. And the Pakistani ISI made sure most of the CIA's dollars went to Hekmatyar, who they expected would succeed and eventually run Afghanistan in co-operation with them.

In the BBC interview I asked Sandy Gall about this rivalry between mujahideen leaders.

Purvis: In the commentary you refer to him as the most famous guerrilla commander of them all. Now what's not covered in your report, I suppose, is the background, which is that while the British were supporting one guerrilla leader, Massoud, the Americans were supporting a rival one, Hekmatyar. Would he be one of the lesser commanders you are referring to?

Gall: Yes in terms of efficiency and effectiveness ... I mean he was a political animal, Gulbuddin Hekmatyar. He was also the darling of course of the ISI, the ISI being the Pakistani intelligence.[601]

Purvis: It sounds like you've slightly taken sides with the guerrilla leader that the British backed against the one that the Americans and Pakistanis backed.

Gall: [laughs] Well, that may sound so, Stewart, but really it was my knowledge of the situation. I thought that Massoud was honourable, a straight shooter as you might say, whereas I knew from experience that Hekmatyar was really, I would say, a murderous thug.[602]

Sandy Gall's feelings towards Hekmatyar were personal. He blamed him for the murder of two of his friends. One was Andy Skrzypkowiak, a former SAS soldier who became a freelance cameraman in Afghanistan 'supplying ITN and the BBC with first-class combat footage'. Gall dedicated one of his books to him as a 'travelling companion, warrior and friend, killed in Afghanistan 1987'.[603]

Skrzypkowiak was on his way to meet Massoud when he was kidnapped and murdered. Gall wrote that Skrzypkowiak's 'only crime was his friendship with Massoud'.[604]

I then moved on to the issue of Western arms supplies to Massoud and whether he was supporting on air the argument that Massoud should get more.

Purvis: Now after that report the Foreign Office sent a telegram about the situation to Washington and deliveries of American arms were resumed to Massoud the following year, that's the account in your book. Was that what you had been hoping for as a result of your trip?

Gall: Do you know, I'd forgotten that ... you know, Stewart, I hope I'm an impartial journalist, I never manoeuvred for anything like that to happen. The deal was that Reagan and Mrs Thatcher worked through General Zia, who deputed the ISI, the Pakistani intelligence, to run the war. So the ISI ran the war on behalf of Zia and Zia was running the war on behalf of Reagan and Thatcher and this meant that the arms were going to the people that Zia and the ISI decided to send them to and Hekmatyar was the chief client, he got most of the money, he got a huge amount of money from the Americans. It was only very late in the day that the Americans decided that he was not what they thought he was and they kind of dropped him and said to the British, you were right, we were wrong, that was amazing.

Finally I turned to whether, with his unrivalled access to people and places on the mujahideen side, he had told British viewers of the depth of British involvement. He said that he knew the British were sending in people to train the mujahideen but hadn't reported it. However, it had been obvious. It was also clear from the British walkie-talkies that the mujahideen were using.

> Purvis: What do you think the audience – and we're talking about millions of people back in Britain seeing your reports – do you think they understood just how deeply Britain was involved in helping the mujahideen at this point?
> Gall: Maybe not.
> Purvis: Did you think it was any part of your role to tell them?
> Gall: I think in all those reports there was hardly any mention of British involvement. I don't feel at all guilty about it, I didn't think I'd overstepped my area of journalistic impartiality.

So what are we to make of the ethics of Sandy Gall's close relationship with British intelligence?

News is news...
Hacks talking to spooks has always been a sensitive subject in British journalism. The fact is that when British journalists return from places where diplomats find it hard to get to the Foreign Office will invite them in for a chat. If they go along it is, in effect,

a de-briefing. Some will go along out of a patriotic duty, others because they think that in return they will get information which means they will hopefully get to know more about what's going on. Sandy Gall was never anything other than totally honest with me when he was invited to the Foreign Office and I never questioned his decision to go.

However, when Sandy Gall revealed his full connections with British intelligence in his book *News from the Front: The Life of a Television Reporter* in 1994, there was unease among Gall's former colleagues at ITN about what he had written about his trips – even among editors such as me who had happily relished the exclusivity of the material he brought back to us. The context of the time was that ITN was perceived by some as having been too close to the Conservative governments of Margaret Thatcher and John Major. So anything that looked like a 'joint venture' between ITN and the Tories aroused suspicion.

His book also prompted a scathing review in *The Guardian*. It described how 'an ageing, grey-haired reporter on a horse, riding across the range with an assorted bunch of Afghan guerrillas' was now revealed to be 'one of the secret weapons used by MI6 to force the British public – otherwise cosmically uninterested – to take some notice of the anti-Soviet battles going on in Afghanistan'. [605]

The headline was 'Playing the Great Game with Incredible Gall' and the author was the literary editor of *The Guardian*, Richard Gott. Later that year Gott had to resign from *The Guardian* amidst allegations that he had been a KGB agent during the Cold War. Gott denied the charges, published in *The Spectator* magazine, but admitted he had gone on expenses-paid trips to Vienna, Athens and Nicosia to visit a senior Russian official in the 1980s. [606]

But Gott had at the very least been talking to intelligence-gatherers too – they just happened to be from the other side. But surely if it is defensible for a journalist to give unclassified information to a diplomat in return for a briefing who should care what 'side' they are on? If it is not illegal, information is information, news is news. Journalists take information from a range of sources and assess it before using it. In principle an intelligence source is no different from any other.

But there are four problems which can arise with material from intelligence sources. The first is that by its very nature it is often difficult to check. This can create the second problem, which is that the story achieves an outcome which the journalist may not anticipate. The chief of the defence staff during the Falklands War, Lord Lewin, considered it perfectly justifiable to feed misinformation to the media, especially if it helped to deceive an enemy. The other two problems involve 'deals' – either that the intelligence sources expect that they will receive something in return from the journalist or that they ask the journalist not to use other information which they have gathered from other sources.

Applying these principles and pitfalls to Sandy Gall's relationship with MI6, he believes his lunches were nothing secret, he was simply looking for information and they were looking for information. Of what he got from them, he says that if journalists are offered something, and it sounds like an interesting story which they would be interested in, their natural inclination would be to say yes. Of the information he gave MI6 he says it was effectively in the public domain because there was nothing that he had not or would not use in his broadcasts.

In terms of trying to achieve an outcome he clearly had common ground with MI6 in wanting to highlight what the Russians were doing in Afghanistan. But in his case there seems to have been an additional personal motive based on his past experiences: 'When the Afghan thing started I thought, well, I do know how the Soviets act, I mean I have seen them in action, and it's not very pleasant. And so this looks to me like a re-run.'[607]

Massoud does seem to have received more arms from the West after Gall pointed out the guerrilla leader's problem with re-supplies but there is no evidence that has yet come to light to make a direct linkage between Gall's reports and those arms supplies. Gall told me, 'I never manoeuvred for anything like that to happen. I felt that was not my job.' His reports on the problems the mujahideen were having getting the right kind of missiles to shoot down Russian helicopters may have influenced a sequence of events which led to the United States supplying the very effective Stinger missile and this in turn may well have led the Russians to decide to withdraw. But again it is difficult to prove direct linkage.

On this issue of deal-making with 'spooks' the only reference which Gall makes to any such discussion is an incident in 1988 when the Pakistani ISI were escorting the satellite dish into Afghanistan. Gall recalls a conversation with an ISI colonel who asked him, 'What sort of line will you be taking in your reports, Mr Sandy Gall?'

'Why, the same as I always do. I shall be impartial.'

'We hope you will be positive, very positive, Mr Sandy Gall.'

Gall remembered that this line was delivered as a not very veiled threat. But he maintains it had no effect on his impartiality.

It was two decades after Gall's reports before an explanatory note was included in the broadcasting regulations about 'due impartiality'. It explained: 'The approach to due impartiality may vary according to the nature of the subject, the type of programme and channel, the likely expectation of the audience as to content, and the extent to which the content and approach is signalled to the audience. Context ... is important.'[608]

Citing the importance of context has given regulators the flexibility and freedom to adjust to particular circumstances but it has also allowed enforcement to be influenced by the prevailing political winds. It would be possible to argue that Sandy Gall's open endorsement of 'the most famous guerrilla commander of them all' over 'lesser commanders' was a breach of the requirement for due impartiality. But it could also be argued that this was within the context of British support for a guerrilla army which was fighting what was still seen as Britain's potential enemy in the world, the Soviet Union.

It would certainly have been better if we at ITN had ever transmitted a report which provided a different kind of context – one which fully explained Britain's underreported role in the war, thus allowing viewers to have a wider picture in which to consider Gall's report from one battlefield.

Whatever our collective shortcomings over telling the full story about Britain and the mujahideen, nobody can ever doubt Sandy Gall's bravery, his humanitarian commitment to the people of Afghanistan and his knowledge of the country. One British ambassador in Kabul said, 'He always reminded me how much I didn't know about Afghanistan.'[609] The charity Sandy Gall's Afghanistan Appeal continues to train Afghan professionals to provide artificial limbs, mobility aids and physiotherapy. In 2010, like Charles Wheeler, he was made a Companion of the Order of St Michael and St George, in his case for 'services to the people of Afghanistan'. It is the class of honour usually awarded for non-military foreign service, typically to FCO officials at department head level and above. His wife, Eleanor, and two of his daughters, Fiona and Michaela, help run the charity. A third daughter, Carlotta, has covered Afghanistan extensively for the *New York Times*.

Two of the key figures in Gall's work in Pakistan and Afghanistan died violent deaths. Zia ul-Haq was killed in 1988 when his presidential plane crashed in mysterious circumstances. Ahmed Shah Massoud helped to overthrow the Communist government left behind by the Russians and became a minister in the power-sharing government which was then formed between different mujahideen groups. But he fell out with the Taliban and a war began between them. In August 2001 two men claiming to be Belgian newsmen of Moroccan origin arrived at Massoud's camp asking for a TV interview. They waited three weeks before they met him. As they began the interview they detonated explosives inside the camera and the battery belt. Massoud died on his way to a field hospital. The Taliban had got their man, probably with the help of al Qaeda. Two days later 9/11 happened and partly in retaliation, a whole new Afghan war began.

12

LINDSEY HILSUM

On Monday 20 January 1997 in a sweltering, airless African courtroom, award-winning reporter Lindsey Hilsum says she crossed a line. In the dock, behind a bullet-proof glass screen, was a mayor from Rwanda, Jean-Paul Akayesu, accused of organising mass killings in an area near the country's capital, Kigali.

Hilsum says, 'I did something journalists have gone to prison to avoid. I testified in a court of law on information gathered in the course of my work.' But she adds, 'I did so, but not without doubts.'

Helping to bring those responsible to justice might seem a noble cause. But in the intriguing world of media ethics nothing is that simple. She was an eyewitness for the prosecution in a case that would go on to make legal history. Wouldn't any journalist welcome the opportunity to make that sort of mark for posterity? Well, no. It is exactly the sort of decision that most journalists hope never to have to make because it places them in an invidious position: choosing between their professional ethics – being impartial observers of events – and, in extreme cases, placing those to one side in favour of being human beings with feelings and passions and cares. It is not an easy choice to make, but a number have had to face up to making it.

Lindsey Hilsum was placed in that difficult position because she had seen what had happened in Rwanda. Her reports, which had been broadcast on the BBC and published in the Western press (*The Guardian*, *The Observer* and *The Independent*), were a record of the horrors that she witnessed during those first days of the Rwandan massacres in 1994. That was why the prosecution wished to call her as a witness: she could tell the court what she had seen and confirm that what she had written was true. Before the prosecution could move on to specific instances and charges, it had to establish general historical facts that were beyond doubt: that there had been massacres, how events had unfolded and what had happened. Likewise, the prosecution needed to prove that the massacres amounted to genocide.

Hilsum's testimony was special because she had been one of only two Western journalists in the country when the massacres began; she was therefore in a 'privileged' position as an impartial observer. The case was being heard by the International Criminal Tribunal for Rwanda (ICTR). It was a parallel companion of the tribunal that was trying those responsible for war crimes and crimes against humanity committed in the former Yugoslavia. At the time both tribunals were 'at the cutting edge of a growing movement to establish international institutions of justice and accountability for mass violence'.[610] So it was an important process, not just a sideshow.

Rwandan paradise

The conflict within Rwanda – nominally between the Hutu and the Tutsi peoples – had become mass murder on a truly dreadful scale. No one will ever know how many died, but estimates range between half a million and a million dead. Victims were often chopped to death with a machete, or clubbed to death with heavy pieces of wood or metal. Many victims were killed by groups of people: that was how many of the perpetrators gained strength for their acts of murder.[611] Shooting was considered to be too quick a release by many of the killers – even those who had access to guns – because the deaths were seen as punishment for being Tutsi (or a 'moderate' Hutu, i.e. a supporter of an opposition political group). They were an act of vengeance. For many victims – perhaps the majority – death did not come easily or quickly. It was lingering. There are many stories where people pleaded to be shot because it was quick, but most pleas were rejected by killers fuelled by bloodlust.

Lindsey Hilsum came to get involved in Rwanda because for most of the 1980s she had been a freelance journalist, working mainly in Africa. Sometimes she worked for aid agencies in countries where war had introduced poverty, hunger and disease. She had been mainly based in Nairobi. In 1993 she was offered a two-month contract in Rwanda by UNICEF, the United Nations Children's Fund. She had never visited the country before, but had been engaged to produce a newsletter that would help aid agencies operating in Rwanda and Burundi work together more coherently and understand what was going on in both countries politically.[612]

What would she have learned about the unknown country? Land-locked Rwanda is a small but densely populated country by African standards. Roughly halfway between the size of Wales and Scotland, and with a population greater than both, it is mountainous and fertile. Described by some as a paradise, and others as a heaven-on-earth, its lush hills are home to mountain gorillas; it is a predominantly agrarian society and its main exports are coffee and tea, but also some tin ore.

Hilsum discovered that Rwanda is populated by two main ethnic groups, the minority Tutsi and the majority Hutu, although most experts agree that that is a distinction that obfuscates rather than clarifies the picture; in the south of the country live the Twa, who are the forest, or pygmy people. In truth, in 1994 she would find that the Tutsis and Hutus shared the same language, culture and religion and lived on the same hills together. The main languages are Kinyarwanda and French, which is the second language. In the years since the massacre English has also been added to the list. The distinction, what Hilsum refers to as the 'ethnie', is probably closer to the ancient Roman division between patricians and plebeians; in pre-colonial Rwandan society, which was essentially feudal, the Tutsis were the traditional overlords of the Hutus, but there was considerable intermarriage and social mobility between the two groups. Stereotypical descriptions of stature say that Tutsis are tall and slender, whereas Hutus are shorter and stockier, but there are many members of one group who very closely resemble those from the other. What was not in doubt, however, was that Rwandans were conscious of the distinction; they could tease it out through conversation. Perhaps uniquely among post-colonial African states, the country retained a colonial requirement that individuals' ethnicity was entered on their personal identity cards. So it was documented for all to see.

Rwandan society was described as obedient and orderly. When Hilsum arrived she noted that nearly everyone turned out to do a form of national service, unpaid communal work that had in the past enabled roads to be built, forests planted and terraces to be constructed in order to combat soil erosion.

The country was a colony for around eighty years, beginning in the late 1880s. It was first a part of German East Africa then, during the First World War, it was taken over by Belgium, which had also taken control of its neighbour, Burundi, where Tutsis formed the majority and Hutu the minority. Belgium retained control until 1962, when it decamped from the whole of central Africa almost overnight. Both the German and Belgian colonists delegated some local control to the Tutsis, who were accorded privileges and educational advantages in return: in effect the Tutsis did the colonial master's dirty work, and the Hutus resented it.[613]

When Hilsum arrived in Kigali, the country's capital, in 1994 she stayed first in a hotel and then, after a few weeks, moved to a suburban house, with its own nightwatchman, a sort of guard. She found a country in the grip of a war of insurgency. It had begun three years earlier when an army of well-organised and mainly Tutsi insurgents invaded from bases they had established years earlier along the Ugandan borderlands with Rwanda. They demanded the right to settle in Rwanda. The insurgents, the Rwandan Patriotic Front (RPF), had been established by Tutsi refugees and their descendants who had fled the country after the Belgian colonists had been evacuated in the early 1960s. In October 1990, in the commune of Kibilira, local Hutus took revenge on Tutsis living in the area, killing more than 300 people. By the end of the month the war reached a stalemate and the RPF decided to resort to guerrilla warfare to break the deadlock.

Reacting to the insurgency, Rwandan President Juvénal Habyarimana, a Hutu, announced the introduction of a multi-party system, and the abolition of the ethnic identity cards. He introduced the former, but never abolished the latter. In 1991 there were ceasefires, political demonstrations and political and ethnic violence. It seemed that the country was slowly beginning to fall apart. The demonstrations and ethnic violence continued into the next year. But the year also saw the establishment of the CDR (Coalition pour la Défense de la République) and the creation and consolidation of militias by extremist Hutu nationalists, including one called *Interahamwe* (a term that translates roughly as 'those who attack together'). Initially posing as a self-defence organisation its members were trained in weapons use and in killing techniques. Its members were instructed to make lists of all Tutsis living in each area.

That spring saw a new RPF offensive which caused up to 350,000 Hutu refugees to move southward to escape the fighting. But in August a peace conference formally opened in Arusha, Tanzania.

Over the following sixteen months extremist militia-inspired political violence escalated. There were hundreds of deaths. Early in 1993 the RPF extended the territory under its control, leading to the displacement of further large numbers of people. Habyarimana resisted signing a power-sharing agreement.

In the spring the presence of French troops briefly became an issue. It already had a small military presence in the country, ostensibly to protect its interests and citizens. But, as conditions in the country deteriorated, it sent in reinforcements. Its garrison became a sticking point in the peace negotiations and a timetable was agreed for the troops to be withdrawn, to be replaced by troops either from the United Nations or from the Organization of African Unity (OAU). In March a new ceasefire agreement was signed in the Tanzanian capital, Dar-es-Salaam.

But as conditions deteriorated the International Committee of the Red Cross (ICRC) warned that with almost one million displaced people the country faced famine and a major humanitarian catastrophe.

In July 1993 an independent commercial radio station opened in Kigali. Only later would the full significance of this event be appreciated. It was set up by people who had close links to President Habyarimana; the studios were even powered from a link to the presidential palace electrical supply. Radio Télévision Libre des Mille Collines (RTLMC) began broadcasting a mix of programming, including talk shows presented by 'shock jocks', which were loosely modelled on their Western radio counterparts, although there much of the similarity stopped. Some presenters were clearly drunk while on air, and their brand of shock-jock presentation was virulent bigotry. Other programmes included phone-ins, interviews and commentaries; but no news programming was included in the mix. Broadcasts were mostly in the vernacular Kinyarwanda language, with a small minority also in French. RTLMC's language was both earthy and raw. It was radically different to the staid state-owned Radio Rwanda. People RTLMC regarded as enemies were called cockroaches,[614] among other names; and in case listeners were in any doubt they were told where the 'enemies' lived, so that they could easily be found; some were described as those who 'deserved to die'.[615] The station was able to assess what impact it was having because some of its targets phoned in. For instance, on 20 November 1993 one caller complained to a broadcaster that he had been stoned after being named in a broadcast.[616] RTLMC implied that all Tutsis were 'traitors'. It did not openly support Habyarimana's government, thus appearing to be independent.

While Western diplomats dismissed the new radio station as a joke, its raw Hutu-extremist message struck a chord with many listeners and its programmes were heard by a rapidly growing audience. It appealed particularly to the unemployed, delinquents, and 'gangs of thugs in the militia': an underclass of people who were ill educated and illiterate and not able to discover for themselves the facts about what was going on in the country around them.[617] It seemed to give 'a mute population' a voice.[618] By a coincidence, the station had opened at a time when small portable radios had suddenly become cheaply and widely available in the country.

A month after RTLMC went on air Rwanda's government and the RPF signed an accord in Arusha to end the civil war. The agreement included power-sharing arrangements and the return of Tutsi refugees to their homes. Two months later, in October 1993, the UN Security Council approved a 2,500-strong peacekeeping force for Rwanda, the UN Assistance Mission for Rwanda (Unamir), a title that was eventually to prove grander than either the powers or the resources allotted to it.

That same month over the border in Burundi there was a coup. Its President, who had been a party to the Arusha talks, was killed. In the violence that followed tens of thousands lost their lives and up to 600,000 fled into neighbouring countries. Meanwhile, RTLMC's audiences grew and its language became more graphic and violent.

By all accounts a few brave souls in the Rwandan Ministry of Information did try to persuade RTLMC to rein in its broadcasts. Just after the Burundian coup the government minister responsible for broadcasting wrote to the station asking it to tone down its programmes, but to little effect. He was criticised on air when broadcasters twice read a letter that had been written by a 'high-level Hutu Power official', who had written that the minister had evil intentions.[619] Misleadingly, the station accused 'Tutsi dog-eaters' of killing the Burundian President, mutilating his body and burying it secretly. It was untrue, but it had given the radio station an opportunity to reinforce its audience base and play on its fears.[620] The ministry's calls for compliance were ignored.

So just as Hilsum was preparing to travel to Kigali, the country was in a state of turmoil: there was insurgency in the north, there were large numbers of refugees fleeing the war, there was inter-community ethnic violence, the Burundian coup on Rwanda's borders generated yet more refugees; extremism was growing, centred around militias, and the UN had just arrived in the country with a very limited mandate and even more limited resources.

In the opening months of 1994, and despite the efforts of many, the broad-based transitional government failed to take off. Each side blamed the other for the failure. Unamir's military commander, a Canadian general, Roméo Dallaire, picked up intelligence about arms shipments, but was forbidden by his UN masters to do anything. He also learned of deliberate attempts to weaken Unamir's mandate. Worryingly, Dallaire learned that young men in the militias had been told to go home and wait for 'a call to arms'.[621] He warned the UN about these developments, but there was no approval for him to do anything about it.

Massacre

It was on 6 April 1994, however, that events were to take their tragic turn and place Hilsum in a unique and difficult position. There were extreme nationalist factions within Habyarimana's Hutu-dominated party that were violently opposed to the prospect of any peace deal being signed with the RPF. Those sentiments may well also have been shared by the President himself, but realpolitik determined that he would sign a peace accord of some sort. That day, having placed his signature on a document he flew back to Kigali in his luxury private aircraft, a Mystère Falcon 50, in the company of his Burundian counterpart, President Cyprien Ntaryamira, who had been in office for barely eight weeks. But something went wrong. As Habyarimana's aircraft approached the city's airport it was blown up, most likely by a surface-to-air missile fired from somewhere in Kigali's suburbs. There were no survivors.

There are a number of theories about who fired the missile

and a number of suspects, although no conclusive proof has so far emerged.[622]

As soon as the aircraft exploded it seemed that all hell broke loose. To some it was as if it had all been planned in advance. The army and the militias started to kill people. Over the next ten days Hilsum travelled around Kigali mostly by car and kept notes about the appalling sights she saw. What follows is a brief sketch taken from some of her newspaper reports.

Her first story was published in *The Guardian* on 8 April. She wrote that the capital had 'descended into chaos' and that 'troops, presidential guards and gendarmes swept through the suburbs killing the Prime Minister, United Nations peacekeepers and scores of civilians'.[623] The dead UN peacekeepers were ten Belgian soldiers, all members of General Dallaire's command. They had gone to investigate the missile attack, and had been disarmed and detained by troops of the Rwandan presidential guard. Their bodies were later found in Kigali. 'They were dead from bullet wounds,' Hilsum quoted a UN spokesman saying. 'You can call it an execution.'[624] She noted that Unamir, which was monitoring the ceasefire between the RPF and federal forces, was powerless to stop the slaughter.

She wrote about 'gangs of soldiers and youths' who 'kidnapped opposition politicians and killed members of the minority Tutsi tribe, clubbing them to death with batons, hacking them with machetes and knives, or shooting them'. The pattern was to be repeated countless times over the next three months. In just thirteen weeks up to 800,000 people – Tutsis and 'moderate' Hutus – were estimated to have been killed: a hundred days of extreme violence, which according to one author matched or even surpassed the numbers killed in an equivalent period in the Nazi Holocaust.

The day after Habyarimana's death the Prime Minister, Agathe Uwilingiyimana, unable to broadcast to Rwanda's people, had been interviewed by telephone by Radio France Internationale. Hilsum quoted her: 'There is shooting, people are being terrorised, people are inside their homes lying on the floor. We are suffering the consequences of the death of the head of state.'[625] Within hours both she and her husband were dead.

In the days that followed, taking risks that she later recognised to have been considerable, Hilsum drove around Kigali witnessing the crowds and the death. On 9 April she wrote about thousands of bodies lying in the streets, after a 'two-day orgy of violence and looting'. She described how 'soldiers entered a religious centre, locked six priests and nine novice nuns in a room and then killed them' sparing only two Belgian Jesuits.[626] She said that it was not apparent why religious groups were targeted, but priests from both Tutsis and Hutus seemed to be victims. In the confusion that followed she said it was not 'clear who is a Hutu and who is a Tutsi'. A Rwandan journalist had described to her how 'youths armed with knives attacked a young couple with a baby, because, although they were Hutus, they looked like Tutsis'.[627]

One day she visited a house where she saw a pile of bodies, partially covered by a blanket, 'all women, and all had been hacked to death with machetes'. She described walking

through the wreckage of the house, through shards of broken glass and china, torn newspapers and broken furniture. A young man and a woman lay on the bed groaning with pain. Both had serious wounds – the woman had been hit by shrapnel from a grenade that had left a huge and bloody hole in her knee.[628]

She wrote that 'massacres like this have occurred all over the capital, and in some parts of rural Rwanda'. It would take months for the real scale of the killings to emerge.

A few Westerners were killed while Western governments accelerated their efforts to evacuate their own nationals. On 9 April French paratroopers landed at Kigali airport, temporarily seized control and began evacuating their nationals. Once it had been completed the forces withdrew and abandoned the Rwandans to their fate.

Unamir was unable to restore law and order because its

mandate was restricted only to monitoring the peace agreement and helping government troops maintain peace. There had been no mention of what it should do if the government itself was the cause of the unrest. Unamir personnel were confined to the national stadium, where eventually thousands of terrified people fled pleading for protection.

In her reports Hilsum tried to make sense of why the carnage was happening: it was not simply an inter-ethnic issue, because opposition party supporters had also been attacked, regardless of their ethnic classification. Religious communities were also prominent targets.

A day after her visit to the house Hilsum wrote about 'one of the most horrific incidents so far', where 'thugs from a Hutu extremist movement attacked a religious centre' near the Zairian border. The extremists had 'separated out all the Tutsis and killed them in front of the nuns and several expatriate aid workers'.[629]

A week after the murder of the Belgian troops the rest of the contingent was withdrawn from the Unamir force, further limiting what the remainder of the force could do. Unamir was in a difficult position because 'if shot at, they did not have permission to return fire'.[630] Hilsum said General Dallaire had asked for a change of mandate so that he could try to control the chaos, but 'the request was apparently rejected'. She concluded:

Unamir's weakness and the UN's moral failure as it leaves Rwandan staff to the mercy of marauding soldiers have once more battered its image. 'We have to look at Somalia, at Angola, and now Rwanda,' a UN official said. 'We really need to think again about what we are doing.'

One evening the extreme stress of the events caught up with her: she had not realised how vulnerable she had been when travelling around and living alone in a suburb where many people were killed. She had shown remarkable courage and tenacity in following stories, but probably without realising it until later, had placed her life at considerable risk. She eventually contacted UN staff and moved to safer accommodation – first to a house shared with other Europeans, and then a hotel, before being evacuated to Nairobi. But within days, she was filing reports from Burundi about events following the death of its President. She returned to Rwanda two months later, as the massacres were coming to an end.

In a comment piece for *The Independent* she was more forthright about the UN's refusal to let Unamir intervene: 'Unamir, the UN peace-keeping force in Rwanda, has done almost nothing to stop the bloodshed in Rwanda. One journalist saw UN troops standing and watching as a band of armed men butchered a woman. Challenged on their inaction, they explained they had no mandate to intervene.'[631] She continued, 'So while thugs and drunken soldiers rampaged through the suburbs hacking babies to death, UN troops retreated to barracks to await orders.'[632] But she acknowledged:

> If they had shot their way through the roadblocks to try to stop the slaughter, they could have been accused of becoming party to the conflict, like the US troops in Somalia. But the problem is deeper than that. The UN force in Rwanda had no credibility. No one was scared of it. An adequately trained and equipped force could at least have asserted its authority over disorganised mobs more interested in killing civilians than fighting rebels. But though many more people are losing their lives in massacres than in fighting, the energies of General Dallaire are still spent trying to broker peace between the RPF and the government.[633]

She concluded, 'The practice of assembling multilateral forces with mandates that cannot adapt to changing circumstances must stop. Failure was predictable, but the UN is not learning from experience ... UN bureaucrats cannot run military operations in Africa from New York.' If it couldn't then the UN could never really protect people. But, of course, it was susceptible to political pressure. American journalist Bill Berkeley wrote in 2001, 'We know that the US actually blocked the UN from intervening in Rwanda. The Clinton administration, soured by its experience in Somalia, was reluctant to intervene in another African nation in which American interests were not obvious.'[634] Berkeley also noted that, like Dallaire's warnings to the UN, the CIA had warned its own government that a massacre was on the cards. But American policy toward the UN was then that the organisation had to learn when to say no. Months after the Akayesu trial President Bill Clinton acknowledged that the US for one had been too slow to react; some critics considered that to be only half the story.

To testify, or not?

It is not without a hint of irony that the UN, which had proved itself so poor at managing peacekeeping operations, should set up criminal tribunals to catch up with the perpetrators of the crimes that its peacekeeping operations had been unable to stop in the first place. The 1990s not only witnessed the Rwandan massacre, but also the conflict in the former Yugoslavia. Until then no international and impartial mechanism had existed that could try people accused of war crimes. The Nuremberg process that followed the Second World War was an ad hoc arrangement. But the scale of the crimes witnessed in both those conflicts was such that few states had any liking for the best that was on offer: a form of national judicial retribution. Opponents were likely to see that as the dispensation of victor's justice; judgments would be open to criticism as tainted by prejudice.

Recognising the scale of the potential crimes and the issues involved in the former Yugoslavia, the UN established a special international criminal tribunal (ICTY) in 1993 to undertake the job of prosecuting war crimes, crimes against humanity and genocide. Its lawyers and judges were drawn from many different national legal systems, and it was hoped the very diversity would demonstrate and deliver impartial justice. As the scale of the

Rwandan massacre became clear moves were quickly made to set up another tribunal to try those responsible. In November 1994, and using ICTY as the model, the UN set up the International Criminal Tribunal for Rwanda (ICTR). The tribunal began working with a dedicated and talented team of international jurists and lawyers and was determined to make an impact.[635]

ICTR decided it was essential for the broad factual background to be established, which was why Hilsum's testimony was considered so important. Like its counterpart, ICTY (*see Chapters 1 and 9*), the tribunal decided it was necessary to establish broadly agreed facts, a historical context and timeline against which events and individual acts could be assessed. Both tribunals looked to journalists who had covered events on the ground to help establish those historical facts as they could provide first-hand and impartial testimony. However, the responses that the tribunals received were diverse. Most journalists refused to give evidence, citing professional ethics. A few agreed because they either did not see the ethical issues in the same way as their colleagues, or because they felt that they had to take sides when it came to the crunch.

Lindsey Hilsum recognised that in her case the decision would be difficult. But she was used to hard choices: the horrors in Rwanda had been far worse than this dilemma. So why did she agree to go to that airless courtroom in Arusha? Why, for that matter, was it based in Arusha? The location was a simple logistical solution: Rwanda was still too dangerous. Some witnesses had already met with fatal 'accidents'. Others had been killed more openly. But it was also not without significance that Arusha was where the RPF peace talks had been held.

What was the case against Akayesu? Jean-Paul Akayesu, a Hutu, was mayor, or *Bourgmestre*, of the Taba commune, which was situated to the west of Kigali. In the two weeks after the massacres began he kept his head down and by all accounts did nothing. He may actually have resisted the genocide.[636] But then he attended a meeting where everything changed. Leading

Interahamwe figures were present; it was chaired by the newly appointed Prime Minister, Jean Kambanda. Whatever happened at it Akayesu came away a changed man. He went on to hold meetings in his commune, often flanked by local Interahamwe leaders, and assumed leadership of the killings. This change of heart witnessed by his constituents encouraged hundreds of them to pick up their machetes and join him. He ordered Tutsis to be beaten or hacked to death. For the victims it was a cruel surprise because until then they had trusted him to protect them and had flocked for safety to his office compound. Many were massacred. But what made Akayesu's actions more noteworthy was that he incited the crowd of killers to go and commit sexual offences: principally gang rape. This last action was the key because the ICTR prosecutors wanted to establish that premeditated sexual offences on this scale could also be considered acts of genocide.[637]

Hilsum is by no means alone in testifying before a tribunal. Ed Vulliamy of *The Guardian*, Martin Bell, formerly of the BBC, Tom Gjelten of the American National Public Radio, Christiane Amanpour of CNN, and Jacky Rowland of the BBC testified in various cases. But many more journalists refused, and the debate continues. What are the arguments? And why is the issue so important?

Those who refuse argue that if journalists act as witnesses in such tribunals they expose themselves to charges of bias because they cross the line between being observers and participants in a story. Moreover, by doing so they possibly place themselves or their fellow professionals in danger – particularly those trying to cover events where it is possible that war crimes and other human rights violations will at some stage be uncovered. Journalists, they argue, are not official witnesses, nor are they police. They are observers and nothing more. But, as Hilsum rightly notes, reporters 'will be among the few outside observers to witness the horror'.[638] It is a privileged position, but also a highly sensitive and dangerous one to be in when bullets and shrapnel are flying and the knives are out.

When the American journalist Marie Colvin was killed while on assignment for the *Sunday Times* in Syria early in 2012 some argued that the journalism of attachment, as advocated by Martin Bell (*see Chapter 9*), could end up with reporters becoming 'moral combatants, crusaders against "evil"'. The editor of *Spiked*, Brendan O'Neill, wrote that by 'emphasising attachment over neutrality, and emotionalism over objectivity, the new breed of attached reporter' will be 'more like an activist, an international campaigner, rather than a dispassionate recorder of fact and truth'.

But Hilsum was careful to say that her own involvement was not about Akayesu – no matter what she, as a human being, may have thought about the charges levelled against him. She felt herself able to participate because she had witnessed widespread slaughter. She had no professional views about Akayesu, the prisoner in the dock who sometimes shuffled nervously and betrayed the fact that like many of his victims he too was very scared. She had not witnessed his crimes. She wrote, 'I do not know if Akayesu is guilty or innocent.'[639]

But she was conscious of the need for the historical record to be set straight by the court if any justice was to be done to the victims. And she felt committed enough to want to help. The prosecution needed to establish that 'the alleged crimes of individuals were "crimes against humanity", part of a "widespread and systematic" plan to kill civilians for reasons of ethnicity, race, religion or politics'.[640] She was adamant that it was: 'Of that I have no doubt.' But, she also recognised, without ego, that there were few alternative witnesses available:

> By accident of history, I happened to be there. The only other foreign correspondent in Kigali at the time was unable to leave her house because, as a Belgian, she was under threat. So I ... was the only foreign journalist to report those first, critical days in the capital. This gave me responsibilities beyond my job as a reporter which I could not avoid.[641]

There had been other outside observers in Kigali – those working for the ICRC, for instance – but they were prevented from
giving testimony precisely because they would undermine their
employer's impartiality, which, crucially, it could never risk. So
the burden fell on her, a freelance cameraman who had actually
recorded some footage of killings[642] and a doctor from the charity
Médecins Sans Frontières, who argued that his human duty over-
rode his 'medical loyalty' to his employer.

So Hilsum told the court what she had seen: 'the hundreds of
hacked bodies spilling out of the morgue, the blood running in
the hospital gutters, the baby whose leg had been partially severed
by a machete, the drunken soldiers and young men on the road-
blocks'.[643] But she attempted to 'distinguish between what I saw
and what I later learnt'. She confessed that in 'those first, terrify-
ing, days I failed to realise how well organised' the campaign
was. 'I saw the horror without understanding the meaning.' Only
later did she realise that the massacre had been well organised,
and not some chaotic event: weapons had been distributed, training given, instructions delivered over RTLMC by the station's
broadcasters. Over the months following the massacre she interviewed 'survivors and some of the killers' leaders' and came to
appreciate that 'far from being "ancient tribal hatred"', it had
been 'a well-planned campaign to try and exterminate Rwanda's
Tutsis and eliminate anyone who opposed the murderous plan'.[644]
Comparisons with the Nazis were not lost on her.

But for Hilsum, the bottom line was simply that it was 'the
right thing to do. The normal rules of journalistic ethics are over-
whelmed by murder on this scale,' she wrote.[645] She saw herself
crossing that line, but felt that 'it was a moral duty to use my
unique position to influence the historical record in the court'.

Two-pronged test
Several years after she had appeared in Arusha, a war crimes
case came before the Rwanda court's sister tribunal, ICTY. It

involved Jonathan Randal, an American journalist who had reported about the civil war in the former Yugoslavia for the *Washington Post*. He had been subpoenaed to give evidence in a trial of a suspected war criminal. Randal refused, citing some of the reasons that have already been outlined. He received backing from his newspaper and many journalists and fought the order. It went to appeal and, in the view of the court, which supported his application, 'a two-pronged test needs to be satisfied in order for a Trial Chamber to issue a subpoena to a war correspondent who, having been requested to testify, refuses to do so'. First, the legal team summoning the journalist should be able to show that 'the evidence sought is of direct and important value in determining a core issue in the case'. So, it needs to be a key fact, or event, not some by-the-way factoid, not, to use a judicial term, obiter dicta. But more importantly, the legal team would have to 'demonstrate that the evidence sought cannot reasonably be obtained elsewhere'. In other words, journalists should not be used just because they were there, or as lazy evidence-gathering. Their potential contribution had to have an element of uniqueness about it, something that could not be gleaned from any other source, not matter how hard they tried. Just as Lindsey Hilsum's testimony could not really be provided by anyone else. So the summoning of journalists to testify as a matter of routine was not acceptable to the court.

The judges had also recognised the dangers for the journalists stemming from overuse. 'Compelling war correspondents to testify before the tribunal on a routine basis may have a significant impact on their ability to obtain information,' they had felt. The Appeal Court recognised the potent dangers of 'the perception that war correspondents can be forced to become witnesses against their interviewees'. That could – and maybe would in some cases – 'result in war correspondents facing difficulties in gathering significant information', but it could also put their lives at risk.[646] The journalist Nina Bernstein recalled that John Kifner, a veteran *New York Times* war correspondent, had told her that if she co-operated with prosecutors 'I would put him at greater risk of being shot the next time he approached some warlord with his press tags dangling, saying, "I just want to tell your story."'[647] It is a powerful injunction.

Roy Gutman, the journalist who first revealed the existence of detention camps in Bosnia to the world, refused to attend the Yugoslav tribunal, after an informal approach. He was not insensitive to the request. 'Make no mistake,' he wrote, 'many reporters, myself included, feel a moral obligation to assist the tribunal, as reporters frequently do with local district attorneys and prosecutors in domestic settings.' But the issue was really whether journalists should testify about articles written years earlier. 'My own standard', Gutman wrote, 'is that if my testimony would make the difference between conviction and release of a person I know was a killer or the planner of killings, I would testify out of conscience.' Anything else

> seems to me I am either there to self-advertise my role in nailing the culprit, being used as window dressing for a weak case, or being made vulnerable to a perfectly legal demand for discovery by the defense and, where that ends, heaven only knows. I would not, as Vulliamy did, make my notes available to the court.[648]

American journalist Bill Berkeley went to Rwanda as the massacres were coming to an end. He heard the stories from both victims, many of whom bore terrible wounds, and perpetrators. His reports appeared in the *New Republic*. He has written how, five years later, he was asked to appear as a prosecution witness at ICTR in the trial of Colonel Théoniste Bagosora, whom many called the Rwandan Himmler. He agreed. But as the years passed in case preparations, and he wrote several editorials for the *New York Times* that were critical of ICTR, he began to have doubts; but so too, it seems, had the prosecution. In the end Berkeley says that for reasons not entirely clear he was never called, but by then he had decided that he would have refused to appear in any case. Stressing that he was only invited, never subpoenaed, he wrote about it saying that not only would it have compromised his impartiality, but his safety.

> I believe that the perception of journalists as potential arms of a criminal prosecution should be avoided at all costs, not least for the safety of future war correspondents and for their ability to do work that ultimately is as essential to the pursuit of truth as any criminal proceeding is likely to be.[649]

But, to be clear, he does accept one of the appeal judges' prongs, and thus supports Lindsey Hilsum's position: 'I believe there might be extraordinary circumstances in which a journalist could well be persuaded to testify if he or she has unique and invaluable evidence that can be gotten nowhere else. But that should be the exceptional case, and the decision should be the journalist's own.'[650] He wrote, 'Journalism, my life's work, is an expression of my humanity and the best contribution I have to make to justice as well as truth.'

But Gutman adds another point when he says that his evidence was published for all to see and there is nothing more that he can contribute. It was a view shared by his editors. 'My worry in this context is that you can give the appearance of being tainted by taking a stand,' he said. Crossing the line and testifying may make it difficult for journalists to sustain the appearance of objectivity in their further coverage. In his view the job of a reporter is simply to report the facts, nothing more, and nothing less. But that is a powerful role. He said, 'At times journalism can have the same impact as a tribunal and a lot faster. A timely, well-documented, irrefutable exposé can pack such a wallop that the mere shining of additional multiple spotlights on a scene can change the behaviour of the culprit.'[651]

Testifying might affect a person's objectivity. It was a reason cited when CNN's Catherine Bond, who had reported on Rwanda for Channel 4 News, refused to testify at the tribunal after CNN's editors pointed out that it would affect her impartiality. But it had less resonance with Ed Vulliamy or his employers: he covered the trial process in which he also appeared as a prosecution witness, both before and after he took the stand.

Roy Gutman does not see what extra value a journalist can add by standing up in court. Hilsum quotes him: 'My editors would say, if all (the court) wants is a recapitulation of what's been written or filmed, then just submit that. They don't need you in person. What do you actually add to the proceedings?'[652] It is a good point. But some would argue, as we saw in the previous chapter about Bosnia, that personal testimony is valuable. A court can probe and satisfy itself as to the witness's candour. But there are times when, for instance, a testimony can make all the difference, as Dr Merdžanić's testimony in the *Living Marxism* trial showed.

But there is perhaps another reason why many – maybe the majority – of American journalists are uneasy about the prospect of testifying before a war crimes tribunal. In the late 1960s and early 1970s some were assailed by the Nixon administration, which wanted to find the sources of news stories that caused it difficulty. A number of journalists refused and elected to go to prison rather than comply, and that prompted a minor change in the law in some states. But it also helped to reinforce the tradition of independence. Many with long memories, and still influential in the profession, see a link and see the profession as an essential bulwark against infringements of freedom of speech.[653] It is a strong argument.

Like Gutman, Hilsum would rather just have submitted written evidence. But in her view 'appearing at the tribunal was a deliberate, personal commitment to justice. I was telling the story to set straight the historical record.' Not that crossing the line, however, meant that she had complete confidence that the court would 'deliver justice or an accurate historical record'.[654] Courts rarely do, it would seem.[655] For the privilege of helping to set the record straight she had to accept attacks from a defence team which questioned her professionalism: by criticising her for not setting out immediately to start investigating the plane crash site, she had failed, they alleged. They heard back that that would have been foolhardy in the extreme. She might have added that, but probably didn't, that had she done so, then like so many others, her body might never have been found either.

But testifying at the tribunal did not turn her into a stool pigeon. She proved that she was still able to maintain a journalist's ethical principles. When she interviewed the former Bosnian Serb leader, Radovan Karadžić, who was then a fugitive wanted by the International Criminal Tribunal for the Former Yugoslavia, she did not pass on any details of where the meeting had taken place – he remained a fugitive for a further ten years. She acknowledged that a balance between 'the practical and ethical demands of reporting, and our responsibility as citizens – or human beings' needs to be struck. But she was also clear that she did not think that she could testify against people like Karadžić 'as individuals, using information gleaned from interviews, because this would be a breach of trust. Even if an interviewee is a mass murderer, the rules of "off the record" and guarding sources apply.' That may be a fair point, but one that may trouble some people. Could one really say for certain that having interviewed a fugitive Himmler or Hitler they would not then tell where they were hiding? That would be a massive moral and professional dilemma, but shows the extremes to which the issue reaches. But no one has yet come up with a checklist that navigates a clear path through these ethical dilemmas. The debate still rages.

But what of Akayesu, the man whose trial started this chapter? He was not a demon. He was a middle-ranking local government official. He was not a simpleton, nor a psychopath. He was literate, obedient and an unexceptional member of the relatively rigid Rwandan society. But he still managed to persuade others to kill upwards of 2,000 of his constituents, and to incite them to commit gang rape. Some thought he was an opportunist who waited to see which way the wind was blowing before acting, joining the winning side. One of the prosecutors thought his motivations were all about power and, in that sense, that he was completely amoral. A poor witness who 'squirmed' in the witness box and contradicted himself while giving evidence, he lost the sympathy of the court as he struggled to lie his way out of several of the holes that he had dug for himself. He was found guilty and was sentenced to life imprisonment, a sentence that was upheld on appeal.[656]

13

ANDREW GILLIGAN

It became known as 'the regime change video'. Two men stood reading short speeches into a TV camera with only a background logo and a pot plant for company. This was the way leaders of a coup d'état, having seized the TV station, used to address the nation. The two men announced that they had been asked to take over power because the former leaders had fallen. They needed a few attempts to read their speeches to camera without making a mistake before the video recording was ready to roll to a waiting world.[657]

The location was not somewhere in a banana republic in the last century but a conference room in Broadcasting House, the London headquarters of the British Broadcasting Corporation, in 2004.

The two men were the acting chairman of the BBC, Lord Ryder, a former Conservative minister, and the acting director-general, Mark Byford. They were an interim regime at the request of the BBC Board of Governors.

The men whom they temporarily replaced, Gavyn Davies and Greg Dyke, were the victims of one of the most acrimonious rows between the BBC and a British government.

When Gavyn Davies resigned as chairman of the BBC he said an attack on the corporation by the Labour government of Prime Minister Tony Blair had 'undoubtedly scrambled our radar screens at the top of the BBC'.[658] Now, a decade later, our investigations have revealed that the BBC's underlying problem was a misunderstanding between an editor and a reporter that could have been avoided and should have been spotted. The changing of the guard at Broadcasting House and one of the biggest traumas in its history need never have happened.

The crisis had been caused by what one reporter had said in one radio programme.

What became known simply as 'Hutton', after the judge who held a public inquiry into it, was a battle between a broadcaster and a government. But it was the death of one man, Dr David Kelly, who had been caught up in the middle, that made the saga so traumatic for everyone involved.

'Hutton' mattered because the BBC appeared to challenge Blair's claim that he had acted in good faith in joining George W. Bush's war in Iraq to overthrow Saddam Hussein and to find the 'weapons of mass destruction' which, it transpired, never existed. There have been four inquiries into different aspects of the Iraq War and related events; many thousands of documents have been submitted in evidence, probably over a million words spoken in testimony and countless more written in news coverage. In this chapter we focus on the role of one editor and one reporter who were at the heart of this particular crisis, but who in the words of one of them 'don't seem to meet too often'.

The editor was Kevin Marsh. Educated at Christ Church, Oxford, he joined the BBC in 1978 as a news trainee and was a BBC News lifer. He had just one short career excursion outside the corporation, a spell as a producer on ITN's *News at Ten*.

The reporter was Andrew Gilligan. Also an Oxbridge man, he studied history at St John's, Cambridge, but took a different path into national journalism. He began on a local paper, the *Cambridge Evening News*, and then freelanced for newspapers such as *The Independent*, for whom he wrote an article in 1995 headlined 'So You Think You Can Hack It on the Nationals?' about students who wanted to become journalists. He then set about hacking it on a national with his first staff job on the *Sunday Telegraph*.

Kevin Marsh never chose Andrew Gilligan to work for him,

but inherited him when he became editor of *Today*, the flagship programme on BBC Radio 4, in 2002. One former BBC and ITN editor, Richard Tait, was later to say that Kevin 'picked up the bill for somebody else's lunch'.[659]

The man who ordered the 'lunch' (but wasn't around to pay for it) was Marsh's predecessor, Rod Liddle. Keen to break more exclusive stories on *Today*, Liddle had been given the freedom to hire investigative reporters such as Gilligan, a man he later described as 'in many ways a strange fellow, with his incessant supply of sugary drinks and chocolate bars and crisps'.[660]

Liddle encouraged his recruits to 'push it'. At the time a *Guardian* article quoted a member of BBC Radio's editorial staff as saying, 'I think there is a feeling around the place that some of them push things a bit too far in an effort to make something sound new.' But the BBC went one step further with Liddle; he was allowed to write a column for *The Guardian*. Initially the column was only about radio, but the BBC then allowed him to develop as a more general columnist, offering observations on a wide range of topics.

The experiment ended in what one BBC executive at the time, Mark Damazer, called 'a lot of broken glass'. Liddle was taken to task by the corporation over a column in which he criticised a Countryside Alliance march in London. The article was deemed 'not acceptable' and did 'not square with the BBC's obligation to be impartial and to be seen to be impartial'. Liddle stepped down as the editor of *Today*.

At that point, Marsh was the editor of another major Radio 4 programme, *The World at One*, where he'd been involved in what amounted to a running battle with the director of communications and strategy at Downing Street, Alastair Campbell. Marsh was the obvious candidate to succeed Liddle but wasn't sure about it. However, after *Today* had been without an editor for nearly three months, he made his mind up. 'I decided I'd do it. For eighteen months. Two years max. Clear up the broken glass. And move on.'

Enter Andrew Gilligan

Among those awaiting him on *Today* were Liddle's recruits including the defence and diplomatic correspondent, Andrew Gilligan. He had previously worked on the *Sunday Telegraph* and in an article headlined 'The Extraordinary World of Andrew Gilligan' his former colleagues were later to describe him as 'insecure yet arrogant, teetotal yet over-indulgent, gentle yet controlling' which made him 'almost impossible to understand or empathise with'.[661] One colleague was quoted as saying that Gilligan was 'a brilliant writer and an extremely intelligent man' but – and there were many buts in the article – 'he was incapable of producing copy on time'.[662]

According to this account, Gilligan was notoriously private, and rarely went to the *Sunday Telegraph* office, preferring to work at night in his flat in south London, where he ingested large amounts of junk food, left the packaging lying around and filed late copy.

Kevin Marsh discovered early on at *Today* that it appeared that no producer worked with the very private Gilligan and no one checked his scripts. When Marsh read one script, about a British arms company's dealings with Zimbabwe, it seemed 'full of holes'. It was not a good start to their relationship.

He also later wrote of Gilligan's habits during this period: 'He would routinely present his stories at the last possible moment and only occasionally at one of the routine editorial conferences. I always assumed he was hoping to smuggle them past an inattentive or indifferent editor.'[663]

It was now December 2002 and all the British media were focused on preparing for what seemed an inevitable Anglo-American invasion of Iraq in the spring to overthrow Saddam Hussein and neutralise what, it was claimed, were his 'weapons of mass destruction' (WMD). Marsh said he was nervous when he discovered that Gilligan was the first, and so far only, BBC reporter to get a visa to go to Baghdad.

He told his immediate boss, Steve Mitchell, that he was against Gilligan going. The reply was 'tough'; if Gilligan was the only person with a visa he'd have to go. And when Marsh told Mitchell that he 'wasn't entirely thrilled he [Gilligan] was on the books at all', Mitchell told him this wasn't Fleet Street where they just fired people, Marsh would have to 'manage him out' using procedures that could take at least two years.

Over in Downing Street they had been keeping an eye on Gilligan too. They disliked a story he had broadcast in November 2000 about whether discussions to codify the European Union's treaties amounted to a draft constitution for a European super-state. To try to damage his credibility they christened him 'gullible Gilligan'.

The wider battle begins

On the morning of 20 March 2003 Andrew Gilligan broadcast from Baghdad on the bombing of the Iraqi capital. The 'Coalition' of American and British forces hoped the bombardment would inspire 'shock and awe' in enemy troops before the land war began. About the same time a letter from Downing Street was arriving at the BBC possibly intending to inspire its own version of 'shock and awe'. Tony Blair wrote to the director-general of the BBC, Greg Dyke, criticising the corporation's coverage.

According to Dyke, Blair wrote: 'It seems to me there has been a real breakdown of the separation of news and comment. I know that Alastair has been pressing you to ensure more reference is made to reports from inside Iraq about the restrictions under which the media operate.' The letter also complained that the BBC had not got the balance right between support and dissent.[664]

No names were mentioned but undoubtedly whoever drafted the letter for Blair – most observers believe it was Alastair Campbell – had Gilligan's reports partly in mind.

Dyke's reply began in robust style:

Firstly, and I do not mean to be rude, but having faced the biggest ever public demonstration in this country and the biggest ever backbench rebellion against a sitting government by its own supporters, would you not agree that your communications advisors are not best placed to advise whether or not the BBC has got the balance right between support and dissent.

The battle lines between a government and the BBC had been drawn, just as they had at so many times of conflict before, from the Suez invasion of 1956 to the Falklands War of 1982.

How very different from much earlier times at the BBC, when during the Munich crisis of 1938 the BBC recorded that its role was to fall 'into line with Government policy'.[665]

This exchange of letters was to prove the opening of the latest front in Alastair Campbell's battle with the BBC. Dyke came to the conclusion that Campbell was obsessed with the corporation. The two men each had a background in the media and in the politics of 'New Labour' but they were never friends and now they were on different sides.

According to one shrewd political observer, Andrew Rawnsley of *The Observer*, Alastair Campbell had become 'one of the most powerful non-elected officials ever to operate from 10 Downing Street'.[666] With unrivalled access to the Prime Minister and almost unlimited freedom to operate, Campbell commanded respect, even fear, from Labour Party politicians for his ability to confront and sometimes to control the media. Originally a newspaper reporter himself, taming political reporters and their editors had become an obsession for Campbell. So much so that Tony Blair is said to have told one friend, 'The trouble with Alastair is that he hates the media.'[667] The BBC's unrivalled position as the nation's biggest news operation had made them an obvious target for him. Over at the BBC a different mindset developed. Campbell was now complaining so often that the default response to a complaint from him was that he was wrong; the BBC was right and must fight back with renewed vigour.

Greg Dyke was the director-general of the BBC but he did not come from the dominant tribe of BBC lifers. Like his predecessor John Birt, his career had been mainly in commercial television and he had been recruited at a senior level by Sir Christopher Bland, who was then chairman of the BBC but had formerly been his chairman at London Weekend Television. Dyke's appointment was controversial because he had been a donor to the Labour Party. Another Labour supporter, Gavyn Davies, became Dyke's boss when he succeeded Bland as chairman of the BBC. Their mutual Labour connection was a coincidence, but it was to turn out to be a significant one.

During the war in Iraq Dyke received many complaints from Campbell about Gilligan's reporting, and on one occasion an identical complaint came from Gerald Kaufman, the chairman of the Commons Select Committee on Culture, Media and Sport. Dyke concluded that Campbell's department had written the letter for Kaufman. On another occasion, the BBC had to accept that Gilligan was wrong to talk about 'more rubbish from Central Command' in reference to the Anglo-American-led coalition.[668] The director of BBC News, Richard Sambrook, wrote to Alastair Campbell: 'This particular phrase was unacceptable, which I regret, and will take it up with Andrew Gilligan. Thank you for drawing it to my attention.'[669]

A very short peace
When American troops entered Baghdad on 9 April 2003 and helped to pull down a statue of Saddam Hussein, BBC executives might have been entitled to a measure of relief that their battle with Downing Street over Iraq was probably over. In fact the worst was yet to come.

The first escalation came a few days later when Andrew Gilligan reported from the Iraqi capital that

> Baghdad may in theory be free but its people are passing their first days of liberty in a greater fear than they've ever known. The old fear of the regime was habitual, low level. This fear is sharp and immediate – the fear that your house will be invaded, your property will be taken away and your daughters will be raped.[670]

Campbell and his team complained but the BBC stood by their man.

Andrew Gilligan came home after the war. The director of BBC News thanked him, told him that some of his reporting had been very good, but that too often he went ten per cent too far. After a short break Gilligan went back to work and played a central role in what was to be a second, and much more significant, escalation in post-war hostilities between the government and the BBC.

On 28 May the *Today* team who were planning the next morning's programme prepared, as usual, their 'master prospects' list which they would hand over to the overnight team that evening. Item number six on the 'foreign' section of the list read:

> WMD: The dossier on Iraq which the government produced last September (24th) was jazzed up at the last minute to include new information based on dubious sources – including the claim that chemical and biological weapons could be deployed at 45 minutes' notice. Live 0700–0730 Andrew Gilligan illustrated two-way. Gilligan has got this from a senior source who shall remain anonymous.[671]

Kevin Marsh says that although the *Today* journalist in charge of the prospects list said Gilligan claimed he had spoken to Marsh about it, in fact this was the first time Marsh discovered that the story was being pursued. He was told that Gilligan's source had said the government's dossier published the previous September had been 'sexed up' in the week before publication. And the source had said 'that was down to Campbell'.[672]

Marsh has said he 'rattled off' to the *Today* journalist a series of questions which Gilligan would need to answer before the story could run, including more details about the source. She went back to Gilligan and then told Marsh enough to satisfy him. She didn't have the source's name because Gilligan hadn't told her, but Marsh didn't regard the name as essential.

Marsh was shown two sides of paper which Gilligan had typed up after his meeting with his source. Only much later would it become known that Gilligan had been to the Charing Cross Hotel in London on 22 May 2003 to meet a Dr David Kelly. He was a British expert on biological warfare who had been employed to undertake certain tasks by the Ministry of Defence and had also been a United Nations weapons-inspector in Iraq.

Gilligan's two sides of paper were headed 'What My Man Said' and they appeared to be a full question and answer (Q&A) transcript of a conversation.

The key section said:

A: The classic was the statement that WMD were ready for use within 45 minutes. Most things in the dossier were double-sourced but that was single source. And we believed that the source was wrong. He said it took 45 minutes to construct a missile assembly, and that was misinterpreted (in the dossier) to mean that WMD could be deployed in 45 minutes. What we thought he actually meant was that they could launch a conventional missile in 45 minutes. There was no evidence that they had loaded missiles with WMD, or could do so anything like that quickly.

Q: So how did this transformation happen?

A: Campbell.

Q: What do you mean? They made it up?

A: No, it was real information. But it was included in the dossier against our wishes because it wasn't reliable. It was a single source and it was not reliable. He said Downing Street had asked if there was anything else on seeing the full original dossier and had been told about this and other things.[673]

Marsh thought it looked like a 'good note of a good source. Enough to go with.' Only later did it become clear that this document was not exactly a 'note'. What the reporter had done was that while he talked to his source he tapped away at the miniature keyboard of a personal organiser device. He later typed up this as a 'Q&A' doubling the number of words and making it easier to read. This apparent transcript was regularly referred to by others

as Gilligan's 'notes', but in truth the words on his personal organiser were really his notes.

As he reflected on Gilligan's proposed story Marsh remembered
conversations with a Cabinet minister and the head of MI6 which
confirmed the doubts he'd had about the dossier when it was first
published. This had been the first government dossier effectively
preparing the case for war to be put to the British public. This is
sometimes confused with a second dossier published the following year which became known as the 'dodgy dossier'.

The first, the September dossier, was titled 'Iraq's Weapons
of Mass Destruction' with a sub-heading 'The Assessment of
the British Government'. In the foreword by Tony Blair was a
sentence which said of Saddam Hussein: 'The document discloses
that his military planning allows for some of the WMD to be
ready within 45 minutes of an order to use them.'[674]

Marsh made his decision. He would go with the story but he
wanted the allegations put to the government. He was told a
Ministry of Defence minister was coming in to be interviewed
live on the programme about another subject. Ministers were
used to being asked additional questions about breaking stories.
But no formal request for a response to Gilligan's story was sent
to the government.

Separately, a *Today* producer began writing a background
briefing for the presenters. Although it was headed 'Gilligan
and Campbell brief', and the name of Alastair Campbell had
appeared in Gilligan's Q&A document written after his interview
with Kelly, it wasn't in this brief. Nor would it appear anywhere
in the coming day's coverage.

That evening Gilligan worked late in his flat in Greenwich on
his contributions to the *Today* programme. At about 1 a.m. he
rang the team preparing the radio news bulletins for breakfast-
time outlets and told them about his story. They asked for him
to file copy and he did. A journalist suggested one small change to
the news script; he agreed and then recorded a voice report for
use on the various bulletins.[675]

On air

The first transmission of any kind was not on *Today* but on the 0500 BBC Radio News bulletins on Radio 2 and Radio 5 Live. On Radio 2 an announcer, Alice Arnold, read a short introduction to part of Gilligan's voice report.

> Alice Arnold: Tony Blair is to become the first Western leader to visit Iraq since the fall of Saddam Hussein. He will meet British troops when he travels to the country later this morning. BBC News has learned that intelligence officials were unhappy with the dossier published by the government last September which claimed that Iraq had the ability to launch weapons of mass destruction in 45 minutes. Andrew Gilligan reports.
>
> Andrew Gilligan: One senior British official has now told the BBC that the original version of the dossier produced by the intelligence services added little to what was already publicly known but one week before publication, said this official, the dossier was transformed on Downing Street's orders. The 45-minute assertion was one of several claims added against the wishes of the intelligence agencies who said it was from a single source which they didn't necessarily believe.[676]

There was no comment from the government because none had been asked for.

At 6 a.m. *Today* itself went on the air and the opening news summary was also based on the copy Gilligan had sent through overnight. Gilligan's major contribution to the programme – a full 'package', with extracts of his source's quotes read by an actor – was not scheduled until about 7.30. The script for this had been seen and approved. However, as part of the usual *Today* format of reporters doing short live interviews looking ahead to later in the programme, Gilligan was interviewed live by *Today* presenter John Humphrys at 6.07.

Humphrys was in the *Today* studio, Gilligan was talking 'down the line' from his flat. At one point in their live interview Gilligan went further than in any previous version of the story that he had written or recorded and said: 'What we've been told by one of the senior officials in charge of drawing up the dossier was that, actually the government probably, erm, knew that the 45-minute figure was wrong, even before it decided to put it in.'

In just two hours the story had gone from an allegation that 'the intelligence agencies ... didn't necessarily believe the claim' to one that 'the government probably knew it was wrong'. In addition, the official who in the 5 a.m. news bulletin was 'involved' in the dossier had, by 6.07, been promoted to become 'one of the senior people in charge of drawing it up'.

Gilligan's editor, Kevin Marsh, has said he was in the back of a minicab on his way to work as he listened to his reporter continuing to stumble through the live transmission:

> Well, erm, our source says that the dossier, as it was finally published, made the Intelligence Services unhappy, erm, because to quote, erm, the source, he said, there was basically, that there was, there was, there was unhappiness because it didn't reflect the considered view they were putting forward, that's a quote from our source and essentially, erm, the 45-minute point, er, was, was probably the most important thing that was added.[677]

Nine years later in his book *Stumbling over Truth*, Marsh remembered his response in the back of the cab as being, 'Just read the fucking script. What's wrong with you? ... It sounded as if Gilligan had got up late and was doing it off the top of his head. Bad call. He needed a bollocking for that.'[678]

When Marsh got to the *Today* office he saw his deputy with a phone clamped to his ear. The deputy 'pointed to the handset and mouthed the words "Downing Street"'. The battle had started, but Marsh's priority at that point was overseeing the rest of that day's programme, especially Gilligan's main report, which went out at 7.32. At no point does it seem that Gilligan was challenged on or off air about the difference between what he had said in the interview at 6.07 and what he said in his approved 7.32 script. The government 'probably knew it was wrong' line was not repeated but nor was it corrected during the programme.

Meanwhile other BBC outlets were reporting the story in slightly different ways. The new allegations had variously originated from 'a security source' or 'security sources' or a 'senior official involved in preparing the dossier'. Sometimes changes to the dossier had been 'at the behest of Downing Street', sometimes 'ordered by Downing Street' or 'asked for', and on one occasion 'Downing Street asked for it to be hyped up to help convince the doubters'. This had apparently either been done 'against the wishes of the intelligence agencies' or 'the security services'; but in other broadcasts the agencies were merely 'unhappy'. As to the government's role, in some reports it had asked 'can we make this a bit more exciting please' or for it to be 'hyped up to help convince the doubters', but in other outlets the document had been 'transformed on Downing Street's orders' or 'at the behest of Downing Street'.

If this was to become some kind of BBC campaign against Downing Street, the inconsistency in the allegations suggested it wasn't a very well-organised one.

Significantly, what had been the strongest allegation reported by Gilligan – that the government probably knew the claim was wrong – never appeared again in any BBC news bulletin on that day. At the time no one seems to have found that odd.

Given the prominence Gilligan's story was getting on BBC Radio, it is striking how little coverage it got on BBC Television.

Some of those who worked in BBC TV news have told me that scepticism about Gilligan's work had grown over the previous months and they steered clear of the story.

However, the BBC *Ten O'Clock News*, regarded as BBC One's flagship news, commissioned a report not by Gilligan but by one of its 'special' correspondents, Gavin Hewitt. He reported: 'I have spoken to one of those who was consulted on the dossier.' Understandably he did not disclose who this person was, nor did he know at the time that this source, Dr David Kelly, was the person who had talked to Gilligan. After an off-the-record conversation with Kelly, Hewitt concluded: 'In the final week before publication, some material was taken out, some material put in. His judgement, some spin from No. 10 did come into play. Even so the intelligence community remains convinced weapons of mass destruction will be found in Iraq.'[679]

With hindsight, this was a significant paragraph. A senior BBC correspondent had looked into a story originating from another part of the corporation, had carried out his own checks and come to a much less dramatic conclusion. Hewitt's 'some spin from No. 10 did come into play' was a contrast with the way the news-reader had introduced his report. The introduction mentioned 'accusations that the government's dossier on Iraq's weapons was distorted by Downing Street'.

Downing Street's response to all this coverage on the BBC was to deny the whole basis of Gilligan's story, although it had accepted that the 45-minute claim was indeed single sourced. At this stage the complaints about the story were being made to the BBC by Alastair Campbell's team rather than by the man himself. Gilligan's remarks at 6.07 were not highlighted for particular complaint by Downing Street.

'We don't seem to meet too often'

As this row between the BBC and the government began to develop, the relationship between Kevin Marsh and Andrew Gilligan remained distant. The two men had hardly spoken before the trans-mission of the report and nothing much seemed to change after-wards. What, for instance, ever happened to that 'bollocking' that Marsh thought Gilligan needed? According to Marsh he bumped into Gilligan later that day in a corridor in BBC Television Centre. He told Gilligan it was a good story and well done but that he had been 'fucking awful' at 6.07. They needed to talk.

Rather than deliver a full 'bollocking', the following day Marsh sent Gilligan an email which struck a rather different tone:

Statement of the obvious I guess but it's really good to have you back here in the UK. Great week, great stories, well handled and well told. Course it's meant *Today* has had a great week too, and that has lifted everyone. We still have to have that conversation [which is my annual appraisal] but since you are entirely nocturnal while I'm a normal human being we don't seem to meet too often. Maybe you could creak the coffin lid open next week during daylight hours. Anyway, it's great to have you back on your beat. Talk soon.[680]

Marsh's subsequent explanation of this email was that Gilligan had been avoiding him, but he thought insincerity might encourage Gilligan to open that coffin lid a little. Gilligan's response was to go on holiday; Marsh could hardly say no. His need to do an 'annual appraisal' of Gilligan would turn out to be more significant.

Before then there would be a new twist in their relationship. In their encounter in the corridor the previous day Gilligan had told his editor that he wanted to write a piece for the *Mail on Sunday*. Marsh said the idea 'didn't thrill' him and as he, Marsh, would be away that weekend Gilligan would have to get another BBC News executive to vet the article.[681]

Marsh said Gilligan told him his piece for that weekend's *Mail on Sunday* would 'add nothing' to what he'd already broadcast on the BBC. In fact he added one very significant word and this was the first time he had used it in public, since he typed up his notes after seeing Dr Kelly. The word was Campbell. The *Mail on Sunday* were not slow to spot it and so that no one missed the point they put the word into capital letters in the headline: 'I asked my intelligence source why Blair misled us all over Saddam's weapons. His reply? One word ... CAMPBELL.'[682]

Gilligan's article told of his meeting with his source and their conversation: 'I asked him how this transformation [of the document] happened. The answer was a single word. "Campbell." What? Campbell made it up? "No, it was real information. But it was included against our wishes because it wasn't reliable."'

This wasn't quite the same thing as what the *Mail* headline claimed, but it was certainly enough to infuriate the Downing Street enforcer. Many listeners would have guessed that Gilligan referring on air to 'Downing Street' was probably a proxy for saying 'Alastair Campbell', but for him to be named in a headline that talked of how 'Blair misled us' was a major escalation in the story. Perhaps it was inevitable it would come out at some point because the name had been in Gilligan's notes from the start, but oddly it had never been mentioned on the air before. For it to be done now, not by the BBC – in their own way and in their own time – but by a BBC reporter without BBC permission and in a newspaper hostile to both the BBC and Campbell was bizarre.

Gilligan has since admitted that, in Marsh's absence that weekend, he did not get another BBC News executive to vet the article before it was sent to the *Mail on Sunday*; but nowhere in his book does Kevin Marsh record reprimanding Gilligan face to face for this, or even email to email.

His view of their relationship seems best summed up in the six words which Marsh uses about a later conversation they had as they walked around the circular open space of Television Centre. 'We walked. He talked. I despaired.' This was not exactly what the BBC would call 'talent management'.

The row between No. 10 and the BBC had been slowly building up. Campbell only got directly involved in the process himself about a week after Gilligan's broadcast. Greg Dyke and Richard Sambrook, who had both been away at the time of the broadcast, also began to get involved.

In an email to one of his bosses on 9 June, headed 'Campbell letter', Marsh was derisive about the complaints from Downing Street, writing 'it's all drivel'; of Campbell he wrote 'the man is flapping in the wind'. Marsh defended Gilligan's story without reservation; there was no mention of any mistakes in what Gilligan had broadcast.[683]

Nearly three weeks later Kevin Marsh sat down and composed

a very different email to his BBC boss, Stephen Mitchell. It was headed 'From here':

> Some thoughts: clearly I have to talk to AG early next week. I hope by then my worst fears – based on what I'm hearing from the spooks this afternoon – aren't realised. Assuming not, the guts of what I would say are:
>
> - This story was a good piece of investigative journalism, marred by flawed reporting – our biggest millstone has been his loose use of language and lack of judgement in some of his phraseology.
> - It was marred also by the quantity of writing for other outlets that varied what was said and was loose with the terms of the story.
> - That it is in many ways a result of the loose and in some ways distant relationship he's been allowed to have with *Today*.

He then set out eight bullet points for how Gilligan's working methods could be changed for the better. For example:

> - That he works substantially in the office
> - That he comes in to TVC[684] to put his pieces together and to file (he usually files from home)
> - That all his proposed stories are discussed with me, in detail as early as possible in the process – face to face if possible

The email ended, 'Does this sound too harsh?? Thoughts?? I'd like anything I say to him to be consistent with anything anyone else above me in the hierarchy. K.'[685]

Kevin Marsh has since explained that the email was a 'draft appraisal', the first stage of an annual BBC process where staff eventually get told what their bosses and colleagues think of how they are performing in their jobs. Marsh has said that his draft appraisal for Gilligan was just one of a 'dozen and a half' he'd prepared and they were 'pretty dull except to the reporter concerned'.[686]

That may well have been Marsh's intention and he had signalled in his previous email to Gilligan that an appraisal was coming up, but to an external reader there was little to indicate that. The email appeared to be an update on Marsh's latest thinking about what had been transmitted and the lessons learned from it, including editorial and managerial shortcomings. Whatever he meant by sending that email, being honest with his boss about his views on Andrew Gilligan turned out to be one of the worst things Kevin Marsh ever did.

At the time it seemed to the BBC that after the opening volley of complaints this particular row with Downing Street just might die down and fizzle out like so many others had before. BBC News executives even went to lunch with Tony Blair at Downing Street and the dispute wasn't mentioned then, although it was commented on afterwards by one of Campbell's team, showing that the issue hadn't entirely gone away.

Then over the next month there were a series of dramatic developments.

Campbell raises the stakes

On 25 June, Alastair Campbell appeared before the House of Commons Foreign Affairs Select Committee, where he was expecting a tough time over his role in the second dossier, the so-called 'dodgy dossier' of February 2003. Some of this document had been plagiarised without attribution, including extracts from one graduate student's thesis which were reproduced with typographical errors uncorrected.

Campbell chose the committee hearing to re-ignite the row with the BBC, thumping the table and almost shouting: 'I simply say, in relation to the BBC story, it is a lie … that is continually repeated, and until we get an apology for it I will keep making sure that Parliament and people like yourselves know that it was a lie.'[687] In Marsh's view Campbell had decided to re-open the attack on the BBC as a diversion from the pressure he was likely to be under at the committee because of the 'dodgy' dossier.

Campbell followed up the next day with a letter to Sambrook

posing twelve very specific questions and asking for 'yes or no' answers to many of them.

Question number three to the BBC was: 'Does it still stand by the allegation made on that day that both we and the intelligence agencies knew the 45-minute claim to be wrong and inserted it despite knowing that? Yes or no?' Campbell had put his finger right on what was to turn out to be the BBC's weak spot, late in the day but not too late for Campbell.[688]

The next day Sambrook's reply to the twelve questions included a very straightforward answer to number three: 'Andrew Gilligan accurately reported the source telling him that the government "probably knew that the 45-minute figure was wrong" and that the claim was "questionable".'[689] Sambrook had stood by the story unreservedly. The BBC's case was clear. The source had spoken those words.

But in fact nothing in Gilligan's notes – either the version on his personal organiser or the 'Q&A' he typed up later – can be interpreted as quoting Kelly as saying that the government probably knew the 45-minute claim was wrong.

Having got Sambrook's reply, Campbell immediately engineered an opportunity to press home his attack by appearing on that night's *Channel 4 News* for what turned into a bad-tempered encounter with presenter Jon Snow.[690] If there had been any doubt before it was clear now: Campbell had become the story.

On 6 July the BBC governors convened a special meeting, which was most unusual as it was a Sunday. They had been sent an email the previous day by Richard Sambrook headed 'How we reported what the source said and what we know'.[691]

After a detailed discussion they concluded that 'BBC journalists and managers sought to maintain impartiality and accuracy during this episode'.[692]

On 8 July there was a meeting in the Prime Minister's study in Downing Street. Andrew Rawnsley of *The Observer* has written that this meeting 'put Tony Blair at the heart of a devious strategy which would lead to Dr David Kelly being outed less than forty-eight hours later'. Rawnsley wrote that Blair had sanctioned a 'naming strategy' which 'guaranteed that the scientist's identity got out while making it hard to prove that Downing Street had done the deed itself'.[693] The government released enough individual pieces of information to allow journalists who knew this patch to guess the identity. If the right name was put to the Ministry of Defence they would helpfully confirm it. One reporter worked out the name of Kelly by typing various clues into a search engine, another – according to Rawnsley – put twenty-one names to the MoD before he got the right one confirmed.

On 9 July Dr David Kelly was named in the press as Gilligan's source. A week later he was up before a Commons committee. It was a messy affair with confused questioning. One MP told Kelly he was a 'fall-guy' and 'chaff'. A Liberal Democrat MP, who in an extraordinary development had been secretly briefed by Andrew Gilligan, asked Kelly if he had been the source of a different BBC story, one by Susan Watts of *Newsnight*. Kelly said no. He lied to Parliament.

According to Andrew Rawnsley, the outing of Kelly had not worked out the way Alastair Campbell hoped. 'It did not fuck Gilligan.' Campbell, he says, concluded that with other troubles on the government's horizon 'this was something which we were going to have to sort of put behind us and forget'. It would not be as simple as that.

On 17 July Dr Kelly left his home in Oxfordshire and walked five miles into the local countryside. According to the official account, he sat down, swallowed some painkillers and cut his left wrist. He bled to death. The next day his body was found. As a writer on the BBC website later observed, 'British politics – public life even – would never be quite the same again.'[694]

Lord Hutton is sent for

A visibly shaken Tony Blair promised a full inquiry and his close friend and Lord Chancellor, Lord Falconer, set about choosing someone to hold it, someone 'utterly impeccable, impartial, someone who no one could allege was New Labour or even knew us'.[695] Tony Blair has recalled that Falconer came with the suggestion of someone 'who definitely fitted the description'. Brian Hutton was a Belfast barrister who had worked his way up to become Lord Chief Justice of Northern Ireland and then a Law Lord in London.

Lord Hutton was portrayed in the press as a slightly conservative, often cautious judge who had sometimes demonstrated his independence in the courts.

The media welcomed the open way in which Hutton went about his business. Hundreds of previously confidential and often embarrassing emails from the main players were disclosed. In recognition of the arrival of the digital age, most of the documents were available to press and public on the Hutton Inquiry website, preserved for posterity on the National Archives website. Hutton's courtroom would become a forum for the inquisition of leading BBC and government figures. It would be the best show in town.

To prepare for it, the BBC formed what was effectively their Hutton squad. The core team were two of Greg Dyke's most trusted advisers and two of the most senior executives in BBC News. They were supported by BBC lawyers, public relations professionals and past and present BBC journalists who were set specific tasks. Some of them made themselves experts on Iraq and weapons of mass destruction.

The only true outsider was probably the most influential member of the team. Andrew Caldecott QC would be the barrister to stand up in front of Lord Hutton, putting forward the BBC's case and questioning key witnesses. He would be supported by junior barristers from his chambers.

In the same way that a news organisation would hire a QC to fight a libel case for them and leave it to him or her to decide the courtroom tactics, the BBC looked to Caldecott to lead their Hutton strategy. Caldecott already had an impressive track record in defamation cases. His website lists tributes such as 'the best libel barrister around bar none', equipped as he is with 'more grey cells between his ears than you or I will ever have'.[696]

Being at heart a libel lawyer he fought the case like a libel trial – to prove that what the BBC had said about Downing Street and the WMD dossier was true. It was as simple as that. As it turned out, there were a number of problems with this strategy of focusing so much on WMD. Greg Dyke later realised one of them:

> Lord Hutton explained that he had decided to limit the scope of his inquiry and completely ignore the crucial question of what sort of weapons of mass destruction the Government was warning us about in the dossier. With this one inexplicable decision Lord Hutton had wiped out key parts of the BBC's evidence and a critical foundation of our case.[697]

Another problem was that the BBC arguably underplayed the importance of the editorial process that Gilligan's story had been put through by his producers and editors. The BBC's preliminary statement to the inquiry made absolutely no mention of any process or checks between the date when Gilligan talked to Kelly and the day he went on air.[698]

The other key person besides Caldecott in the BBC's planning team was obviously the director-general himself. Dyke and his close advisers were based in Broadcasting House (BH) in Central London. The advisers had a background in legal and business affairs and brought a cool detachment to the process of putting forward the BBC's case. The BBC News executives were based in the newsroom in Television Centre. More than once his BH team observed that Greg Dyke, never a shrinking violet, would become even more passionate, especially about Alastair Campbell, once immersed in the editorial hub of his organisation.

It subsequently became conventional wisdom outside the BBC that Dyke was not on top of the detail and also did not question his own team hard enough because of his disputes with Campbell and a desire to show that, despite his own previous Labour links, he was now truly independent. But Kevin Marsh has subsequently written that 'Dyke grilled Gilligan and he grilled me before he took up the fight with Campbell'.[699] It is also clear that the BBC had, like Campbell, realised the potential significance of Gilligan's one-off remarks at 6.07. Marsh has written that Dyke asked Gilligan outright whether Kelly had used the words 'the government probably knew the 45-minute claim was wrong'. Marsh's account is that 'Gilligan assured him more than once that he had'.[700]

On one of those occasions Marsh said Dyke told Gilligan 'you'd better be fucking right', then turned to the rest of those in the room and said 'he'd better be fucking right'.[701]

Internal tensions at the BBC

The legal team was based in a third location, an office in the BBC's White City complex in west London. It was here, amidst the boxes of files and papers and leftover food, that the decision was made that had the most impact on Kevin Marsh. He later recalled that when he first went there he did not feel especially welcome. The problem was the 'draft appraisal' email to Steve Mitchell on 27 June, which the BBC was having to disclose, along with countless other BBC emails and documents. Revealing it to Hutton meant showing it to Gilligan too, who had never previously seen this list of his faults. Marsh encountered Gilligan in the legal team's office. The reporter said to his editor, referring to the email, 'It's surprising what you find out about people at times like this.' Marsh replied, 'But you knew that's what I think, I've told you often enough. You know it's true, too.'[702] Such encounters did not exactly foster team spirit among those working for the BBC's cause.

The email raised the obvious question: if the editor of Today had these doubts about a reporter, why had he allowed the man to go on air with such a controversial story without the toughest of editorial controls? There wasn't an easy answer but in Marsh's mind he had, as editor, put the story through proper editorial checks. It subsequently became clear to Marsh that the lawyers didn't want him to give evidence in Hutton's courtroom for fear that he would be 'ripped apart' especially by Jonathan Sumption QC, counsel for the government and considered one of the most agile legal minds at the bar.

Greg Dyke has said that the BBC didn't put Marsh forward because

> our legal advice was that you didn't nominate witnesses; you waited for the inquiry team to call them. This was based on our QC's firm belief that all your bad days would come when your witnesses were in the witness box and all your best days would come when it was the turn of the government witnesses.

Whether or not the BBC could have done more to get Marsh into the witness box, there was certainly relief among their Hutton team that the editor of the *Today* programme wasn't called by the judge.

Dyke later accepted that Marsh was therefore never given the chance to explain the editorial processes and 'as a result Hutton has been allowed to create the myth that Gilligan's report went to air without any proper editorial control being exercised beforehand'.[703]

Marsh's role became a backroom one helping the team preparing the BBC's submissions to the Hutton Inquiry. In Marsh's absence as a witness, the director of BBC News, Richard Sambrook, who had played no role whatsoever in the preparation or transmission of Gilligan's report or in Marsh's 'draft appraisal' of Gilligan, was now to answer in public for both.

The Hutton hearings begin

Once Lord Hutton's hearings started Marsh was left unsure what, if anything, he was meant to be doing to help the BBC's case. He was getting more alarmed by the BBC's emerging strategy.[704] He said he felt like botulinum, the most acutely toxic substance known to mankind.

The BBC would have liked to have been able to prove that

everything they had transmitted on the story was one hundred per cent correct. The 'Preliminary Statement of the BBC' made only one small concession: 'The BBC accepts that on one occasion the source was described specifically as a source from the intelligence services. Although Dr Kelly did have access to intelligence material, this was an error which the BBC regrets.'[705]

Apart from that the BBC did not accept any mistakes and made six headline submissions stating boldly either that they had 'accurately recorded what Dr Kelly told' them or that 'the BBC was right to broadcast' what they had.

However, back in their offices it was becoming clearer to the BBC team that although most of what *Today* had broadcast was what Dr Kelly had told Gilligan, there were some mistakes. This left the BBC with two problems: one was being sure of what was true and what was a mistake before they went into the Hutton courtroom, and the other was deciding which mistake to admit to and when. Neither was going to be easy to solve.

On 12 August 2003, Andrew Gilligan made his first appearance before Lord Hutton in a crowded courtroom in the Royal Courts of Justice in London. The transcripts of the cross-examination of Gilligan and other BBC witnesses reveal a constantly changing position on key issues.

The most significant was Gilligan's own position on his 'government probably knew it was wrong' allegation at 6.07. The counsel for the inquiry, James Dingemans QC, contrasted it with Gilligan's note of Kelly's quote: 'It was real information but included against our wishes because they considered it unreliable.'

Was this line from Kelly enough to support his own allegation about the government knowing the claim was probably wrong?

Gilligan: Well, I think it is a reasonable conclusion to draw from what he said. But I have to say that with the benefit of hindsight, looking at it now with a fine-tooth comb, I think it was not wrong, what I said, but it was not perfect either, and in hindsight I should have scripted that too.[706]

In just one exchange, the principal allegation by the BBC against the government, which Gilligan had 'been told' by his source, was now something that he hadn't actually been told but which he had concluded and while 'not wrong' was 'not perfect either'.

In a later exchange Gilligan conceded more ground:

> I think in hindsight as I say, particularly that 6.07, quite unwittingly and unintentionally but I did give people the wrong impression about whether this was real intelligence or whether it was made up or not; and I never intended to give anyone the impression that it was not real intelligence or that it had been fabricated, but I think I must have done; and so in that sense I agree to that, I think.[707]

It came as no surprise that when Gilligan returned at a later hearing Jonathan Sumption QC, for the government, took him back to that, by now infamous, line at 6.07.

> Sumption: You accept, I think, that it was expressed by you as something that your source had said, whereas in fact it was an inference of your own?
> Gilligan: Yes, that is right, that was my mistake.

Greg Dyke later listed Gilligan's admission as one of the 'particularly bad moments for the BBC' during the inquiry. 'This was not what we believed he had told us.'

Kevin Marsh was asked about Gilligan's belated admission on a radio programme nearly a decade later by the BBC's political editor, Nick Robinson.[708]

> Marsh: To misattribute one of your key claims to a single, anonymous source the moment when you have to have maximum trust in your reporter, to misquote and misattribute something its journalistically criminal.
> Robinson: And yet the BBC didn't find out until a judicial inquiry found out for them?

Marsh: Well, Andrew continued to insist that those were exactly
the words that Dr Kelly had used.

In the hearings the bad news for the BBC kept on coming. It was
put to their witnesses that Gilligan was wrong to say in some
broadcasts that Kelly was a member of the intelligence services;
he wasn't. To compound the offence, the corporation had wrongly
denied in a press statement that Gilligan had ever said that. It was
suggested that Kelly had never told Gilligan that he had been one
of those in charge of the dossier, that Gilligan had allowed an
unsupported headline in the *Mail on Sunday* to go uncorrected,
that the BBC governors had not been given the full facts. The
charge sheet seemed endless.

What the BBC didn't tell Hutton

In Marsh's mind there was a much simpler story but the BBC
weren't telling it. It could be summed up in the five words which
Marsh said he muttered to himself that morning in a minicab as
he listened to Gilligan stumbling through that live interview: 'Just
read the fucking script.'

Marsh subsequently wrote:

> I expected Gilligan to have his script in front of him for that 6.07
> two-way. I expected to hear the allegations expressed exactly as
> they were in the script. I certainly didn't expect him to use different
> words, changing both meaning and attribution. I would have liked
> to have explained this to Lord Hutton.[709]

Although the BBC's main submission to Hutton has never been
published I have been able to confirm that it stated that the 6.07
broadcast was 'unscripted'.

That submission never mentioned any script for 6.07, no document was ever submitted as a 6.07 script and nor did any of the
BBC witnesses who appeared before His Lordship ever mention
any such script. Nor was there any mention of any agreement

between Marsh and Gilligan that the allegations would, in Marsh's subsequent words, be 'expressed exactly as they were in the script'.

Instead the BBC's version that it had been an 'unscripted' broadcast was set out from the moment Gilligan was asked about 6.07 in his first cross-examination:

> Dingemans: Was this contribution to the programme scripted?
> Gilligan: No, it was not.
> Dingemans: So this was you speaking from the studio or from home?
> Gilligan: From home. I have an ISDN line at home because it is an early morning programme. This is me speaking live and unscripted.
> Lord Hutton: You are speaking?
> Gilligan: Speaking live and unscripted.
> Dingemans: Live and unscripted.
> Gilligan: Yes.[710]

When Gilligan returned for further cross-examination the following month the subject came up again:

> Dingemans: This was a very serious charge, as it turned out, or a matter of great public interest, where you broadcast words simply unscripted. Do you accept that that was unfortunate?
> Gilligan: Yes, we should have scripted it.[711]

In his book *Stumbling over Truth*, Marsh wrote that there was a script which Gilligan 'was supposed to have in front of him as he did this live two-way with John Humphrys'.[712] Marsh explained that he had been able to look at this script overnight from home using a laptop linked to the BBC's computer system. His book has an appendix described as 'Andrew Gilligan's script for *Today*, 29 May 2003'. The words which are in that appendix match exactly the words which are in the BBC's transcript of the 7.32 portion of *Today* which was submitted to Hutton. In other words there is no dispute that they are the words Andrew Gilligan spoke at 7.32. But nowhere in the BBC's evidence was it ever suggested that these same words were what Gilligan should have used earlier at 6.07. Nor does Marsh explain when or how Gilligan agreed with him that the reporter would have a script 'in front of him' at 6.07. But it is clear that despite whatever Andrew Gilligan and the director of BBC News, Richard Sambrook, later told Lord Hutton, the editor of *Today* believed there was a script which Gilligan was told to 'have in front of him' at 6.07.

Subsequently the BBC did a complete volte-face on this issue. In direct contradiction with its evidence to Hutton, a BBC internal disciplinary process held after Hutton's report concluded: 'In relation to the broadcast on the *Today* programme, on 29 May 2003, we are satisfied that a core script was properly prepared and cleared in line with normal production practices in place at the time, but was then not followed by Andrew Gilligan.' It added: 'We consider that the BBC's evidence to the Hutton Inquiry could have been clearer in this respect.'[713]

The full findings and rationale of the internal investigation by BBC executives Stephen Dando and Caroline Thomson, known as 'the process', have never been published. I have tried to get the BBC to release the details of how they came to this new conclusion but they refuse.[714] But Kevin Marsh has been told the full findings and regards them as a vindication of his own position.

So was there a script or not?

So the BBC fought the Hutton Inquiry on one basis: that the 6.07 interview was 'unscripted' and then after Hutton it decided that there was a script after all? To try to get to the bottom of this I contacted the two main protagonists a decade later and after hearing both sides I have concluded that it all depends on what you mean by 'a 6.07 script'.

Andrew Gilligan told me:

I have no recollection of producing any kind of script for the live two-way – we were generally told not to, because it made you sound stilted. Can I absolutely swear that nothing of that nature was done? No: it was ten years ago. But as you say, nothing of the sort appears in the copious documentation submitted by the BBC to the Hutton Inquiry.[715]

Andrew Gilligan also pointed to what Marsh had later said about him in his 27 June 'draft appraisal email': that in future, among other things, they 'agree on a script or on core elements of a script that he does not subsequently vary'. This, Gilligan said, 'clearly suggests, of course, that no script was prepared for the offending 29 May item'.

I then put Andrew Gilligan's response to Kevin Marsh and the misunderstanding that the two seemed to have had for nearly ten years began to become a little clearer. In part of his reply Marsh said:

> Gilligan's 'script' was the one he wrote for his 7.32 substantive piece – and that was the script the night editor approved and which, later, I read and the one which, in all material substance, he was supposed to keep to.
>
>   He's right to say that he wasn't required to write a specific script for his 6.07 two-way – but he was required to deliver the allegations etc. in that two-way in exactly the form he'd scripted them for 7.32. If you think about it, anything else would be absurd.[716]
>
>   So, to be clear; I read the 'substantive' or 'core' script on my laptop, the script that was going to be read in full at 7.32. I expected to hear the allegations in that form whenever Gilligan was on air, whether 'live and unscripted' or in the substantive piece. As you'll know, he did stick to the 'core' script in some dozen and a half live broadcasts during the day. He only went off-piste the once – and that was in the 6.07.

In summary – in my words not theirs – Marsh says he wanted Gilligan to use the 7.32 script as the basis of his 6.07 live interview. Gilligan says he didn't know he was meant to.

What a pity this couldn't have been sorted out a long time before. If it had been agreed between Marsh and Gilligan that the 7.32 script was also to be regarded as a 6.07 script and kept to, the BBC's biggest problem would never have happened. But, now, months later in the middle of a judge-led inquiry it was becoming clear that there were other problems.

Would it have mattered if the BBC's evidence had been clearer from the start that there had been an editorial process but there had been a misunderstanding over a 6.07 script? The trouble is that this wasn't the only 'misunderstanding' or mistake. Before the inquiry began, the BBC agreed there had been one mistake, that Downing Street should have been given advance notice of Gilligan's story. In its 'Preliminary Statement' to Hutton the BBC admitted one further mistake, but by the end of Hutton the BBC's own in-house magazine, *Ariel*, had counted four more:

1. Gilligan's 6.07 broadcast should have been scripted.
2. The early broadcast did not distinguish sufficiently between what David Kelly had said and Gilligan's interpretation of what he had said. The BBC accepted that Kelly did not say that the government had put in the 45 minutes claim when they probably knew it was wrong.
3. A BBC reply to Alastair Campbell – made under considerable time pressure – contained some factual errors. Greg Dyke told the inquiry he should have taken longer to consider Campbell's twelve-point letter and passed it to the programme complaints unit for investigation.
4. Richard Sambrook said he should have looked at Gilligan's notes earlier than he did.[717]

In fact a close reading of the court transcripts suggests there were yet more admissions. But at the end of the day there was to be only one admitted mistake that really mattered.

As the hearings came towards their end in late 2003 Lord Hutton made one telling intervention which signalled where he was coming from. He pointed out to counsel for the BBC that in June Alastair Campbell had asked Richard Sambrook in a letter if he stood by Gilligan's story over the 'government probably knew' line. Sambrook replied that he did. Yet eighty-two days later Andrew Gilligan changed that story in court and accepted it was 'my mistake'.[718] It was therefore probably no surprise that Hutton's very first conclusion in the BBC section of his final report was that the allegation was 'unfounded'. But he also said that when the BBC management looked at Gilligan's notes after 27 June they failed to appreciate that the notes did not fully support this allegation. The management 'therefore failed to draw the attention of the Governors to the lack of support in the notes for the most serious of the allegations'.[719]

Hutton's verdict

In Hutton's mind there were effectively two counts of guilty, one of 'defective' editorial processes and the other being a failure of both management and governors to investigate Campbell's complaints properly.

Where Hutton went disastrously wrong in the opinion of most independently minded observers was in failing to give the BBC any credit at all for the journalistic enterprise which first surfaced the story and for the many facts Gilligan got right. The most common response in the next morning's papers was that Hutton's report was a 'whitewash' of the government.

Some insight into why Hutton expressed his verdict the way he did has come from no less than Tony Blair himself. He has written that there was genuine amazement in Downing Street that from their perspective Hutton, having found for the government, 'had had the courage not to dress it up for the BBC, but to call it as it was'. With his own background in the legal world Blair offered this rationale for what outsiders might call a 'winner takes all' verdict:

> When I was his pupil, Derry [Irvine] used to tell me that there were
> two types of judges: those who made up their mind, but left loose

ends, something for the losing side to cling to, something that expressed the judge's own inner hesitation about making a clear decision; and those who made up their mind, and once of that view, delivered the decision complete, unadulterated and unvarnished, with every allegation covered and every doubt answered. Lord Hutton was of the latter kind.

A decade on from Hutton's verdicts there is a further, wider and still relevant issue to consider: the BBC's strategy in handling major complaints from governments of the day. The corporation almost conceded in their final submission to Hutton that they had played the whole row with Campbell the wrong way. In a very telling section, referring to Richard Sambrook's reply to Campbell's 'yes or no' challenges, the BBC said: 'As to the drafting of the letter of 27 June Mr Dyke has stated that, with hindsight, if he were in the same position again he would have conducted a fuller investigation or else referred the matter to the Programme Complaints Unit.'[720]

That Programme Complaints Unit option might well have worked. If Campbell's complaints had been referred there as complaints from everyone else in the world were, the BBC would not have had to make replies by return of post, especially to those twelve questions.

Back on 16 June – at the height of their row – Richard Sambrook had written to Alastair Campbell:

I am sorry that we still seem far apart on the validity of our reporting on the concerns about the September dossier. I should remind you that we have a Programme Complaints Unit which functions completely separately from production arms of the BBC, such as BBC News and reports to the Director-General with a right of appeal to the Governors. If you feel it would help, you could make a formal complaint to the Head of the PCU, Fraser Steel.

Alastair Campbell was never going to 'feel it would help' to go to the Complaints Unit. From his point of view he needed to keep the row in the public eye. But the BBC could have created some process that didn't require his consent. Many of the detailed critiques of the BBC's handling of Hutton can fairly be described as being 'with the benefit of hindsight'. This 'kick it into the long grass' option cannot be so easily dismissed. It was always an obvious route, but one which the BBC chose not to pursue very hard. It is almost as if the two sides were enjoying the fight too much.

The BBC could also have directed Campbell to the independent Broadcasting Standards Commission, in its final year before its absorption into the new Office of Communications (Ofcom). There was a third possible course: to have set up a special complaints inquiry headed by outside and independent figures, as Thames Television had done at the time of its dispute with Margaret Thatcher over the *Death on the Rock* programme in 1988, which reported on the shooting of an IRA team in Gibraltar.

Either an internal process or some kind of independent inquiry would have isolated the BBC chairman and the governors from the row and probably ensured their survival. The regime change video need never have happened. As it was, the chairman resigned and the governors were later abolished and replaced by the BBC Trust.

Counting the bodies

If the chairman, Gavyn Davies, had hoped his own sacrifice would save his director-general, he was wrong. By the same time the next day, Greg Dyke was gone too.

With hindsight was there an honourable deal he could have done to resolve the row with Downing Street?

Greg Dyke said a decade later: 'There were a number of discussions during this period that went on between Tony Blair and Gavyn Davies, who was then the chairman of the BBC. We then got phoned up by Peter Mandelson, who said "look, there is a deal to be done here". But the deal required us to say that although we were right to broadcast the story when we did it actually the story was wrong. We were not prepared to do that.'[721]

His director of policy at the time, Caroline Thomson, has said there was the possibility of a compromise 'but the thing escalated and the more aggressive the response got from Alastair the less likely it was that the BBC was going to back off because it felt that its independence was at stake ... This was part of a long series of complaints and this was the one where you finally had to see him off.'

She said that with her former boss's 'pugnacity' and Alastair Campbell's background, 'It was a car crash waiting to happen.'

The former director-general prefers, perhaps understandably, to focus blame on the man who did the investigation into the car crash. 'The mistake we made at the BBC was that we believed he would be an independent judge. And he did run a very interesting and independent inquiry, the only trouble is his conclusions in no way reflected the evidence that was given at the inquiry.'

In his account of 'Why Hutton Was Wrong' Greg Dyke concluded:

> ... most of the story broadcast on the *Today* programme on that May morning was right, and while Gilligan made mistakes they were nowhere near as serious as those made by Downing Street when producing the two dossiers warning about the threats from Iraq: the BBC was not sending British soldiers to war.

Dyke's principal adversary went too. Even before Hutton published his report Alastair Campbell had left Downing Street. Tony Blair had witnessed him 'out of control' and concluded that he would have to take a chance on life without Alastair. Blair's successor, Gordon Brown, invited Campbell back to Downing Street to help run what was to be an unsuccessful general election campaign. Campbell later went to work for an international public relations company.

Back at the BBC Andrew Gilligan was soon on his way. He later wrote: 'An internal inquiry into the Hutton fiasco concluded that I, the most junior person involved, was wholly responsible. I did wonder why, if that was genuinely the case, the BBC's management had ever come to my defence in the first place.'[722]

Some of the BBC management have told me the answer to this is that with hindsight they had been more concerned to protect Gilligan, who was seen to be under a lot of pressure, than to challenge him.

Gilligan successfully returned to print journalism and became a regular broadcaster on commercial radio.

He rarely appears on the BBC but there was an exception near the tenth anniversary of his broadcast. *The Reunion* is a BBC Radio 4 series which 'reunites a group of people intimately involved in a moment of modern history'. One characteristic of the series is that the atmosphere of each reunion is nostalgic, even collegiate, among those brought together again from different perspectives.

'The Hutton Inquiry', the *Reunion* episode of Friday 10 May 2013, could not have been more different. The guests were Andrew Gilligan, Greg Dyke and from the government of 2003, Defence Secretary Geoff Hoon and Downing Street spokesman Tom Kelly. Although a decade had passed since the events they were discussing, the mood around the table was argumentative and bad tempered. The presenter, Sue McGregor, at one point told her guests, 'Gentlemen, nobody can hear what any of you are saying.'[723]

As if to show nothing much had changed Andrew Gilligan was at the heart of it. When Tom Kelly asked Gilligan to stop interrupting him Gilligan said, 'You've got to tell the truth, though, otherwise I will interrupt you.'

Gilligan said in this programme that his 6.07 error had been 'corrected within the hour' and 'swiftly corrected'. In fact the error was never corrected during the programme, it just wasn't repeated.

Kevin Marsh stayed on as editor of *Today* before becoming editor at the new BBC College of Journalism, set up following the criticisms of the BBC in the Hutton report. He left the BBC in 2011 to start his own company and write his book about how 'my reputation had been trashed by Hutton'.[724]

And what of the reputation of the man who unwittingly started all this, Dr David Kelly?

In July 2004, a committee chaired by the former Cabinet Secretary Lord Butler concluded that the claim that Iraq could use weapons of mass destruction within 45 minutes should not have been made in the government's weapons dossier without explaining what the claim referred to. It recorded that MI6 subsequently believed that the intelligence report on the claim 'has come into question', with doubts cast about one of the links in the reporting chain. The Butler Committee also concluded that it was a 'serious weakness' in the dossier that the warnings from intelligence chiefs about the limitations of their judgements 'were not made clear enough'.[725]

At the later Chilcott Inquiry into the invasion, Michael Laurie, who had been a director-general in Defence Intelligence, commented on Alastair Campbell's claim that the purpose of the dossier was not 'to make a case for war'. Laurie said he 'had no doubt at that time this was exactly the purpose and these very words were used'. A previous paper had been 'rejected because it did not make a strong enough case. From then until September we were under pressure to find intelligence that could reinforce the case.'[726]

So everything we have learned from this and other subsequent official inquiries and documents confirms that one man got it absolutely right in what he said at the Charing Cross Hotel in London on 22 May 2003. But he died. As Andrew Marr of the BBC reported at the time of the death of Dr David Kelly, 'In the so-called war between the government and the BBC a useful, decent man today became a real casualty.'

14

THE HACKERS

In November 2005 a royal prince and a former royal correspondent sat down at St James's Palace and over a beer wondered if someone had been listening to the messages they had been sending each other.

It began a process that over the following decade unravelled into the biggest media scandal of recent times, bringing about the closure of Britain's bestselling newspaper, a long and controversial public inquiry into the press and the arrest of more than fifty journalists. What became known as 'phone-hacking' or 'Hackgate' illustrated all the downsides of an absence of clear lines in the news business.

The unlikely origins of the royal trigger point were in the African state of Lesotho where Prince Harry did voluntary work in 2004 as part of a gap year. Tom Bradby, then the royal correspondent of ITV News, made a documentary about the prince's time in Lesotho. The two men got on well and after the programme was transmitted Bradby made a video from pictures shot during Harry's gap year, set it to music and presented it to him for his personal use.

Bradby moved on to a new role as political editor of ITV News but kept up his royal contacts and had lunch with Harry's elder brother, Prince William, whom he had also got to know from his time as a royal correspondent. The prince told Bradby that he had heard about the Harry video and that he would like a

similar one about his own travels. But there would be a difference: Prince William would like to edit this video himself. The
two men discussed how they would need Bradby's employers
at ITN to lend some editing equipment and how Bradby would
teach him to edit. (Some of the reporter's colleagues were later to
comment that this idea sounded like the blind leading the blind.)

In a series of texts and calls between Tom Bradby, Prince
William and his closest staff it was arranged that the two men
would meet on the evening of Monday 14 November. On the
day before the scheduled meeting the 'Blackadder' column in
the *News of the World* reported:

> If ITN do a stocktake on their portable editing suites this week
> they might notice they're one down. That's because their pin-up
> political editor Tom Bradby has lent it to close pal Prince William
> so he can edit together all his gap-year videos and DVDs into one
> very posh home movie.

Tom Bradby was 'pretty shocked'. The next evening he went to
St James's Palace as planned and set up the editing equipment
in a room in Prince William's private quarters. The prince came
downstairs and before they started the editing lesson the two men
discussed the story.

Bradby later remembered the conversation:

> We basically sat there and discussed – look, how on earth could
> this have got out? We worked out that he and I and only two other
> people close to him had known about it.[727]

> When you're in a situation where you've had a conversation with
> someone, and it's confidential and then an aspect of it is splat-
> tered all over a newspaper, that is uncomfortable. So that was
> why I felt it was right to explore what really happened. We talked
> about it and we agreed that there was some potential security

implication and it was then up to them to go to the police, as they did.[728]

Prince William thought the theory that there had been a breach of security made sense because he was already baffled how a story about a sports injury he had picked up had appeared the previous week in the very same column. 'Blackadder' called itself 'the snake in the grass of the rich and powerful'.

Bradby had a hunch that stories like these might have been gathered by reporters hacking into mobile phones. He later explained:

> As ITV's royal correspondent (a post I held a few years previously) I had heard that this was an absolutely routine way of doing business in tabloid newspapers. In fact, during the Diana years phone hacking was the least of it. How did the Squidgygate tape (in which Diana shared intimacies with a lover) get recorded and find itself into the public domain? And what about the tape in which we heard Charles asking Camilla if he could be re-incarnated as her tampax? One can only suspect that someone, somewhere did a lot worse than hacking voice messages.[729]

A few weeks later Bradby's hunch had been proven right. Scotland Yard detectives had checked with a major mobile phone operator and discovered that as many as nine 'rogue' phones were being used to call into the mobile inboxes of the two royal staff who had known about Bradby's scheduled meeting with Prince William. One of those nine phones was the home number of a reporter on the *News of the World*. Detectives separately discovered that a man had been calling another mobile phone company, posing as a member of staff, trying to get details which would have enabled him to access the voicemails of royal staff. That inquiry led them to the offices of a private investigator.

One year later, in January 2007, the royal editor of the *News of the World*, Clive Goodman, was convicted at the Old Bailey after pleading guilty to intercepting phone messages. He was sentenced to four months in jail. His employers were to describe him as a single 'rogue reporter' acting without any authorisation. A private investigator, Glenn Mulcaire, also pleaded guilty and was sentenced to six months. The judge, Mr Justice Gross, described their behaviour as 'low conduct, reprehensible in the extreme'. Only Goodman and Mulcaire were charged at this time. It seemed that it was the end of the matter. It was not.

The full sequence of events from this 'rogue reporter' defence through to the investigations into phone-hacking by *Guardian* reporter Nick Davies, his revelation that the *News of the World* had hacked the phone of missing schoolgirl Millie Dowler, the closure of the *News of the World* and the establishment of the Leveson Inquiry into the press are best set out in *Dial M for Murdoch* by Tom Watson and Martin Hickman. Watson was one of the parliamentarians who pushed for the truth when others, including most of the British press, decided this was not a story worth pursuing.

The whole phone-hacking episode is perhaps the best recent example of the confusion about if, when and where reporters are justified in crossing vaguely drawn ethical lines. The press has fairly put the case that phone-hacking was primarily a criminal matter. The editor-in-chief of the *Daily Mail*, and the doyen of tabloid and mid-market editors, Paul Dacre, attacked the creation by David Cameron of Lord Justice Leveson's Inquiry into the Culture, Practice and Ethics of the Press. At his very first encounter with Sir Brian Leveson at a preliminary seminar he told the judge, 'The truth is the police should have investigated this crime properly and prosecuted the perpetrators.'

But the phone-hacking scandal can't solely be blamed on the police. There are a series of reasons why wider ethical ambiguity and confusion contributed to it.

The first was the existence of a cultural issue in the media.

In my own experience over four decades, the vast majority of British journalists respected and observed the law of the land. But occasionally, and it was only occasionally, a few of them believed that they had the right to opt in and out of observing certain laws as if these applied to ordinary citizens but not to journalists.

Paul Dacre told the Leveson Inquiry that this was a thing of the past. He looked back on what the British press was like when he started in newspapers in the 1970s:

> ... much of its behaviour was outrageous. It was not uncommon for reporters to steal photographs from homes. Blatant subterfuge was commonly used. There were no restraints on invasions of privacy. Harassment was the rule rather than the exception.[730]

Dacre was keen to point out that the press was now 'vastly better behaved'.

In March 2003 two editors from News International, the British newspaper arm of Rupert Murdoch's News Corporation, appeared before a parliamentary committee. The then editor of *The Sun*, Rebekah Brooks (née Rebekah Wade) told the House of Commons Culture, Media and Sport Select Committee, 'We have paid the police for information in the past.' Andy Coulson, then editor of *The Sun*'s sister paper the *News of the World*, was sitting beside her and interjected, 'We have always operated within the code and within the law.' Labour MP Chris Bryant told them he believed it was illegal for police to be paid for information. Mr Coulson replied, 'As I said, we have always operated within the code and within the law.'

The contradiction between Rebekah Brooks saying *The Sun* had paid policemen in the past, which was illegal, and Coulson saying they operated within the law was obvious for all to see.

Mrs Brooks later said that what she had meant was that there was a widely held belief in the industry that police officers were sometimes paid, but that didn't mean it was a widespread practice.

She had never paid a policeman herself or sanctioned such a payment.

Private eyes

One long-standing practice which illustrates the attitude of parts of the media concerns police radio messages, which for many years could easily be heard on public airwaves. Under the Wireless Telegraphy Act of 1949 it was and is perfectly legal to listen to police radio transmissions in the UK but illegal to 'act upon any information' picked up from such broadcasts. So, for instance, journalists should not, in law, go to the scene of a crime to report the story if they were alerted to it by what was said in a police radio message. But one training manual for broadcast journalists still advises:

> The surest way to keep in touch with major breaking news is to listen to emergency services radio. By monitoring the transmissions of police and fire services you can hear the news as it is actually happening, instead of waiting for the official version to be collated and sanitised by a spokesperson.[731]

Some newsrooms decided to get this done for them. Private firms would be paid to monitor police radios and then alert news desks when a big story was breaking or developing. Thus a practice arose whereby 'journalism' of this kind could be outsourced to a third party who would be paid for it and carry the can if and where the line was crossed between lawful and unlawful investigation. This approach began to be emulated in other investigative fields and lines became increasingly blurred. Significantly the first (mobile) phone-hacking case taken to court involved a collaboration between a reporter and a private investigator.

These arrangements had the benefit of offering editors a certain distance from potential exposure to risk in the information-gathering process. The former BBC correspondent and now media commentator Nicholas Jones has highlighted how in News International senior journalists with their 'own sources' had access to a 'payment process' to reward 'external providers of information, not just private investigators but also individual sources'. The need to involve an editor would not be triggered until a reporter exceeded limits set by a managing editor.[732] If the reporter wanted a higher cash limit that was something the reporter could agree with his or her managing editor directly.

As new forms of electronic communication and data transmission blossomed at the end of the last century the authorities struggled to keep track of what private investigators, many of them former police officers, were up to, especially on behalf of the media. And when they did occasionally stumble across illegal activity underlying news-gathering, the lines of responsibility for taking action were not always clear.

In May 2006 the Information Commissioner's Office (ICO) published a report titled 'What Price Privacy? The Unlawful Trade in Confidential Personal Information'. The ICO referred to 'a major case' where private information about individuals had been supplied to 305 journalists on various newspapers by a private detective. The apparent thoroughness of this report was praised at the time. But in 2011 there was evidence that rather than being a symbol of success for the authorities it symbolised their failure. The ICO's senior investigator revealed his frustration at what he felt to be unjustifiable delays in publishing what he had found.

In his written evidence to the Leveson Inquiry, Alec Owens wrote:

> The publication in May 2006 of 'What Price Privacy?' was no more than an attempt to lock the stable door after the horse had bolted in an effort to cover up the fact that the ICO had failed in its duty to conduct a full and proper investigation into the conduct of journalists at the time when they could and should have.

Owens said that in 2003 the then Information Commissioner, Richard Thomas, decided that the involvement of the press would not be dealt with by the ICO and the police through the courts. Owens was told not to contact any of the many newspapers which had used the detective's services.

Instead Thomas would write to the chairman of the Press Complaints Commission (PCC), Sir Christopher Meyer, formerly John Major's press secretary in Downing Street and British ambassador in Washington. Thomas told Meyer that he and the PCC would first be given a chance 'to deal with the issue in a way which would put an end to these unacceptable practices across the media as a whole'.

He proposed that the PCC should revise its code of practice and that this 'could provide a more satisfactory outcome than legal proceedings'.[733]

In June 2004 the PCC code was amended for a number of reasons, one of them to reflect developments in technology. But relying on the PCC and the updating of its code caused some problems. This approach fundamentally failed to comprehend the role and the powers (or lack of them) of the PCC. Confusion about the 'self-regulation' of the press became another factor in the failure to get to the heart of phone-hacking.

Although Sir Christopher Meyer and his predecessors regularly called the PCC a 'self-regulator', it never was, something a new PCC chairman, Lord Hunt, confirmed in 2011. It was a body for handling complaints about what appeared in newspapers, no more, no less. It did not have the powers, or indeed the resources, pro-actively to investigate media standards and impose sanctions on wrong-doers in the press.[734]

During the phone-hacking affair ambiguity and confusion about where lines should be drawn was not confined to the press, its 'self-regulators' and those like the ICO who believed naively that the regulators represented a solution to a problem. The police and the public prosecutors were not immune either. Even after the first prosecutions came to court and resulted in a conviction there seems to have been confusion about the law of the land.

As Tom Bradby remembered at the time of the royal phone-hacking, the British media had form when it came to publishing information from royal phone calls in tabloid exclusives.

The origins of the so-called 'Squidgygate' and 'Camillagate' tapes in the early 1990s were never fully revealed. But no one was ever charged and one legacy of the saga was that if the media published the contents of private phone calls, it seemed it was unlikely that there would be any legal implications.

The Regulation of Investigatory Powers Act 2000 (RIPA), which contained a section about the interception of communications, should have changed that.

Differing views

In July 2009, the House of Commons Select Committee on Culture, Media and Sport, which had been battling against the indifference of much of the rest of the British Establishment to get to the truth about phone-hacking, was making progress. Nick Davies had published a story in *The Guardian* about the scale of illegality at the *News of the World*. The new Director of Public Prosecutions (DPP), Keir Starmer QC, called for an internal review of the evidence which the police had given the Crown Prosecution Service back in 2006. A week later he announced there was no need to formally re-open the case. He told the Commons committee that the law covering phone-hacking required that 'to prove the criminal offence of interception the prosecution must prove that the actual message was intercepted prior to it being accessed by the intended recipient'.

In effect, the DPP was saying that it was only an offence to listen to a voicemail if the message was on its way into the recipient's inbox or sitting in there waiting for him or her to listen to it, but not once they had listened to it and saved it. This became known as a 'narrow' interpretation of the RIPA and the police said it presented a real obstacle in bringing prosecutions on behalf of victims. How could anyone be sure whether a phone-hacker heard a voicemail before or after the intended recipient?

But then Britain's state prosecutor did an about-turn; he decided that the opposite of what he had just said was true. 'An offence may be committed if a communication is intercepted or looked into after it has been accessed by the intended recipient.'[735]

How could Keir Starmer QC have performed such a volte-face on such an important issue? He explained to the Leveson Inquiry that he had relied on the advice of David Perry QC, who had been the prosecuting counsel in the only phone-hacking trial to date and who would have known if the 'narrow view' had been taken then. And who or what did the learned QC consider and consult before advising the DPP? Why, none other than a document prepared by a policeman, Detective Chief Superintendent Williams.

Mr Perry explained to Leveson that his own recollections and those of the detective 'were at fault. And the moral of the story is: don't do advices overnight if you don't have the papers.'[736]

It turned out that MPs had been given important legal advice from the DPP who had got it from a QC who had got it from a policeman who had allegedly got it wrong. But now it was clear that it didn't matter if the voicemail was hacked before or after the recipient had heard it; to do so without prior authorisation which was provided for in RIPA was unlawful.

Another significant moment occurred in January 2011, when Scotland Yard had announced that it was launching a new inquiry into phone-hacking.

In the face of increasing public and political concern and with all the enthusiasm of a convert, Scotland Yard found substantial resources for initially one, but eventually three, parallel investigations: Operation Weeting into allegations of illegal mobile-phone voicemail interception, Operation Tuleta into allegations of computer-hacking and Operation Elveden into allegations of illegal payments made to public officials. In addition, Operation

Rubicon investigated allegations surrounding the former MSP Tommy Sheridan's defamation action against the *News of the World* and his subsequent conviction for perjury.

Investigations have resulted in a spate of dawn raids, arrests and charges affecting both tabloid journalists, police and other public servants. They were still ongoing at the time of writing and will have a serious impact on media–police relations for a very considerable time to come.

This was extensively addressed in the Leveson Inquiry and a succession of witnesses from the media, the police and the world of politics was processed at the televised hearing. Rupert Murdoch's newspaper empire and many of its key personnel were subjected to a particularly thorough investigation given its connections with and influence over decades of successive governments irrespective of colour. Leveson probed not only in relation to phone-hacking but also into the branding of innocent people as murder suspects without adequate evidence and stories published which prejudiced the due process of criminal cases. It was also becoming widely known that News International was settling civil actions for violation of individuals' right to privacy, despite extensive attempts to hush them up through confidential settlements. Confronted with the savaging it was getting during the inquiry, hostility from the public and attacks from elsewhere in the printed and broadcast media, the proprietors of the *News of the World* (the Murdoch empire's British flagship Sunday tabloid) panicked.

The company's mother ship in the US, News Corporation, had become worried about the possibility of legal action in America over the failure of the London management to be seen to be getting to the bottom of phone-hacking.

At its headquarters in New York, News Corporation set up a Management and Standards Committee (MSC) with a mixture of British and American executives, and started re-opening the files at NI's headquarters at Wapping in London. Material, the existence of which had previously been denied, was found and indiscriminately handed over to the police.

Naming names

News Corporation breached one of the few lines that almost all journalists agree should not be crossed. Its knee-jerk attempts to staunch public criticism of the wider group, unalloyed by the closure of the *News of the World* as a result of revelations in the Leveson Inquiry, would reveal the names of public officials who gave them information or stories. The decision caused a former reporter on the *News of the World*, Tim Wood, to say that News International had broken 'the first rule of journalism by failing to protect a confidential source'.

As Wood came towards the end of a night shift on a Saturday morning in September 2010 he had taken a seven-minute phone call. On the line was someone who identified themselves as a detective and told him that Scotland Yard was launching a new phone-hacking investigation into his paper. Wood sent an email to his bosses but the paper did not follow up the call; they were suspicious that it might be a 'sting' by someone looking for money. Wood thought that that would be the end of it – eighteen months later he was contacted by the police and shown the email. It had been handed over to the police by the MSC executives.

Wood's disclosed email made him a reluctant prime witness against Detective Chief Inspector April Casburn, aged fifty-three, from Essex. She was found guilty and sent to jail for fifteen months for misconduct in public office. The judge said her call was 'a corrupt attempt to make money'. Other policemen and public officials were to follow her to prison on other charges.[737]

After the trial of April Casburn, Tim Wood wrote:

> The MSC's betrayal threatens the confidence of any future source who is thinking of going to News International's four newspapers and hoping to remain anonymous ... It also threatens the ability of reporters on the publisher's titles – *The Sun*, *The Times* and their

sister Sundays – to operate effectively in the future. Indeed, the MSC's actions jeopardise the work of all journalists.[738]

Soon after, Nick Cohen, the *Observer* columnist and anti-censorship campaigner, wrote that 'one of the largest news operations in Europe is collaborating with the state with a vigour and thoroughness unmatched in the history of democratic nations'.[739]

15

THE MORALS OF THE STORIES

During Lord Justice Leveson's public hearings his star inquisitor came face to face with the man whose decision to withdraw his newspapers from the Press Complaints Commission had become known as 'the Desmond problem'. The exchange between the QC and the proprietor of four national newspaper titles[740] seemed to summarise the gap between the law and the media at its widest.

> Robert Jay QC: What interest, if any, do you have in ethical stand-ards within your papers, or is that purely a matter for the editors?
> Richard Desmond: Well, ethical, I don't quite know what the word means, but perhaps you'll explain what the word means, ethical.
> Robert Jay QC: I think it is paragraph 22, perhaps, of your state-ment. You make it clear everybody's ethics are different: 'We don't talk about ethics or morals, because it's a very fine line...' The very use of that term or language would suggest that certain things are on the right side of the line and certain things are on the wrong side of the line. Can we agree about that?
> Richard Desmond: As I say in my statement, we don't talk about ethics or morals because it's a very fine line and everybody's ethics are different.

When Leveson finally reported at the end of 2012 it was inevita-ble that frustrating moments such as these would leave a trace.

In an article for the *Guardian* website's 'Comment is Free' section, I reduced his 2,000 pages to one paragraph of seventy words:

> Leveson: The press – but not politicians or the police – have been very naughty boys. Your 'independent regulation' plan is useless – adopt mine. I can help you cut your libel bills via an arbitration arm but we need a law to make this happen.
> Cameron: I like the 'Leveson principles' but not a Leveson law.
> Clegg: I like them both.
> Cameron: Let's have another debate to get me off this hook.

The Prime Minister's advisers told him that the way off the hook was to create a statute that wasn't a statute but a 'Royal Charter'. When the press didn't like the Royal Charter that Parliament endorsed, they came up with their own. Six months on from Leveson's report the two sides were still miles apart; whatever regulatory structure finally develops from the post-Leveson debate, it will be more independent and more rigorous than any previous attempt.

The dispute about regulatory models has overshadowed many of the benefits which I believe have been derived from the Leveson process and which are also relevant to the issues we have raised in earlier chapters. Buried away in the transcripts of the hours of hearings is a useful Leveson tutorial. More specifically it is Leveson explaining how the law recognises that sometimes it is acceptable to break the law.

> I think there's a perfectly legitimate distinction between invading privacy, with all the civil responsibilities that that entails, and deceptively obtaining material, if it's in the public interest, where there is a strong public interest, and deciding: 'Well, I'm prepared to break the criminal law to do this.' Now, there is a distinction between the two. Whether you want to apply it is obviously a matter for you.

He outlined four 'backstops' that were available to journalists news-gathering and reporting 'in the public interest'. There were, he said, 'a number of hoops through which a journalist would jump or not jump, as he might prefer, which could cover the situation'.

Sometimes, but not always, a statute can specifically provide for a defence. For instance, under the Data Protection Act of 1998 there is a specific defence in section 55 which says 'in the particular circumstances the obtaining, disclosing or procuring was justified as being in the public interest'.

Secondly there are the guidelines for prosecutors which Leveson says he 'encouraged' the Director of Public Prosecutions (DPP), Keir Starmer QC, to set out. These suggest journalists should not be charged when 'the public interest served by the conduct in question outweighs the overall criminality'. The guidelines offer what the DPP called 'examples of conduct ... capable of serving the public interest'.

The third Leveson 'backstop' is the British jury system, which in the case of the senior civil servant Clive Ponting acquitted him of charges under the Official Secrets Act even though he admitted to leaking key documents after the Falklands War.

'Finally,' said Leveson, 'there is, I hope, at the end of the line, a sensible judge who would take a view that even if it is a strict breach of the law, and even if there isn't a public interest defence, then this is not a very egregious problem.'

Which just leaves the small problem of defining what exactly is in the 'public interest'.

The Guardian's investigations editor, David Leigh, was asked at Leveson about another journalist's statement that the public interest is what the public is interested in. He called that 'an absurd proposition'. He preferred a quote from Lord Northcliffe that 'news is something that somebody wants to suppress. All the rest is advertising.' That, he said, was 'a starting point'.

The problem of converting the concept of 'public interest' into the terminology of statute and regulation is best illustrated by the dispute about one line in the Press Complaints Commission's Editors' Code of Practice: 'There is a public interest in freedom of expression itself.'

John Lloyd, a contributing editor for the *Financial Times* and director of journalism at the Reuters Institute for the Study of Journalism at the University of Oxford, is not a fan of this sentence. He has called it 'an absurd claim when left at that'.

On the other hand, the editor of *The Guardian*, Alan Rusbridger, who has often been a critic of the PCC itself, has written, 'I'm one of those who think the PCC's definition of the "public interest" is actually rather good.'

There have been some new attempts to define the public interest in more precise terms. Professor Steven Barnett offered one to the Leveson Inquiry:

> There is a clear public interest in:
> * Exposing or detecting crime, incompetence, injustice or significant anti-social behaviour among private or public officials in positions of responsibility;
> * Protecting the public from potential danger;
> * Preventing the public from being misled by erroneous statements or by the hypocrisy of those attempting to create a false image for potential material gain;
> * Revealing information which fulfils a democratic role in advancing a better understanding of issues that are of importance to a significant portion of the public, or that assists the public in making important decisions in public life.

The search for the perfect definition of the public interest goes on.

But, helpfully, in addition to new guidelines and draft definitions, we now have a case where a news organisation argued a public interest defence for hacking to both the Crown Prosecution Service and the broadcasting regulator. The news organisation is, by coincidence, also a part of a Murdoch-controlled media enterprise, BSkyB. The man Sky News hacked was the so-called 'canoe-man' who paddled off to sea one day and, it appeared at the time, never came back.

In March 2002, John Darwin from County Durham was

reported missing in his canoe in the North Sea. He was presumed dead and his wife Anne collected more than £500,000 in life insurance pay-outs. In fact he was hiding in their home. He had even allowed their two sons to think he was dead.

In July 2008 John and Anne Darwin were both sentenced to six years in prison. Sky News transmitted a report about 'John and Anne Darwin's masterplan', quoting from emails that the 'canoe-man' had written to his wife and to a lawyer.

Four years later, John Ryley, head of Sky News, issued a press release which said, 'On two occasions, we have authorised a journalist to access the email of individuals suspected of criminal activity... We stand by these actions as editorially justified and in the public interest.'[741]

When John Ryley appeared before the Leveson Inquiry the Lord Justice himself immediately joined in the questioning. Firstly, about the law.

> Lord Justice Leveson: What you were doing wasn't merely invading somebody's privacy; it was breaching the criminal law.
> Ryley: It was.

Then about regulation.

> Lord Justice Leveson: Well, where does the Ofcom Broadcasting Code give any authority to a breach of the criminal law?
> Ryley: It doesn't.

But Sky News and its staff were subsequently not proceeded against by the UK's public prosecutors and broadcasting regulator. In March 2013 the Crown Prosecution Service announced:

> The evidence indicates that the public interest served by the conduct in question outweighs the potential overall criminality... In reaching this decision, we took into account that the emails were accessed with a view to showing that a criminal offence had been committed.[742]

In July 2013 Ofcom decided that Sky News had not breached the Broadcasting Code by 'obtaining and subsequently broadcasting material accessed improperly by gaining unauthorised access to the email accounts' because 'the broadcaster's right to freedom of expression, including the freedom to receive and impart information and ideas without interference, in the exceptional circumstances of this case, outweighed Mr and Mrs Darwin's expectation of privacy'. However it also noted that 'BSkyB's conduct is at the boundaries of what is appropriate'.[743]

The hacking affair and the Leveson Inquiry had brought – among many other things – new guidelines, a new awareness that the media couldn't just opt in and out of observing the law and the 'canoe-man' case. One other benefit may turn out to have an even wider and longer-lasting impact.

'Transparency' is arguably the most overused word in the English language but that doesn't mean the value of the concept is completely diminished. It doesn't come much more transparent than an editor being interrogated live on television in front of a senior judge by a top barrister. At the Leveson Inquiry public hearings, the live television coverage and the simultaneous commentary on social media made a powerful combination for holding journalists to account in the same way as they, rightly, hold others to account.

There were moments when editors and reporters sat, heads down, as they struggled to remember why and how certain deeds were done. On Twitter, colleagues, competitors and citizens congratulated, criticised and challenged them. John Ryley of Sky News looked uncomfortable being questioned by Leveson about the 'canoe-man' but his openness probably helped his case with the CPS and Ofcom.

My own conclusion is that nothing will ever be the same again after Leveson and that real journalism has nothing to fear from the transparency and accountability it represented.

I am not advocating regular 'trial by television' of journalists. It wouldn't be right and it wouldn't be needed. I believe that the outside possibility of being questioned in public, the possible chance of the disclosure of internal emails (as reinforced by the disclosures to both the Hutton Inquiry and the Pollard review for the BBC of the Savile affair), and the likelihood of peer review on social media have changed behaviours and will continue to do so. Those who believe they can meet the public interest should have nothing to fear.

So I commend one new 'line' and I call it the 'Leigh line' after the investigations editor of *The Guardian*, David Leigh, who said at a Leveson hearing:

> I think I would say a journalist ought to be prepared to face up to the consequences of what they've done. I mean, if I do something that I think is OK in the public interest, I have to be prepared to take the consequences.

UNIVERSITY OF CHESTER, WARRINGTON CAMPUS

APPENDIX

What is an ambitious young journalist to conclude from these stories of what their predecessors got up to in the news business?

I feel we owe it to would-be journalists, some of whom I help to teach, to at least offer them some specific guidance based on our research.

Jeff Hulbert and I have distilled some of the lessons learned into a 'Purvis–Hulbert List' – a checklist that a journalist can refer to at significant moments.

First ask yourself: is there a law, an industry code or in-house guideline covering what you are about to do? You can find out most of the rules by reading them yourself and by asking an expert in the newsroom. The best advice is to follow the rules, but if you feel you would be justified in breaking them check with your editors, who in turn will consult their legal advisers. They can help decide if your organisation would have a public interest defence that they would be confident to put forward under public scrutiny, potentially before a jury.

There are ten other situations where we would advise a pause for thought:

- If you are about to attack your rivals in public, have you controlled your competitive instincts and ensured that any allegations you make will be seen to be fair when the full facts are made public?

- If you are relying on a whistle-blower, have you got all the facts in your story right so that you respect their motives and help protect their identity?
- If you are getting a story from intelligence sources, where does the balance of benefit lie? They will get planted propaganda, what exactly will you get?
- If you are giving information to intelligence sources, is there a good reason why you are doing this if the story wasn't interesting enough for you to put in the public domain by publishing or broadcasting it yourself?
- If you are self-censoring a story, can you justify this because it will facilitate an eventual greater truth?
- If you are giving evidence in a court case, have you thought through what you think it is right and wrong to reveal? If you are taking sides, are you being honest about it?
- If you've done a defensible deal with a source to omit a key fact, are you sure your report won't end up misleading people?
- If your editors and sub-editors have changed your copy substantially, can you still stand behind it?
- If you are a broadcast journalist subject to the due impartiality rules, is your knowledge of the subject enough for you to offer a 'professional judgement' without it being a 'personal view'?

If the answer to these ten questions is 'yes', then go ahead and if necessary cross somebody's line; you'll be ready. As David Leigh put it, 'If I do something that I think is OK in the public interest, I have to be prepared to take the consequences.'

ENDNOTES

1   Fitzroy Maclean, *Eastern Approaches* (London: Penguin, 1991), p. 311
2   Ed Vulliamy, *The War is Dead, Long Live the War: Bosnia: The Reckoning* (London: Bodley Head, 2012), p. xxvii
3   Mark Curtis, *Secret Affairs: Britain's Collusion with Radical Islam*, 2nd edn (London: Serpent's Tail, 2012)
4   For a view that the images were not sanitised see Jean Seaton, *Carnage and the Media* (London: Allen Lane, 2005), Chapter 6. Some of the incidents initially attributed to Bosnian Serbs were later found to have been perpetrated by Bosnian Muslims.
5   See Brendan Simms, *Unfinest Hour* (London: Penguin, 2002)
6   John Burns, 'The Media as Impartial Observers or Protagonists: Conflict Reporting or Conflict Encouragement in Former Yugoslavia', in James Gow, Richard Paterson and Alison Preston (eds), *Bosnia by Television* (London: British Film Institute, 1996), p. 92
7   John Simpson, *A Mad World, My Masters: Tales From a Traveller's Life* (London: Pan, 2001), p. 322
8   Roy Gutman, 'Prisoners of Serbia's War', reprinted in Roy Gutman, *A Witness to Genocide: The First Inside Account of the Horrors of Ethnic Cleansing in Bosnia* (Shaftesbury: Element, 1993), pp. 28–33
9   Roy Gutman, 'Like Auschwitz, Serbs Pack Muslims into Freight Cars', reprinted in Gutman, *A Witness to Genocide*, pp. 36–40
10 Maggie O'Kane, 'Muslims' Nightmare under the Long Hot Yugoslav Sun', *The Guardian*, 29 July 1992; and Roy Gutman interview, 'All Things Considered', National Public Radio, 2 August 1992; see also: Roy Gutman, *A Witness to Genocide*
11 Roy Gutman, 'Death Camps, Survivors Tell of Captivity, Mass Slaughters in Bosnia', reprinted in Roy Gutman, *A Witness to Genocide*, pp. 44–49
12 See Ed Vulliamy, 'Concentration Camps', in Roy Gutman and David Rieff (eds), *Crimes of War: What the Public Should Know* (New York: W. W. Norton & Co., 1999), p. 102
13 Bill Nasson, *The Boer War: The Struggle for South Africa* (London: History Press, 2011), pp. 241–246; Thomas Pakenham, *The Boer War* (London: Abacus, 1991), pp. 507, 509–510, 517 and 572. Up to 155,000 (111,000 whites and 44,000 blacks) had been held in the camps; 'official' estimates of the death rate varied between 18,000 and 28,000.
14 See Primo Levi, *If This is a Man* (London: Abacus, 1995), for his experience in one of the labour camps in the Auschwitz complex. Auschwitz comprised three main camps, including Auschwitz-Birkenau, and forty-five satellite camps; see also Hannah Arendt, *Eichmann in Jerusalem* (London: Penguin, 1994).

15 Gitta Sereny, *Into That Darkness: From Mercy Killing to Mass Murder*, new edn (London: Pimlico, 1995)

16 There is a picture of the 'restored' Treblinka site on which a farmhouse had been built at the end of 1943 and in which a Ukrainian farmer named Strebel was housed. If questioned he was expected to claim that his family had lived there for a long time. The photograph is reproduced in Sereny, *Into That Darkness*, between pages 192 and 193; for the closure and disguising of the camp, see pages 249–250. Sereny quotes from a report to Heinrich Himmler by the SS general in direct charge of the three camps, Odilo Globocnik. It confirmed that the same method of disguise was adopted to mask all of the Operation (*Aktion*) Reinhardt camps (p. 249).

17 See Martin Gilbert, *The Holocaust* (London: Collins, 1986); I. C. B. Dear and M. R. D. Foot, *The Oxford Companion to the Second World War* (Oxford: Oxford University Press, 1995); Sereny, *Into That Darkness*; Rudolf Hoess, *Commandant of Auschwitz* (London: Phoenix, 2000), (especially Primo Levi's introduction); Yisrael Gutman and Michael Berenbaum (eds), *Anatomy of the Auschwitz Death Camp* (Bloomington: Indiana University Press, 1998) (in particular Part II); and Hanna Arendt, *Eichmann in Jerusalem*, p. 1

18 Transcript, Independent Television News, Penny Marshall and Ian Williams v. Informinc (LM) Ltd, Michael Hume and Helene Guldberg, (Sue Inglish) day 5 am, p. 40, lines 1–5

19 Nik Gowing interview with Radovan Karadžić, *Channel 4 News*, 29 July 1992: http://www.itnsource.com/en/shotlist//ITN/1992/07/29/BSP290792023/?s=bosnia&st=0&pn=1

20 Ibid.

21 Transcript (Sue Inglish), day 5 am, p. 40, lines 8–12. See also: Nik Gowing, 'Real-time TV Coverage from War: Does It Make or Break Government Policy?', in James Gow, Richard Paterson and Alison Preston (eds), *Bosnia by Television*, p. 89

22 Transcript (Sue Inglish), day 5 am, p. 40, lines 14–21

23 Vulliamy, *The War is Dead, Long Live the War*, p. 5

24 See Vulliamy, *The War is Dead, Long Live the War*, p. 5

25 Transcript, day 2 pm, p. 36, lines 28–41

26 Vulliamy, *The War is Dead, Long Live the War*, p. 6; trial transcript, day 2 PM, p. 37, lines 6–19

27 Vulliamy, *The War is Dead, Long Live the War*, p. 6

28 Yigal Chazan and Foreign Staff, 'US Confirms Camps Exist', *The Guardian*, 4 August 1992, p. 6

29 Ibid.

30 Transcript, day 2 pm, p. 37, lines 49–55

31 Ed Vulliamy, 'Shame of Camp Omarska', *The Guardian*, 7 August 1992, p. 1

32 Ibid.

33 This was the notorious camp at Keraterm, which held mostly Bosniak Muslim prisoners, although some Croats were held, too. The camp was located at a former ceramic works and was the scene of beatings and executions, according to the UN Committee of Experts – see final report of the United Nations commission of experts established pursuant to security council resolution 780 (1992), S/1994/674, Annex VIII; and Ed Vulliamy, *Seasons in Hell, Understanding Bosnia's War* (London: Simon and Schuster, 1994), pp. 111–112, 202–203.

34 Transcript, day 2 pm, p. 40, lines 20–25

35 Transcript, day 6 pm, p. 55, lines 34–42

36 Vulliamy, *The War is Dead, Long Live the War*, p. xxiv

37 Transcript, day 2 pm, p. 42, lines 23–31

38 Vulliamy, *The War is Dead, Long Live the War*, p. 7

39   Transcript, day 6 pm, p. 53, lines 41–44

40   Transcript, day 6 pm, p. 54, lines 15–18

41   Transcript, day 2 pm, p. 44, lines 28–31

42   Transcript, day 2 pm, pp. 44–45; Transcript, day 6 pm, p. 55, lines 34–42

43   Transcript, day 2 pm, p. 44, lines 47–51

44   Transcript, day 2 pm, p. 46, lines 9–23

45   Sandra Sanchez, 'Horror in Serbian Prison Camps', *USA Today*, 7 August 1992, p. 4A

46   Paul Lewis, 'Conflict in the Balkans: U.S. and Allies Divided Over Role of U.N. Forces', *New York Times*, 9 August 1992, p. 12

47   Craig R. Whitney, 'Conflict in the Balkans: What Price Bosnia? Atrocity Reports Make West Consider How Far It Should Go to End Violence', *New York Times*, 10 August 1992, p. 8

48   Ibid.

49   Paddy Ashdown, 'When Will You Act? The Leader of the Liberal Democrats Paddy Ashdown Sent This Letter to Mr Major on his Return from Bosnia', *The Guardian*, 13 August 1992

50   Vulliamy, *The War is Dead, Long Live the War*, p. 6

51   Final report of the United Nations commission of experts established pursuant to security council resolution 780 (1992), S/1994/674, 27 May 1994. Annex VIII acknowledges that most camps had closed by the middle of August 1992.

52   John Taylor, *Body Horror: Photojournalism, Catastrophe and War* (Manchester: Manchester University Press, 1998), p. 63

53   Vulliamy, 'Concentration Camps', p. 102

54   Ibid., p. 103

55   UN Human Rights Committee document, GE.93–16824 (E), 27 April 1993, paragraph 7. In paragraph 6 the document uses the term 'concentration camp' to describe the camps and lists over ninety Bosnian Serb-controlled camps in paragraph 7. Later paragraphs provide details of the numbers of detainees, organisation, conditions and deaths.

56   The commission reported: '"Informative talks" or interrogations basically took place in the Omarska and Keraterm camps ... more than 6,000 adult males were taken to these concentration camps in the short period they existed (from the end of May to the beginning of August 1992). Since only 1,503 were moved on to Manjača camp according to Mr Drljača [Deputy Minister of Interior of the Serb Republic of Bosnia], a limited number transferred to the Trnopolje camp and almost none released, it may be assumed that the death toll was extremely high.' See final report of the United Nations commission of experts established pursuant to security council resolution 780 (1992), S/1994/674, 27 May 1994, paragraph 170, pp. 40–41.

57   The UN commission's report (Annex VIII) identified 639 camps: Serb-controlled: 331 (of which 204 were corroborated and 128 were uncorroborated); Muslim-controlled: 83 (of which 38 were corroborated and 45 were uncorroborated); Croat-controlled: 51 (of which 30 were corroborated and 21 were uncorroborated); unknown (i.e. no controlling group was positively established): 174 (of which 102 were corroborated and 72 were uncorroborated).

58   Ed Vulliamy's other journalism awards for his Bosnia coverage were: 1992 Granada TV International Reporter of the Year; 1992 Amnesty International Reporter of the Year; and 1994 James Cameron Memorial Award.

59   Final report of the United Nations commission of experts established pursuant to security council resolution 780 (1992), Annex V, The Prijedor report, S/1994/674/Add.2 (Vol. I), 28 December 1994

60   Ibid.

61   See: (Milošević) Carlotta Gall, 'Serbian tells of Spiriting Milosevic Away', *New York*

Times, 1 July 2001, and Chris Stephen, *Judgement Day: The Trial of Slobodan Milosevic* (London: Atlantic Books, 2004), especially Chapter 7; (Karadžić) 'Serbia Capture Fugitive Karadžić', BBC News, 21 July 2008, http://news.bbc.co.uk/1/hi/world/europe/7518543.stm (accessed 26 November 2012); (Mladić) 'Ratko Mladic Arrested: Bosnia War Crimes Suspect Held', BBC News, 26 May 2011, http://www.bbc.co.uk/news/world-europe-13561407 (accessed 26 November 2012)

62   See ICTY Tadić summary, http://www.icty.org/x/cases/tadic/cis/en/cis_tadic_en.pdf (accessed 26 November 2012)

63   'Germany Prosecutes Serb for War Crimes in Bosnia', Agence France Presse – English, 14 February 1994

64   Lindsey Hilsum, war crimes trial: http://www.pbs.org/newshour/bb/bosnia/war_crimes_5-7.html

65   Ed Vulliamy, 'Tadić Stood Where No Man Has Since Goering and Hess, Ed Vulliamy at the first Bosnian war-crimes trial in The Hague', *The Guardian*, 8 May 1996, p. 2

66   Ed Vulliamy, 'Testimony for the Terrorised', *The Guardian*, 15 June 1996, p. 29

67   Transcript, day 8 am, p. 17, lines 21–22

68   Transcript, day 8 pm, p. 72, lines 40–54

69   David Campbell, 'Atrocity, Memory, Photography: Imaging the Concentration Camps of Bosnia – The Case of ITN Versus Living Marxism, Part 1', *Journal of Human Rights*, vol. 1, no. 1 (March 2002), pp. 8–9

70   Transcript, day 8 pm, p. 73, lines 1–11

71   Transcript, day 8 am, p. 18, lines 44–55

72   Transcript, day 8 am, p. 17, lines 46–47

73   Transcript, day 8 am, p. 19, lines 3–8

74   Thomas Deichmann, 'The Picture that Fooled the World', *Living Marxism*, no. 97, February 1997

75   Private information

76   Martin Bell, *Through Gates of Fire: A Journey into World Disorder* (London: Phoenix, 2004), p. 166

77   Luke Harding, 'Second Front: A Shot that's Still Ringing', *The Guardian*, 12 March 1997

78   Ibid.

79   Mick Hume, 'Letter: The Rocky Road From Dunblane', *The Guardian*, 18 March 1996, p. 10 ('Nothing like the school gym shooting has ever happened in Britain before. There is nothing to suggest that it will happen again. So why should we allow this extraordinary incident to determine the degree of security, surveillance and controls we are prepared to accept in our society?')

80   Mick Hume, 'Letter: Battle Rages over Bosnia', *The Guardian*, 14 March 1997, p. 16

81   Andy Beckett, 'Licence to Rile', *The Guardian*, 15 May 1999

82   Ed Vulliamy, 'I Stand by My Story', *The Observer*, 2 February 1997, p. 25

83   Andrew Culf, 'ITN Wins Apology over Bosnia Libel, Press Release Alleged Camps Stories Fabricated', *The Guardian*, 18 April 1997, p. 9

84   Private information

85   Martin Bell, *Through Gates of Fire*, pp. 164–65

86   Richard Tait, Letter to the Editor, *The Times*, 23 October 1998, p. 27

87   John Simpson interview with Vin Ray at Frontline Club, London, 16 January 2013

88   John Simpson, *Strange Places, Questionable People* (London: Pan, 1999), p. 449

89   Eddie Gibb, 'John Simpson to Act for Defence Against ITN in Libel Trial', *Sunday Herald*, 6 February 2000, p. 6

90   Eddie Gibb, 'Ready for Another War', *Sunday Herald*, 6 February 2000, p. 4

91   John Simpson, witness statement for LM in ITN v LM libel case, London, 2000

92   Deborah Lipstadt, *History on Trial: My Day in Court with a Holocaust Denier* (New York: HarperPerennial, 2006); Richard Evans, *Telling Lies about Hitler* (London: Verso, 2002)

93   Transcript, day 8 am, p. 27, lines 53–54

94   Mick Hume, 'Spare Any Change Guv?', *The Times*, 17 March 2000

95   David Campbell, 'Atrocity, Memory, Photography: Imaging the Concentration Camps of Bosnia – The Case of ITN Versus Living Marxism, Part 2', *Journal of Human Rights*, vol. 1, no. 2 (June 2002), pp. 143–172

96   Transcript, day 7 am, p. 3, lines 5–16

97   Transcript, day 1, pp. 11–12, lines 48–55 and 1

98   Ibid., p. 10, lines 53–54

99   Transcript, day 7 am, p. 11, lines 18–27

100   Ibid., p. 11, lines 42–46

101   Ibid., p. 12, lines 13–26

102   Ibid., p. 12, lines 28–32

103   Ibid., p. 13, line 1

104   Ibid., p. 13, lines 14–19

105   Ibid., p. 13, lines 30–32

106   Ibid., p. 14, lines 1–22

107   Ibid., p. 14, lines 24–29

108   Ibid., p. 15, lines 41–52

109   Ibid., p. 16, lines 45–50

110   Ibid., p. 17, lines 9–19

111   David Campbell, 'Atrocity, Memory, Photography: Imaging the Concentration Camps of Bosnia – The Case of ITN Versus Living Marxism, Part 1', p. 25

112   Transcript, day 11 am, pp. 10–14

113   Transcript, day 11 pm, pp. 17–19

114   Ibid., p. 20

115   Broadcasting Standards Commission, Adjudication, 2 October 2000

116   Ibid.

117   Ibid.

118   Hume, 'Spare Any Change Guv?'

119   Mick Hume, *There is No Such Thing as a Free Press: And We Need One More Than Ever* (Exeter: Imprint Academic, 2012), Kindle location 2711

120   John Simpson, *A Mad World, My Masters*, p. 321

121   Ibid., p. 322

122   Ed Vulliamy, *The War is Dead, Long Live the War*, p. 83

123   Email exchanges: Stewart Purvis with Henry De Zoete (special adviser to Michael Gove), April and May 2013

124   John Simpson, 'Book Review: *The War is Dead, Long Live the War: Bosnia: The Reckoning* by Ed Vulliamy', *The Observer*, 22 April 2012, p. 37

125   TNA KV2/1016, 172532/ME/16, 26 January 1920

126   TNA CAB 24/132 CP 3209, weekly report on revolutionary organisations in the United Kingdom, no. 138

127   John Callaghan and Kevin Morgan, 'The Open Conspiracy of the Communist Party and the Case of W. N. Ewer, Communist and Anti-Communist', *Historical Journal*, vol. 49, no. 2 (June 2006), p. 553

128   Federated Press of America, FPA, based in London's Strand.

129   TNA KV2/1016, s809a, p. 12

130   TNA KV2/1016, folio 1101, p. 5

131   TNA KV2/485; Keith Jeffery, *MI6: The History of the Secret Intelligence Service, 1909–1949*, revised edn (London: Bloomsbury, 2011), pp. 230–231

132   Francis Williams, *Nothing So Strange* (New York: American Heritage Press, 1970), p. 113

133   TNA FO 371/56885/N 6092G, Kirkpatrick memorandum; minutes, 7 May 1946

134   Sir John Rennie (MI6); Sir Ray Whitney (Conservative MP)

135   Paul Lashmar and James Oliver, *Britain's Secret Propaganda War* (Stroud: Sutton, 1998)

136   John Jenks, *British Propaganda and News Media in the Cold War* (Edinburgh: Edinburgh University Press, 2006), p. 82

137   Alter Litvin and John Keep, *Stalinism: Russian and Western Views at the Turn of the Millennium* (London: Routledge, 2005), p. 11

138   See Timothy Snyder, *Bloodlands: Europe Between Hitler and Stalin* (London: Bodley Head, 2010), Chapter 1; Robert Conquest, *The Harvest of Sorrow: Soviet Collectivisation and the Terror-Famine* (London: Pimlico, 2002); Robert Service, *A History of Twentieth Century Russia* (London: Allen Lane, 1997); Lynne Viola, *Peasant Rebels Under Stalin: Collectivization and the Culture of Peasant Resistance* (New York: Oxford University Press, 1996); for the unreliability of records see Litvin and Keep, *Stalinism*; Sheila Fitzpatrick, *Everyday Stalinism: Ordinary Life in Extraordinary Times* (New York: Oxford University Press, 1999; D'Ann Penner, *The Agrarian Strike of 1932–33*, Kennan Institute for Advanced Russian Studies at the Hoover Institution, occasional paper, no. 269, 1998

139   Walter Duranty, *I Write as I Please* (London: Hamish Hamilton, 1933), p. 287

140   Harrison E. Salisbury, *Without Fear or Favor: The New York Times and its Times* (New York: Times Books, 1980), p. 458

141   Walter Duranty, *Search for a Key* (New York: Simon and Schuster, 1943), p. 1. The book mixes fiction and fact.

142   S. J. Taylor, *Stalin's Apologist: Walter Duranty, The New York Times's Man in Moscow* (New York: Oxford University Press, 1990), p. 4

143   Ibid., p. 23

144   Ibid., p. 18

145   Crowley, Duranty, Jane Chéron and Victor Neuberg took part in a series of twenty-three satanic, sexual and magic rituals, the so-called 'Paris Workings', which lasted for seven weeks from 31 December 1913. The *New York Times* would not have approved. Richard Kaczynski, *Perdurabo: The Life of Aleister Crowley*, revised edn (Berkeley: North Atlantic Books, 2010); and Aleister Crowley, *The Equinox: The Vision and The Voice – With Commentary and Other Papers*, v. 4, no. 2, new edn (York Beach, ME: Red Wheel/Weiser, 1999), pp. 351–395

146   S. J. Taylor, *Stalin's Apologist*, p. 32

147   Tobias Churton, *Aleister Crowley: The Biography* (London: Watkins Publishing, 2011), p. 306

148   Williams said Duranty uttered 'the first mention that I remember of the word "war" in connection with the events that followed so fast for the next few weeks...', Wythe Williams, *Passed by the Censor*, 1916 (Forgotten Books reprint, 2012), p. 3

149   Duranty, *I Write As I Please*, pp. 283–284

150   The Kapp Putsch was an uprising that sought to overthrow the German government which had accepted the terms of the Versailles Treaty ending the First World War.

151   Duranty, *I Write As I Please*, pp. 74–75. The diplomat only found out about the story when Washington asked for details.

152   Ibid., p. 93

153   W. Lippmann and C. Merz, 'A Test of the News', *New Republic*, 4 August 1920

154   Ibid., p. 3

155   Ibid., p. 45

156   Duranty, *I Write As I Please*, p. 99

157   TNA FO 371/16323, (William) Strang to Collier, 6 December 1932

158   Salisbury, *Without Fear or Favor*, p. 462

159   Ibid., p. 462

160   Ibid., p. 463

161   David C. Engerman, 'Modernization from the Other Shore: American Observers and the Costs of Soviet Economic Development', *American Historical Review*, vol. 105, no. 2 (April 2000), pp. 390–391; see also the articles: Walter Duranty, *New York Times*: 'All Russia Suffers Shortage of Food'; 'Supplies Dwindling', 25 November 1932, p. 1; 'Food Shortage Laid to Soviet Peasants', 26 November 1932, p. 9; 'Soviet Press Lays Shortages to Foes', 27 November 1932, p. 4; 'Soviet Not Alarmed over Food Shortage', 28 November 1932, p. 6; 'Soviet Industries Hurt Agriculture', 29 November 1932, p. 4; 'Bolsheviki United on Socialist Goal', 30 November 1932, p. 4.

162   Engerman, 'Modernization from the Other Shore', p. 206

163   Ibid., p. 200

164   Walter Duranty, 'Red Russia', *New York Times*, 14 June 1931

165   Engerman, 'Modernization from the Other Shore', p. 384

166   Walter Duranty, 'Red Square', *New York Times*, 18 September 1932

167   For 1932 Pulitzer Prizes: http://www.pulitzer.org/awards/1932

168   Taylor, *Stalin's Apologist*, p. 182

169   TNA FO 371/16323/N7289 Strang to Collier, 6 December 1932

170   Engerman, 'Modernization from the Other Shore', p. 391

171   David C. Engerman, *Modernization from the Other Shore: American Intellectuals and the Romance of Russian Development*, (Cambridge, MA: Harvard University Press, 2003) p. 197

172   William Henry Chamberlin: 'The Russian Peasant Sphinx', *Foreign Affairs*, vol. 7, no. 3 (April 1929), pp. 477–487; 'Making the Collective Man in Soviet Russia', *Foreign Affairs*, vol. 10, no. 2 (January 1932), pp. 280–292; 'The Balance Sheet of the Five-Year Plan', *Foreign Affairs*, vol. 11, no. 3 (April 1933), pp. 458–469; 'What is Happening in Russia?', *International Affairs*, vol. 12, no. 2 (March 1933), pp. 187–204.

173   Chamberlin, 'What is Happening in Russia?', p. 189

174   Engerman, 'Modernization from the Other Shore: American Observers and the Costs of Soviet Economic Development', p. 392.

175   Duranty's interview with Stalin was published in the *New York Times* on 1 December 1930. It is reprinted in Walter Duranty, *Russia Reported* (London: Victor Gollancz, 1934), pp. 202–207.

176   Originally published by the Alton Press Inc., Pittsburgh, USA in 1932. A PDF is available online: http://www.garethjones.org/soviet_articles/experiences_in_russia_1931.pdf (accessed 19 September 2012)

177   TNA FO 371/16336/N6494, Strang, record of meeting with Mr Duranty, 14 November, 1932

178   Engerman, *Modernization from the Other Shore: American Intellectuals and the Romance of Russian Development*, p. 201

179   See Snyder, *Bloodlands*, Chapter 1

180   Simon Sebag-Montefiore, *Stalin: The Court of the Red Tsar* (London: Weidenfeld & Nicolson, 2003), p. 80. Stalin had told Churchill that collectivisation 'had been a terrible struggle, "in which he had to destroy ten million. It was fearful. Four years it lasted. It was absolutely necessary ... there was no use arguing with them"', (citing Winston Churchill, *The Second World War*, vol. 4, pp. 447–448).

181   Whitman Bassow, *The Moscow Correspondents: Reporting on Russia from the Revolution to Glasnost* (New York: William Morrow and Co., 1988), p. 67

182   Richard Ingrams, *Muggeridge* (London: Harper Collins, 1996), p. 72

183   Investigation of the Ukrainian Famine, Report to Congress by the Commission on

the Ukraine Famine, 19 April 1988 (submitted to Congress, 22 April 1988), United States Government Printing Office, Washington: 1988, p. 168 (hereafter referred to as Congressional report)

184   Gareth Jones, Letter to the Editor, *New York Times*, 1 May 1933

185   Malcolm Muggeridge (unattributed – 'From a Correspondent in Russia'), 'The Soviet and the Peasantry, an Observer's Notes, II, Hunger in the Ukraine', *Manchester Guardian*, 27 March 1933, pp. 9–10

186   Malcolm Muggeridge (unattributed – 'From a Correspondent in Russia'), 'The Soviet and the Peasantry, an Observer's Notes, III, Poor Harvest in Prospect', *Manchester Guardian*, 28 March 1933, pp. 9–10

187   Malcolm Muggeridge, ed. John Bright-Holmes, *Like It Was: The Diaries of Malcolm Muggeridge* (London: Collins, 1981), p. 74

188   For a comprehensive account of Jones's life and supporting information, as well as transcripts of many relevant articles: http://www.garethjones.org

189   From the 1933 diary of Gareth Jones, vol. 2: http://www.garethjones.org/diaries/1933-2/gareth_jones_1933_diary_2_part_2.pdf, accessed 18 September 2012

190   Gareth Jones was the subject of a *Storyville* documentary, *Hitler, Stalin and Mr Jones*, (BBC4, 5 July 2012, 9 p.m.) while Duranty was the subject of a Radio 4 documentary, *But They Are Only Russians*, (12 January 2013, 11.30 a.m.).

191   Ingrams, *Muggeridge*, p. 72

192   Edgar Ansel Mowrer, 'Russian Famine Now as Great as Famine of 1921 says Secretary to Lloyd George', *Chicago Daily News*, 29 March 1933, p. 2

193   'Millions Starving in Russia', *Daily Express*, 30 March 1933, p. 2.

194   '"Keep Cool" says Soviet Ambassador', *Daily Express*, 30 March 1933, p. 2. The engineers were all released. See Gordon W. Morrell, *Britain Confronts the Stalin Revolution: Anglo-Soviet Relations and the Metro-Vickers Crisis* (Waterloo, ON: Wilfrid Laurier University Press, 1995)

195   Walter Duranty, 'Russians Hungry, but Not Starving', *New York Times*, 31 March 1933

196   Thirty-five agriculture bureaucrats were shot as a result.

197   Walter Duranty, 'Soviet Industry Shows Big Gains', *New York Times*, April 6, 1933

198   [George] Bernard Shaw and Twenty Others, Letter to the Editor, *Manchester Guardian*, 2 March 1933

199   Ingrams, *Muggeridge*, p. 75

200   Dana G. Dalrymple, 'The Soviet Famine of 1932–1934', *Soviet Studies*, vol. 15, no. 3 (January 1964), p. 250

201   Ingrams, *Muggeridge*, p. 69

202   Lyons mistakenly telephoned a despatch to London without clearing it first with the censor; failing to stop its circulation on the newswires was the end of his career in Moscow. He left in January 1934. See: Bassow, *Moscow Correspondents*, pp. 86–87.

203   James Crowl, *Angels in Stalin's Paradise: Western Reporters in Soviet Russia, 1917 to 1937* (Washington: University Press of America, 1982) p. 141

204   Eugene Lyons, *Assignment in Utopia* (New York: Harcourt Brace, 1937), p. 575

205   Ibid.

206   Ibid.

207   Congressional report, p. 169

208   Crowl, *Angels in Stalin's Paradise*, p. 142

209   Ibid.

210   Bassow, *The Moscow Correspondents*, pp. 75–78; Engerman, *Modernisation from the Other Shore: American Intellectuals and the Romance of Russian Development*, Chapter 9

211   Congressional report, p. 168

212 Williams, *Passed by the Censor*, pp. 11–16

213 Malcolm Muggeridge, *Winter in Moscow*, 1934 (Thirsk: House of Stratus, 2003), p. vii

214 See: Taylor, *Stalin's Apologist*, p. 160; a facsimile of the memorandum is available at: http://www.garethjones.org/Embassy-1.pdf. The Congressional Commission gave the full National Archives reference for the document: 193 V p. 2; 861.5017-Living Conditions/268; T1249; Records of the Department of State; NA.

215 According to Lyons Duranty, when asked if he really meant ten million deaths, replied, 'Hell I don't … I'm being conservative!' He allegedly continued, 'But they're only Russians.' Lyons, *Assignment in New York*, p. 580; Congressional report, p. 172.

216 Dalrymple, 'The Soviet Famine of 1932–1934', p. 278

217 Congressional report, p. 170

218 TNA FO 371/17253, N 7182/114/38, Strang minute, 26 September 1933, T A Shone note to King, Cabinet, Dominions, 2 October 1933

219 Bassow, *The Moscow Correspondents*, p. 88. 'Indeed, despite his flaws as a reporter, during the years he covered Moscow, Walter Duranty informed the world that from the ashes of the Czar's empire a new power had risen that would have to be reckoned with and would henceforth play a paramount role in international affairs.'

220 'Roosevelt Confers on Russian Policy, Consults Walter Duranty in Regard that Our Policy Should Change', *New York Times*, 26 July 1932, p. 1

221 Jacob Heilbrunn, 'The *New York Times* and the Moscow Show Trials', *World Affairs*, vol. 153, no. 3 (Winter 1991), pp. 87–101

222 Sebag-Montefiore, *Stalin*, p. 34: 'No man, no problem.' See also: TNA FO 676/215

223 Louis Fischer, *Why Recognize Russia?* (London: Jonathan Cape, 1931)

224 See: 'US "hushed up" Soviet Guilt over Katyn', BBC News, http://www.bbc.co.uk/news/world-europe-19552745 and 'Records Relating to the Katyn Forest Massacre at the National Archives', National Archives, http://www.archives.gov/research/foreign-policy/katyn-massacre/ (both accessed 19 September 2012)

225 Congressional report, pp. xxiii–xxiv

226 Ibid. p. 151

227 Ibid. p. 173

228 Engerman, 'Modernisation from the Other Shore: American Observers and the Costs of Soviet Economic Development', p. 401

229 Joe Alsop, 'Columnist Makes Assessment of American Fourth Estate' (31 December 1974), *Sarasota Journal*, 2 January 1975, p. 38, http://news.google.com/newspapers?nid=1798&dat=19750102&id=8QwfAAAAIBAJ&sjid=UI0EAAAAIBAJ&pg=3908,552897 (accessed 14 September 2012)

230 Salisbury, *Without Fear or Favor*, p. 460

231 See Ronald Grigor Suny, *The Cambridge History of Russia, Vol. 3: The Twentieth Century* (Cambridge: Cambridge University Press, 2006), pp. 39–40, in which he makes observations about the background of the historian Robert Conquest. See also David C. Engerman, 'Social Science in the Cold War', *Isis*, vol. 101, no. 2 (June 2010), pp. 393–400; David C. Engerman, *Know Your Enemy: The Rise and Fall of America's Soviet Experts* (New York: Oxford University Press, 2012); David C. Engerman, 'The Ironies of the Iron Curtain: The Cold War and the Rise of Russian Studies in the United States', *Cahiers du monde russe*, vol. 45, no. 3/4 (July–December 2004), pp. 465–496

232 See the 1984 made-for-TV film *Harvest of Despair*, which presented a harrowing and, in the view of many critics, one-sided account of the famine. It was produced by Yurij Luhovy and Slavko Nowytski, and directed by Slavko Nowytski. The decision to screen the film was debated on US Public Broadcasting Service television by Robert Conquest, Christopher Hitchens and Harrison Salisbury and, chaired by William F. Buckley Jr, the session was taped in New York on 4 September 1986.

233 http://www.projectcensored.org/about

234   'CIA Operating Drone Base in Saudi Arabia, US Media Reveal', http://www.bbc.co.uk/
      news/world-middle-east-21350437; Alex Spillius, Diplomatic Correspondent, 'Saudi
      DroneBlackoutRaisesDoubtsaboutUSMediaIndependence',*DailyTelegraph*,6February
      2013, http://www.telegraph.co.uk/news/worldnews/northamerica/usa/9853693/Saudi-
      drone-blackout-raises-doubts-about-US-media-independence.html
235   'Rescued from Tehran: We Were There', *Argo*, Warner Home Video, March 2013, UK
      edition
236   'Ukrainian Famine Was "Genocide"', BBC News, http://news.bbc.co.uk/1/hi/world/
      europe/6193266.stm
237   Russian grain exports during the years of the famine were as follows: 1931, 5.06
      million metric tons; 1932, 1.73 million metric tons; and in 1933, 1.68 million metric
      tons. Source: Commission on the Ukraine Famine, Report to (US) Congress, 22 April
      1988, p. 167.
238   KGB files say Blunt claimed Hewit as his lover; others claim Hewit as Burgess's long-
      term lover whom he 'lent' to his friends and those he wanted to do favours for.
239   Goronwy Rees, *A Chapter of Accidents* (London: Chatto & Windus, 1972), p. 122
240   His name does not appear on the list of members in the 1935/36 annual report. Philby's
      does, as well as the Marquess of Lothian and Thomas Cook and Company. See TNA
      KV5/3
241   Noel Annan, *Our Age: The Generation That Made Post-war Britain* (London: Fontana,
      1991), pp. 160–161
242   Robert Cecil, *A Divided Life: A Biography of Donald Maclean* (London: Bodley Head,
      1988), p. 132
243   BBC Written Archives Centre, L1/68/1
244   Ibid.
245   During his last undergraduate year Burgess helped to organise a strike among Trinity
      College waiters, who up to that time had been employed on a casual basis and only
      during term times.
246   Tom Driberg and Baron Bradwell, *Guy Burgess, a Portrait with Background* (London:
      Weidenfeld & Nicolson, 1956), p. 33; Barrie Penrose and Simon Freeman, *Conspiracy
      of Silence: The Secret Life of Anthony Blunt* (London: Grafton, 1986), p. 207
247   Dr P. Lousel to Sir Richard Maconachie, Director Talks, 14 March 1938, BBC Written
      Archives, Guy Burgess, Left Staff File L1/ 6/18
248   Internal memorandum about the Munich crisis, BBC WAC file C41. The memorandum
      says Neville Chamberlain's No. 10 adviser, Sir Horace Wilson, asked the corporation to
      'pay particular attention to opinions expressed in talks such as Harold Nicolson's "The
      Past Week"'. During September, the memorandum records 'consultation between the
      BBC and Whitehall became extremely close and news bulletins as a whole inevitably
      fell into line with government policy at this critical juncture'.
249   BBC WAC R1 Contributors file 3A, 5 September 1938
250   Driberg and Bradwell, *Guy Burgess*, pp. 44–46.
251   Guy Burgess to DT (Director, Talks), part of conversation with Mr Churchill, 4 October
      1938, BBC Written Archives Centre, L1/68/1
252   'A memo from Burgess about Winston Churchill', BBC, http://www.bbc.co.uk/archive/
      burgess/7705.shtml
253   'Cambridge Five Spy Ring, Part 33 of 42', FBI Records, http://vault.fbi.gov/
      Cambridge%20Five%20Spy%20Ring/Cambridge%20Five%20Spy%20Ring%20
      Part%2033%20of%2042/view
254   Some believe that Sir Joseph Ball, who ran the Conservative Party's research depart-
      ment during the 1930s, had some hand in this. Until Isaiah Berlin revealed that
      Burgess had worked for the department for a period no obvious connection had been
      established.

255 Its designation was 'Section IX or D (allegedly for 'Destruction')', Keith Jeffery, *MI6: The History of the Secret Intelligence Service 1909–1949* (London: Bloomsbury, 2010), p. 320. An internal history written in 1945 said Grand adopted the designation 'D' for himself (see W. J. M. Mackenzie, *The Secret History of SOE* (London: St Ermin's, 2000), p. 4; Mark Seaman, *Special Operations Executive* (London: Routledge, 2006), p. 10).

256 Mackenzie, *The Secret History of SOE*, p. 13

257 Burgess was not entirely inactive, however, as he had played his own discreet part during the Munich crisis by passing secret messages between the French and British governments via his Homintern contacts: Christopher Andrew and Oleg Gordievsky, *KGB: The Inside Story of its Foreign Operations from Lenin to Gorbachev* (London: Hodder & Stoughton, 1990), p. 236; Driberg and Bradwell, *Guy Burgess*, pp. 40–41.

258 Jeffery, *MI6*, p. 386

259 The saga is revealed in the following: Driberg and Bradwell, *Guy Burgess*, p. 59; Verne Newton, *The Butcher's Embrace* (London: Macdonald, 1991), pp. 19–20; Harold Nicolson, *Diaries and Letters, 1939–1945, Volume 2* (London: Fontana Books, 1970), entry for 17 June 1940 (and unpublished diary, June 1940 at Balliol College archives); Yuri Modin, *My Five Cambridge Friends* (London: Headline, 1994), p. 83; TNA FO 371/24847/N6063G, Telegram 1488, 'Burgess to "D" through "C", 24 July 1940'; TNA FO 371/24847/N6063G, Telegram 1683, FO to Lord Lothian (British Ambassador, Washington), 27 July 1940; Michael Ignatieff, *Isaiah Berlin: A Life* (London: Vintage, 2011), Kindle locations 1874–1916; Isaiah Berlin (Henry Hardy, ed.), *Flourishing: Letters 1928–1946* (London: Random House, 2012), Kindle locations 9371–9509). Miriam Rothschild then lived in Washington.

260 Harold Nicolson, unpublished diary, 19 August 1940

261 Lord Gladwyn, *The Memoirs of Lord Gladwyn* (London: Weidenfeld & Nicolson, 1972), p. 101

262 TNA HS 8/334

263 BBC Written Archives Centre, Caversham (WAC), L1/68/1, W R Baker, for General Establishment Officer to S D Charles, Ministry of Information 15 January 1941

264 BBC WAC L1/68/1

265 Christopher Andrew, *The Defence of the Realm: The Authorized History of MI5* (London: Allen Lane, 2010), p. 270. Burgess ran an agent for MI5 – see: Nigel West (ed.), *The Guy Liddell Diaries, Volume 1: 1939–1942* (London: Taylor and Francis, 2007), p. 174; and *Volume 2: 1942–1945*

266 Andrew, *The Defence of the Realm*, p. 270

267 Four of the Cambridge Five (Blunt, Burgess, Cairncross and Philby) fell under suspicion of being planted British double agents by NKVD officer Elena Modrzchinskaya: their information was considered to be too good, voluminous and consistent, arousing suspicions in Moscow that it was a plant. See Genrikh Borovik, *The Philby Files* (London: Little, Brown, 1994), Chapters 20 and 21; Christopher Andrew and Vasili Mitrokhin, *The Mitrokhin Archive* (London: Allen Lane, 2000), pp. 112, 156–60, 207–208; Andrew and Gordievsky, *KGB*, pp. 334–7; Nigel West and Oleg Tsarev, *Crown Jewels: The British Secrets at the Heart of the KGB Archives* (London: HarperCollins, 1998), pp. 159–162; Nigel West and Oleg Tsarev (eds), *Triplex: Secrets from the Cambridge Spies* (New Haven, CT: Yale University Press, 2009), pp. 317–334

268 Harold Nicolson unpublished diary, 6 May 1943

269 Hailsham quotation taken from Dame Stella Rimington, *Adventures in the BBC Archive, A Former Head of MI5 Investigates the Cambridge Spies*, Radio 4 (first broadcast 8 November 2008), 56 minutes, http://www.bbc.co.uk/archive/cambridg-espies/7816.shtml

270 HL Deb 21 March 1989 vol. 505 cc. 581–648

271   George Orwell, entry for 2 June 1942, *The Orwell Diaries* (London: Penguin, 2010), Kindle locations 8033–8068

272   BBC Written Archives, March 28 1944, BBC WAC L1/68/1: Left Staff, Burgess, Guy

273   David Graham in *Rebels: Guy Burgess – A Portrait Of An Unlikely Spy*, Radio 4 (first broadcast 5 October 1984), 27 minutes, http://www.bbc.co.uk/archive/cambridg-espies/7811.shtml

274   Peter Smollett was recruited and run as a sub-agent by Kim Philby, and shared with Anthony Blunt and Guy Burgess. This broke Moscow's cardinal rule that one agent should not know the identity of any other agent.

275   Miranda Carter, *Anthony Blunt: His Lives* (London: Macmillan, 2001), p. 457; Peter Wright with Paul Greengrass, *Spycatcher* (Melbourne: Heinemann Australia, 1987), pp. 242–243

276   TNA INF 1/147, Smolka [Smollett] to Mrs Atkins, 2 August 1942

277   Andrew and Gordievsky, *KGB*, p. 268; see also Andrew and Mitrokhin, *The Mitrokhin Archive*, pp. 158–9; Ian McLaine, *Ministry of Morale* (London: Allen & Unwin, 1979), pp. 202–3; Christopher Andrew, 'Moscow's Literary Agents', *The Times*, 9 December 1994; Timothy Garton Ash, 'Orwell's List: Love, Death and Treachery', *The Guardian*, 21 June 2003.

278   BBC WAC, L1/68/1

279   BBC WAC, L1/68/1

280   West and Tsarev, *Crown Jewels*, pp. 149–150, 162

281   See Jenny Rees, *Looking for Mr Nobody: The Secret Life of Goronwy Rees* (London: Weidenfeld & Nicolson, 1997) and Guy Liddell diary for 1951 (TNA KV4/473)

282   Harold Nicolson, unpublished diary, 5 January 1944

283   Michael Luke, *David Tennant and the Gargoyle Years* (London: Weidenfeld & Nicolson, 1991), p. 177

284   An Old Etonian friend of Burgess and a wartime MI5 officer.

285   Harold Acton, *More Memoirs of an Aesthete* (London: Faber & Faber, 2008), p. 87

286   See, for instance, TNA FO 366/1392, Ridsdale to Minister (Richard Law) 1 March 1944

287   TNA FO 954/23A, Ridsdale minute, 7 May 1943, Folio 196

288   Ibid., folio 200, Ridsdale to Harvey (Eden's principal private secretary), 21 May 1943

289   Ibid., folio 227

290   Ibid., folio 228

291   Harold Nicolson unpublished diary entries for 26 January 1944 and 2 February 1944

292   Various emails from Mary Pring (FCO) to Jeff Hulbert, March and April 2013. The document, which has yet to reach the National Archives, is described as 'Extract[s] from Three minutes headed "G F De M Burgess" (all undated)', Box 12, File 7.

293   TNA FO 800/272, Pierson Dixon to Sir Orme Sargent, handwritten note dated 4 June 1946

294   Churchill gave personal responsibility for MI5 to Eden in December 1943: Andrew, *The Defence of the Realm*, p. 309.

295   BBC WAC L1/68/1

296   Nicolson, *Diaries and Letters, 1939–1945, Volume 2*, entry for 26 February 1945

297   Driberg and Bradwell, *Guy Burgess*, Appendix

298   Record of a telephone conversation between the BBC and the Foreign Office, BBC, http://www.bbc.co.uk/archive/burgess/7723.shtml

299   BBC WAC L1/68/1, Barnes note for staff file, 11 July 1944

300   Stefan Berger and Norman LaPorte, 'John Peet (1915–1988): An Englishman in the GDR', *History*, vol. 89, no. 293 (January 2004), p. 49

301 Donald Read, *The Power of News: The History of Reuters*, 2nd edn (Oxford: Oxford University Press, 1999), p. 441

302 East German TV newsreel, '*Der Augenzeuge*', copy held by Thomson Reuters archivist, seen by authors.

303 Berger and LaPorte, 'John Peet'. Peet delivered his statement in German; this extract is taken from the translation used by Berger and LaPorte. A slightly different translation appears in John Peet, *The Long Engagement: Memoirs of a Cold War Legend* (London: Fourth Estate, 1989), p. 185

304 Peet, *The Long Engagement*, p. 50

305 Kathleen McLaughlin, 'British Reporter Quits the West', *New York Times*, 12 June 1950

306 Yuri Korolkov, 'John Peet Crosses Over to Peace Camp', *Pravda*, 13 June 1950, p. 6

307 Peet, *The Long Engagement*, p. 185

308 Ibid., p. 1

309 McLaughlin, 'British Reporter Quits the West'

310 Author's interview with former Reuter correspondent Sandy Gall

311 Michael Nelson, *Castro and Stockmaster: A Life in Reuters* (Leicester: Matador, 2011), p. 108

312 Peet, *The Long Engagement*, p. 1

313 Ibid.

314 Ibid., p. 186

315 Documents in Thomson Reuters archive, seen by author

316 Peet, *The Long Engagement*, p. 186

317 Nelson, *Castro and Stockmaster*, p. 109

318 Ibid., p. 5

319 Letter from Hubert Peet to Reuters in Thomson Reuters archive

320 Peet, *The Long Engagement*, pp. 8–9

321 Ibid., p. 11

322 Ibid., p. 12

323 Ibid.

324 Ibid., p. 6

325 John Peet audio interview with Imperial War Museum

326 Peet, *The Long Engagement*, p. 17

327 Ibid., p. 19

328 Ibid., p. 22

329 Ibid., p. 26

330 John Peet audio interview with Imperial War Museum

331 Ibid.

332 Ibid.

333 Peet, *The Long Engagement*, p. 100

334 Ibid., p. 141

335 Read, *The Power of News*, p. 441

336 Peet, *The Long Engagement*, p. 175

337 Ibid., p. 180

338 Ibid., p. 181

339 Ibid. In Berger and LaPorte's translation Keightley is misspelt as Keepley.

340 McLaughlin, 'British Reporter Quits the West'

341 See publisher's note at start of Peet, *The Long Engagement*

342 Peet, *The Long Engagement*, p. 227

343 Ibid., p. 2

344 Ibid., p. 5

345 Ibid., p. 186

346   Documents in Thomson Reuters archive
347   Elizabeth Paterson, *Postcards from Abroad: Memories of P. E. N.* (London: Sinclair Stevenson, 2001), p. 98
348   Read, *The Power of News*, p. 443
349   Derek Jameson, *Touched by Angels* (London: Ebury, 1988), p. 116
350   Interview with Derek Jameson
351   Read, *The Power of News*, p. 440
352   Interview with Derek Jameson
353   Read, *The Power of News*, p. 441
354   Interview with Derek Jameson
355   Read, *The Power of News*, p. 440
356   Ibid. p. 441
357   Peet, *The Long Engagement*, p. 189
358   Ibid., photographs
359   Berger and LaPorte, quoting *Berliner Zeitung*, 'John Peet', p. 56
360   Ibid.
361   Peet, *The Long Engagement*, photographs
362   Berger and LaPorte, 'John Peet', p. 56
363   Ibid.
364   Ibid.
365   McLaughlin, 'British Reporter Quits the West'
366   Berger and LaPorte, 'John Peet', p. 58
367   Peet, *The Long Engagement*, p. 238
368   Ibid., p. 239
369   Nelson, *Castro and Stockmaster*, p. 109
370   Interview with Sandy Gall, 2011
371   Peet, *The Long Engagement*, front-cover sleeve note.
372   Ibid., p. 101.
373   Ibid., p. 102
374   Ibid.
375   Ibid., p. 230
376   Ibid., p. 231
377   Berger and LaPorte, 'John Peet', p. 52
378   Documents in Thomson Reuters archive
379   TNA Foreign Office file FO371/85097
380   TNA PREM 11/264, Liddell to Hunt, 28 April 1952
381   Berger and LaPorte, 'John Peet', p. 67
382   Peet, *The Long Engagement*, p. 231
383   Ibid., p. x
384   'Aber wo ist das Omelett?', Zeit Online, http://www.zeit.de/1989/08/aber-wo-ist-das-omelett/seite-1; Moor wrote the article in German for *Die Zeit* and quoted the letter in German. We have translated the letter back into English.
385   'A Reporter You'd Trust', *Daily Mail*, 29 November 1994, p. 10
386   Ibid.
387   Ibid.
388   'Obituary: Reg Foster', *The Times*, 27 January 2000, p. 27
389   Susanna Gross, 'Obituary: Brendan Mulholland', *Daily Mail*, 21 May 1992, p. 39
390   'On This Day: 14 July 1962 – Seven Ministers out of Cabinet', *The Times*, 14 July 1992, p. 17; Harold Macmillan (Peter Catterall ed.), *The Macmillan Diaries, Volume II, 1957–1966: Prime Minister and After* (London: Pan, 2011), pp. 483–485
391   That scandal had seen Royal Navy Portland base employees Harry Houghton and his lover, Ethel Gee, jailed along with their KGB contacts, Peter and Helen Kroger, and

KGB controller Gordon Lonsdale; see *The Times*, 17 January 1961, p. 7; *The Times*, 24 March 1961, p. 3. They had been caught as the result of a tip-off by a Polish defector, Michael Goleniewski. Superintendent Smith and Chief Inspector Smith had arrested them, too.

392   George Blake, an MI6 officer, was jailed for forty-two years after a trial held in camera: '42-year Sentence on Man Who Spied For Russia', *The Times*, 4 May 1961, p. 12.

393   'US and British Tanks Out in Berlin', *The Times*, 26 October 1961, p. 12; Michael R. Beschloss, *Kennedy v. Khrushchev: The Crisis Years, 1960–1963* (London: Faber & Faber, 1991), pp. 333–335; Macmillan, *The Macmillan Diaries, Volume II*, p. 423 (27 October entry)

394   Alistair Horne, *Macmillan: 1957–86, Volume II* (London: Macmillan, 1989), p. 457

395   The news had been broken to Macmillan by Defence Minister Peter Thorneycroft and First Lord of the Admiralty Lord Carrington on 12 September. Macmillan recorded, 'What they had to tell me was indeed distressing in the present nervous atmosphere': Harold Macmillan, *At the End of the Day, 1961–63* (London: Macmillan, 1973), p. 429. Macmillan's published diaries first record Vassall on 28 September 1962; see *The Macmillan Diaries, Volume II*, p. 501: 'There will be another big row, worked up by the Press, over this ...'

396   Alistair Horne, *Macmillan: 1957–86, Volume II*, p. 461

397   Ibid. Macmillan held a dim view of the head of MI5, Sir Roger Hollis, thinking him insignificant.

398   Vassall had been caught as a result of information passed on by a Soviet defector, Anatoly Golitsyn; see Christopher Andrew, *The Defence of the Realm: The Authorised History of MI5* (London: Allen Lane, 2010), p. 492.

399   'Obituary: Reg Foster', *The Times*

400   'Vassall Sentenced to 18 Years Imprisonment', *The Times*, 23 October 1962, p. 6. Vassall served ten years. He was released on parole on 25 October 1972.

401   *Daily Sketch*, 23 October 1962

402   Macmillan, *At the End of the Day*, p. 430

403   The Romer report was published in June 1961; see for instance, 'Security Breach Report Blames Admiralty', *The Times*, 14 June 1961, p. 12.

404   Security Procedures in the Public Service, The Radcliffe Report, April 1962, Cmnd 1681

405   John Vassall (Committee of Inquiry), HC Deb 1962, 8 November 1962, vol. 666, cc. 1148–1152

406   TNA TS 58/658, Minutes of the first meeting held on 25 October 1962

407   Macmillan, *At the End of the Day*, p. 431

408   Peter Hennessy, 'The Eternal Fireman Who Always Answers the Call to Duty', *The Times*, 30 January 1976, p. 16

409   'Obituary: Viscount Radcliffe', *The Times*, 4 April 1997, p. 14

410   Ibid.

411   Report of the Tribunal Appointed to Inquire into the Vassall Case and Related Matters (hereafter called Radcliffe report), Cmnd 2009, April 1963, para 9, p. 3

412   Radcliffe report, Appendix

413   TNA TS 58/643, P 39, Written statement by Reginald Foster

414   Transcripts for sessions 16, 17, 18 and 19, all in TNA TS 58/652, are lost.

415   There is an interesting point here about records held in archives. The photocopy of the article that is lodged in Foster's file held at TNA is clearly marked up to show what was of interest to Radcliffe. The words 'women's clothes' appear in the first of three bulleted paragraphs on page 10 of the *Daily Sketch*, 23 October 1962. They are clearly marked in red and black ball-point pen. The edition that is available on microfilm at the British Library's Newspaper Library at Colindale is different. In that version

the words from the three bulleted paragraphs appear on page 1, under a different banner headline and with no by-line. The three 'bulleted' paragraphs in fact are not bulleted at all, but are marked by bold capitals, ONE ... TWO ... THREE ... instead. Paragraphs 244 and 251 of the Radcliffe report suggest either that the paper's assistant editor, Donald Todhunter, or its lead Vassall reporter, Louis Kirby, would have helped Radcliffe identify who had supplied those words. Foster had told Radcliffe, his trial and his appeal that he had not supplied the word 'wore'. See [1963] 1 All ER 767, Denning MR.

416   TNA TS 58/704, the case against Reginald Foster, extract from transcript, Writ of Summons, 21 January 1963, Queens Bench Division papers

417   Ibid.

418   TNA TS 58/653, Session 20, p. 34

419   L. C. J. McNae (ed.), revised by R. M. Taylor, *Essential Law For Journalists*, 3rd edn (London: Staples Press, 1967), p. 76

420   TNA TS 58/703, the case against Desmond Clough

421   Radcliffe report, p. 77

422   Radcliffe report, p. 78

423   TNA TS 58/653, P. H. Hoskins testimony, day 21, p. 50 and p. 45

424   '"Express" Crime Reporter at Vassall Tribunal Refuses to Disclose Who Confirmed Story', *The Times*, 18 January 1963, p. 12

425   'I Won't Tell Man Allowed to Keep his Secret', *Daily Sketch*, 18 January 1963, p. 14

426   TNA TS 58/705, the case against Brendan Mulholland, TNA. See Brendan Mulholland, Alfred Draper and Gilbert Lewthwaite, 'Epitaph on a Spy', *Daily Mail*, 23 October 1962, p. 13

427   TNA TS 58/654, Mulholland transcript, session 22, 18 January 1963, p. 34

428   TNA TS 58/566, Todhunter transcript, session 30, 31 January 1963, p. 14

429   See Andrew Roth, 'Obituary: Ian Waller: A Progressive Voice on the Sunday Telegraph', *The Guardian*, 2 September 2003, p. 25

430   See 'Sentence on Journalist', *The Times*, 26 January 1963, p. 5; '6 Months', *Daily Sketch*, 26 January 1963, p. 1

431   TNA TS 58/643, P54 and P54a

432   TNA TS 58/655, Day 29A, p. 10

433   Ibid., p. 2

434   Ibid., p. 3

435   Ibid., p. 3

436   Ibid., p. 5

437   Ibid., p. 6

438   Ibid., p. 9

439   Ibid., p. 8 and p. 14

440   Ibid., p. 12

441   Ibid., p. 15

442   Ibid., p. 21

443   *The Times*, 8 July 1947, p. 1

444   'Vassall's Denial in Evidence before Tribunal', *The Times*, 30 January 1963, p. 10; TS 58/655 Day 29, WJC Vassall, oral evidence, p. 23

445   See *The Times*, various reports, 11–27 July 1961

446   For her OBE see Supplement to the *London Gazette*, 8 June 1950, p. 2787

447   'Two Years for Woman Information Official', *The Times*, 8 December 1962, p. 5. The £3,800-a-year director of the Central Office of Information's Photographic Division, she had been trapped by a 'Romeo spy'.

448   '6 Months and 3 Months for Journalists', *The Times*, 5 February 1963, p. 10

449   'Three Unexpected Witnesses at Vassall Inquiry', *The Times*, 9 February 1963, p. 6

450   'Police See Students about "Isis" Article', *The Times*, 20 March 1958, p. 5; 'Official Secrets Act Summons', *The Times*, 3 May, 1958, p. 3; 'Three-month Sentence on "Isis" Case Undergraduates', *The Times*, 19 July, 1958, p. 4. The editor of *Isis* at the time was the future playwright Dennis Potter.

451   [1963] 1 All ER 767

452   Brendan Mulholland, *Almost a Holiday* (London: Macmillan, 1966)

453   Radcliffe report, paragraph 17, p. 5

454   Ibid., paragraph 184, p. 56

455   Ibid., paragraph 187, pp. 57–58

456   Ibid., paragraph 226, p. 68

457   Ibid., paragraph 64, p. 20

458   'The SKETCH Says', *Daily Sketch*, 8 May 1963, p. 20

459   Court of Appeal: 'Press against State', *The Times*, 13 February 1963, p. 15; 'Appeals by Journalists Dismissed', *The Times*, 14 February 1963, p. 6. In the judgment Denning said, 'How is anyone to know that this story was not a pure invention, if the journalist will not tell the tribunal its source? Even if it was not invention, how is anyone to know that it was not the gossip of some idler seeking to impress? ... He must remember that he has been directed by the tribunal to disclose it as a matter of public duty, and that is justification enough.' [1963] 1 All ER 767, p. 772.

460   See D. R. Thorpe, *Supermac* (London: Chatto & Windus, 2010), p. 791, fn. 70: Anthony Howard to Thorpe, 3 March, 2008; private information.

461   Private information

462   Betty Williams, with addendum by Matthew Engel, 'Obituary: Reg Foster: Crime Reporter Jailed in the Aftermath of the Vassall Spy Case', *The Guardian*, 12 January 2000

463   Richard Davenport-Hines, *An English Affair: Sex, Class and Power in the Age of Profumo* (London: HarperCollins, 2012), Kindle location 3968

464   Geoffrey Levy, 'Sex, Lies and the Smearing of a Brave Man: Why is a Historian Blackening the Name of this Mail Reporter who went to Jail Rather than Betray a Source?' *Daily Mail*, 27 December 2012, http://www.dailymail.co.uk/news/article-2251958/Why-historian-blackening-Mail-reporter-went-jail-betray-source.html#ixzz2I3eEQgvx. Graham Lord's book *Lord's Ladies and Gentlemen: 100 Legends of the 20th Century* (Fern Hill Books, 2012) is dedicated to Brendan Mulholland: 'In memory of Brendan Mulholland, a fine reporter and a great friend.'

465   'Three Unexpected Witnesses at Vassall Inquiry', *The Times*, 9 February 1963, p. 6

466   Address by Mark Thompson, then director-general of the BBC, at the memorial service for Charles Wheeler held at Westminster Abbey on 20 January 2009

467   'Berlin Wall Archive: "Pure Monty Python"', *Newsnight*, BBC, http://news.bbc.co.uk/1/hi/programmes/newsnight/8359845.stm

468   'Charles Wheeler in His Own Words', BBC Radio 4, 5 July 2008

469   'National Monument' quote from Francine Stock in 'A Roving National Monument' by James Rampton, *Sunday Times*, 2 August 1992

470   Sir Charles Wheeler, *Oxford Dictionary of National Biography*, http://www.oxforddnb.com/view/article/100220 (last accessed 12 June 2013)

471   'Representing Reality', BBC document on impartiality, 1989

472   John Bridcut, 'From Seesaw to Wagon Wheel: Safeguarding Impartiality in the 21st Century', BBC Trust, 2007, p. 25

473   Joseph Trenaman and Denis McQuail, *Television and the Political Image* (London: Methuen, 1961), p. 67

474   Ibid., p. 26

475   Sir Charles Wheeler, *Oxford Dictionary of National Biography*

476 Catherine Hurley (ed.), *Could Do Even Better, More School Reports of the Great and the Good* (London: Simon & Schuster, 2005), p. 55

477 'Charles Wheeler in His Own Words', BBC Radio 4, 5 July 2008

478 Sir Charles Wheeler, *Oxford Dictionary of National Biography*

479 Interview with Michael Peacock, 'Charles Wheeler in His Own Words', BBC Radio 4, 5 July 2008

480 Stephen Brant, translated by Charles Wheeler, *The East German Rising: 17 June 1953* (1957, 1979), p. 11

481 'Charles Wheeler in His Own Words', BBC Radio 4, 5 July 2008

482 Michael Nelson, *War of the Black Heavens* (Syracuse, NY: Syracuse University Press, 1997), p. 33

483 Ibid., p. 34

484 Michael Evans, 'MI6 Fed Cold War Propaganda to BBC', *The Times*, 20 October 1997

485 Michael Nelson, *Castro and Stockmaster* (Leicester: Matador, 2011), p. 169

486 'Hungarian Revolution of 1956', BBC, http://news.bbc.co.uk/1/hi/uk/7498495.stm

487 'Obituary: Sir Charles Wheeler', BBC, http://news.bbc.co.uk/1/hi/entertainment/7402172.stm

488 Martin Bell, 'Charles Wheeler: An Inspiration', *The Guardian*, http://www.guardian.co.uk/commentisfree/2008/jul/04/bbc

489 'Los Angeles Race Riots 1965', *Newsnight*, BBC, http://news.bbc.co.uk/1/hi/programmes/newsnight/7502600.stm

490 'Charles Wheeler in His Own Words', BBC Radio 4, 5 July 2008

491 'Charles Wheeler's Finest Moments', BBC, http://news.bbc.co.uk/1/hi/uk/7489866.stm

492 'From Managed Media to Active Representation: The Gulf War and the Kurdish Refugee Crisis', Part 3 of Martin Shaw, *Civil Society and Media in Global Crises: Representing Distant Violence* (London: Pinter, 1996), pp. 71–124

493 'Charles Wheeler in His Own Words', BBC Radio 4, 5 July 2008

494 'A Tribute to Charles Wheeler', *Newsnight*, BBC, http://news.bbc.co.uk/1/hi/programmes/newsnight/charles_wheeler/default.stm

495 Ibid.

496 'Broadcasters to Fight Plans for Impartiality Rules', *The Independent*, 27 August 1990, p. 5

497 See John De St Jorre, *The Brothers' War* (London: Faber & Faber, 2009); Chibuike Uche, 'Oil, British Interests and the Nigerian Civil War', *Journal of African History*, vol. 49, no. 1 (2008), pp. 111–135; TNA, FCO 38/202, Sir David Hunt (British High Commissioner, Lagos) to Sir Eric Norris (Commonwealth Office), 23 June 1967: 'We have reached the stage where whatever we do one or other parties will stop the flow of oil. Perhaps the companies can drag things out and perhaps they will drag them out long enough for the Federal Government to invade the East and put down the rebellion quickly…'

498 Sir David Hunt to Charles Curran (BBC), 24 February 1969, BBC WAC R78-690-1, Nigerian Civil War, vol. 1

499 BBC WAC, News Divisional Meeting, 26 January 1967, minute 25

500 Frederick Forsyth, 'The BBC Has Never Been Neutral on Anything', *Daily Express*, 2 November 2012

501 TNA FCO 25/199: Nicol Morton (British Consulate, Buea, Cameroon) to G. D. Anderson (British High Commission, Lagos), 4 August 1967

502 TNA FCO 25/199: Anderson to Morton, 14 August 1967

503 TNA FCO 38/253, Telegram 1747, 16 August 1967, British High Commission, Lagos to Foreign Office, London

504 BBC WAC, ENCA Minute 481, 18 August 1967

505 BBC WAC, ENCA Minute 491, 1 September 1967

506 John Simpson, 'My Part in the Fall and Rise of Freddy Forsyth, a Writer of Great Fiction Foreign Affairs', *Sunday Telegraph*, 2 March 2003, p. 27; Frederick Forsyth, 'Forsyth Bites Back at John Simpson...', *Sunday Telegraph*, 9 March 2003, p. 30

507 BBC WAC, ENCA Minute 510, 5 September 1967

508 BBC WAC, News Divisional Meeting, minute 329, 2 November 1967. Two weeks later, the News Divisional Meeting learned that 'Frederick Forsyth would be joining the News Reporting Staff on 4 December 1967' (minute 353).

509 TNA FCO 65/448, Sir David Hunt (High Commissioner, Lagos) to Sir John Wilson, Foreign and Commonwealth Office, 1 May 1969

510 BBC WAC, R 88/690/1, Nigerian Civil War, vol. 1, letter from Charles Curran (possibly to Sir David Hunt), 7 August 1968. Unfortunately, the letter shows to whom it was copied, but not to whom it was addressed.

511 TNA FCO 95/225; St Jorre, *The Brothers' War*

512 'Biafra: Fighting a War Without Guns', *Timewatch*, BBC, 30 July 1995

513 Michael Nicholson, *A Measure of Danger: Memoirs of a British War Correspondent* (London: Fontana, 1992), pp. 25–6 and p. 32. Nicholson repeated the claims about Forsyth in the *Sunday Telegraph* (9 March 2003). Forsyth dismissed them (Letter, *Sunday Telegraph*, 16 March 2003). For an earlier claim, see A. B. Akinyemi, 'The British Press and the Nigerian Civil War', *African Affairs*, vol. 71, no. 285 (October 1972), pp. 408–426; and Peter Sissons, *When One Door Closes* (London: Biteback Publishing, 2011), pp. 96–98

514 TNA FCO 65/446, H. J. Arbuthnott (British High Commission, Lagos) to E. G. Lewis (Foreign and Commonwealth Office), 23 August 1969. See also TNA FCO 65/448, Lewis to Wilson (West Africa Department) and Haydon (News Department), 2 May 1969.

515 TNA DO 186/9, Sir Eric Norris to Sir David Hunt, 18 July 1968. Norris: 'Forsyth's first call was, as you know, on Paul Gore-Booth [Permanent Under-Secretary, Foreign Office] to deliver a message from Ojukwu. I was present...' Hunt's reply (26 July 1968) included: 'I am reluctant, however, to believe Forsyth, who has not been very truthful in the past...'

516 Walter Schwarz, *The Ideal Occupation: A Memoir* (Brighton: Revel Barker Publishing, 2011), pp. 148–9

517 Sissons, *When One Door Closes*

518 Sandy Gall, *Don't Worry About the Money Now* (London: Hamish Hamilton, 1982), p. 304

519 Not all accepted that the starvation was as bad as depicted: see TNA FCO 65/446, John Wilson [Foreign and Commonwealth Office] to E. G. Willen, British High Commission, Lagos, 24 November 1969.

520 Schwarz, *The Ideal Occupation*

521 Maurice Chittenden, 'Forsyth: My Real Life Dogs of War Coup', *Sunday Times*, 11 June 2006, p. 7

522 *HARDtalk*, BBC, Wednesday 18 August 2010 – BBC News Channel at 0230 and 0430 BST; BBC World News at 0330, 0830, 1530, 1930 GMT

523 Ibid.

524 Forsyth was invited by David Cameron to chair the Conservative Party's Military Covenant Commission in 2008. See *Restoring the Covenant*, Conservative Party, September 2008.

525 Peter McKay, 'Bosnia, Let's Go', *Evening Standard*, 11 February 1993

526 Bell, *In Harm's Way* (London: Penguin, 1996), p. 116

527 Ibid. p. 120

528 Bell speech at Frontline Club, London, 27 September 2011

529 Martin Bell, *In Harm's Way*, p. 122

530 Richard Sambrook, *Delivering Trust: Impartiality and Objectivity in the Digital Age*, Reuters Institute for the Study of Journalism, July 2012, p. 5

531 The Radio Newsroom, News Guide, BBC, 1967, held in BBC Written Archive, Caversham

532 Bell interview, *When Reporters Cross the Line*, BBC Radio 4, 3 December 2011

533 'Prime Minister on the Issues', *The Times*, 28 September 1938, p. 10

534 Douglas Hurd, 'We Can at Least Save Civilian Lives', *The Independent*, 12 December 1994

535 Bell, *In Harm's Way*, p. 114

536 Ibid., p. 132

537 Martin Bell, 'Forcing a Peace', *Panorama*, BBC, 8 February 1993

538 McKay, 'Bosnia? Let's Go!'

539 Andrew Marr, 'A Dumb Witness Mouthing Horror', *The Independent*, 10 February 1993

540 Simon Jenkins, 'The Swamp of Civil War', *The Times*, 10 February 1993

541 John Naughton, 'Engaged in the Conflict', *The Observer*, 14 February 1993, p. 64

542 Glenwyn Benson, Letter to the Editor, *The Times*, 17 February 1993

543 *When Reporters Cross the Line*, BBC Radio 4

544 Charles Dickens Jr, *Dickens's Dictionary of London*, 1879

545 Michael Binyon, 'Media's Tunnel Vision Is Attacked by Hurd', *The Times*, 10 September 1993

546 Michael Leapman, 'Media: Do We Let Our Hearts Rule Our Headlines?', *The Independent*, 15 September 1993, p. 19

547 John Simpson, 'War of the Worlds', *The Guardian*, 17 September 1993

548 Martin Bell, lecture to the Ulster Museum, Belfast, October 1993, reprinted in *British Journalism Review*, vol. 4, no. 4 (1993).

549 Hurd, 'We Can at Least Save Civilian Lives'

550 Bell, *In Harm's Way*, p. 128

551 Martin Bell, lecture to the Ulster Museum

552 'Martin Bell Slates "Neutral reporting"', *The Guardian*, 23 November 1996

553 Martin Bell, 'The Journalism of Attachment' in Matthew Kieran (ed.), *Media Ethics* (London: Routledge, 1998)

554 John Lloyd, 'Babel', *Prospect*, 20 July 1997

555 Philip M. Taylor, *Munitions of the Mind*, 3rd edn (Manchester: Manchester University Press, 2003), p. 303

556 'John Simpson Spoils for Battle on Home Front', *The Independent*, 5 August 1997

557 Robert Fox, Peter Naylor Memorial Lecture on Defence, Gresham College, 2009

558 *When Reporters Cross the Line*, BBC Radio 4

559 Martin Bell, 'The Truth Is Our Currency', *From Our Own Correspondent*, BBC Radio Four, 1997, repeated on BBC World Service, 28 December 2011

560 John Bridcut, 'From Seesaw to Wagon Wheel: Safeguarding Impartiality in the 21st Century', BBC Trust, 2007

561 See http://www.bbc.co.uk/blogs/collegeofjournalism/ethics-and-values/impartiality/ Some of the text remains, but not the video.

562 See the impartiality section of the BBC College of Journalism website.

563 Kevin Marsh, 'Issues of Impartiality in News and Current Affairs: Some Practical Considerations', in Leon Barkho (ed.), *From Theory to Practice: How to Assess and Apply Impartiality in News and Current Affairs* (Chicago: University of Chicago Press, 2013)

564 Sambrook, *Delivering Trust*

565 Martin Bell report on the massacre at Ahmici, BBC News, 1993

566 Paragraph 4.4.31 of the current BBC guidelines, Section 4: Impartiality, Personal

View Content, http://www.bbc.co.uk/editorialguidelines/page/guidelines-impartiality-personal-view/ (last accessed 18 July 2013)

567 Martin Bell, *Desert Island Discs*, BBC Radio 4, 15 July 2001

568 Martin Bell, 'Here is the War Live by Satellite', *The Guardian*, 8 March 1997

569 Poem read by Martin Bell at the Frontline Club, September 2011

570 All the documents quoted in this chapter unless otherwise stated are in the 'due impartiality' files of the ITA, stored at Bournemouth University.

571 Ray Fitzwalter, *The Dream that Died: The Rise and Fall of ITV* (Leicester: Matador, 2008), p. 2

572 Denis Forman, *Persona Granada* (London: André Deutsch, 1997), p. 163

573 TNA KV2/3221 and TNA KV2/3222

574 *The Times*, 8 March 2010

575 R. R. Ford, 'British Film Officer in New York, February 1941', quoted in Kay Gladstone, *British Interception of German Export Newsreels and the Development of British Combat Filming 1939–1942*, Imperial War Museum Review. no. 2, 1987

576 Ibid.

577 Forman, *Persona Granada*, p. 49

578 Bernard Sendall, *Independent Television in Britain: Volume II, Expansion and Change 1958–68* (London: Macmillan, 1983), p. 335

579 Fitzwalter, *The Dream that Died*, p. 2

580 Minutes of 93rd meeting of the ITA, 3 June 1958

581 Forman, *Persona Granada*, p. 125

582 Ibid., p. 214

583 Ibid., p. 125

584 Ibid., p. 217

585 Ibid., p. 223

586 'A Painful Reminder: Evidence for All Mankind', ITN Source, http://www.itnsource.com/shotlist/ITVProgs/1985/09/08/306430001/?s=*

587 Sandy Gall, *News from the Front* (London: Heinemann, 1994), p. 117–118

588 IRA Demonstrations, ITN Source, http://www.itnsource.com/en/shotlist/BHC_ITN/1965/01/20/X20016501/?s=IRA+demonstration&st=2&pn=1

589 Sandy Gall interviewed on *Reporters' Notes*, BBC Radio 4, 18 December 2001

590 Sandy Gall, *Don't Worry About the Money Now*, p. 83

591 Sandy Gall interviewed on *John Dunn Show*, BBC Radio 2, 17 October 1983

592 Sandy Gall interviewed by Steve Jones, BBC Radio 2, 29 September 1983

593 Gall, *News from the Front*, p. 2

594 Ibid., p. 28

595 Zia ul-Haq interview with Sandy Gall, ITN, April 1979

596 Sandy Gall, *War against the Taliban* (London: Bloomsbury, 2012), pp. 7–8

597 Ibid., p. 10

598 Gall, *News from the Front*, p. 158

599 Ibid., p. 162

600 Sandy Gall, report on ITN, 6 December 1989

601 Hekmatyar was a leading rebel commander who received financial support from the United States, Pakistan and Saudi Arabia. A long-time rival of Massoud, it has been alleged that in 1975 he received Pakistani help in trying unsuccessfully to assassinate him.

602 Sandy Gall interviewed on *When Reporters Cross the Line*, BBC Radio 4

603 Gall, *News from the Front*, dedication

604 Ibid., p. 173

605 Richard Gott, 'Playing the Great Game with Incredible Gall', *The Guardian*, 12 February 1994

606   Moira Whittle, 'Guardian Journalist Quits over KGB's Spy Claims', PA News, 8 December 1994

607   Sandy Gall, recorded interview with author for BBC radio, November 2011

608   Section 5, Ofcom Broadcasting Code, http://stakeholders.ofcom.org.uk/broadcasting/broadcast-codes/broadcast-code/impartiality/ (last accessed 9 July 2013)

609   Sherard Cowper-Coles, Cables from Kabul (London: HarperPress, 2011), p. 264

610   Bill Berkeley, The Graves Are Not Yet Full: Race, Tribe and Power in the Heart of Africa (London: Basic Books, 2002), p. 249. ICTR and ICTY were 'dry runs' for the International Criminal Court, which was established by the 1998 Rome Conference.

611   Berkeley, The Graves Are Not Yet Full, p. 269

612   Lindsey Hilsum, 'Where is Kigali?', Granta 51, Autumn 1995, p. 148

613   Berkeley, The Graves Are Not Yet Full, p. 257

614   The word in Kinyarwanda was inyenzi (Roméo Dallaire, Shake Hands with the Devil (London: Arrow, 2005), p. 142)

615   Linda Melvern, A People Betrayed (London: Zed, 2000), pp. 70–73

616   Simone Monasebian, 'The Pre-genocide Case against Radio-Television Libre des Mille Collines', in Allan Thompson (ed.), The Media and the Rwanda Genocide (London: Pluto Press, 2007), p. 310

617   Ibid., p. 71

618   Dina Temple-Raston, Justice on the Grass: A Story of Genocide and Redemption (New York: Simon & Schuster, 2005), p. 3

619   Monasebian, 'The Pre-genocide Case...', p. 310

620   Ibid., p. 311

621   Dallaire, Shake Hands with the Devil, p. 156. Dallaire saw paperwork that showed the shipment included material from companies operating in Belgium, Israel, France, the United Kingdom, the Netherlands and Egypt.

622   See Melvern, A People Betrayed, pp. 115–116; 'Rwanda: des missiles qui pointent Paris', http://journal.liberation.fr/publication/liberation/943/#!/0_2; subsequent French judicial investigations have unearthed contradictory evidence and France's role has also been questioned: Christophe Châtelot, 'Rwanda: un rapport de l'ONU pose la question du rôle de la France', Le Monde, 4 June 2012.

623   Lindsey Hilsum, 'Rwandan PM Killed as Troops Wreak Carnage', The Guardian, 8 April 1994, p. 1

624   Years later the Belgian government purchased the building in which they died. Heavily pock-marked with bullet holes it is now maintained as a permanent monument in Kigali.

625   Hilsum, 'Rwandan PM Killed as Troops Wreak Carnage'

626   Lindsey Hilsum, 'Thousands Massacred in Rwanda', The Guardian, 9 April 1994, p. 1

627   Ibid.

628   Lindsey Hilsum, 'Bloody Vengeance in Rwanda', The Observer, 10 April 1994

629   Lindsey Hilsum, 'Foreigners Flee Bloody Horrors of Rwanda', The Guardian, 11 April 1994, p. 8

630   Lindsey Hilsum, 'Rwandan Blood Flows as Foreign Forces Depart', The Guardian, 16 April 1994, p. 12

631   Lindsey Hilsum, 'The UN's Scuttle Diplomacy; Somalia, Angola and Now Rwanda', The Independent, 17 April 1994, p. 21

632   Ibid.

633   Ibid.

634   Berkeley, The Graves Are Not Yet Full, p. 250

635   This is more than can be said for how the massacre of between 100,000 and 300,000 Hutus by Tutsis in Burundi in 1972 was handled. In a world focused on the Vietnam

War, and other conflicts, it barely caught international attention at all. See Lord Brockway, 'Need for UN Peace Initiatives', Letter to the Editor, *The Times*, 12 June 1972, p. 13.

636   Berkeley, *The Graves Are Not Yet Full*, p. 246

637   Ibid., pp. 245–248, 277–284

638   Lindsey Hilsum, 'Crossing the Line to Commitment', *British Journalism Review*, vol. 8, no. 1, 1997, p. 29

639   Ibid.

640   Ibid., p. 30

641   Ibid., pp. 30–31

642   Nick Hughes, an independent cameraman. See Nick Hughes, 'Exhibit 467: Genocide Through a Camera Lens', in Allan Thompson (ed.), *The Media and the Rwanda Genocide* (London: Pluto Press, 2007), pp. 231–234

643   Hilsum, 'Crossing the Line to Commitment', p. 30

644   Ibid.

645   Ibid.

646   Prosecutor v. Radoslav Brdjanin, 'Decision on Prosecution's Second Request for a Subpoena of Jonathan Randal, ICTY', case no. IT-99-36-T, para. 11

647   Nina Bernstein, 'Testing Different Expectations of Journalism', http://www.nieman. harvard.edu/reports/article/101207/Testing-Different-Expectations-of-Journalism. aspx (last accessed 11 December 2012)

648   Roy Gutman, 'Consequences Occur When Reporters Testify', http://www.nieman. harvard.edu/reports/article/101208/Consequences-Occur-When-Reporters-Testify. aspx (last accessed 6 December 2012.)

649   Bill Berkeley, 'A Reporter Decides to Testify, Then Decides Against It', http://www. nieman.harvard.edu/reports/article/101242/A-Reporter-Decides-to-Testify-Then-Decides-Against-It.aspx (last accessed 6 December 2012)

650   Ibid.

651   Ibid.

652   Hilsum, 'Crossing the Line to Commitment', p. 31

653   Bernstein, 'Testing Different Expectations of Journalism'

654   Hilsum, 'Crossing the Line to Commitment', p. 31

655   See Richard Ashby Wilson, *Writing History in International Criminal Trials*, Chapters 1 and 7, (Cambridge: Cambridge University Press, 2011)

656   Jean-Paul Akayesu, Hague Justice Portal, http://www.haguejusticeportal.net/index. php?id=8778 (last accessed 11 December 2012)

657   For videos of both Ryder and Byford see http://news.bbc.co.uk/1/hi/uk_poli-tics/3441869.stm

658   For Gavyn Davies's resignation statement see http://news.bbc.co.uk/1/hi/uk_poli-tics/3439595.stm

659   Richard Tait speaking at the Frontline Club, 19 September 2012, at an event to mark the publication of Kevin Marsh's book *Stumbling over Truth*.

660   Rod Liddle, 'Labour's Attack on Gilligan is Just Nit-picking', *The Guardian*, http:// www.guardian.co.uk/politics/2003/aug/13/iraq.davidkelly

661   Elizabeth Day, 'Fallout From a "Rubbishy Piece of Journalism": The Extraordinary World of Andrew Gilligan', *Sunday Telegraph*, 1 February, 2004

662   Ibid.

663   Kevin Marsh, *Stumbling over Truth* (London: Biteback Publishing, 2012), p. 102

664   Greg Dyke, *Inside Story* (London: HarperCollins, 2004), p. 253

665   BBC WAC file C41

666   Andrew Rawnsley, *The End of the Party* (London: Penguin, 2010), p. 204

667   Ibid., p. 206; Blair's friend Barry Cox is quoted by Andrew Rawnsley.

668   Dyke, *Inside Story*, p. 257
669   Transcript: http://webarchive.nationalarchives.gov.uk/20090128221550/http://www.the-hutton-inquiry.org.uk/content/bbc/bbc_4_0156to0162.pdf
670   Quoted in Dyke, *Inside Story*, p. 257
671   The Hutton Inquiry, document no. BBC/4/0213
672   Marsh, *Stumbling Over Truth*, p. 90
673   Transcript: http://webarchive.nationalarchives.gov.uk/20090128221550/http://www.the-hutton-inquiry.org.uk/content/bbc/bbc_4_0203to0204.pdf
674   'Iraq's Weapons of Mass Destruction: The Assessment of the British Government': http://news.bbc.co.uk/nol/shared/spl/hi/middle_east/02/uk_dossier_on_iraq/pdf/iraqdossier.pdf
675   Author interview with former BBC newsroom journalist, December 2012
676   Hutton Inquiry, BBC evidence BBC/18/0014
677   Hutton Inquiry, BBC evidence BBC/4/0223
678   Marsh, *Stumbling over Truth*, p. 127
679   Hutton Inquiry, BBC evidence BBC/4/0262
680   Hutton Inquiry, BBC evidence BBC/8/0001
681   Marsh, *Stumbling over Truth*, p. 136
682   *Mail on Sunday*, 1 June 2003, p. 26
683   Hutton Inquiry, BBC evidence BBC/5/0066
684   TVC is BBC Television Centre, where both the radio and TV newsrooms were based in 2003.
685   Hutton Inquiry, BBC evidence BBC/5/0118
686   Marsh, *Stumbling over Truth*, p. 156
687   'Timeline: David Kelly', *The Conspiracy Files*, BBC, http://news.bbc.co.uk/1/hi/programmes/conspiracy_files/6380231.stm
688   Hutton Inquiry, Cabinet Office evidence CAB/1/0352-0354
689   Hutton Inquiry, Cabinet Office evidence CAB/1/0355-0366
690   *Channel 4 News*, 27 June 2003; Nicholas Watt, 'Master of Spin Storms Studio to Become the Story', *The Guardian*, 28 June 2003
691   Hutton Inquiry, BBC evidence BBC/6/0006
692   Hutton Inquiry, BBC evidence BBC/14/0115
693   Rawnsley, *The End of the Party*, p. 211
694   'A Year on From the Death of David Kelly', BBC, http://news.bbc.co.uk/1/hi/uk_politics/3901183.stm
695   Tony Blair, *A Journey* (London: Hutchinson, 2010), p. 459
696   Andrew Caldecott, QC, One Brick Court, http://www.onebrickcourt.com/barristers.aspx?menu=main&pageid=25&barristerid=24
697   Dyke, *Inside Story*, p. 3
698   Preliminary statement of the BBC to the Hutton Inquiry
699   Kevin Marsh, 'Lord Hutton Did Us All a Disservice', *British Journalism Review*, vol. 23, no. 3, September 2012
700   Marsh, *Stumbling over Truth*, p. 157
701   Ibid., p. 172
702   Ibid., p. 206
703   Dyke, *Inside Story*, p. 258
704   Marsh, *Stumbling over Truth*, p. 207
705   Preliminary statement of the BBC to the Hutton Inquiry, para. 13
706   Andrew Gilligan cross-examination at the Hutton Inquiry, 12 August 2003
707   Ibid.
708   *Battle for the Airwaves*, Episode 7, BBC Radio 4, 5 March 2013
709   Marsh, *Stumbling over Truth*, p. 215

710　Andrew Gilligan cross-examination at the Hutton Inquiry, 12 August 2003

711　Andrew Gilligan cross-examination at the Hutton Inquiry, 17 September 2003

712　Marsh, *Stumbling over Truth*, p. 125.

713　'Decisions reached in the BBC disciplinary process', Appendix 2, in 'The BBC's Journalism after Hutton, The Report of the Neil Review Team', June 2004

714　Email exchange between the BBC and authors

715　Email from Andrew Gilligan to Stewart Purvis, 14 February 2013

716　Email from Kevin Marsh to Stewart Purvis, 19 February 2013

717　Hutton Special, *Ariel* (BBC in-house staff magazine), BBC, 29 January 2004, p. 6

718　Andrew Gilligan cross-examination by Jonathan Sumption QC at the Hutton Inquiry, 17 September 2003

719　For the Hutton Report see http://webarchive.nationalarchives.gov.uk/20090128221550/ http://www.the-hutton-inquiry.org.uk/content/rulings/statement280104.htm

720　For the Hutton Report see http://webarchive.nationalarchives.gov.uk/20090128221550/ http://www.the-hutton-inquiry.org.uk/content/fsb/fsb_1.pdf

721　'The Hutton Inquiry', *The Reunion*, BBC Radio 4, 10 May 2013

722　'Whether It's the Hutton Report or Jimmy Savile, the BBC is Hopeless in a Crisis, *The Telegraph*, http://www.telegraph.co.uk/culture/tvandradio/bbc/9633399/Whether-its-the-Hutton-Report-or-Jimmy-Savile-theBBC-is-hopeless-in-a-crisis.html

723　'The Hutton Inquiry', *The Reunion*, BBC Radio 4

724　Kevin Marsh, Frontline Club, London, 19 September 2012

725　'At-a-glance: Butler Report', BBC, http://news.bbc.co.uk/1/hi/uk_politics/3892809.stm

726　Iraq inquiry website: http://www.iraqinquiry.org.uk/media/52051/Laurie-statement-FINAL.pdf

727　Interview with Tom Bradby, *Channel 4 News*, 9 August 2006

728　Interview with Tom Bradby, *Radio Times*, 24 August 2012

729　'Phone-hacking: The Movie', Tom Bradby Blog, 10 November 2011

730　'Paul Dacre's Speech at the Leveson Inquiry – Full Text', *The Guardian*, http://www.guardian.co.uk/media/2011/oct/12/paul-dacre-leveson-speech

731　Andrew Boyd, *Broadcast Journalism: Techniques of Radio and Television News* (Oxford: Focal Press, 2001), p. 32

732　Nicholas Jones, 'Great Political Theatre Mr Jay, Shame About the Questions', in Richard Keeble and John Mair (eds), *The Phone-Hacking Scandal: Journalism on Trial* (Bury St Edmunds: Abramis, 2012), p. 131

733　Tom Watson and Martin Hickman, *Dial M for Murdoch* (London: Allen Lane, 2012), p. 31

734　For the role of the PCC see http://www.pcc.org.uk/about/index.html; and its role in the phone-hacking affair is reviewed at http://mediastandardstrust.org/publications/did-the-pcc-fail-when-it-came-to-phone-hacking/

735　'Ripa and the Phone-hacking Investigation', *The Guardian*, http://www.guardian.co.uk/media/2011/mar/13/phone-hacking-newspapers

736　Oral evidence from David Perry QC to the Leveson Inquiry

737　'April Casburn Jailed for News of the World Leak Offer', BBC News, http://www.bbc.co.uk/news/uk-21292338

738　'Commentary: Why I Gave Evidence in Trial of Senior Police Office', Exaro News, http://www.exaronews.com/articles/4824/commentary-why-i-gave-evidence-in-trial-of-senior-police-officer

739　'Murdoch Has Betrayed Us All', *The Spectator*, 9 February 2013

740　Richard Desmond, owner of Northern and Shell, the publishers of the *Daily* and *Sunday Express* and *Daily Star* and *Daily Star Sunday*.

741　John Ryley's statement regarding Sky News Darwin story, Sky News press release, 5 April 2012

742　'CPS Rules Sky News Email Hacking Canoe-man John Darwin Was Public Interest', *Press Gazette*, http://www.pressgazette.co.uk/cps-rules-sky-news-email-hacking-canoe-man-john-darwin-was-public-interest

743　*Ofcom Broadcast Bulletin*, issue no. 233, 1 July 2013, http://stakeholders.ofcom.org.uk/binaries/enforcement/broadcast-bulletins/obb233/obb233.pdf

PICTURE CREDITS

p. x © Mike Webster / Rex Features

p. 40 © National Archives

p. 58 © Press Association

p. 88 © TopFoto

p. 122 © TopFoto

p. 146 © Reg Warhurst / Associated Newspapers / Rex Features

p. 176 © Press Association

p. 190 © Press Association

p. 212 © Press Association

p. 228 © ITV / Rex Features

p. 246 © ITV / Rex Features

p. 262 © Twitter

p. 286 © Tom Pilston / The Independent / Rex Features

INDEX

Acton, Harold 112, 113
Afghanistan
   under control of Soviet Union 248,
      249–50, 251–2
   Sandy Gall's reports from 249–52,
      253–6, 258–60
   support for mujahideen 254–6
   death of Ahmed Shah Massoud
      260–61
Akayesu, Jean-Paul 263, 276–7, 278,
   284–5
Al Fayed, Mohamed 31
Alić, Fikret 16, 17–18, 21, 22, 32–3
Allport, G. J. B. 111
Alsop, Joe 85
Amanpour, Christiane 277
Anda, Carr Van 63
Anderson, G. D. 196
Andrew, Christopher 51, 92, 110
Arnold, Alice 297
Ashdown, Paddy 14, 17
Attlee, Clement 53, 54
Austin, John 164

Bagosora, Théoniste 281
Baker, W. R. 104–5
Baldwin, Stanley 53
Banja Luka 8, 10
Barnaby, J. 95

Barnes, George 96, 98, 99, 107, 111,
   117, 118, 120–21
Barnes, Ralph 71
Barnett, Steven 342
Bell, Adrian 214
Bell, Martin 277, 278
   and ITN's writ against *Living
      Marxism* 24, 26
   on Biafran conflict 193
   on Freddie Forsyth 199, 206
Benson, Glenwyn 214, 217
Berger, Stefan 136, 141
Berkeley, Bill 275, 281–2
Berlin, Isiah 103
Bernstein, Nina 280
Bernstein, Sidney
   early life and career 230–33
   founds Granada TV 233–4
   and impartiality 234–5, 236, 240
   on *Cuba Si* 236, 237, 238
   later career and retirement 243–4
Bevin, Ernest 54
Bhutto, Zulfikar Ali 251
Biafran conflict 191–207
Birt, John 292–3
Blair, Tony 287, 288, 291, 292, 296,
   305, 306, 318–19, 321
Blake, George 150
Bland, Sir Christopher 293

Blazević, Azra 20, 33
Blunt, Anthony 90, 91, 96, 105, 109, 112
Bond, Catherine 282–3
Bosnia and Herzegovina
  civil war in 2–5, 213–27
  camps in 5–9
  media visits to camps 9–15
  reports from visits to camps 15–18
  and Hague trial 18–24
  John Simpson on camps in 28–30, 31, 34, 37–8
  Martin Bell reports on 213–27
Boucher, Richard 12
Bowra, Sir Maurice 93
Bracken, Brendan 116, 155
Bradby, Tom 325–7, 333
Brčko 8
British Broadcasting Corporation (BBC)
  and ITN's writ against Living Marxism 23, 24, 26, 35–6
  W. N. Ewer on 56–7, 116
  Guy Burgess works for 90, 94–8, 104–11, 120–21
  impartiality in 179–80, 214–15, 222–4, 225–6, 289
  Charles Wheeler works for 180–88, 189
  and Information Research Department 182–4
  and Biafran conflict 193–4, 195, 196–200
  and Bosnian conflict 214–15, 222–4, 225–6
  and World in Action 239, 240
  and Hutton Inquiry 287–8, 307–18, 319–21, 322–3
  and invasion of Iraq 291–2
  and dossier on WMD reports 294, 299–300, 302, 304–5

Brockway, Fenner 53
Brooks, Rebekah 320–30
Bryant, Chris 329
Buerk, Michael 219, 224
Bulger, James 30
Burgess, Guy
  description of 89–90, 93–4
  works for BBC 90, 94–8, 104–11, 120–21
  works for NKVD 91, 92
  flees to Moscow 92
  early career 92–3, 94–5
  and Harold Nicolson 97–100, 106, 117, 119
  works for MI6 100–104
  works for KGB 108–9, 110, 111–12, 119–20
  works for Foreign Office 113–19
  absconds to Soviet Union 120
Burns, John 5
Bush, George H. 16, 17
Bush, George W. 288
Butler, Lord 323
Butler, R. A. 'Rab' 42
Byford, Mark 287

Cadogan, Sir Alexander 113–14, 115, 117–18
Cairncross, John 91
Caldecott, Andrew 307
Cameron, David 328, 340
Campbell, Alastair 289, 291, 292, 296, 301–2, 304–5, 306, 308, 317, 318, 319–20, 321, 323
Campbell, David 20, 35
Campbell, Naomi 30–31
Can I Help You? 107–8
Carleton Greene, Hugh 189, 214
Carr, E. H. 96
Carrington, Lord 248
Carter, Jimmy 87

Casburn, April 336
Cecil, Robert 94
Chamberlain, Neville 98
Chamberlin, William Henry 64, 67,
    68, 71
Chancellor, Christopher 135
Channel 4 News
    visit to camps in Bosnia 9–15
    reports on visits to camps 16, 17,
        32
    reports on massacre in Rwanda
        282–3
    Alastair Campbell appears on 305
Chéron, Jane 62
Chicago Daily News 71, 73
Churchill, Clarissa 109–10
Churchill, Winston 54, 90, 100–101,
    109, 113, 127, 142–3, 231
Clark, Douglas 159
Clinton, Bill 87
Clough, Desmond 159, 163, 168
Cohen, Nick 337
Cole, G. D. H. 43
Colvin, Marie 278
Conquest, Robert 55
Cook, Phyllis 166
Cornelius-Wheeler, Sir Selwyn 178
Čosić, Dobrica 17
Coulson, Andrew 329
Craxton, John 113
Cripps, Sir Stafford 107
Crowl, James 79
Crowley, Aleister 62
Cuba Si 236–8
Cunningham, Sir Charles 154
Curran, Charles 199
Curzon, Lord 44
Cusack, R. V. 158, 164, 167, 169

Dacre, Paul 328, 329
Daily Express 73, 159, 210

Daily Herald 42, 43–5, 46, 47–8,
    49–50, 52–4, 56–7, 148, 149
Daily Mail 148, 149, 153, 162
Daily Mirror 31
Daily Sketch 153, 157, 162, 164,
    171, 172
Daily Worker 129, 136, 143
Dale, Walter 48, 49
Dallaire, Romeo 270, 271, 273, 275
Damazer, Mark 289
Dando, Stephen 315
Darwin, Anne 343, 344
Darwin, John 342–3, 344
Davenport-Hines, Richard 173
Davies, Gavyn 287, 293, 320–21
Davies, Nick 328, 33
Davis, Evan 225
Deichmann, Thomas 20–23, 24–5,
    28, 29, 32, 35
Deighton, Len 144
Delahunty, Patrick 169
Democratic German Report (DGR)
    136–7, 143
Denning, Lord 172–3
Denny, Harold 82
Desmond, Richard 339
Deutsch, Arnold 92
Dingemans, James 311, 314
Donaldson, John 158, 159
Dowler, Millie 328
Driberg, Tom 90
Duranty, Walter
    description of 60–61
    early life and career 61–3
    reports from Soviet Union 63–7,
        68
    and famine in Ukraine 70, 72,
        73–7, 79–81, 83, 85–7
    later career and death 82–3, 84–5
Dyke, Greg 287, 291–3, 302, 308–9,
    310, 312, 317, 319, 321, 322

Eden, Anthony 90, 115, 116, 117, 118
Eisler, Gerhart 124, 125
Elton, Lord 96
Empson, William 107
Engel, Matthew 173
Engerman, David 67, 68, 77, 84
Enwright, Anna 83
Equatorial Guinea 207–10
Ewer, Monica 44, 52
Ewer, W. N. 116
    at reception with Foreign Secretary 41–2
    starts work for *Daily Herald* 43–5
    under MI5 surveillance 44–51, 52
    in Soviet Union 45–7
    attempts to spy on MI5 47–50
    moderates political views 52–4
    recruited by Information Research Department 54–7
Experiences in Russia 1931 – A Diary (Jones) 69

Feather, Vic 56
Fischer, Louis 67, 68, 77, 78, 83
Fitzwalter, Ray 230
Fleming, Ian 180
Foot, R. W. 113, 115
Footman, David 101–2
Forest, Baron de 43
Forman, Denis 238, 239, 241–2
Forsyth, Frederick
    and John Peet 137
    reports on Biafran conflict 191–207
    role in attempted coup in Equatorial Guinea 207–10
Foster, Reg
    description of 147–9
    works on John Vassall story 152, 153

at Vassall tribunal 157–9
charged with contempt 163, 164, 168–70, 173, 174–5
release from prison 171
Fox, Robert 224
Fraser, Sir Robert 234–6, 237, 239
Furse, Aileen 108

Galbraith, Thomas 'Tam' 153, 156, 161, 162
Gall, Sandy
    on John Peet 138–9
    on Freddie Forsyth 200, 205
    connections with MI6 247–8, 252, 257–8
    early career 248–9
    reports from Afghanistan 249–52, 253–6, 258–60
Gallacher, Willie 106
Gardiner, Alexander 244
Gay, Alexander 207, 209–10
Geiringer, Alfred 133, 141–2
German Democratic Republic (GDR)
    John Peet defects to 123–6, 132–5
    John Peet works in 135–45
    Charles Wheeler reports from 181–4
Gibb, Eddie 28–9
Gilligan, Andrew
    early career 288
    works on *Today* programme 288–91
    reports on invasion of Iraq 291–2, 293–4
    reports on dossier on WMD 294–302, 303
    and Hutton Inquiry 309, 311–12, 313–17, 322
Ginhoven, Hubertus van 49, 50
Gjelten, Tom 277
Goebbels, Josef 123

Goodman, Clive 328, 331
Goodman, Geoffrey 57
Gorman, Sir William 168–9
Gott, Richard 257–8
Gove, Michael 26–7, 39
Gowing, Nik 9, 31
Graham, David 108
Granada TV 233–45
Grand, Lawrence 101
Green, John 90
Gross, Mr Justice 328
Guardian, The 5
    visit to camps in Bosnia 9–13
    reports on visits to camps 16, 17
    and Hague trials 19, 20
    and ITN's writ against *Living
        Marxism* 24
    reports on famine in Ukraine 71–2
    on Charles Wheeler 189
    on Sandy Gall 257
    reports on massacre in Rwanda
        271
    reports on phone-hacking 328,
        333
    on Leveson Inquiry 339–40
Gutman, Roy 5–6, 8–9, 10, 23, 281,
    282, 283

Habyarimana, Juvénal 267, 268, 270
Hallworth, Rodney 172, 173
Hamilton, Neil 31
Harding, Luke 24
HARDtalk 208–9
Harry, Prince 325
Harvey, Oliver 116
Hayes, Jack 48, 51
Healey, Denis 56
Hekmatyar, Gulbuddin 254–5
Henri, Ernst 110
Hewat, Tim 236–8, 239
Hewit, Jack 90, 98

Hewitt, Gavin 299–300
Hickman, Martin 328
Higham, Nick 23, 35, 36
Hill, Christopher 109
Hill, Lord 240
Hilsum, Lindsay
    testifies at International Criminal
        Tribunal for Rwanda 263–4,
        276, 277–9, 283–4
    first reports from Rwanda 265,
        266
    reports from massacre in Rwanda
        271–2, 273–5
Hilton, John 107
Hindus, Maurice 70
Hitchcock, Alfred 232
Hitler, Adolf 6–7, 98
Hobson, Sir John 152, 161, 174
Hogg, Quintin 106
Holness, Bob 237
Hoon, Geoff 322
Hoskins, Percy 159–61
Houghton, Douglas 106
Howard, Anthony 173
Howard, Brian 113
Hudson, Lucian 223
Hulbert, Jeff 103, 109, 114, 115, 158,
    164, 167, 192, 203
Hume, Mike 21–2, 24–5, 26, 31, 32,
    35, 36–7
Humphrys, John 179, 297, 314
Hunt, Bryan 208
Hunt, Sir David 193, 199, 200
Hunt, Lord 332
Hurd, Douglas 16–17, 187, 215, 216,
    219–21
Hussein, King 250, 251
Hussein, Saddam 288
Hutton Inquiry 306–20

In Harm's Way (Bell) 222

Independent, The 217, 221, 274
Independent Broadcasting Authority
    (IBA) 243–4
Independent Television Authority
    (ITA) 234–6, 237, 239–42
Independent Television News (ITN)
    visit to camps in Bosnia 9–15
    reports on visits to camps 15–16,
        17–18
    and Hague trials 19–21, 22–3
    issues writ against *Living Marxism*
        22–31
    libel hearing against *Living
        Marxism* 31–5
    effect of libel hearing 35–9
    links to Conservative governments
        257
Information Research Department
    54–7, 182–4
Inglish, Sue 9–10
Ingrams, Richard 76–7, 79
International Criminal Tribunal for
    the Former Yugoslavia (ICTY)
    18–19, 33, 275, 276, 279–81
International Criminal Tribunal for
    Rwanda (ICTR) 263–4, 275–9,
    281–4
Inter-Services Intelligence Directorate
    (ISI) 252, 255–6, 259
Iraq 186–8, 204–5, 288, 291–2,
    293–4
Izetbegović, Alija 3

Jalalabad 253
Jameson, Derek 134–5
Jane, Charles 49, 50
Jay, Robert 339
Jebb, Gladwyn 103, 118
Jenkins, Simon 217
Johnston, Sir Russell 14
Jones, Gareth 69, 72–8, 83, 85

Jones, Nicholas 331

Kambanda, Jean 277
Kamenev, Lev 65
Karadžić, Radovan 3, 9–10, 11, 19,
    31, 284
Katz, Otto 231
Keeler, Christine 175
Keightley, Charles 132
Kelly, David 295, 296, 300, 301, 305,
    306, 311, 317, 323
Kelly, Tom 322
Kennedy, John F. 9–10, 153–4
Keraterm 19
Keynes, John Maynard 97
KGB 108–9, 110, 111–12, 119–20
Kifner, John 280–81
Kirby, Louis 162, 164
Kirkpatrick, Ivone 235, 237
Kirwan, Lawrence 135
Kliefoth, A. W. 80, 81
Knight, Maxwell 51, 57
Knightley, Phillip 31
Korolkov, Yuri 125

Lansbury, George 43
LaPorte, Norman 136, 141
Laski, Harold 43
Laurie, Michael 323
Leapman, Michael 205
Leeper, Rex 98
Leigh, David 341, 345
Leveson Inquiry 328–30, 331–2, 334,
    335, 336, 339–43
Levy, Geoffrey 173
Liddle, Rod 289
Lidell, Alvar 99
Lippmann, Walter 63, 64
Litvinov, Maxim 64, 72, 82
Living Marxism 21–39
Lloyd, John 223, 342

Lloyd, Selwyn 42

Lloyd George, Megan 106

Lockhart, Sir Robert Bruce 56

London Evening Standard 217

Long Engagement, The: Memoirs of a Cold War Legend (Peet) 139–40

Lonsdale, Gordon 159

Lord, Graham 173

Lyons, Eugene 67, 70–71, 77–8

McCullin, Don 202

McDermid, Angus 195

MacDonald, Ramsay 50

McKay, Peter 217

McLaughlin, Kathleen 125

Maclean, Donald 91, 92, 120

Macmillan, Harold 150, 151, 154–5, 175

Macnamara, Jack 92–3, 95

McNeil, Hector 106

Maconachie, Sir Richard 109

Mail on Sunday 301–2, 313

Major, John 17, 187

Maletér, Pál 249

Mallett, Ivo 119

Manchester Guardian see *Guardian, The*

Mandelson, Peter 320

Manjača 11

Mann, Simon 208, 210

Marr, Andrew 217, 323

Marsh, Kevin 225, 288–9, 290–91, 294–6, 298–9, 300–304, 309, 312–13, 314–15, 316, 322–3

Marshall, Penny 10, 12, 14, 16, 18, 21, 32–3, 35

Martin, Kingsley 53

Massoud, Ahmed Shah 248, 250, 253, 254, 255, 258–9, 260–61

Matheson, Hilda 102

Mayhew, Christopher 54, 56

Merdžanić, Idriz 12, 33–4, 283

Merz, Charles 63, 64

Meyer, Sir Christopher 332

Meynell, Francis 43

MI5

surveillance on W. N. Ewer 44–51, 57

Anthony Blunt works for 91, 105

and Guy Burgess 105, 118

and Sidney Bernstein 231

MI6

Guy Burgess works for 100–104

connection with Sandy Gall 247–8, 252, 257–8

Millar, Frederick Hoyer 103, 118

Millar, Gavin 32–3

Miller, Harry 162

Milmo, Helenus 'Buster' 160

Milosevic, Slobodan 3, 19

Mitchell, Steve 290–91, 303, 309

Mitterrand, François 17

Mladić, Ratko 3, 19

Modin, Yuri 119

Moor, Paul 144–5

Morland, Mr Justice 30–31, 35

Morton, Nichol 195, 196

Mowrer, Edgar Ansel 73

Muggeridge, Kitty 71

Muggeridge, Malcolm 71–2, 76, 80, 84

Mulcaire, Glenn 328, 331

Mulholland, Brendan

description of 149

works on John Vassall story 152, 153

at Vassall tribunal 161–3

charged with contempt 163, 168–70, 173, 174–5

later career 172

Murdoch, Rupert 335

Nagy, Imre 249

Naughton, John 217

Nelson, Michael 182, 183–4

Neues Deutschland 136

New Republic 281

New York Herald Tribune 71

New York Times 16, 60, 61, 62, 63, 66, 67, 75, 77, 80, 81, 83, 85, 125, 137, 281

News at 5.45 15, 16

News at Ten 16, 288

News Corporation 335–7

News from the Front: The Life of a Television Reporter (Gall) 257

News of the World 326, 327–8, 333, 335

Newsday 5

Newsnight 177–8, 186

Nicolson, Harold 90, 97–100, 102, 103, 106, 112, 115, 116, 117, 119

Nicholson, Michael 192, 202

Nine O'Clock News 36

Northern Ireland 229–30

Ntaryamira, Cyprien 270

Observer, The 217

O'Daire, Paddy 130

Ojukwu, General 194, 200, 202, 204, 205, 206

O'Kane, Maggie 5, 8, 9, 10

Omarska 8–9, 10, 11, 12–13, 19, 21, 28, 29, 32

O'Neill, Brendan 278

O'Neill, Terence 230

Orwell, George 107

Osborne, Bridget 210

Other Side of Jimmy Saville, The 244–5

Oumansky, Konstantin 79

Owen, David 55

Owens, Alec 331–2

Panorama 213, 216–17, 220, 226, 239

Pasic, Jusuf 33

Past Week, The 98

Paxman, Jeremy 177–8, 188

Peacock, Michael 182

Peet, Hubert 127–8

Peet, John
defects to GDR 123–6, 132–5
early life and career 128–31
works for Reuters 131–2
works in GDR 135–45

Peet, Stephen 127, 141

Perry, David 334

Philby, Kim 91, 93, 105

Pilger, John 242

Ponting, Clive 341

Poulson, John 243

Pragnell, tony 239–40

Pravda 125

Pritt, D. N. 56

Proctor, Denis 95

Profumo, John 175

Pugh-Pugh, Ivy 163–8, 171, 174

Radcliffe, Lord 154–6, 157, 158–9, 163, 164, 167, 169, 170–71, 172

Randal, Jonathan 280

Rawnsley, Andrew 305–6

Read, Donald 134

Rees, Goronwy 112

Reuters 123–6, 131–2, 133, 134, 135

Richardson, Kenneth 166

Ridsdale, William 115–17, 119

Romer, Sir Charles 154

Roosevelt, Franklin D. 82, 83, 113

Rothschild, Miriam 103

Rothschild, Tess 90

Rothschild, Victor 90, 103

Rowland, Jacky 277

Rusbridger, Alan 342

Russell, Bertrand 56
Rwanda
    and International Criminal
        Tribunal for Rwanda 263–4,
        275–9, 281–4
    background to massacre 264–70
    massacre in 270–75
Ryder, Lord 287
Ryley, John 343, 344

Sackur, Stephen 208–10
Sackville-West, Vita 97, 102
Salisbury, Harrison 60–61, 85
Sambrook, Richard 225–6, 302,
    304–5, 310, 315, 317, 318, 319
Sarajevo 4, 29, 218, 221
Savile, Jimmy 1, 244–5
Scene at Six Thirty 229
Schapiro, Leonard 56
Schwarz, Walter 205, 207
Seckelmann, Peter 182
Sendall, Bernard 237
Seton-Watson, Hugh 96
Shaw, George Bernard 76
Sheilds, Tom 31
Sheridan, Tommy 335
Shone, T. A. 81
Simpson, John
    and Jimmy Savile scandal 1
    on biased reporting 5
    and camps in Bosnia 28–30, 31,
        34, 37–8
    on Charles Wheeler 178
    on Frederick Forsyth 192, 198
    on Martin Bell 220, 223
Sissons, Peter 205
Six O'Clock News 35
Skrzypkowiak, Andy 255
Sky News 342–4
Sloan, P. A. 73
Slocombe, George 51

Smith, Ferguson 149
Smith, George 149
Smollett, Peter 109–10
Snow, Jon 305
Soviet Union
    E. W. Ewer in 45–7
    and Zinoviev letter 50
    attacks by E. W. Ewer 55–7
    famine in Ukraine 59–60, 69–87
    Walter Duranty reports from
        63–7, 68
    press coverage of 67–9
    and 'Cambridge Spies' 91–2
    Guy Burgess absconds to 120
    in Afghanistan 248, 249–50,
        251–2
Spectator, The 257
Stalin, Joseph 82, 113
Starmar, Keir 333, 334, 341
Stoneman, William H. 64, 71
Strachey, John 106
Strang, William 67, 81
Strange Places, Questionable People
    (Simpson) 28
Stumbling over the Truth (Marsh)
    298, 314
Sumption, Jonathan 310, 312
Sun, The 329
Sunday Telegraph 288, 290
Sunday Times 207, 278
Swett-Escott, Bickham 56

Tadić, Düsko 19–21, 22, 33
Tait, Richard 23–4, 26, 27, 38, 289
Tapsell, Peter 156
Taylor, A. J. P. 76
Taylor, Philip 223
Taylor, Sally 61
Ten O'Clock News 299
Thatcher, Margaret 251
Thomas, Richard 332

Thompson, O. 111

Thomson, Caroline 315, 321

Thorneycroft, Lord 107

Thorpe, Jeremy 150

Thwaites, General 44

Times, The 52, 57, 92, 151, 217

Timewatch 201–2

Tindall, David 198

Today 289–91, 294, 296–9, 311

Todhunter, Donald 162, 164

Toynbee, Philip 113

Trevelyan, G. M. 94–5

Trnopolje 8, 10, 12, 13, 16, 18, 19, 21, 22, 23, 27, 28, 29–30, 32–3, 35, 37–8, 39

Trotsky, Leon 47

Uwilingiyamana, Agathe 271–2

Vassall, John 149–53, 154, 157, 161, 162, 164–8, 169

Vulliamy, Ed 10, 11, 13, 14–15, 16, 17, 18, 19–20, 38, 277

Walpole, Hugh 61

War is Dead, Long Live the War, The: Bosnia: the Reckoning (Vulliamy) 38

War of the Black Heavens (Nelson) 182

Washington Post 280

Watson, Tom 328

Watts, Susan 306

Webb, Beatrice 71

Webster, Paul 10

Week in Westminster, The 105–7

Weeks, Romilly 205

Wheeler, Charles
    interviewed by Jeremy Paxman 177–8
    anti-Establishment views 178–9

early life and career 180–81
    reports on East Berlin uprising 181–2
    and Information Research Department 182–4
    reports on Hungarian uprising 184–5
    as Washington correspondent 185–6
    reports on first Gulf War 186–8
    later career and death 188–9

Wheeler, Frances 135

Why Recognize Russia? (Fischer) 83

William, Prince 325–7

Williams, Francis 53

Williams, Ian 10, 11, 12–13, 15–16, 18, 21, 35

Williams, Wythe 61

Willis, Ramsay 161

Wilson, Harold 175

Winster, Lord 107

Wladimiroff, Mischa 21

Wood, Mark 26

Wood, Tim 336–7

World in Action 238–9, 240, 242–3, 244

World at One, The 289

Wylie, Tom 97

Yugoslavia 2 *see also* Bosnia and Herzegovina

Zia ul-Haq 250–52, 255–6, 260

Zinoviev, Grigory 65

Zoete, Henry de 39